# Making of
# Optical Space

Peter Brown

# Chaucer and the Making of Optical Space

PETER LANG

Oxford · Bern · Berlin · Bruxelles · Frankfurt am Main · New York · Wien

Bibliographic information published by Die Deutsche Bibliothek
Die Deutsche Bibliothek lists this publication in the Deutsche
Nationalbibliografie; detailed bibliographic data is available on
the Internet at ‹http://dnb.ddb.de›.

British Library and Library of Congress Cataloguing-in-Publication Data:
A catalogue record for this book is available from The British Library,
Great Britain, and from The Library of Congress, USA

ISBN 978-3-03911-340-8

© Peter Lang AG, International Academic Publishers, Bern 2007
Hochfeldstrasse 32, Postfach 746, CH-3000 Bern 9, Switzerland
info@peterlang.com, www.peterlang.com, www.peterlang.net

Printed in Germany

# Contents

# Illustrations

# Acknowledgements

I am grateful to have had opportunities to air the ideas developed in this book at various conferences and research colloquia. They include ones held at the University of Birmingham; University of Durham; Rice University, Houston; the Sorbonne; Trinity College, Oxford; University College, London; and the University of York. On these occasions I have learnt much from the comments and responses of fellow medievalists. Also of great benefit have been discussions with colleagues and postgraduate students within the School of English and the Canterbury Centre for Medieval & Tudor Studies at the University of Kent.

Individuals who have given valuable and generous feedback on particular aspects of my research include Derek Brewer, Andrew Butcher, Steve Ellis, Nicky Hallett, David C. Lindberg, Alastair Minnis and Derek Pearsall. Three anonymous readers made detailed comments on earlier versions of the text and helped me to make some improvements. I am entirely responsible for the short-comings that remain.

I acknowledge with gratitude the granting of a Research Leave award by the Arts and Humanities Research Council, and research leave given by the School of English at the University of Kent. Without such support this book could not have been completed.

Staff at the University of Kent have provided invaluable practical help, especially Angela Faunch and Dot Turner in the Document Delivery section of the Templeman Library and Lesley Farr in the Design Unit.

The second section of Chapter Five (pp. 152–60) is based on my article, 'An Optical Theme in the Merchant's Tale', *Studies in the Age of Chaucer: Proceedings* 2 (1986), 231–43.

Unless otherwise indicated, quotations from Chaucer's works refer to *The Riverside Chaucer*, ed. Larry D. Benson et al., 3rd edn (Boston Mass.: Houghton Mifflin, 1987).

Permission to reproduce photographs is acknowledged in the captions to the illustrations.

Design and production have been in the capable hands of Graham Speake and Andrew Ivett, whose professional skills have saved me from numerous pitfalls.

The interest and enthusiasm of my son, Oliver, and daughter, Louisa, have made the task of preparing the text for publication a cause of enjoyment and celebration.

This book is dedicated to its first reader, Anjela Gallego-Sala.

# Abbreviations

| | |
|---|---|
| EETS | Early English Text Society |
| *ELH* | *English Literary History* |
| es | extra series |
| FrP | Friar's Prologue |
| GP | General Prologue |
| *LGW* | *Legend of Good Women* |
| *MED* | *Middle English Dictionary*, ed. Hans Kurath, Sherman M. Kuhn and Robert E. Lewis (Ann Arbor: University of Michigan Press, 1954–2001) |
| MerchT | Merchant's Tale |
| NPT | Nun's Priest's Tale |
| *OED* | *The Oxford English Dictionary*, 2nd edn, ed. John Simpson and Edmund Weiner, 20 vols (Oxford: Oxford University Press, 1989) |
| os | original series |
| PardPT | Pardoner's Prologue and Tale |
| PardT | Pardoner's Tale |
| *PMLA* | *Publications of the Modern Language Association of America* |
| RP | Reeve's Prologue |
| SATF | Société des Anciens Textes Français |
| SqT | Squire's Tale |
| SumT | Summoner's Tale |
| WBPT | Wife of Bath's Prologue and Tale |

# Introduction

> For the truths are obscure, the ends hidden, the doubts manifold, the minds turbid, the reasonings various; the premises are gleaned from the senses, and the senses (which are our tools) are not immune from error. The path of investigation is therefore obliterated and the inquirer, however diligent, is not infallible. Consequently, when inquiry concerns subtle matters, perplexity grows, views diverge, opinions vary, conclusions differ and certainty becomes difficult to obtain.[1]

This book has two complementary aims. First, it is intended as a contribution to a developing interest among medievalists in the links between Chaucer's writings and the medieval science of optics, or *perspectiva*. Those links bring into play a number of issues, among them Chaucer's reception and reworking of sources and analogues (including ones in the neglected area of scientific writing), his understanding of subjectivity and his representation of visual experience. Such topics are given due coverage, but my main emphasis is on space as an optical phenomenon; in particular, how the authors of scientific treatises (especially Alhacen, Grosseteste and Bacon) conceptualized or 'made' space and how such ideas affected Chaucer's writings through encyclopedias, sermons and vernacular literature. My other aim is a broader study of the ways in which Chaucer created a sense of space in his narratives, and the functional and thematic uses to which he put it – what might in general terms be called his politics of space. Here, due account is taken of the influence of *perspectiva*, but I have not limited the literary discussions of whole works to a catalogue of cause and effect. Rather, I have wanted to allow his works to speak for themselves

---

1    Alhacen, *Optics*, trans. Sabra, vol. 1, p. 3. The first three chapters of Alhacen's work were not translated into medieval Latin.

and to allow optical matters their due place, but not necessarily a dominant position.

These two aims find expression in the earlier and later chapters of the book, which fall into two mutually supporting parts. The first part concerns the construction of space from a medieval perspective: it summarizes key optical theories and shows in detail how they affected the ways in which Chaucer created spatialized scenes. To that end it considers a number of examples and test-cases and plots as closely as possible the affinities between scientific and literary texts. The book then moves through a transitional chapter, covering certain features of the Squire's Tale and Reeve's Tale, before changing its focus to whole narratives. The emphasis of the second part of the book is on space as construed from the standpoint of a modern critic, albeit one alert to the optical context previously explored. The shift of emphasis as between the two parts of the book is one of methodology and is designed to underline the reciprocal relationship between *perspectiva* and Chaucer's poetry. While the earlier chapters stress the optical tradition, and see Chaucer's poetry through that lens, the later chapters prioritize narrative and view its optical content from a literary standpoint. It follows that they entertain constructions of space other than those that are purely optical: ones determined by chivalric values, urban life, erotic love or religious belief. In such contexts, *perspectiva* continues to play a key part – sometimes explicitly, sometimes implicitly – in enabling Chaucer to achieve his distinctive sense of narrative space.

Space is a topic now enjoying wide currency across a range of disciplines and theoretical approaches, from geography to anthropology, from postcolonial studies to postmodernism and feminism.[2] In responding to such developments it has seemed important

---

2    For summative treatments, see Soja, *Postmodern Geographies* and the first part of his *Thirdspace*. As examples of distinct theoretical approaches, see Carter, *Road to Botany Bay*; Casey, *Fate of Place*, pp. 285–330; Giddens, 'Time, Space and Regionalisation'; Gregory, *Geographical Imaginations*, esp. ch. 6; Grosz, 'Women, *Chora*, Dwelling'; Harvey, *Condition of Postmodernity*,

to anchor my work in an established body of theory with wide cultural horizons and a strong historical awareness. Here, my choice fell on Henri Lefebvre's *La Production de l'espace*, first published in 1974 but not translated into English until 1991. It is discussed explicitly in the next chapter and in the conclusion, but its presence is felt in many other parts of the present book.[3] Inevitably, there are occasional inflections deriving from other theorists, especially Michel Foucault.[4] At a more local level I have paid due attention to the steadily increasing number of studies on the nature and meaning of space in late medieval English narrative, in particular those on Chaucer.

In writing this book I have returned to my doctoral thesis, written at the Centre for Medieval Studies at the University of York under the joint supervision of Elizabeth Salter and Derek Pearsall.[5] Its two volumes now read as a clumsy account of *perspectiva*, its influence on Chaucer, and his spatial designs. But it has been useful as a starting-point for some of the arguments presented here, or as a basis for updating the more empirical data. At the time it was written, theories of space were thin on the ground, studies of visual perception and space in Chaucer's writings few and far between, the general interest in medieval optics barely visible. The subsequent enrichment of scholarly writing in all of these areas, coupled with the appearance of new editions and translations of optical works, means that I have been able to undertake a fundamental rethinking of the positions adopted in my thesis. That process has been slow and difficult, but also deeply satisfying. No doubt my new synthesis will seem sketchy and

esp. ch. 3; Hillier and Hanson, *Social Logic of Space*; Lawrence and Low, 'Built Environment and Spatial Form'; Massey, *Space, Place and Gender*, esp. ch. 11; Soja, 'Spatiality of Social Life'; and Tuan, *Space and Place*.

3    As examples of other recent readings of medieval literature (including Chaucer's works) within a Lefebvrian framework, see Evans, 'Production of Space'; and Strohm, 'Three London Itineraries'.

4    See esp. Foucault, 'Of Other Spaces'; and his 'Space, Knowledge and Power'; also Soja, *Thirdspace*, ch. 5.

5    Brown, 'Chaucer's Visual World'.

erroneous twenty years hence, but that is the nature of the process by which scholarly enquiry advances, as Alhacen himself knew.

The end result is that approximately two-thirds of the present book is brand new, while the remainder, represented chiefly by Chapters Two, Three and Four on the science of optics, has been extensively revised, updated and condensed. At the same time, I have extended the range of works studied to include, as well as the *Canterbury Tales*, Chaucer's dream poems and *Troilus and Criseyde*. In broad terms, the new study endorses the old, and confirms that *perspectiva* forms a rich and rewarding context for understanding key aspects of Chaucer's poetry and especially its spatial content. But whereas my thesis dealt with three optical topics – light, vision and space – the present emphasis is on the latter. At the same time the theoretical framework of my argument has moved away from the ideas of J. J. Gibson and Ernst Gombrich[6] and towards those of Lefebvre. The consequence is a less mechanistic account of the relationship between medieval optics and Chaucer's compositions, and (it is to be hoped) a more nuanced one. The empirical evidence speaks for itself, showing Chaucer's debt to this body of writing. It is also demonstrable that the basis of his fascination with optics extended to its account of visual error, to its inbuilt contradictions and to a broader understanding of the nature of social space.

The first chapter is a sampling of representative studies of space, both critical and theoretical, that provide a basis for an approach to Chaucer's works. Early empirical pieces provoke a range of hypotheses, while more recent studies stress the close connections between space and visual perception, and between space and power. The latter also suggest that the human body is crucial in mediating and representing a sense of space, particularly as it affects the boundary between public and private awareness. The

6    Gibson, *Perception of the Visual World* (on which see now Bruce and Green, *Visual Perception*, pp. 189–204; and Reed, *Gibson and the Psychology of Perception*); and Gombrich, *Art and Illusion*. See Brown, 'Chaucer's Visual World', vol. 1, pp. 34–9.

significance of the body in this respect is borne out in studies that focus on non-literary aspects of medieval culture (such as archaeology and medicine). Other attempts to deal with space as an historical phenomenon indicate the extent to which it is a product of its culture, laden with symbolic freight, and a means of asserting and contesting power. Chaucer's writing is, in its own ways, actively engaged in representing and questioning the ways in which space is produced by individuals and groups. However, the concepts of modern theory need to be balanced by an understanding of the spatial ideas available to Chaucer, whether in his literary models or in the science of *perspectiva*.

The second chapter considers the perception of space, the conditions which make it possible, and the eye's proneness to error, as fundamental concerns of medieval optical treatises. Robert Grosseteste was in an influential position from which to promote his ideas about light as the essential component of extension in space – a light which, in its transcendent form, was the material basis of the universe. Accordingly, the study of light rays provided insights into the nature of God. Alhacen, writing within Arabic and Aristotelian traditions, concentrated instead on the changing and deceptive aspects of the seen world, and especially on the psychology of vision – including the perception of solidity and distance. His work was extended, and embedded in Western scholastic culture, by the Silesian scholar, Witelo. Roger Bacon, for his part, effected a synthesis of Arabic and Christian theories, on the basis of which he promoted a particular theory about the propagation of images (*species*) from object to onlooker. By the mid fourteenth century *perspectiva* was an established component of arts courses at Oxford and Cambridge, and featured as an important topic in writings by a wide range of scholars.

Less specialized accounts of *perspectiva*, deriving from the scholarly treatises, were soon available in encyclopedias and sermons, as Chapter Three shows. These accounts of visual phenomena were more accessible to Chaucer and his audience, and provide further evidence of a broad intellectual context that stimulated awareness of optical topics. In abbreviated and eclectic form, Bartholomaeus Anglicus in his *De proprietatibus rerum* synthesized available information on the eye, the prerequisites of vision and the act of seeing. Vincent of Beauvais, in his *Speculum naturale*, incorporated more of the metaphysics of light and vision. The optical data available in encyclopedias in turn became the basis for moralized exempla – a practice encouraged by Grosseteste. In the hands of the Dominicans and Franciscans, such exempla enjoyed widespread currency, as the collection by Peter of Limoges, *De oculo morali*, and other compilations, demonstrate.

The next chapter shows how recent studies have attempted to map Chaucer's affiliations with optical writings, and there can be little doubt that, in principle, he was receptive to optical ideas. He had a well-substantiated interest in Latin science, and his familiarity with encyclopedias and sermon exempla has long been established. The case of the Squire's Tale, in which Chaucer refers specifically to Alhacen and Witelo, indicates the extent to which he was interested in combining optical ideas with narrative. The tale also serves as a first exploration of some of the interconnections of sight, space, power, knowledge, identity, and self-awareness. The Reeve's Tale, by contrast, is a narrative whose optical ideas (which have close parallels in a range of scientific texts) are fully integrated with a central theme on the control of space.

Chapter Five concerns two literary models affecting Chaucer's spatial practices. The passage on optics in the Squire's Tale derives from Jean de Meun's *Roman de la Rose*, where there is an extended account of scientific explanations for the marvellous effects created by mirrors. As others have shown, the nature and the idea of the mirror is a central and unifying motif of the entire poem. The optical influence of the *Rose* is also felt in the ending of the Merchant's Tale, when May attempts a rational explanation for January's apparently defective sight. However, May's discourse also has analogues in scientific writings by Alhacen, Witelo, Vincent, Bartholomaeus and Robert Holcot. Dante's *Divina commedia* provided Chaucer with another kind of model for combining optical science with narrative poetry. There, Dante integrates his working knowledge of optics with the symbolic applications of light, vision and space: as Dante approaches paradise, the light becomes more intense, his vision sharper and less prone to error, space more expansive. For his part, Chaucer is less responsive to the symbolic dimensions of optics, as the *House of Fame*, influenced by Dante's work, shows.

Chaucer's distinctive handling of optical ideas is best demonstrated through an analysis of an entire, complete, poem. In the *Book of the Duchess*, the subject of Chapter Six, his emphasis falls on the extent to which the production of space is a personal and subjective activity, closely linked to visual perception. The story of Ceyx and Alcyone indicates that a sense of identity is also associated with the ability to produce space – an activity in which the imagination plays a key role. The narrator's own retrieval of a sense of personal space, and with it a renewed vitality, results from his reading of Ovid's tale, and is a foretaste of what is in store for the man in black. In his case the dreamer himself, rather than a book, becomes the *messager* urging an end to reductive inertia and a reintegration with social space. The idea of the intermediary, connecting persons and things across distance, has affinities with the theory of *species*, and is instanced within the poem in the historiated glass through which the sun projects light into the dreamer's virtual bedchamber. The theory, as developed by Bacon, was the object of academic controversy when Chaucer wrote. The poem achieves its final act of recuperative mediation through the visual memorializing of White.

The kind of space to which the man in black is about to be restored is distinctively aristocratic, such as that found in the Knight's Tale, the subject of the next chapter. It is characterized by absolute control and by the dominance of public and masculine values. At the same time, it is susceptible to subversion and disruption by chance events, private desires and the feminine. In order to represent space as an important element in his mimetic and symbolic schemes, Chaucer used and adapted the techniques of Boccaccio, whose *Teseida* is his main source. It is especially in episodes at the grove, the prison and the amphitheatre that Theseus' control of space is contested. He is at first successful in maintaining control by adapting to changing circumstances, but with the death of Arcite his approach is deeply compromised. The grounds for questioning it extend also to the iconographic design of the poem, by means of which Chaucer offers his audience alternative readings of Theseus' world. Insofar as the space of that world is constructed from visual experience, Chaucer shows a familiarity with the principles of Alhacen's *De aspectibus*.

The Miller's Tale demonstrates that, further down the social scale, and in an urban setting, space is constructed differently – as Chapter Eight shows. Only in parody, through the figure of a jealous old carpenter, does one individual attempt to exert absolute power over the space inhabited by others. John's presumption is roundly chastized: his domestic space is feminized through the sexual allure of his wife, Alisoun, and its control usurped by the cleverness of his lodger, Nicholas. Whereas Theseus dwelt on the virtues of boundaries, hierarchical stability, and containment, the Miller's Tale rejoices in acts of spatial transgression, acts that are in part enabled by the complex overlaying of social networks in medieval Oxford. Within this setting, each protagonist invents his or her space in different ways: Nicholas as a theatrical producer, John according to moral and religious stereotypes, Alisoun through her body, Absolon by restless socializing. With the exception of Alisoun, each is susceptible to delusions about their own percipience and for both John and Absolon the tendency to be deceived extends also to visual experience.

*Troilus and Criseyde*, the topic of my ninth chapter, is Chaucer's most complex account of space. In the narrative the expansion and contraction of emotions are represented in spatial terms and, similarly, spiritual attitudes are framed according to a sense of where heaven and hell might be. In turn, the gods have power to effect devastating changes on earth. Thus, subjective and physical spaces are closely connected. At the same time the different spaces of Troy – religious, emotional, political, military – are in conflict with each other and the scene of their struggle is the city. Troy is carefully delineated through its buildings, streets and other topographical features, and in ways that echo the appearance and nature of London itself. Domestic space epitomizes the complexity of urban space: it is subject to competing claims, and is deceptive to the untutored eye.

Chapter Ten continues and concludes the discussion of *Troilus*. It shows, first, how the different parts of Troy are linked in a variety of ways – for example, by the to-ing and fro-ing of Pandarus. However, the gaze is the subtlest kind of link, at once connecting objects and people, and constituting the space between them, as Troilus' first sight of Criseyde demonstrates. All such visual links are fragile and fleeting, and there is a persistent tendency towards the separation of the different parts of Troy, as well as a counter-tendency towards making them whole. The love affair achieves wholeness, only to be replaced by an anguished fragmentation, in which Troilus is acutely aware of the space that separates him from Criseyde. Later, he recovers a more profound sense of unity and of the integration of the diverse aspects of his experience and knowledge. The optical context for the poem as a whole lies in the differences between Alhacen's account of the psychological interpretation of visual data, and Grosseteste's belief in the symbolic nature of space.

The final chapter observes that Chaucer's representation of space was affected by optical ideas available to him in a wide range of texts, including theological, scientific, encyclopedic, homiletic and literary. His interest in optical space fed his imagination and the uses to which he put *perspectiva* were highly distinctive. In particular, he subjected a purely visual account of space to a critique that emphasized both the eye's proneness to error and the variety of means by which individuals and groups produce and contest space. In this respect, the evidence from Chaucer's poetry complies with Lefebvre's strictures on the dominance of the visual. While making visuality central, Chaucer shows how space is also constructed by the other senses, by mental processes and by patterns of belief and emotion. These in turn suggest other cultural contexts, such as Giottesque perspective and affective piety, which might be used alongside the optical tradition further to thicken our understanding of the ways in which Chaucer fabricates narrative space.

# 1 Prospect

To underestimate, ignore and diminish space amounts to the over-estimation of texts, written matter, and writing systems, along with the readable and the visible, to the point of assigning to these a monopoly on intelligibility.[1]

Until recently, discussions of space in medieval literature were neither frequent nor extensive. However, they are now sufficiently numerous and complex to act – together with studies of space in medieval culture more generally – as an introduction to some of the ramifications and pitfalls of the topic. What follows is an overview, a representative sample of approaches with especially interesting implications for a more detailed and thorough examination of Chaucer's use of space. I consider first of all the models and precedents from critical studies of medieval authors, including Chaucer, and in order to provide a sense of chronological development I examine in turn two early articles, by Charles Muscatine and Gerhard Joseph, and then the more recent work of Sarah Stanbury and A. C. Spearing. Next, the focus widens to studies by Roberta Gilchrist and Marie-Christine Pouchelle, who consider medieval ideas of space in non-literary contexts. Finally, I introduce some theoretical positions, as developed by Aron Gurevich, Jacques le Goff, Paul Zumthor and Henri Lefebvre. A number of studies mentioned here reappear in subsequent chapters, where they are discussed in more detail in relation to individual texts. Similarly, I have reserved for later use some items which, while of great intrinsic interest, have little to add to the range of approaches exemplified below.

1    Lefebvre, *Production of Space*, p. 62.

ɔ short pieces illustrate the largely empirical approach taken
ɩy years ago. Following the art historians, Muscatine identified
ɔ types of pictorial space in Gothic art. One is flat or plani-
.etric, tending towards the symbolic representation of ideas and
.oncepts; the other is realistic, involving the illusion of depth and
the plastic modelling of figures. The presence of both types of
space in a single composition produces an aesthetic tension which
is a hallmark of the Gothic style. Muscatine then described the
spatial content of examples of medieval narrative from different
periods. The space of early medieval allegory is conceptual – moral
and unrealistic. Prudentius' *Psychomachia* illustrates the point: 'This
space, suspended somewhere outside the naturalistic world, is
completely discontinuous with it.'[2] It is elaborated in *Anticlaudianus*,
where Alan of Lille brings into play a cosmological space in order
to articulate such schematic, spiritual relationships as those be-
tween Prudence and God. Here, Alan creates a kind of 'spatial
epistemology'. In spite of his apparent attempt to describe a
cosmological journey, 'space itself is not yet *felt* to be natural or
even navigable, despite the continuous navigation'.[3]

The case is different with a later example, Dante's *Divina
commedia*, where space is used both in the traditional way to order
the ideological relationships in and between hell, purgatory and
paradise and also, at a local level, to place the pilgrim in a tangible
realm like that of the experiential world – one registered through
the sensory and psychological perceptions of the narrator:

> Note, on the one hand, the rationalized pattern, with its numerical,
> hierarchic orderings – reflecting by their locations immutable moral re-
> lationships; on the other, the continuously personal and humane response
> of the pilgrim who traverses this moral landscape, suffusing, I repeat, the
> abstract pattern with drama and immediacy.

2    Muscatine, 'Locus of Action', p. 117. Cf. the introduction to Ganim, *Style
     and Consciousness.*
3    Ibid., p. 118 (author's emphasis).

In such ways 'an irregular, humane naturalised setting [is used] to represent psychological and emotional experience'.[4] The combination of schematic and personal space produces that distinctively Gothic tension found also in art – a tension with potential for fracture as well as equipoise. Muscatine detected in Chaucer's contemporary, William Langland, a spatial anarchy or surrealism. Langland uses various types of space, 'but none of these becomes a controlling locus of his narrative'.[5] This instability he associated with the social upheavals of the fourteenth century.

Muscatine's article has important implications for a study of the representation of space in Chaucer's writings, and gives rise to a number of conjectures. One is that the visual arts is a fruitful area of enquiry and comparison. Another is that space may be conceptual, a means of ordering and structuring ideas, as well as perceptual, a representation of a feature of the visual world. It follows that the two, competing spatial codes of Gothic aesthetics enlarge the possibilities for literary design, meaning and mode. Then again, Chaucer's spatial constructs, as well as their effects, are likely to be distinctive: not like Dante's, not like Langland's, although founded on similar principles. Furthermore, such distinctiveness is likely to show in local details, both of protagonists and of their immediate surroundings, which are so crucial in creating a sense of realistic space. That space may also be a co-ordinate of personal experience, expressive of dramatic tension, feeling and thought. Nor can we fully understand Chaucer's use of space unless we also take account of its use by those writers, like Dante, with whose works he was familiar. Finally, an author's distinctive spatial structures may reflect key social formations and disruptions.

Joseph opted for a narrower frame of reference when he wrote in 1970 of 'Chaucer's differentiation of human space' in Fragment I of the *Canterbury Tales*.[6] In the Knight's Tale, he distinguished four enclosures – the prison, grove, temples and lists

---

4    Ibid., p. 119.
5    Ibid., p. 120. Cf. his *Poetry and Crisis*, pp. 87–90, repr. in his *Medieval Literature*, pp. 122–4.
6    Joseph, 'Chaucerian "Game"-"Earnest"', p. 83.

– which are progressively larger, reflecting the attempt of Theseus to impose a containing order on the experience of the Theban knights. The lasting impression, though, is that life is a prison, and this sense of human space contrasts with the more restricting interiors of the ensuing fabliaux which, paradoxically, are experienced as 'utterly congenial to human delight'.[7] Joseph argued that the use of space in Fragment I is Chaucer's means of expressing the 'argument of herbergage' referred to in the unfinished Cook's Tale (4329). It is 'a controlling principle in the entire structure of Fragment I. The Fragment asserts that the quantity and quality of space is relative to the perspective of the human mind contending with it'.[8] This notion, he contended, is applicable to other tales in the Canterbury sequence and to the narrative framework itself. The pilgrimage places the capacious, freely enjoyed and all-inclusive domestic space of the convivial Tabard against the more austere sense of space which the pilgrims experience as they approach, as the Parson would have it, 'Jerusalem celestial', where the limitations of human space dissolve in an all-embracing infinity.

A shortcoming of Joseph's approach is that he does not credit Chaucer's fabliaux with the capacity to sustain anything but a superficial treatment of space. In the Reeve's Tale, however, the subject of space is deeply embedded within the design of both the action and the thematic structure.[9] This cavil apart, Joseph identified some principles of spatial representation in Chaucer's writing which represent an advance on previous discussions of the topic. The first is that Chaucer is quite conscious and deliberate in using space to organize the meaning of his narratives. The second is that space is carefully differentiated to take account of the different mind-sets of the individuals who inhabit it. It means something different to different people: they have their own mental constructs, their own ways of apprehending the space which they occupy. The third, which follows from the first two, is that space

7    Ibid., p. 89.
8    Ibid., p. 91.
9    See below, pp. 136–43.

accommodates a variety of meanings, from a sense of existential imprisonment exacerbated by a restrictive interior, to a theatrical locus where ingenious actors can enjoy and benefit from the manipulation of their surroundings, to the dimensionlessness of God.

More recently, Stanbury and Spearing have begun to explore the connections between space and visual perception in relation to a range of medieval authors. Stanbury has drawn attention to the *Gawain*-poet's tendency to describe enclosed spaces constructed according to the perceptual experience of a narrative eyewitness.[10] At the same time, the limits of an individual's spatial perception are keyed to epistemological horizons (what is seen is what is known), so that the way in which space is perceived and understood becomes an index of intellectual and spiritual awareness – a point made previously by Muscatine in relation to Dante. Simultaneously, the reader is given access to broader dimensions and so can situate the protagonist's experience in relation to a more complex spatial structure. Thus the dreamer's experience in *Pearl* is related according to an optically coherent *erber* and landscape of paradise. In *Purity*, even when there is no textual witness, scenes are framed according to perceptual logic, and this is then used as metonym for the moral or spiritual life. Distinctive to *Sir Gawain and the Green Knight* is the extent to which enclosed space is constructed according to the returned gaze (a feature which heightens the spatial nature of his experience) as well as the sense that his choices and decisions are susceptible to a variety of possible interpretations. In *Patience* the *Gawain*-poet makes the fullest use of space, constructed according to lines of sight. Repeatedly, Jonah believes he can hide from God (in the hold of the ship, in the whale), but he finds that there is no escape from the divine, all-

10  Stanbury, *Seeing the Gawain-Poet*. See also her 'Space and Visual Hermeneutics'. As precursors, see Clark and Wasserman, 'Pearl Poet's City Imagery'; Eldredge, 'Sheltering Space and Cosmic Space'; Renoir, 'Descriptive Technique' and his 'Progressive Magnification'; and Spearing, *Gawain-Poet*, pp. 37–9 and 231–2.

penetrating gaze, that his personal and immediate space exists within larger spaces ultimately enclosed and controlled by God.[11]

Complementing Stanbury's work is Spearing's account of medieval European romance, connecting secrecy and looking with the organization of private and public space, and with the power exercised within them.[12] Central to his study is sexuality, insofar as sexual relations depend upon privacy and secrecy. In a culture that denied private space to most individuals, privacy was a privilege enjoyed by the élite. Within aristocratic households, private and public spaces were carefully differentiated in the forms respectively of chamber and hall, the latter a predominantly masculine domain and the former, with its curtained bed, predominantly feminine. Other forms of enclosure, such as gardens, window embrasures and darkness, also repay consideration because they too can be used to articulate the tense interconnections of private and public, secrecy and sexuality. The boundaries between public and private domains become crucial insofar as sexual privacy can be breached by spies, windows, light. But the privacy in question is not just that of lovers acting in defiance of the prevailing organization of space; it is that of the individual's innermost thoughts and feelings. Physical space is thus associated with subjectivity, whether by metaphors of inwardness or by seeking out places in which to be alone. In all this, the gaze is fundamental. It can be used to exert public power, to express unfulfilled and illegitimate desire, or to confirm the mutuality of secret love.[13] Insofar as the gaze requires distance, it is again a cornerstone of spatial design.

Both Stanbury and Spearing have themselves demonstrated the applications of such approaches to Chaucerian narrative. Stanbury has suggested that while Chaucer was at times indifferent to the visual coherence of his descriptions, there are a number of

11   On the shifting perspectives of *Patience* see also Clark and Wasserman, 'Jonah and the Whale'; and Padolsky, 'Steering the Reader's Heart'.
12   Spearing, *Medieval Poet as Voyeur*. Most of what follows is drawn from the first chapter. See also Gilchrist, *Gender and Archaeology*, ch. 6.
13   Cf. Baldwin, '"Gates Pure and Shining and Serene"'; Cline, 'Hearts and Eyes'; and Donaldson-Evans, 'Love's Fatal Glance'.

extraordinary exceptions. In subsequent work, she has made the crucial connection between a sense of space and acts of vision as they are represented in *Troilus and Criseyde*.[14] Insisting, as others have done, on the importance of subjectivity in the apprehension of space, she shows how Chaucer uses space to articulate the complex and dynamic relationships between private and public zones, as well as the varieties of power encountered in each. The oscillation between private and public is mapped by movement in and out of architectural constructs. Within and across these personal and public boundaries, space is devised through lines of sight, space which may nevertheless collapse into self-consciousness once the lover's gaze turns in upon itself. By such means the lovers, Pandarus and the audience become implicated in a species of voyeuristic activities. Pandarus, in particular, exults in the manipulation and control of space which, in the case of his house, becomes a feminized structure complete with secret passages and within which he exerts unquestioned power. Yet even he is in turn mastered by the intrusion of the public sphere, once the political situation demands Criseyde's departure from Troy. The final gaze of the narrative belongs to Troilus who, powerless to affect human actions, and no longer embroiled in private emotions, is reconfigured through an unprecedented perspective on his former self.

Spearing finds in *Troilus* seemingly contradictory features in its narrative organization and content: intense curiosity coupled with a strong sense of distance, and the presence of others at moments of great intimacy. Different kinds of space – closed and unenclosed, private and public – articulate these opposites, while at the same time showing the extent to which they interlock and interpenetrate. Sight plays a key part in the evocation of space, but so do hearing, light, temperature, darkness and touch. Yet the idea of space has less tangible outcomes: it applies also to the psychological and imaginative dimensions of the narrative. These include both the metaphysical realm to which Troilus departs, and memories of the past, anticipations of the future, dreams and the possibilities opened up by written texts. In gaining privileged access to such

14    Stanbury, 'Lover's Gaze'; and her 'Voyeur and the Private Life'.

mental spaces the reader is, like Pandarus and the narrator, frequently engaged in a process of prying, of intrusion, of violating the boundaries of private space. In *Troilus*, private space is frequently associated with the interior life, but more specifically with feminine or feminized experience. In the Knight's Tale, by contrast, such experience is allowed no room. Consequently public, masculine considerations dominate, and acts of vision no less than significant spaces tend to be open rather than secret, structured to convey general philosophical and cultural, rather than personal, import. Private life, along with Theseus' conquest of 'Femenye', has been expunged or at least suppressed.

Of all bodily senses, it is especially sight that is responsible for registering the complexity of spatial relations, however much touch, hearing or movement are also involved. Stanbury and Spearing have shown the extent to which Chaucer capitalized on lines of sight to create a sense of space in his narratives. Their careful analyses in these areas provide significant advances in our understanding of the means whereby Chaucer created spatial effects, and the uses to which they are put. Spearing has also recognized that Chaucer deploys additional sensory information to the same end. Stanbury has indicated how the apprehension of space in the act of visual perception can register a personal process of understanding and enlightenment. The idea that space is used to express the contest of power, realized in terms of public and private, male and female, has placed spatial representation at the heart of current critical discourse about medieval literature. That in its turn should not blind us to the possibility that the functions of space in Chaucerian narrative are, in practice, considerably more diverse. For example, Spearing has indicated that the spatial structures of Chaucer's narrative (in *Troilus*) might be regarded as extending to the representation of memory and the imagination and to the reader's subjective interpretation of these topics.

Another welcome tendency of the approaches taken by Stanbury and Spearing is their emphasis on the individual as mediating subject in the apprehension and interpretation of space. As they imply, an individual's sense of space derives in the first instance from the ministrations of the body. For the human body is at once object, having three-dimensional form in relation to ambient space, and subject, perceiving its own and other forms and interpreting them, including their spatial identities and relations.[15] Chaucer's accounts of the human body, as the meeting place of object and subject, are central to his representation of narrative space, for he focuses both on the space occupied by an individual and how that location, and its complex relationship to the surrounding space, are subjectively perceived and construed.[16] The relationship between body as affective subject and other, contingent spatial forms is mediated primarily through the sense of sight and yet, as Spearing has reminded us, it is also expressed through movement (including posture and gesture), touch, smell, sound, speech and sexual attraction. Thus it is by means of the body that space is perceived, lived and produced. Alternatively, one might conclude that it is by means of space, which is suceptible to endless redefinition, that the body achieves its sense of place and identity, that it is through space that the relations of power, gender and status are articulated and negotiated as an individual interprets, and reinterprets, his or her place in the world.

Such observations are applicable not only to literary texts, but also to a wider range of cultural products. Some archaeological studies of medieval culture have approached space in relation to the human body, taking into account landscape, urban topography, architectural structure and boundary.[17] The spaces within which bodies were limited, enclosed, classified, controlled, segregated, liberated, are expressive of social values and order, but space is also dynamic and provides a means for transforming social relationships and personal identity. Gilchrist has explored the links between space and body in the case of medieval hospitals which, positioned on the

15  Cf. Thomas, *Time, Culture and Identity*, pp. 83–91.
16  A number of studies have begun to explore Chaucer's poetry 'in corporeal terms' – a phrase used by Gallacher, 'Chaucer and the Rhetoric of the Body', p. 218. On the more general neglect of the body in cultural studies, see Porter, 'History of the Body', p. 223.
17  Gilchrist, *Gender and Material Culture*, ch. 6; and her 'Medieval Bodies'.

edges of towns, were the sites for both the incarceration and display
of stigmatized (diseased and sinful) bodies such as those of lepers.
She also shows how 'Space is fundamental in the construction of
gender'[18] by examining the design of space for women in castles,
where their numbers were strictly limited, and where chastity was
protected by enclosure, and in nunneries, where female religious
were subject to more strict control than their male counterparts. In
these cases, space was deployed to limit the potential for sexual
corruption and transgression and to maintain hierarchy and bodily
purity. Similarly, the radical reorganization of space is expressive of a
concomitant change in female status and power.[19]

No less promising than the evidence from material culture are
the traditional and extensive linguistic correspondences between the
body and images of enclosure. These have been mapped by Pouch-
elle in relation to a medieval treatise on surgery written between
1306 and 1320 by Henri de Mondeville, surgeon to Philip the Fair
of France, but she also draws on a much wider range of medieval
writings.[20] Human constructs, especially buildings, and topography,
are used as metaphors for describing different parts and functions
of the body: the body is a building, a castle, a prison, a city, a ship, a
cave; its mouth a door; its eyes, windows; its insides figured by other
containers such as a cage, coffer, pot or purse. Typically, domestic
interiors are associated with the female body, especially the womb
(man's first dwelling-place), and as femininity is linked with a pro-
tected, inner, enclosed domestic space, so masculinity is linked to
the outside, to unrestricted, 'wild' space. Thus, sexual and personal
identity are bound up with forms of spatial representation which are
frequently concentric in design, so reflecting the structure of the
universe itself.[21]

18    Ibid., p. 49.
19    For an overview of the approach exemplified by Gilchrist, see Fairclough,
      'Meaningful Constructions'; and Grenville, *Medieval Housing*, pp. 14–22.
      Gilchrist's ideas are also influential in Raguin and Stanbury (eds), *Women's
      Space*.
20    Pouchelle, *Body and Surgery*, ch. 8 and Table 2.
21    See also Camille, *Gothic Idol*, pp. 87–101, on the connections between
      sexual taboo and bodily boundaries.

What are the implications for Chaucer's poetry of non-literary studies such as these? In general terms they tend to confirm one of the findings of critical writings: that his spatial representations are deliberate and artificial, and therefore need to be interpreted as significant aspects of his overall meaning. That meaning cannot be dissociated from the symbolic forms which space took in Chaucer's own culture. So it behoves the reader to be aware of social space as expressed through the organization of, say, houses, courts or towns, while at the same time recognizing that spatial design in the material world expresses power relations and reflects divisions and separations of estate and gender. More than this – there is the distinct likelihood that Chaucer is not merely representing spatial formations and what they customarily expressed in his own culture but also contesting them, much as he represents but interrogates other received ideas, whether in the form of source material, rhetorical convention or ideology. Thus, his delineation of boundaries, enclosures, and their transgression, and his explorations of liminal states, are likely to be revealing both of dominant social forms of space and of his own account of them.

The theoretical positions emerging from Stanbury, Spearing, Gilchrist and Pouchelle receive some support from those cultural historians of the Middle Ages who have considered space as subject to temporal and cultural change. Gurevich's focus is not so much on space as a feature of the physical world as on the subjective experience of that space, which alters according to society, social development and the individual. According to him, we are not born with an innate sense of space: like the sense of time, with which it is closely related, it has to be learned. In the Middle Ages, space is charged with emotional and spiritual potential:

> time and space can be good or evil, beneficial for certain kinds of activity, dangerous or hostile to others; there is a sacral time, a time to make merry, a time for sacrifice, a time for the re-enactment of the myth connected with the return of 'primordial' time; and in the same way there exists a

sacral space, there are sacral places or whole worlds subject to special forces.[22]

The painted or written representation of space produces its own categories, its own conventions for delineating spatial phenomena. These representational codes are affected by the special creative and ideological problems which a particular artist faces. The implication is that spatial representation in literature is not something which is merely transcribed from the material world, but on the contrary an artificial construct with its own particular valences and functions. Thus in looking at the representation of space in narrative we are looking at the reconstruction of an existing construct, itself posited on one of the naturally occurring structures of the physical world.

To clarify: the visual world exists as an array of forms which occupy space, and which exist in spatial relations with each other. This visual array, as the psychologists of perception remind us, we learn to see, to interpret, in order to identify objects, move about, touch, interact.[23] Merely at this operational level the nature of spatial awareness varies from culture to culture and from individual to individual. There is then superimposed a whole range of symbolic structures and values particular to culture, time and protagonist. Narrative poets cannot ignore their own circumstances in this respect – they are enmeshed in them – but that need not prevent the introduction of a further layer of spatial design, one which responds to a writer's particular reading of the cultural environment, and to his or her own intentions for the narrative work in question.

For le Goff, the representation of space in literary narrative provides crucial evidence for that larger enterprise, a history of the medieval imagination, to which he has dedicated an exploratory book. His approach requires that we regard 'space' as an elastic term, applicable both to geographical areas and to the individual

---

22    Gurevich, *Categories of Medieval Culture*, p. 29.
23    See esp. Gibson, *Perception of the Visual World*.

conscience.[24] In one way this may be a liberating approach to the concept because it breaks down the sense of boundary between outer and inner experience.[25] At the same time, le Goff's approach draws attention to the symbolic as well as to the literal dimensions of space.[26]

Paul Zumthor's *La Mesure du monde*, subtitled *La Representation de l'espace au moyen âge*, builds upon the work of Gurevich and le Goff, among others. Although a literary scholar, Zumthor takes a topographical and geographical approach: he includes literary material but it enjoys no special privilege alongside the other evidence. Ranging over one thousand years of cultural history, he creates a *summa* of typical places (village, house, city, church, monastery, garden) in order to describe the essential features of their social functions and spatial design. He then proceeds to consider in similar terms how such places were separated (say by desert or forest), linked (roads, pilgrimage, chivalric adventure), or sought to expand their influence and power (territory, conquest, crusade, travel, trade, exploration, missionary activity). The forms of representation Zumthor examines extend to maps and painted and sculpted images. Although he expresses an interest in optical representations of space, it centres on the emergence from medieval theory of artificial perspective with its emphasis on a single point of view – a development seen as expressive of a fundamental shift in the relationship between the individual and the surrounding world. Zumthor also explores ways in which attitudes towards personal, public and political space and distance were affected through the symbolic structures of belief, myth and alienation. He stresses, once again, the importance of the human body and mind as mediators between the world 'out there' and the world 'in here' in creating a sense of individual or collective identity, or of the marginal, the exiled, the other and the monstrous. A concluding chapter on 'l'espace des textes' focuses on the make-up of the manuscript page and the function of book

24   Le Goff, *Medieval Imagination*, p. 13.
25   Cf. Porter, 'History of the Body', p. 212.
26   Le Goff, *Medieval Imagination*, p. 65.

as object rather than what Zumthor terms *espace décrit*, the subject
of the present study.

There is also much to be learned from theorists whose
primary focus is not the medieval period. Lefebvre shares with
Gurevich, le Goff and Zumthor the conviction that space is a
cultural product with its own history and he has drawn attention to
its inherent complexity and richness. There is a multitude of spaces
to bear in mind: not only the sacral, as Gurevich describes it, but
also the geographic, economic, demographic, sociological, political,
commercial or national, each interlocking with the others.[27] The
organization of social space, whether in the form of territorial
arrangements, within towns, or within buildings themselves, serves
the dominant social group, but by that token space also becomes
the means whereby power is challenged and contested. Inevitably,
social space becomes embodied in representations of space:
demarcations, limits, boundaries, walls, and the relationships of
symbolic objects within them, articulate structures of belief, power
and control. They also delineate the territory which must be chal-
lenged, invaded or negotiated by rival claimants. Social space is a
product, artificially made, susceptible to decoding, expressive of a
society's values and aspirations. Literature is full of it: 'any search
for space in literary texts will find it everywhere and in every guise:
enclosed, projected, dreamt of, speculated about'.[28] This flexibility
of the literary imagination enables it both to reflect existing models
of spatial organization, but also to change, appropriate, propose
alternatives, so redesigning their prescribed limits and contesting
their symbolic content.[29] Thus, an analysis of narrative space needs
to be based on some understanding of what cultural space, in the
larger sense, might mean.[30]

---

27  Lefebvre, *Production of Space*, p. 8. Like Spearing, he places a stress on
    sense-perception, gesture and sexual energy in the creation of inter-
    personal space (pp. 162, 169–71, 182–3, 194–205, 212–18 and 363).
28  Ibid., p. 15.
29  Ibid, p. 39.
30  For a reading of Lefebvre alongside the work of Frederic Jameson, see
    Dear, 'Postmodern Bloodlines'. For an attempt to conceptualize the issues
    from a geographical standpoint, see Harrison, *Medieval Space*.

The studies discussed above lay the groundwork for a wide-ranging account of Chaucer's use of space. They suggest several possible categories of analysis: representational technique (descriptions of architecture, the gaze, visual cues, the body), symbolic function (space as an index of knowledge, of subjective states, as articulating the contest of public and private, or the play of power) and cultural context (social space, pictorial space). There have been valuable contributions in each of these areas but, viewed as a whole, the work done on Chaucer's use of space is localized and fragmentary. His representational techniques, the meanings expressed through spatial design, and the cultural contexts, are all categories that may be considerably expanded. There is also a need for a more complex explanatory model than any of those advanced thus far, one that provides a fuller framework of understanding.

All of the scholars considered above endorse the notion that space is something deliberately made or, to use Lefebvre's term, produced. This idea promises the best theoretical starting-point for an analysis of Chaucer's writings, for it enables us to consider various levels of spatial representation under a common principle. Thus, one can look at the way in which space was produced within the context of Chaucer's society, his appropriation and redefinition of spatial forms, and then at the construction of space within narrative on the part of the protagonists. To regard space as produced by the agency of social groups, authors or fictive individuals helps to explain its dynamic nature, the extent to which it is subject to perpetual negotiation between, say, the demands of public life and private life or between individuals whose perceptions of each other differ. Seen like this, it becomes more explicable as an instrument of political power or sexual desire, and as a means whereby personal or social identity is translated into the actions and settings of the material world. It also raises questions of function and technique. Thus, space may be made to express knowledge stored in the memory, or to articulate emotion, using methods which range from architectural description to accounts of visual experience. It follows that we should not think of space as undifferentiated but as a phenomenon that subdivides into many different kinds: personal, dramatic, architectural, cosmic, each bearing its own hallmark according to the proclivities of its 'producer' and each, as often as not, in contention with other, rival, spatial schemata.

The possibility of developing a fuller and more satisfactory account of Chaucer's use of space, based on the best that modern critical and theoretical writing has to offer, should not be allowed to obscure one uncomfortable fact. Chaucer himself did not have access to a Stanbury, a Zumthor or a Lefebvre, and so did not conceptualize his practices in ways that are open to us. To state this is not to invalidate modern studies of space, and even less to imply that Chaucer's own conceptual framework was comparatively unsophisticated. On the contrary, modern studies of space have opened up for Chaucerians an important new area of enquiry. But its significance *in a medieval context* is only now becoming apparent. The more it does, the more necessary it is to question and modify modern interpretations, whether theoretical or empirical, in order to avoid imposing on Chaucer anachronistic models of spatial representation. The priorities are to identify in as much detail as possible the precise forms in which he represented space, the meanings they express and the conceptual ideas that underpin them. To this end, we need to ask a key question that has been largely omitted from current critical studies, namely: What concepts of space were available to Chaucer?

One obvious answer, which bears repetition, is that he discovered his spatial models in the literary works with which he was familiar. Certainly, it is of crucial importance that we take account of the texts that inform Chaucer's compositions. But they provide only half an explanation for, as the published research has led us to expect, Chaucer performs on his received material feats of transformation, reconfiguring received symbolic codes to make his spatial designs his and his alone. In doing so he manifests a high level of awareness about space and its cultural uses. That awareness is informed by an understanding that space is produced in different ways by different people and agencies, that it is a flexible semiotic system capable of expressing a range of meanings from political power to personal aspiration, that his readers and audience are necessarily involved in the process of constructing and interpreting the spaces he describes. So we need to look to broader cultural contexts for a fuller answer to the question, which might be rephrased as: What were the precedents and models, other than those found in his immediate sources, that enabled him to create his distinctive spatial designs?

As the concluding chapter of this book indicates, a full answer lies in a range of diverse cultural topics including affective piety, memory systems and pictorial perspective, that could not possibly be given their due weight within the scope of a single monograph. Instead, the contextual emphasis of the present study lies in a body of thought and writing well suited to Chaucer's spatial imagination: the science of optics, or *perspectiva*. Specialized and more popular texts on the science of sight were of widespread influence and appeal and, it will be argued, they provided Chaucer and his public with new and powerful ways of understanding the production of space. *Perspectiva* acted as a catalyst, a stimulus to regarding space as interesting in its own right, and as a subtle instrument for exploring and articulating the complex connections of a range of related issues.

Medieval optical writings represented space as predominantly a visual phenomenon, a product of the gaze; stressed the fundamental importance of light in the perception of spatial relations; showed how spatial perception could be transliterated into terms descriptive of visual cues and subjective judgement; and embedded the treatment of light, vision and space within a traditional symbolic system while allowing for the possibility that such phenomena might be regarded as value-free objects of scientific enquiry. The discipline of *perspectiva* put space on the cusp between personal and public, the imagined and the real, the body and other objects, demonstrating the very ways in which it was a constructed phenomenon, its making and interpretation the products of an interplay between the human intelligence and the physical world. It exemplified ways in which personal space interacts with spaces determined by others, thus undergoing a continual process of adjustment and revision. And it identified the extent to which human vision and spatial experience, far from being reliable indicators of knowledge gained, are subject to deception. It refused a simple correlation between space and cognition, replacing it with an altogether more problematic formula: what we see is what we think we know.

# 2 The Making of Optical Space

> The existence of the spatial depends on the interrelations of objects [...] space is not absolute, it is relational.[1]

What Stanbury refers to as 'lines of sight'[2] is the subject-matter of *perspectiva*. A central concern of this important and influential discipline is the perception of space, understood as the product of a human interpreter engaged in deciphering visual cues, especially those that indicate the distance between the eye and an array of forms and textures. It also covers the conditions which make the perception of space possible (light, colour, form) or which make it difficult or prone to error. The scientific and theological traditions from which the medieval science of optics developed are varied, and the long process of synthesis from Greek, Arabic and Western ideas is a complex one.[3] In the present chapter I provide an introduction to the treatment of space in key optical works circulating in England during the later fourteenth century, especially those by Robert Grosseteste, Ibn al-Haytham (Alhacen) and Roger Bacon. I then proceed to evaluate the status of *perspectiva* as part of my general aim of providing a sense of a significant intellectual context within which Chaucer used space as an expressive device.

---

1 Massey, *Space, Place and Gender*, p. 261.
2 Stanbury, *Seeing the Gawain-Poet*, p. 5 and *passim*.
3 The leading authority is David C. Lindberg, whose writings are referred to frequently below. For a thorough survey, see especially his *Theories of Vision*. Many of his key articles are collected in his *Studies in the History of Medieval Optics*. For a succinct history of *perspectiva*, see *Witelonis perspectivae liber quintus*, ed. and trans. Smith, pp. 18–31.

# Robert Grosseteste (*c*.1168–1253)

The high standing of *perspectiva* as an intellectual discipline in the second half of the fourteenth century may be traced back to the importance attached to optical ideas a century earlier by Robert Grosseteste, and to the powerful positions and lengthy period during which he disseminated them. He lectured in theology in the Oxford schools from 1225–30, then became first lector to the Franciscan school at Oxford. In 1235 he was elected bishop of Lincoln. He died in 1253 at the age of about eighty-five.[4] Succeeding generations of scholars absorbed his views on the utility and special status of optics among the natural sciences.[5] Grosseteste's original scientific works, and his commentaries on Aristotle, helped to establish the pre-eminence of Oxford in natural philosophy.[6] He considered optics to be 'the fundamental physical science'[7] and wrote a number of works which examined the nature and properties of light. Of these the most remarkable is an early composition, *De luce* (*c*.1226), with the contemporary *Commentary on the Posterior Analytics* (1220–8) providing further material of interest. The other optical works were all written towards the end of his time at Oxford, *c*.1230–3: *De lineis* – *De natura locorum*, *De iride* and *De colore*.[8] Together, they laid the foundations for the discipline

4    For Grosseteste's life, scholarship and influence, see Southern, *Grosseteste*, esp. pp. 1–101 and his 'A Last Review', prefacing the second edition; also Callus, 'Grosseteste as Scholar', pp. 1–11; Crombie, *Grosseteste*; McEvoy, *Philosophy of Grosseteste*, pp. 3–25; and Russell, 'Phases'.

5    Cobban, *Medieval English Universities*, pp. 42 and 277–9; Crombie, 'Grosseteste's Position', pp. 112–13 and his *Grosseteste*, pp. 135–6; and McEvoy, *Philosophy of Grosseteste*, pp. 8–13 and 17–19. On Grosseteste's influence see also below, pp. 87–94.

6    Callus, 'Grosseteste as Scholar', pp. 12–15 and 25–8; and his 'Introduction of Aristotelian Learning', pp. 253–5.

7    Crombie, 'Grosseteste's Position', p. 111.

8    For dating see Dales, 'Grosseteste's Scientific Works', pp. 394–401; McEvoy, 'Chronology', pp. 631–55; and his *Philosophy of Grosseteste*, Appendix B. For lists of extant MSS see Lindberg, *Catalogue*, pp. 57–62. For a bibliography of Grosseteste's writings, see Thomson, *Writings of*

of *perspectiva* as it evolved at Oxford and elsewhere, establishing its credentials as a scientific enterprise consonant with Christian teaching.

The task of assimilation was not entirely straightforward. Grosseteste's sources were texts in the natural sciences, deriving from Greek and Arabic originals, of the sort that had been banned at Paris by papal ordinance in 1210.[9] He was acquainted with optical writings by Euclid, Aristotle, Avicenna, and perhaps Alkindi and Averroes.[10] The success of Grosseteste's act of synthesis may be attributed both to Oxford's relative freedom from papal control, which made it a more fertile ground for the reception of natural science,[11] and to two key procedural strategies which he adopted. In the first place, he foregrounded a methodology – Euclidean geometry – that was non-controversial, and a long-established part of the quadrivium, as the basis for studying the novel subject of optics. The study of geometry is important, wrote Grosseteste, because all the causes of natural effects take place through lines, angles and diagrams ('Omnes enim causae effectuum naturalium habent dari per lineas, angulos et figuras.')[12] Thus, he represented optics itself as a sub-species of an already familiar and accepted discipline.[13] It is 'a science built on visual

*Grosseteste*, which supplement with McEvoy, *Philosophy of Grosseteste*, Appendix A.

9    Coppleston, *History of Medieval Philosophy*, pp. 200–2 and 206–12. On the relations between the papacy and the University of Paris, see Cobban, *Medieval Universities*, ch. 4.

10   Crombie, *Grosseteste*, pp. 116–17. For an assessment of Grosseteste's optical thought in relation to the medieval tradition, see Lindberg, *Theories of Vision*, pp. 100–2.

11   See Camille, 'Illustrations in Harley MS 3487'; Leff, '*Trivium* and the Three Philosophies', pp. 319–25; ten Doesschate, 'Oxford and the Revival of Optics'; and Weisheipl, 'Science in the Thirteenth Century', p. 19.

12   Grosseteste, *De lineis*, in *Philosophischen Werke*, ed. Baur, p. 60; trans. Eastwood, 'Geometrical Optics', p. 90. Eastwood also translates *De natura locorum* and *De iride*. Complete translations by Lindberg of *De lineis* and *De iride* also appear in *Source Book*, ed. Grant, pp. 385–91.

13   Cf. Lindberg, 'Introduction' to *Bacon and the Origins of Perspectiva*, pp. xxxvii–xl; and Molland, 'Geometrical Background', pp. 109–10.

figures and this includes the science which is based upon figures formed by radiant lines and surfaces, whether they are radiating projections from the sun, the stars, or any other radiant body'.[14] Grosseteste went on to elaborate his theory of the way in which these lines of light rays are produced. Objects emit rays not just to the observer but spherically, in all directions, creating a world where space is filled by the radiant light emanating from three-dimensional forms: 'For every agent projects its power spherically, since it does so on all sides and along every diameter: upwards and downwards, before and after, to the right and to the left.'[15]

For Grosseteste, light was much more than the means whereby objects announce and transmit their presence to the world at large. Since light of its nature propagates itself spherically, in three dimensions, it must be the basis of materiality itself (or what Grosseteste calls *corporeitas*). The three-dimensional propagation of light is an idea elaborated in *De luce*, where he describes light as the very origin and essence of corporeity:

> The first corporeal form which some call corporeity is in my opinion light. For light of its very nature diffuses itself in every direction in such a way that a point of light will produce instantaneously a sphere of light of any size whatsoever, unless some opaque object stands in the way. Now the extension of matter in three dimensions is the necessary concomitant of corporeity, and this despite the fact that both corporeity and matter are in themselves simple substances lacking all dimension [...] Whatever performs this function of introducing corporeity into matter is either light or some agent that acts in virtue of its participation in light to which this operation belongs essentially. Corporeity, therefore, is either light itself or the agent which performs the aforementioned operation and introduces dimensions into matter in virtue of its participation in light, and acts through the power of the same light. But the first form cannot introduce

14    'scientia, quae erigitur super figuras visuales, et haec subalternat sibi scientiam, quae erigitur super figuras, quae continent lineae et superficies radiosae, sive proiecta sint illa radiosa et sole, sive ex stellis, sive ex aliquo corpore radiante.' Grosseteste, *De iride*; ed. Baur, p. 72; trans. Eastwood, p. 177.
15    'Omne enim agens multiplicat suam virtutem sphaerice, quoniam undique et in omnes diametros: sursum deorsum, ante retro, dextrorsum sinistrorsum.' Ibid.; ed. Baur, p. 64; trans. Eastwood, p. 118.

dimensions into matter through the power of a subsequent form. Therefore light is not a form subsequent to corporeity, but it is corporeity itself.[16]

Grosseteste is establishing much more than an ingenious analogy between the three-dimensional transmission of light and the three-dimensional nature of material forms. For him, light has a primal quality: it is the informing substance of the physical world, inundating and informing both objects and their ambient space; it is no less than the instrument with which God created the universe. Here then is the second, and the more profound, of those strategies by means of which Grosseteste developed a rationale for *perspectiva*: he coupled it with a long-standing tradition of light metaphysics, neoplatonic in origin and channelled through the writings of pseudo-Dionysius and Augustine, which regarded light as the very essence of existence.[17]

In *De luce*, he makes a distinction between primal light (*lux*), the very first corporeal form, and secondary light (*lumen*). On a cosmic scale *lux*, as was its nature, multiplied itself spherically into a mass the size of the material universe ('in tantam molem, quanta

---

16   'Formam primam corporalem, quam quidam corporeitatem vocant, lucem esse arbitror. Lux enim per se in omnem partem se ipsam diffundit, ita ut e puncto lucis sphaera lucis quamvis magna subito generetur, nisi obsistat umbrosum. Corporeitas vero est, quam de necessitate consequitur extensio materiae secundum tres dimensiones, cum tamen utraque, corporeitas scilicet et materia, sit substantia in se ipsa simplex, omni carens dimensione [...] Corporeitas ergo aut est ipsa lux, aut est dictum opus faciens et in materiam dimensiones inducens, in quantum participat ipsam lucem et agit per virtutem ipsius lucis. Ac vero formam primam in materiam dimensiones inducere per virtutem formae consequentis ipsam est impossibile. Non est ergo lux forma consequens ipsam corporeitatem, sed est ipsa corporeitas.' Grosseteste, *De luce*; ed. Baur, pp. 51–2; trans. Riedl, *On Light*, p. 10. On the three-dimensional propagation of light, see Baur, 'Licht in der Naturphilosophie des Grosseteste', pp. 50–1; his *Philosophie des Grosseteste*, pp. 80–4; Eastwood, 'Geometrical Optics', pp. 18–20; and McEvoy, 'Metaphysics of Light', p. 132.

17   French and Cunningham, *Before Science*, pp. 230–7; and McEvoy, *Philosophy of Grosseteste*, pp. 68–123. Cf. Lindberg, 'Genesis', pp. 7–23; and McEvoy, 'Nature as Light'.

est mundi machina' ).[18] Having completely realized its potential for spherical expansion, the outermost parts of the universe (the firmament) are more extended and more rarefied than those within ('plus extendi et magis rarefieri, quam partes intimas').[19] The firmament can expand no further, and transmits its own reflected or secondary light (*lumen*) concentrically, back towards the centre of the universe. The *lumen* of the firmament also realizes its maximum potential: 'in the outermost parts of the mass in question, the second sphere came into being, completely actualized and capable of no further impression'.[20] In its turn, the second sphere gives out its *lumen*, thus generating a third sphere. This process of propagation continues, the spheres becoming progressively smaller and less rarefied, until the universe is complete, with the earth and its four elemental spheres at the centre.[21] It is a short step from the neoplatonic cosmogony which Grosseteste describes in *De luce* to the account of creation in Genesis 1:4, where light is a product of God's work on the first day, preexisting the sun and moon which were not created until the fourth day. Commentaries on the *Hexaëmeron*, one of which Grosseteste wrote (*c*.1232–5), traditionally stressed the importance of light in the Christian scheme of creation.[22]

---

18    Grosseteste, *De luce*; ed Baur, p. 52; trans. Riedl, p. 11. For commentary see Baur, *Philosophie des Grosseteste*, pp. 85–93; Callus, 'Grosseteste's Place', pp. 161–5; Crombie, *Grosseteste*, pp. 104–31; Eastwood, 'Geometrical Optics', pp. 16–18 and 21–5; Lindberg, *Theories of Vision*, pp. 95–9; Lynch, 'Doctrine of Divine Ideas'; McEvoy, *Philosophy of Grosseteste*, pp. 151–88; and Southern, *Grosseteste*, pp. 136–9.

19    Grosseteste, *De luce*; ed. Baur, p. 54; trans. Riedl, p. 13.

20    'Et ita fiebat in ipsis partibus extimis dictae molis sphaera secunda completa nullius impressionis ultra receptibilis.' Ibid.; ed. Baur, p. 55; trans. Riedl, p. 14.

21    Ibid.; ed. Baur, pp. 55–6; trans. Riedl, pp. 14–15.

22    Grosseteste, *Hexaëmeron*, II. iv–xi; ed. Dales and Gieben, pp. 88–101; trans. Martin, pp. 87–101. See also McEvoy, *Philosophy of Grosseteste*, pp. 60–3; Muckle, 'Hexameron of Grosseteste', pp. 153–4 and 160–3; and Southern *Grosseteste*, pp. 205–11. The relation of Grosseteste's commentary to the expository tradition, particularly to St Basil's commentary on the *Hexaëmeron*, is also described in Baur, *Philosophie des Grosseteste*, pp. 76–81.

By regarding the universe and the corporeity of its forms as a result of the agency of light, Grosseteste was able to give the scientific discipline of optics a theological sanction.[23] If God gave preference to the creation of light and light was, as the informing principle of the universe, corporeity itself, then optics as a study of light was a key to gaining knowledge of God. The external behaviour of light in the physical world therefore has a direct bearing on the internal illumination of the soul; and the analogies that can be drawn between the nature of the outer eye and the inner eye are a means of elucidating scriptural truth.[24] In the next chapter we shall see how traditional comparisons between the outer and inner eye were given new currency both by Grosseteste's interest in the topic and by the rapid spread of optical ideas to homiletic literature.

## Alhacen (*c*.965–*c*.1039)

Informing all parts of the physical world, light for Grosseteste is the fundamental component of the phenomenon of space, whether that occupied by solid objects, or that between them, or that through which they are perceived. Furthermore, he accentuated the functions of light as both the instrument of God's creative power and as an index of spiritual cognition. Grosseteste's metaphysical tendencies are somewhat removed from Chaucer's natural inclinations as a poet of descriptive narrative, although he was fully aware of the epistemological associations of vision and

---

23  McEvoy, *Philosophy of Grosseteste*, pp. 280–9. Cf. Crombie, *Grosseteste*, p. 106; Devons, 'Optics'; and Lindberg, *Theories of Vision*, p. 99. On the traditions of light symbolism, see Bevan *Symbolism and Belief*, lecture 6; and note the useful bibliography by Bremer, 'Licht als universales Darstellungsmedium'.
24  Crombie, *Grosseteste*, pp. 128–31; Eastwood, 'Mediaeval Empiricism'; McEvoy, *Philosophy of Grosseteste*, pp. 106–8, 136–9 and 335–9; and Southern, *Grosseteste*, p. 135.

light, especially through his reading of Boethius and Dante. But as far as optical texts are concerned, his stronger affinity is with an author who concentrates, like him, on the seen world – its surfaces, appearance, changing aspects, capacity for deception and the problems of interpretation that follow.

*Kitab al-Manazir*, written *c.*1000 by the Arabic author Ibn al-Haytham, and translated into Latin in the early thirteenth century as the *De aspectibus* (On visual appearances) of Alhacen, has none of the spiritual overtones of Grosseteste's scientific work. Writing in an Aristotelian and empirical tradition, light for Alhacen is a purely physical phenomenon that is a prerequisite for vision. Vision, in turn, is the sensory means whereby space is apprehended. The 'how' of that apprehension is the subject of much of his book, as the frontispiece to the first printed edition of 1572 illustrates (Fig. 2.1): how the eye perceives and interprets space; what visual cues enable the observer to detect and measure it; the mental and physiological processes that are involved. Again, Alhacen's explanatory model for the 'lines of sight' through which the perception of space is made possible is that developed by Euclid and Ptolemy, but in other areas he introduced innovations and modifications, often with a basis in experimental procedures, that proved persuasive enough to put the entire subject on a new footing.[25] His work was unknown to Grosseteste but, once translated, it rapidly assumed a prominent position and became the most influential of all medieval works on optics.[26]

25   Lindberg, 'Alhazen's Theory of Vision', pp. 331–41; Smith, 'Introduction' to *Alhacen's Theory of Visual Perception*, pp. cxii–cxviii; and Vescovini, 'Fortune de l'optique d'Ibn al-Haitham'. For a succinct account of optical theory prior to Alhacen, see Lindberg, 'Introduction' to *Bacon and the Origins of Perspectiva*, pp. xxv–xxxvii.

26   Smith, 'Introduction' to *Alhacen's Theory of Visual Perception*, pp. clv–clxi, lists 22 Latin MSS. The translation of *Kitab-al-Manazir* into Latin is discussed by Lindberg, *Theories of Vision*, pp. 209–10; and see his 'Introduction' to *Opticae thesaurus*, ed. Risner, pp. vi–vii. The Arabic text of books 1–3 has been translated by Sabra as *Optics of Ibn al-Haytham*, the Latin text of books 1–3 by Smith as *Alhacen's Theory of Visual Perception*.

# VITELLONIS THV
### R I N Ĝ O P O L O N I   O P T I-
#### CAE LIBRI DECEM.

Inftaurati,figuris nouis illuftrati atque aucti:infinitisq; erroribus,
quibus antea fcatebant,expurgati.

A'

F̈ D E R I C Ó  R I S N E R O.

B A S I L E AE,

**Figure 2.1.** The frontispiece to *Opticae thesaurus*, ed. Risner
(1572). [Science and Society Picture Library.]

Alhacen's first important accomplishment was to establish that light originates not in the eye, as some Platonists (including Euclid and Ptolemy) thought, but at the perceived object.[27] He drew attention to the fact that very bright light is painful to the eye and that it leaves an after-image:

> when an observer looks at a pure white body illuminated by intense daylight, even though there may be no [direct] sunlight, if he continues to look at that body for a while and then shifts his focus to a dark location, he will see the form of its light, along with its shape, in that dark location.[28]

This evidence shows that light has some effect in the eye and that illuminated colours have an effect in the eye. It is therefore proposed that in vision the eye receives light from external sources.

Light and colour stream perpetually from each point on the surface of coloured, radiant objects.[29] Light and colour travel in straight lines and in all directions, and it is their property to pass together through any transparent body. Now the eye itself is made up of transparent layers or tunics. Therefore the eye senses light and colour ('visus sentit lumen et colores que sunt in superficie

---

27    Sabra, 'Ibn Al-Haytham's Criticisms'. For general commentary, see Bauer, *Psychologie Alhazens*; Lindberg, *Theories of Vision*, pp. 58–86; Ronchi, *Nature of Light*, pp. 45–57; Sabra, 'Sensation and Inference'; Vescovini, *Prospettiva medievale*, pp. 113–32; and Winter, 'Optical Researches'.

28    'quando inspiciens inspexerit corpus mundum album super quod oriebatur lux diei et fuerit illa lux fortis, quamvis non sit lux solis et moretur in aspectu diu deinde auferat visum suum ad locum obscurum inveniet formam illius lucis in loco obscure illo, et inveniet cum hoc figuram eius. Deinde si clauserit visum et fuerit intuens secundum horam, inveniet in oculo suo formam illius lucis'. Alhacen, *De aspectibus*, I .4. 3; ed. Smith, pp. 3–4. Translations from Alhacen are by Smith unless otherwise stated.

29    'a quolibet punctorum que sunt in superficiebus visibilium illuminatorum extenduntur cum quolibet lumine forme eius super quamlibet lineam rectam, que potest extendi ex illo puncto'. Ibid., I. 6. 20; ed. Smith, p. 30. This proposition is treated at greater length in the first three chapters of the Arabic text. See Lindberg, *Theories of Vision*, pp. 240–1, n. 31. On the propagation of light according to Alhacen, see Rashed, 'Optique géométrique', pp. 273–81.

rei vise, et pertranseunt per diafonitatem tunicarum visus').[30]
In order to receive forms of light and colour the eye has merely to
be placed opposite an irradiated, coloured object.[31] This leads
Alhacen to a further critique and refutation of the Euclidean
argument that visual rays issue from the eye. Such extramission
theories, he says, are an attempt to explain in tactile terms how
objects are apprehended when a space separates them from the
observer. But since the transmission of forms to the eye by light
and colour has already been adequately explained, the idea that
rays issue from the eye is otiose; nor does it explain the perception
of objects at a distance.[32] In denying their physical existence, how-
ever, Alhacen does not jettison the notion of rays as geometrical
symbols. They are useful to mathematicians in demonstrating the
extension of forms across space to the eye, but radial lines are
imaginary.[33]

In stating that each point on the surface of an object sends
out light rays in all directions, Alhacen had introduced a sizeable
problem, although one which he recognized. For from a single
point on the surface of the object many rays will come to the eye.
If the eye is receiving such rays from every visible point, then there
is in the eye a process of superimposition: 'since the parts of a
single visible object have different colors, from any one of those
spots the form of color and light will reach the entire surface of
the eye; and thus the colors of those parts will mingle on the eye's
surface'.[34] Now if the eye cannot discriminate between the diff-
erent points that emit rays, then it cannot apprehend the object
other than as a hopeless confusion of light and colour. In practice,

30   Alhacen, *De aspectibus*, I. 6. 6; ed. Smith, p. 23. See Polyak, *Retina*, figs. 7–20
     for medieval Arabic and Latin diagrams of the eye.
31   Alhacen, *De aspectibus*, I. 6. 1; ed. Smith, p. 22.
32   Ibid., I. 6. 51–8; ed. Smith, pp. 45–8.
33   'quod linee radiales sunt ymaginate, est opinio vera et opinio opinantis
     quod aliquid exit a visu est opinio falsa'. Ibid., I. 6. 59; ed. Smith, pp. 48–9.
34   'Cum ergo fuerint partes unius rei vise diversi coloris, veniet ad totam
     superficiem visus ex unoquoque illorum forma coloris et lucis; et sic
     permiscebuntur colores illarum partium in superficie visus.' Ibid., I. 6. 10;
     ed. Smith, pp. 24–5.

however, objects are seen distinctly.[35] How can this be? In order to explain clear vision, Alhacen must establish that from each point in the visual field only one ray reaches the percipient part of the eye, which is not the surface itself, but the lens or crystalline humour.[36] He first draws attention to the behaviour of light rays when they encounter a transparent medium denser than air. Only a ray perpendicular to the surface of the medium continues in a straight line; those which strike it obliquely are refracted. This is also true of rays which, striking the surface of the eye, pass through the transparent outer layers or tunics to the crystalline lens (Fig. 2.2): 'only the light and color that are incident at right angles upon the surface of the eye will pass through the transparency of the tunics of the eye. The form incident along any other line will be refracted and will not pass straight through'.[37]

From every sheaf of rays issuing from points on the surface of the visible object only one will strike the lens at right angles; all the other rays are oblique and have a nugatory effect, for the effect of light travelling in perpendicular lines is stronger that the effect of light travelling at an angle ('operatio lucis venientis super perpendiculares est fortior operatione lucis venientis super lineas inclinatas'). Thus, at any point on the surface of the eye only one ray will enter at the perpendicular and pass unrefracted through the transparent tunics to the crystalline lens.[38]

The perpendicular lines, grouped together, form an imaginary pyramid:

---

35    *Loc. cit.*; ed. Smith, p. 25.

36    Ibid., I .6. 11–17; ed. Smith, pp. 25–8.

37    'nichil pertransibit ex eis per diafonitatem tunicarum visus secundum rectitudinem nisi illud quod erit super lineam rectam elevatam super superficiem visus secundum angulos rectos. Et illud quod fuerit super aliam lineam reflectetur et non pertransibit recte'. Ibid., I. 6. 19; ed. Smith, pp. 29–30.

38    Ibid., I. 6. 24; ed. Smith, p. 33. For Alhacen's not always convincing discussion of oblique rays, see Lindberg, *Theories of Vision*, pp. 74–8.

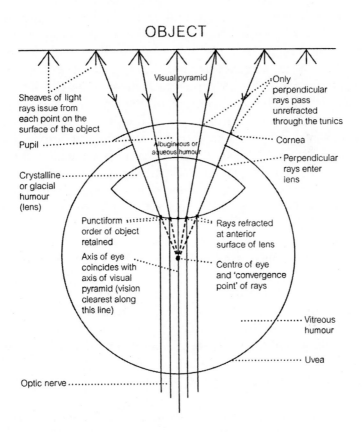

**Figure 2.2.** The geometry of sight: perception at a distance according to Alhacen.

between that point and that whole surface a cone can be imagined with its
vertex at that point and its base formed by that surface. And that cone
contains all the straight lines that are imagined to lie between that [vertex-]
point and all the points on that surface.[39]

Since the rays are rectilinear and converge at a point, they preserve
the same arrangement as the points from which they originated in
the visual field. Through the visual pyramid, therefore, the form
of light and colour of the visible object is conveyed to the eye.
The point of convergence is the centre of the eye, beyond the
crystalline or glacial humour, on which the two-dimensional image
is arranged like the arrangement of the coloured parts on the
surface of the visible object.[40] It is at the glacial humour that the
sensation of seeing is transferred from physical impression to
sense-impression. The axis of the pyramid is coincident with the
straight line connecting the central parts of the eye;[41] vision is most
clear through the axis since it alone of all the straight lines passing
through the crystalline lens proceeds to the centre of the eye
without refraction.[42]

Alhacen, having established an intromission theory of vision,
at the same time succeeded in preserving a geometrical representa-
tion of sight that derives from Euclid, yet without including some
of the more problematic features of Euclidean theory. For ex-
ample, there are no gaps between the rays of the visual pyramid (as
there had been in Euclid's scheme) since they issue from every
point in the visual field. Alhacen's subsequent discussion of direct
vision is lengthy and detailed and it will not be possible to do it
justice here. Instead, I propose to exemplify those other aspects

39    'inter illud punctum et totam illam superficiem est piramis ymaginabilis
      cuius conus est illud punctum et cuius basis est illa superficies. Et illa
      piramis continet omnes lineas rectas ymaginatas que sunt inter illud
      punctum et omnia puncta illius superficiei.' Alhacen, *De aspectibus*, I. 6. 26;
      ed. Smith, p. 33.
40    On Alhacen's geometry of vision, see Crombie, 'Mechanistic Hypothesis',
      pp. 17–22; Lindberg, *Theories of Vision*, pp. 80–5; and Vescovini, *Prospettiva
      medievale*, pp. 120–1.
41    Alhacen, *De aspectibus*, II. 2. 3; ed. Smith, p. 81.
42    Ibid., II. 2. 23; ed. Smith, pp. 93–4.

of his writings relevant to his theories of spatial perception: the conditions which make clear vision possible, the different types of visual stimuli and how they are apprehended, the perception of distance and of depth in objects, and the causes of error.[43]

There are eight prerequisites if vision is to be fully effected.[44] The first is space between the eye and the visible object for, if the object is adjacent to the eye, light will be excluded; and since only a small portion of the object will be facing the pupil, the entire form will not be seen.[45] The second requirement is that there should be no intervening body between the eye and the visible object, which must lie in front; if there is, it will cut off the imaginary straight lines which must run direct from object to eye if it is to be seen in its entirety.[46] Third, the object must be luminous or illuminated, for light is necessary to its extension in air and to the activating of colour, on which awareness of form depends.[47] Fourth, the object must be above a certain size; if it is very small, then when it is extended through the visual pyramid to the eye its impact on the crystalline lens will be negligible.[48] Fifth, it must be present to the eye for a sufficient length of time. Sixth, the medium between the eye and the visible object must be transparent and continuous to allow for the transmission of multiple forms to the eye.[49] Seventh, the object itself must have density because what is dense has colour, which in turn produces the forms that come to the eye.[50] Finally, the eye itself must be healthy.

Alhacen identifies twenty-two properties (*intentiones*) found in visible objects: light and colour, through which are also conveyed

43  For a lucid account of Alhacen on the perception of space, see Hatfield and Epstein, 'Sensory Core', pp. 367–71.
44  Summarized in Alhacen *De aspectibus*, III. 3. 1–3; ed. Smith, p. 285.
45  Ibid., I. 8. 3–4; ed. Smith, pp. 73–4.
46  Ibid., I. 8. 5; ed. Smith, pp. 74–5.
47  Ibid., I. 8. 6; ed. Smith, p. 75. On the connection between colour and light in Alhacen's theory, see Bauer, *Psychologie Alhacens*, pp. 41–4; and Rashed, 'Optique géometrique', pp. 278–80.
48  Alhacen, *De aspectibus*, I. 8. 7; ed. Smith, pp. 75–6.
49  Ibid., I. 8. 8; ed. Smith, pp. 76–7.
50  Ibid., I. 8. 9–10; ed. Smith, pp. 77–8.

distance, place, corporeity, shape, size, discreteness, separation, number, movement, rest, roughness, smoothness, transparency, density, shadow, darkness, beauty, ugliness, similarity and difference.[51] Such properties represent classes of stimulus: for example, straightness, curvature, concavity and convexity would come under 'shape'. The reception by the eye of these properties is only the first stage towards the completion of the act of vision. There follows a rational process of evaluation, inference, remembering and recognition.[52] For instance, comparative judgements are made between different strengths of colour and light, and between different shapes and positions, as in the process of writing:

> Writing, as well, will be deciphered only by [the reader's] discerning the forms of the letters, along with their combinations, and by comparing them with similar ones already known to the writer. And by the same token, when the way many visible characteristics are perceived is examined, it will be found that they are not perceived through brute sensation, but through judgment and differentiation.[53]

The mental faculty which completes the act of vision is called by Alhacen the discriminative faculty or *virtus distinctiva*.[54] It is this

---

51   Ibid., II. 3. 44; ed. Smith, pp. 111–12. Beauty (*pulchritudo*) and ugliness (*turpitudo*) would not seem to belong in this list. They are examined at greater length at II. 3. 200–32; ed. Smith, pp. 204–15. On the aesthetic implications of Alhacen's work, see de Bruyne, *Etudes d'esthéthique médiévale*, vol. 3, pp. 243–51; and Summers, *Judgment of Sense*, pp. 153–7. On his treatment of intentionality, see Witelo, *Perspectivae liber quintus*, ed. and trans. Smith, pp. 38–42.

52   On the faculty psychology relevant to Alhacen's theory, see Bundy, *Theory of Imagination*, ch. 9; and Harvey, *Inward Wits*.

53   'Et etiam scriptura non comprehendetur nisi ex distinctione formarum literarum, et compositione illarum, et comparatione illarum ex sibi similibus, que sunt note scriptori ante. Et similiter multe res visibiles quando considerabitur qualitas comprehensionis illarum, invenietur quod non comprehenduntur solo sensu sed ratione et distinctione.' Alhacen, *De aspectibus*, II. 3. 15; ed. Smith, p. 100.

54   For a fuller account of Alhacen's psychology of vision, see Bauer, *Psychologie Alhazens*, pp. 48–55; and Vescovini, *Prospettiva medievale*, pp. 122–32. Cf. Camille, 'Before the Gaze'.

faculty which is responsible for decoding the two-dimensional image of the crystalline lens into an accurate impression of space and depth in the visual world.

The accurate perception of space depends on the presence between eye and object of an array of contiguous objects (*corpora ordinata continuata*) of known distance and size. The distance of the object can then be judged in relation to the array. Without it, distance cannot be accurately perceived. For example, the height of clouds is difficult to assess unless they are seen in relation to mountains.[55] Alhacen outlines an experiment in which two parallel walls are viewed, one behind the other, but in circumstances where the concomitant visual array, in this case a ground plane, is not visible (Fig. 8.1). In such conditions, the observer finds it impossible to judge the distance of the walls or the amount of space between them. The experiment demonstrates that 'sight does not perceive the magnitude of the distance of a visible object unless its distance is spanned by a continuous, ordered range of bodies, and unless sight perceives those bodies and determines their measures accurately'.[56] The accurate gauging of size also depends on the presence of *corpora ordinata continuata*, since the estimation of size is related to estimated distance. But neither distance, the spatial relations between forms, nor size, can be directly judged if the object concerned is too distant, for then the contingent visual array itself become indistinct and ceases to function as a point of reference.

The process of assessing distance, since it involves comparisons, is a function of the *virtus distinctiva*.[57] When objects are especially far away, or their distance cannot be determined in relation to the contingent array of bodies, the *virtus distinctiva* makes an estimation of distance by referring to former sightings of

55   Alhacen, *De aspectibus*, II. 3. 79; ed. Smith, pp. 131–2.
56   'visus non comprehendit quantitatem remotionis rei vise nisi quando remotio eius fuerit respiciens corpora ordinata continuata, et comprehenderit visus illa corpora et certificaverit mensuras eorum'. Ibid., II. 3. 80; ed. Smith, p. 132.
57   Ibid., II. 3. 86; ed. Smith, p. 135.

the object in question; a similar process of deductive reasoning can lead to conjectures about size, but errors may be made. The discrepancy between estimated and actual distance varies with circumstance, but in favourable conditions it is minimal. Alhacen thus builds up a complex but clear model of the psychology of perception, in which the evaluation of space is central:

> Thus, given a visible object perceived by sight and having its form imagined in the soul, when its distance is spanned by a continuous, ordered range of objects, that distance being moderate, and when sight perceives those bodies ranged in continuous order over its distance, and when the faculty of discrimination has already apprehended these bodies and accurately determined their measures, then the measure of that distance [of that visible object] is accurately determined.[58]

If any of these conditions is absent, then the distance will not be fully ascertained. The same prerequisites obtain for the accurate perception of the space between objects and of volume.[59] In all such gauging processes, the human body is the basis of measurement.[60]

The preceding examples show that Alhacen was acutely conscious of the eye's proneness to deception, and he dedicated the entire third book of his treatise to errors of sight, acknowledging that 'sight is frequently deceived about many of the things it perceives about visible objects, and it perceives them other than they really are. Moreover, sight sometimes perceives that it is being deceived even as it is being deceived, but it sometimes does not'.[61]

---

58  'Mensura ergo remotionis rei vise comprehensa a visu cuius forma est ymaginata in anima, quando illa remotio fuerit respiciens corpora ordinata continuata, et cum hoc fuerit illa remotio mediocris, et cum hoc comprehenderit visus illa corpora ordinata respicientia eius remotionem, et cum hoc iam virtus distinctiva cognoverit ipsa et certificaverit mensuras eorum, tunc mensura certificata est.' Ibid., II. 3. 90; ed. Smith, p. 137.

59  Cf. Vescovini, *Prospettiva medievale*, p. 124.

60  Alhacen, *De aspectibus*, II. 3. 151–6; ed. Smith, pp. 173–8.

61  'multotiens decipitur visus in multis eorum que comprehendit ex visibilibus, et comprehendit illa alio modo ab eo quo sunt. Et forte

He divides the types of error into three categories: those that occur at the moment of perception and which may be caused by adverse physical circumstances, such as excessive distance, or fog; those that occur through misrecognition, when the observer wrongly interprets a set of visual cues, judging (for example) an obliquely-placed square shape to be oblong;[62] and errors of inference, in which the visual data are correctly perceived, but then mismatched with a set of cues long familiar to the observer, as in a case of mistaken identity.[63] As we shall see in Chapter Six, later theorists, building on Alhacen's work, developed his notions of visual error into an interrogation of visual certitude. Chaucer, for his part, had a keen interest in the psychology and effects of visual error and spatial disorientation.

Alhacen's essentially materialist approach to optical matters seems far removed from Grosseteste's insistence on the spiritual nature of the light that informs the physical world. Their differences are instanced when Alhacen defines solidity (*corporeitas*) not as analogous to the behaviour of light, but merely as extension in the third dimension: 'extensio corporis secundum trinam dimensionem, comprehenditur a visu in quibusdam corporibus et in quibusdam non'.[64] It is implicit in the act of perception that what is seen must have some solidity: although when a form presents itself to view only a plane surface may be visible, the third dimension is necessarily present. An object (e.g. a cube) can be so placed that only one flat surface is seen, in which case its solidity, although present, is not directly apprehended.[65] But if it is positioned obliquely, so that two surfaces are visible, then its

62    percipit suam deceptionem cum decipitur, et forte non'. Ibid, III. 1. 1; ed. Smith, p. 245.
62    Ibid., III. 7.6; ed. Smith, pp. 601–2.
63    Ibid., III. 6.4–5; ed. Smith, p. 597.
64    Alhacen, *De aspectibus*, II. 3. 121; ed. Smith, p. 156.
65    According to Alhacen, a convex surface is a special case since it is seems to have depth through the relative nearness of its central portion; but a concave surface is seen in only two dimensions because at its centre there is not extension of the body, but emptiness. Its depth is apprehended only through prior knowledge. Ibid., II. 3. 123–4; ed. Smith, pp. 157–8.

solidity and depth become visually evident. Obliqueness of one surface in relation to another signals depth in the object and in general all bodies are seen in depth: 'in general, whenever sight can perceive two surfaces intersecting one another in a given body, it will perceive its corporeity'.[66] The obliqueness on which generally depends the perception of depth in objects is only effective at moderate distances; in objects at a great distance, obliqueness cannot be detected. Solidity in such cases is apprehended through prior acquaintance with the object.

The assimilation of Alhacen's ideas was accelerated by a book, entitled *Perspectiva*, completed *c*.1274 by the Silesian scholar, Witelo. It was closely modelled on *De aspectibus*, but Witelo also drew on writings by Euclid, Ptolemy and Bacon. At the time of his optical researches he was as at the papal court at Viterbo, an important forum for the exchange of optical ideas during the 1260s and 1270s.[67] Not unlike Grosseteste, he created an imprimatur by expatiating on the importance of light as an informing agent in the scheme of creation, couching his words in the form of a dedication to William of Moerbeke, a papal confessor who was himself a keen student and translator of scientific texts.[68] Witelo's *Perspectiva* soon became an authoritative source of optical theory, and formed one of the major channels through which Alhacen's ideas were

66 'generaliter dico quod quodlibet corpus in quo visus potest compre-hendere duas superficies secantes se comprehendet corporeitatem in illo'. Ibid., II. 3. 122; ed. Smith, p. 157.

67 On Witelo and his optical ideas, see Birkenmajer, 'Etudes sur Witelo' and his 'Witelo, le plus ancien savant'; Lindberg, 'Introduction' to *Opticae thesaurus*, pp. vii–xiii; Tea, 'Witelo prospettico'; Witelo, *Perspectivae liber primus*, ed. and trans. Unguru, pp. 12–25; his *Perspictivae liber quintus*, ed. and trans. Smith, pp. 13–18 and 58–66; and his *Perspectivae liber secundus et liber tertius*, ed. and trans Unguru, pp. 11–32. For evidence of Witelo's early optical interests, see Theisen, 'Witelo's Recension'.

68 The dedicatory letter appears in Witelo, *Perspectiva*, ed. Risner, p. 1; partially translated by Kraft and LeMoine in Lindberg, *Theories of Vision*, pp. 118–19, and at greater length in Crombie, *Grosseteste*, p. 215. On Viterbo as a centre for the transmission of optical literature, see Lindberg, 'Lines of Influence', pp. 72–5.

disseminated.[69] The supplementary material that he introduced derived from other extant optical texts, and is therefore well suited to the task of placing Chaucer's accounts of the visual world within the context of scientific optics.

## Roger Bacon (*c*.1220-*c*.1292)

The writings of Alhacen and Witelo had considerable potential for representations of the visual world, as Italian artists of the early quattrocento were to discover.[70] Later, the pyramid of visual rays from eye to object, intersected by an imaginary plane 'picture' surface, became the means whereby Renaissance and later artists painted according to the rules of *perspectiva artificialis* (Fig. 2.3).[71] More immediately, Alhacen's writings provided a systematic analysis of the process by which vision is effected, examining in turn and at length the constituent parts of that process, placing the perceiving subject at its centre, recognizing the importance of aesthetic considerations, explaining both the physiology and the psychology of perception, and subsuming the whole to a logically consistent theory.[72] Generally, they considerably advanced understanding of visual phenomena such as space, and raised awareness of optical matters to a new height.

---

69  Lindberg, *Catalogue*, pp. 77–9, gives 25 surviving MSS of Witelo's *Perspectiva*. On the relationship between Witelo's work and Alhacen's, see Lindberg, 'Alhacen's Theory of Vision', pp. 330–4. For an account of Witelo's achievement and influence, see *Witelonis Perspectivae liber quintus*, ed. and trans. Smith, pp. 66–72.

70  Crombie, 'Expectation, Modelling and Assent'; Hills, *Light of Early Italian Painting*, ch. 4; and Vescovini, 'Contributo'. For an early example of the application of Alhacen's theories to painting, see Marshall, 'Two Scholastic Discussions', pp. 170–5; and cf. Summers, *Judgment of Sense*, pp. 164–7.

71  Elkins, *Poetics of Perspective*, pp. 46–52; and Smith, 'Introduction' to *Alhacen's Theory of Visual Perception*, pp. civ–cxii.

72  Smith, 'Getting the Big Picture'.

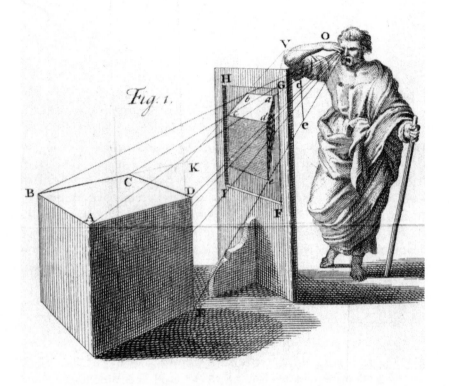

**Figure 2.3.** The principle of linear perspective, using a plane surface to intersect and plot the rays of the visual pyramid. From Taylor, *New Principles of Linear Perspective* (1811). [By permission of the British Library.]

Roger Bacon's work provides a vivid indication of the impact of optical ideas on English scholars. He had access to, and used, all the major optical works that had been written and translated into Latin by the mid-thirteenth century, effecting a synthesis of the different traditions and giving *perspectiva* the appearance of a unified body of thought.[73] He was educated at Oxford, where he is likely to have developed his interest in optics under the influence of Grosseteste's thought. In the 1240s he began lecturing in the faculty of arts at Paris, and it was there that he composed his optical and other scientific writings in the late 1250s or early 1260s.[74] They were then despatched to Bacon's patron, Pope Clement IV, at Viterbo. Bacon worked under difficult conditions, caught in a nexus of controversies about the reception of Aristotelian science in the arts faculty, and in a dispute about the legitimacy of Franciscans pursuing studies and producing books, rather than attending to the normal duties of mendicants. He returned to the Franciscans at Oxford some time after 1278. The number of surviving manuscripts witnesses to the extent of Bacon's influence on optical thought. Of present concern are *De multiplicatione specierum* and *Perspectiva*, which forms the fifth part of his *Opus maius*.[75]

On the propagation of light from the object in straight lines, the visual pyramid, the conditions and properties of vision, the structure of the eye, the perception of distance, the psychology of sight and perception and experimental proof, Bacon stays close to

73 Cf. Lindberg, 'Bacon and the Origins of *Perspectiva*'; and his *Theories of Vision*, pp. 108–9 and 116. See also French and Cunningham, *Before Science*, pp. 237–43; and Steele, 'Bacon and the State of Science'.

74 Recent accounts of Bacon's life and thought include Hackett, 'Roger Bacon'; and Lindberg, 'Introduction' to his *Bacon's Philosophy of Nature*, pp. xxvi–xxxv, which supplement with his 'Introduction' to *Bacon and the Origins of Perspectiva*, pp. xvii–xxv.

75 24 MSS of *De multiplicatione specierum* survive, and 39 of *Perspectiva*, which circulated independently of the *Opus maius*. Lindberg 'Introduction' to *Bacon's Philosophy of Nature*, pp. lxxv–lxxix; and his *Catalogue*, pp. 37–8 and 40–2. In his 'Lines of Influence', pp. 68–9, Lindberg notes Bacon's other optical writings.

Alhacen.[76] But on the question of what exactly crosses the space between object and eye in order to produce vision, and how the effect of that object is transmitted and received, Bacon develops a theory borrowed from Grosseteste, whom he much admired.[77] Grosseteste had maintained that, just as hot objects generate heat, so a visible object generates an emanation or *species* through which its form is transmitted along straight lines to both sentient and inanimate recipients. Precedents for the idea exist in both Greek and Arabic writing:[78]

> A natural agent multiplies its power from itself to the recipient, whether it acts on sense or on matter. This power is sometimes called species, sometimes a likeness, and it is the same thing whatever it may be called; and the agent sends the same power into sense and into matter, or into its own contrary, as heat sends the same thing into the sense of touch and into a cold body. For it does not act by deliberation and choice, and therefore it acts in a single manner whatever it encounters, whether sense or something insensitive, whether something animate or inanimate. But the effects are diversified by the diversity of the recipient, for when this power is received by the senses, it produces an effect that is somehow spiritual and noble; on the other hand, when it is received by matter, it produces a material effect.[79]

76  Lindberg, 'Bacon and the Origins of *Perspectiva*'; and his *Theories of Vision*, pp. 109–12. For summaries of Bacon's optical theory, see Bridges, *Life and Work of Bacon*, pp. 101–11; Matthews, 'Medieval Theory of Vision'; and Wiedemann, 'Bacon und seine Verdienste um die Optik'.

77  On Bacon's doctrine of the multiplication of species, see especially Crombie, *Grosseteste*, pp. 139–62; Crowley, *Bacon*, pp. 21–32; Lindberg, 'Introduction' to *Bacon's Philosophy of Nature*, pp. liii–lxxi; McEvoy, *Philosophy of Grosseteste*, pp. 151–3; Southern, *Grosseteste*, pp. 136–9; Tachau, *Vision and Certitude*, ch. 1; Vescovini, *Prospettiva medievale*, pp. 57–76; and Vogl, 'Bacons Lehre'.

78  Lindberg, 'Introduction' to *Bacon's Philosophy of Nature*, pp. xxxv–liii; his 'Alhazen's Theory of Vision', pp. 332–41; and Siegel, *Galen on Sense Perception*, pp. 124–5. Passages on *species* by various authors are translated in *Source Book*, ed. Grant, pp. 393–7.

79  'Agens naturale multiplicat virtutem suam a se usque in patiens, sive agat in sensum, sive in materiam. Quae virtus aliquando vocatur species, aliquando similitudo, et idem est, quocunque modo vocetur; et idem immittet in sensum et idem in materiam, sive contrarium, ut calidum idem immittit in tactum et in frigidum. Non enim agit per deliberationem et

Once the eye has received a *species*, then reason discerns its full nature.[80] It is this activity of natural bodies that optics studies.

By *species*, Bacon meant both Grosseteste's conception of the word and Alhacen's forms of light and colour, as well as other antecedent ideas about the projection of images from an object to an observer and their subsequent interpretation by the mental faculties. The *species* is the first effect of an agent ('primus effectus agentis')[81] generated by the object into the adjacent medium: 'Every efficient cause acts through its own power, which it exercises on the adjacent matter, as the light (*lux*) of the sun exercises its power on the air (which power is light [*lumen*] diffused through the whole world from the solar light [*lux*]). And this power is called "likeness", "image", and "species".'[82] The impression of the *species* in the medium is made by activating the potentiality of the recipient matter ('per veram immutationem et eductionem de potentia activa materie patientis').[83] Through a process of multiplication the form is transmitted:

> that which is produced [by an object] in the first part of the air is not separated from that part, since form cannot be separated from the matter in which it is unless it should be soul; rather, it produces its likeness in the

electionem; et ideo uno modo agit, quicquid occurrat, sive sit sensus, sive sit aliud, sive animatum, sive inanimatum. Sed propter diversitatem patientis diversificantur effectus. In sensu enim ista virtus recepta facit operationem spiritualem quodammodo et nobiliorem; in contrario, sive in materia, facit operationem materialem, sicut sol per eandem virtutem in diversis passis diversos producit effectus.' Grosseteste, *De lineis*, ed. Baur, p. 60; trans. Lindberg in *Source Book*, ed. Grant, pp. 385–6.

80  Note Grosseteste, *Commentary on the Posterior Analytics*, I. 14; ff. 20v–21r (cited in Eastwood, 'Geometrical Optics', p. 228).

81  Bacon, *De multiplicatione specierum*, I. 1; ed. and trans. Lindberg, pp. 6–7, line 75.

82  'Omne enim efficiens agit per suam virtutem quam facit in materiam subjectam, ut lux solis facit suam virtutem in aere, quae est lumen diffusum per totum mundum a luce solari. Et haec virtus vocatur similitudo, et imago, et species'. Bacon, *Opus maius*, pars 4, dist. 2, cap. 1; ed. Bridges, vol. 1, p. 111; trans. Lindberg in *Source Book*, ed. Grant, p. 393.

83  Bacon *De multiplicatione specierum*, I. 3; ed. and trans. Lindberg, pp. 46–7, lines 51–2; and see Vogl, 'Bacons Lehre', pp. 216–19.

second part of the air, and so on. Therefore, there is no local motion, but a generation multiplied through the different parts of the medium.[84]

The rectilinear constructs of geometry between eye and object plot the route of the *species* which multiply from the object through the adjacent medium: 'Every multiplication is according to lines, angles, or figures. As long as a species advances through a medium possessing a single rarity, as entirely in the heavens, entirely in fire, entirely in air, or entirely in water, it always maintains a rectilinear path'.[85]

The *species* arrive at the eye in a punctiform array that preserves the arrangement and order of the visible form.[86] Since *species* are produced by all that exists in the material world, the eye also must give them out. There is evidence for this in the fact that a person can see the reflection of his or her own eye. Bacon maintains that *species* issuing from the eye are necessary to complete the act of vision.[87] He thus integrates two seemingly opposed theories, describing how the eye sensitizes the medium between it and the perceived object, so making possible the apprehension of forms at a distance:

> the act of sight is the perception of a visible object at a distance, and therefore the eye [must] perceive the visible object through its own power multiplied to the object.

84   'illa que in prima parte aeris fit non separatur ab illa, cum forma non potest separari a materia in qua est nisi sit anima; sed facit sibi simile in secundam partem, et sic ultra. Et ideo non est motus localis, sed est generatio multiplicata per diversas partes medii'. Bacon, *Perspectiva*, pars 5. 1, dist. 9, cap. 4; ed. and trans. Lindberg, pp. 140–1.

85   'Omnis autem multiplicatio vel est secundum lineas, vel angulos, vel figuras. Dum vero species in medio raritatis unius incedit, ut in toto coelo, et in toto igne, et in toto aere, vel in toto aqua, semper tenet vias rectas'. Bacon, *Opus maius*, pars 4, dist. 2, cap. 2; ed. Bridges, vol. 1, p. 112; trans. Lindberg in *Source Book*, ed. Grant, p. 393.

86   Bacon, *De multiplicatione specierum*, I. 2; ed. and trans. Lindberg, pp. 38–41, lines 311–33. See Vogl, 'Bacons Lehre', pp. 213–15.

87   Bacon, *De multiplicatione specierum*, I. 2; ed. and trans. Lindberg, pp. 30–3, lines 180–96. See Lindberg, *Theories of Vision*, pp. 14–16; Crombie, *Grosseteste*, pp. 151–2; and Vogl, 'Bacons Lehre', pp. 213 and 225–6.

Furthermore, the species of mundane things are not immediately suited of themselves to bring to completion an action on the eye, owing to the nobility of the latter. Therefore, they must be assisted and excited by the species [of the eye], which proceeds through the region occupied by the visual pyramid, altering and ennobling the medium and rendering it commensurate with sight.[88]

Addressing himself to the corporeity of objects and their propagation in depth, Bacon observes that a *species* preserves the three dimensions of its source because the medium through which it passes is also three-dimensional ('nec est corpus quod ibi generatur, sed forma corporalis, non habens tamen dimensiones per se, sed fit sub dimensionibus aeris').[89] Bacon is able to support his argument with reference to antecedent writers, such as Alhacen and Alkindi, who said that visual rays do not have only length, but also width and height.[90] The nature of rays therefore reveals the extension in three dimensions of the *species* whose path they trace:

It is to be understood that the lines along which multiplication occurs do not consist of length alone, extended between two points, but all of them have width and depth [as well], as the authors of books on optics determine. Alhacen demonstrates in his fourth book that every ray coming from a part of a body necessarily has width and depth, as well as length. Similarly, Jacob Alkindi says that an impression is similar to that which produces it; now, the impressing body has three dimensions, and therefore the ray has [this same] corporeal property. And he adds that rays do not consist of straight lines between which are intervals, but that multi-

88    'operatio videndi est circa cognitionem visibilis distantis, et ideo visus cognoscit visibile per suam virtutem multiplicatam ad ipsum.
        Preterea species rerum mundi non sunt nate statim de se agere ad plenam actionem in visu propter eius nobilitatem. Unde oportet quod iuventur et excitentur per speciem, que incedat in loco pyramidis visualis, et alteret medium ac nobilitet, et reddat ipsum proportionale visui.' Bacon, *Perspectiva*, pars 5, dist. 7, cap. 4; ed. and trans. Lindberg, pp. 104–5.
89    Ibid., pars 5, dist. 9, cap. 4; ed. and trans. Lindberg, pp. 140–1. Cf. Lindberg, 'Introduction' to *Bacon and the Origins of Perspectiva*, pp. lxxxiv–lxxxvi.
90    Lindberg, 'Alkindi's Critique', pp. 469–89; his 'Intromission-Extramission Controversy', pp. 138–41; his *Theories of Vision*, ch. 2; and Vescovini, *Prospettiva medievale*, pp. 44–7.

plication is continuous, and therefore it does not lack width. And, in the third place, he says that whatever lacks width, depth, and length is not perceived by sight; therefore a ray [if it were to lack width and depth] would be unseen, which it is not. And we know that a ray must pass through some part of the medium; but every part of the medium has three dimensions.[91]

The literary usefulness of Bacon's optical ideas is somewhat different from that of Grosseteste's or Alhacen's, but no less full of possibilities. His emphasis on vision as the means whereby distance and space are experienced; his account of the world as one crowded with forms (human and inanimate) clamouring for attention; his sense that only some of these truly 'connect' with the human observer; that the *species* of object and eye enact a process of communication designed to negotiate the distance that separates them; his insistence that sight is a pro-active process, while the viewer at the same time remains impressionable; his emphasis on the three-dimensional quality of perceived forms and of the medium through which they are seen – all of these features of his work provide a supportive framework for Chaucer's re-creation of the visual and experiential world.

91  'Sed sciendum quod huiusmodo linee, super quas est multiplicatio non sunt habentes solam longitudinem inter duo puncta extensam, sed earum quelibet est habens latitudinem et profunditatem, sicut auctores aspectuum determinant. Alhacen in quarto libro hoc ostendit, quod omnis radius qui venit a parte corporis habet necessario latitudinem et profunditatem, sicut longitudinem. Et similiter Jacobus Alkindi dicit quod impressio similis est cum eo a quo fit; imprimens autem corpus est habens tres dimensiones, que radius habet corporalem proprietatem. Et addit quod radius non est secundum lineas rectas inter quas sunt intervalla, sed multiplicatio est continua; quare non carebit latitudine. Et tertio dicit quod illud quod caret latitudine et profunditate et longitudine non sentitur visu; radius igitur non videtur, quod falsum est. Et scimus quod radius non potest transire nisi per aliquam partem medii; sed quelibet pars medii est habens trinam dimensionem.' Bacon, *De multiplicatione specierum*, II. 1; ed. and trans. Lindberg, pp. 94–5, lines 79–93.

## The Status of *Perspectiva*

Bacon's ideas, together with those of Grosseteste and Alhacen, give some idea of the extraordinary richness, ingenuity, vitality and potential of optical ideas by the 1270s. If they remained accessible to a relatively small group of scholars, that position soon changed as *perspectiva* came to be regarded more generally as a highly significant science, and became established as a subject worthy of study at the highest level. Thus it was steadily assimilated into the intellectual consciousness of the fourteenth century. There are various ways in which to gauge the level of interest in the science of *perspectiva* before and during Chaucer's lifetime. One indicator is the number of surviving manuscripts of the key texts.[92] Another might be the claims made for *perspectiva* by respected authors of optical treatises. A further, less partial, measure is the part played by optics in university curricula. A fourth is the extent to which optical ideas permeated the works of authors not specializing in optical studies.

*Perspectiva* did not lack influential champions. In the opinion of Grosseteste, optics held a pre-eminent position among the sciences since it was devoted to studying earthly manifestations of the light which was the first cause of creation. Through a process of spiritual illumination such a discipline would lead towards an understanding of God himself.[93] Witelo argued for the utility of optics along similar lines: it is a study of light, which is the first of all sensible forms ('primum omnium formarum sensibilium').[94] Bacon claimed that optics was far more pleasing and noble than mathematics or any other science because its subjects are vision, light and colour – the essentials of both beauty and cognition: 'Potest vero aliqua scientia esse utilior, sed nulla tantam suavitatem

92   Lindberg, *Catalogue*.
93   Cf. Crombie, *Grosseteste*, p. 104; McEvoy, *Philosophy of Grosseteste*, pp. 59–63, 107–8, 250–6, 279–80 and 303; Southern, *Grosseteste*, pp. 135, 217–19 and 275; and Vescovini, *Prospettiva medievale*, pp. 13–14.
94   Witelo, *Perspectiva*, ed. Risner, p. 2.

ulchritudinem utilitatis habet. Et ideo est flos philosophiae
is et per quam, nec sine qua, aliae scientiae sciri possunt.'[95]
in Pecham (*c.*1230–*c.*1292), Archbishop of Canterbury from
79, wrote an introduction to optics, *Perspectiva communis*, which
as survived in relatively large numbers of manuscripts, of which
wenty-nine date from the fourteenth century.[96] He introduces his
work in the similarly effusive terms: 'Therefore, perspective, in
which demonstrations are devised through the use of radiant lines,
and in which glory is found physically as well as mathematically so
that perspective is adorned by the flowers of both, is properly
preferred to [all the traditional] teachings of mankind.'[97]

All of these apologists were able to draw on the long-standing
tradition of sight as the superior sense,[98] but they were also arguing
for the importance of a newly established science. What exactly
did the word *perspectiva* denote by the mid-fourteenth century?[99]
It referred to a multifold discipline which included the study
of the nature and transmission of light; the behaviour of light
rays according to Euclidean laws of reflection and refraction; the
physiology of the eye; and the psychology of perception. These
meanings of *perspectiva*, literally 'seeing clearly', were of regular

95   Bacon, *Perspectiva*, pars 1, dist.1, cap.1; ed. and trans. Lindberg, pp. 4–5. Cf.
     Lindberg, 'Introduction' to *Bacon and the Origins of* Perspectiva, pp. xx–xxi.
96   Pecham's interest in optics was probably stimulated by his time at Oxford,
     Paris and Viterbo. See *Pecham and the Science of Optics*, ed. and trans. Lindberg,
     pp. 3–11 and 15–18; his 'Lines of Influence', pp. 75–83; and his '*Perspectiva
     communis* of Pecham', pp. 44–53. In his *Catalogue*, Lindberg lists a total of 64
     surviving MSS (including fragments) of Pecham's treatise.
97   'Perspectiva igitur humanis traditionibus recte prefertur, in cuius area
     linea radiosa demonstrationum nexibus complicatur, in qua tam physice
     quam mathematice gloria reperitur, utriusque floribus adornata.' Pecham,
     *Perspectiva communis*, Prohemium; ed. and trans. Lindberg, pp. 60–1, lines
     9–11.
98   See Jonas, 'Nobility of Sight'; Lindberg and Steneck, 'Sense of Vision', pp.
     33–40; and Summers, *Judgment of Sense*, pp. 32–9.
99   For a discussion of the word's definition within modern and medieval
     contexts, see Ronchi, *Optics*, ch. 1.

occurrence from before 1233 until the fifteenth century.[100] *Perspectiva* meant, in general terms, 'the science of the sight',[101] and formed a convenient title for books devoted to vision in its various aspects. These works were customarily divided into three parts: on direct vision (*optica*), on reflection (*catoptrica*), and on refraction (*dioptrica*).[102]

In England, the places where such books were read and discussed with the greatest intensity were the universities of Oxford and Cambridge, and that fact lent the subject prestige, influence and an aura of difficulty and intellectual excitement. By the end of the thirteenth century, optics was an accepted component of the arts courses at the universities. Geometry had always been one of the subjects of the quadrivium and *perspectiva* found its natural home as a science 'subordinated' to geometry.[103] The surviving curricula and catalogues indicate that the works of Alhacen, Witelo and Bacon were commonly used as textbooks. At Oxford, it was possible by 1350 to substitute Alhacen or Witelo for Euclid's *Elements*,[104] and they retained their prominence in the curriculum for many years: a *forma* of 1431 for inception in the faculty of arts at Oxford lists optical texts in the geometrical section of the

100  Latham (comp.), *Revised Medieval Latin Word-List*, p. 346; and Panofsky, *Early Netherlandish Painting*, vol. 1, p. 3. Cf. French and Cunningham, *Before Science*, pp. 248–50.

101  This is the definition provided by Trevisa in his translation of Bartholomaeus, *De proprietatibus rerum*, cited in *MED*. *OED* uses the formulation 'science of optics' for the vernacular cognate *perspective* (I. 1). Occurrences are noted from 1387 to 1658. Bartholomaeus' treatment of optics is discussed below, pp. 78–81.

102  The foundations of the division lie in ancient science. See Lejeune, *Recherches sur la catoptrique grecque*, pp. 3–4; and Lindberg, *Theories of Vision*, p. 89.

103  See Clagett, 'Some General Aspects of Physics', pp. 31–2; Eastwood, 'Geometrical Optics', pp. 10–15 and 223–5; Vescovini, '*Perspectiva* nell'enciclopedia del sapere medievale'; Weisheipl, 'Classification of the Sciences', pp. 68–72; and his 'Nature, Scope and Classification', pp. 474–80.

104  Kibre and Siraisi, 'Institutional Setting', p. 129. Cf. Lindberg, 'Introduction' to *Bacon and the Origins of Perspectiva*, p. xcvii.

quadrivium.[105] The optical works of Ptolemy, Euclid and Pecham may also have been used.[106] The records of the library at Merton College, which in the fourteenth century was the centre of a scientific school, show that the optical works of Grosseteste, Alhacen, Witelo and Bacon were all available and in use, as were other texts with a significant optical content: Plato's *Timaeus*, Aristotle's *De anima* and *De sensu*, pseudo-Grosseteste's *Summa philosophiae*,[107] Bartholomaeus Anglicus' *De proprietatibus rerum* and Peter of Limoges's *De oculo morali*.[108] A further Oxford resource for those interested in *perspectiva* was the library of the Franciscans, to which Grosseteste had bequeathed his books.[109]

By the mid-thirteenth century all of the major Greek and Arabic optical texts were available to scholars in translation. The second half of the century is marked by a process of assimilation, synthesis and simplification in the works of Witelo, Bacon and Pecham.[110] They in turn stimulated further optical writings by others, such as the Oxford scholars Robert Kilwardby (d.1279),[111] Walter of Odington (*fl.*1301–30), and John of Dumbleton (*fl.*1331–1349).[112] Throughout the fourteenth century, interest in *perspectiva*

---

105  'Geometriam per duos anni terminos, videlicet librum Geometrie Euclidis, seu Alicen Vitulonemve in perspectivam'. Gibson (ed.), *Statuta antiqua universitatis Oxoniensis*, p. 234. See North, 'Quadrivium', pp. 346–8. There are some brief remarks on the study of optics at Cambridge in Leader, *History of the University of Cambridge*, vol. 1, pp. 145–6.

106  Weisheipl, 'Curriculum of the Faculty of Arts', pp. 171–2. On the scholarly interest taken in Euclid's *Optica*, see Theisen, 'Euclid's Optics'; his (ed.) *'Liber de visu'*, 44–54; and his 'Mediaeval Tradition of Euclid's *Optics'*.

107  Crombie, *Grosseteste*, pp. 162–4; and see McKeon, *Study of the* Summa Philosophiae, pp. 156–74 and 206–9.

108  Powicke, *Medieval Books of Merton College*, pp. 23, 36, 47, 49, 50, 60–1, 64, 68, 84, 97, 100, 101–4, 121, 148, 173, 191, 214 and 241. On *De proprietatibus rerum* and *De oculo morali*, see below, pp. 78–81 and 95–103 respectively.

109  Ker, 'Oxford College Libraries', pp. 307–8.

110  Cf. Alessio, 'Per uno studio'.

111  Crombie, *Grosseteste*, pp. 138–9; and note also Clagett, 'Some General Aspects of Physics', pp. 35–6.

112  Crombie, *Grosseteste*, pp. 181–7; and see Weisheipl, 'Place of John Dumbleton'.

became more pervasive as its previous emphasis on geometrical explanations of vision gave way to a bias towards ontological problems about the physical phenomena of sight,[113] a tendency appropriate to the prevailing philosophical climate as represented in the writings of Duns Scotus (*c.*1266–1308),[114] William of Ockham (*c.*1285–1349),[115] John Buridan (*c.*1295–1358),[116] and Nicholas Oresme (*c.*1320–1382).[117] Ockham's optical ideas occasioned controversy (to which we shall return in Chapter Six), his rejection of *species* provoking defences from John of Reading and Walter Chatton, among others.[118] In the later fourteenth century, optics was one of the subjects scrutinized by the scholastic method of *quaestiones*, in which particular points would be raised and supporting and contradictory arguments rehearsed.[119]

113  On the importance of optics in the philosophical thought of the fourteenth century, see Lindberg *Theories of Vision*, pp. 140–2; and Vescovini, *Prospettiva medievale*, ch. 11.

114  McCarthy, 'Medieval Light Theory and Optics'; and Tachau, *Vision and Certitude*, ch. 3. For Grosseteste's influence on Scotus and Ockham, see Crombie, *Grosseteste*, pp. 167–77.

115  On Ockham's discussion of perception, see Alessio, 'Per uno studio', pp. 474–90; Coppleston, *History of Medieval Philosophy*, pp. 239–43; Moody, 'Ockham, Buridan and Nicholas of Autrecourt', pp. 133–7 and his 'William of Ockham'; Tachau, *Vision and Certitude*, pp. 130–5; and Vescovini, *Prospettiva medievale*, pp. 219–21.

116  Alessio, 'Per uno studio', pp. 492–4; and Vescovini, *Prospettiva medievale*, ch. 8.

117  McLuskey (ed. and trans.), 'Oresme on Light, Color and the Rainbow'; and Marshall, 'Oresme on the Nature, Reflection and Speed of Light'. See also Vescovini, *Prospettiva medievale*, pp. 195–204; and, on Oresme's reading of Witelo, Birkenmajer, 'Etudes sur Witelo', pp. 98–120.

118  Tachau, *Vision and Certitude*, pp. 174–9 and 198–202.

119  There are surviving sets of *quaestiones* on optics by Dominicus de Clavasio (*fl.*1349), Henry of Lagenstein (1325–1397) and Blasius of Parma (*fl.*1377–1416). See Lindberg, *Theories of Vision*, pp. 122–32, and for further discussion Vescovini, *Prospettiva medievale*, pp. 206–11, and ch. 12. The first of the six *quaestiones* in the unique MS of Dominicus, whose main authority is Alhacen, has been edited by Vescovini. The question concerns the purpose of *perspectiva* as a science: Vescovini, 'Questions de *perspective* de Dominicus de Clivaxo'; and see Alessio, 'Per uno studio'; and Vescovini, 'Questioni di *Perspectiva* di Biagio Pelacani da Parma'. Cf. Jacquart, 'Rapport', pp. 241–3.

It was not only through scientific and philosophical texts that *perspectiva* won an enthusiastic following in scholarly communities. In the later Middle Ages, the numerous commentaries on Aristotle and on the *Sentences* of Peter Lombard provided opportunities for optical theories to be discussed.[120] For instance, Albertus Magnus (*c.*1206–1280),[121] Richard Fournival (1210–*c.*1260),[122] and Thomas Aquinas (*c.*1225–1274)[123] all display a well-informed knowledge of the subject in their writings on light. Through these less specialized routes, as well as through more direct channels, the substance of *perspectiva* was spread and sustained so that in the fourteenth and fifteenth centuries 'there were more scholars taking a serious interest in vision than during any previous period of comparable duration in the history of mankind'.[124]

120  Lindberg, *Theories of Vision*, pp. 132–40.
121  Albertus Magnus, *De anima*, bk. 2, tract 3, chs. 7–16; ed. Stroick, vol. 7, part 1, pp. 108–23. See Lindberg, *Catalogue*, pp. 16–17; his 'Roger Bacon on Light, Vision', pp. 256–7, his 'Science of Optics', pp. 349–50; and his *Theories of Vision*, pp. 104–7; and Steneck, 'Albert on the Psychology of Sense Perception', pp. 275–6. Cf. Lindberg, 'Introduction' to *Bacon and the Origins of Perspectiva*, pp. xl–xli.
122  Birkenmajer, 'Grosseteste and Richard Fournival', pp. 36–41; and Crombie, *Grosseteste*, pp. 189–200.
123  Aristotle, *De anima*, bk. 2, chs. 7–8; trans Foster and Humphries, pp. 260–76; and see Lindberg, *Catalogue*, p. 36; and McCarthy, 'Medieval Light Theory and Optics', pp. 144–53.
124  Lindberg, *Theories of Vision*, p. 144.

# 3 Encyclopedias and Sermons

The fundamental codes of a culture – those governing its language, its schemas of perception, its exchanges, its techniques, its values, the hierarchy of its practices – establish for every man, from the very first, the empirical orders with which he will be dealing and within which he will be at home.[1]

In the preceding chapter I argued that optics enjoyed a prominent position in the intellectual consciousness of the fourteenth century, and that discussions of spatial phenomena were central to its concerns. I also suggested that it was a complex and sometimes contentious science with a reputation for being arcane and recondite, the preserve of scholars. It if were no more than that, a subject studied and disputed in university circles, then its interest as a context for Chaucer's writings would be correspondingly circumscribed. In fact, its influence spread rapidly to more generalized levels of learning. *Perspectiva*, in its less specialized guises, thus became an accessible subject. This is an important factor to bear in mind when considering Chaucer's use of optical material. To be convincing as an intellectual context, affecting his poetry at a fundamental level, optical ideas need to have been available, if in diluted or indirect forms, to a wider section of the community than the scholarly one, in short to the other kinds of people who constituted Chaucer's audience. If a more general awareness of visual phenomena can be demonstrated, then Chaucer's enlargement of the spatial content of his sources becomes explicable as part of a wider development. The present chapter therefore considers evidence from two types of text – encyclopedias and sermon

1    Foucault, *Order of Things*, p. xx.

exempla – in order to form an impression of the non-specialized knowledge of optics in the fourteenth century.

To consider the receptivity of Chaucer's audience to optical ideas is to broach the question of literacy, and here it is helpful to glance at the types of literacy current in later medieval England, as identified by Malcolm Parkes and elaborated by Joyce Coleman.[2] They were that of the cleric, fluent in both Latin and the vernacular languages; that of the nobility and gentry who used vernacular books for recreation; and that of a professional group, including administrators, lawyers, merchants and craftsmen, who read or wrote English in the course of their work.[3] Members of the second two categories might also possess a pragmatic knowledge of Latin, but it is unlikely often to have extended to the reading of texts on scientific topics.[4] The specialized texts discussed in the previous chapter were accessible only to the first category, whose reading practices might be either scholarly or literary (that is, with an eye to the composition of new texts).[5] The same is true of encyclopedias in Latin, although these works have a much wider appeal within the limits of their readership.[6] Vernacular encyclopedic texts were accessible to clerical and aristocratic readers, but were perhaps especially attractive to certain types of professional reader since these compilations furnished a convenient means of gaining ready access to a modicum of essential knowledge.[7] Thus, encyclopedias were susceptible to

2    Coleman, *Public Reading and the Reading Public*, pp. 88–92; and Parkes, 'Literacy of the Laity', p. 555. The present paragraphs owe much to these discussions.

3    Parkes, 'Literacy of the Laity', pp. 561 and 568. See also his *English Cursive Book Hands*, p. xvi.

4    See Clanchy, *From Memory to Written Record*, chs. 7 and 10 for precedents to 1301; and Orme, *English Schools*, ch. 1, for the fourteenth and fifteenth centuries.

5    For books generally available to clerics see Wilson, 'Contents of the Mediaeval Library'.

6    Seymour, 'Some Medieval English Owners', pp. 158–65.

7    E.g. *Sidrak and Bokkus*, a hybrid of encyclopedia, romance and dialogue, which circulated in English and French versions. It appears among the effects of Sir Simon de Burley (d.1388), William de Walcote, a priest (*fl.*1348–

many kinds of reading – utilitarian, religious, professional and recreational – and provide support for Coleman's claims that types of text should not be allocated rigidly to types of literacy, and that individual readers practised different kinds of reading modes. With exempla it is less a question less of readership than of audience, and while many sermons were primarily intended for court or university circles, others – especially those of the friars – were heard, in English, by a wide range of social estates. Visual topics occupy a significant place in both encyclopedias and exempla, and it is therefore possible to conclude that perceptual ideas were familiar to large sections of the reading and listening communities in the later fourteenth century. Chaucer, writing for the same communities, writing as a bourgeois with aristocratic and academic connections, therefore had the basis for a dialogue with his audience and readership.[8] In using optical and optically derived material he was operating within well-recognized territory.

1370), and Robert de Roos (*fl.*1373–80), a government official. See Scattergood, 'Two Medieval Book Lists'; and *Sidrak*, ed. Burton, vol. 1, p. xxxiii. For an example of its optical content see question 241 (ed. Burton, vol. 2, pp. 492–3), on whether the eye, in the act of vision, gives out something or receives the image of the thing seen. *Sidrak* also appears among fifteenth-century bequests made by London merchants. See Thrupp, *Merchant Class*, pp. 162–3; cf. pp. 155–63 on the literacy of London merchant families. On the attractiveness of vernacular encyclopedias to this stratum of society, see also Parkes, 'Literacy of the Laity', p. 566.

8    Strohm identified Chaucer's audience as the socially mobile lesser gentry, comprising knights and esquires but also lawyers and members of Chancery. See his 'Chaucer's Audience(s)', for arguments subsequently developed in his *Social Chaucer*, ch. 3.

Encyclopedias

The two encyclopedias discussed here are selected both for their widespread dissemination and influence, and because they provide sources or analogues for Chaucer's own writings. Undoubtedly the most popular encyclopedia in the later Middle Ages was *De proprietatibus rerum* by the Franciscan, Bartholomaeus Anglicus, a work completed *c.*1245.[9] It appears with great frequency in the manuscript collections of Europe. For example, Thorndike noted eighteen manuscripts, chiefly of the late fourteenth and early fifteenth centuries, at the Bibliothèque Nationale in Paris – a city where, by 1284, it was prescribed as a university textbook.[10] In English libraries alone, twenty-three manuscripts in English hands survive, of which the majority date from the fourteenth century.[11] The work is a common item in wills of the period,[12] and its continuing usefulness is shown by the number of vernacular versions circulating – including ones in Italian, French, Provençal and Spanish. John Trevisa's English version (used below) appeared in 1398.[13] Bartholomaeus' work is thus 'an illustration of the rough general knowledge which any person with any pretense to culture was then supposed to possess'.[14]

In dealing with optical matters, Bartholomaeus names Pliny, Isidore and Bede; Chalcidius, Aristotle, Hippocrates and Pythagoras; Augustine, pseudo-Dionysius, Basil and Ambrose; and Alhacen, Constantinus (the translator of Hunain), Albumasar, Haly

9    French and Cunningham, *Before Science*, pp. 212–17. The evidence for dating is considered by Seymour et al., *Bartholomaeus*, ch. 4.

10   Ibid., p. 34; and Thorndike, *History of Magic*, vol. 2, p. 405.

11   Seymour, 'Some Medieval English Owners', pp. 156–8.

12   In the case of English wills, Seymour shows that the owners of the encyclopedia were almost invariably churchmen in high office. Ibid., pp. 164–5. Cf. Sandler, *Omne Bonum*, vol. 1, pp. 31–2; and Scattergood, 'Literary Culture'.

13   Michaud-Quantin, 'Petites Encylopédies', p. 587; and Se Boyar, 'Bartholomaeus Anglicus', pp. 186–8.

14   Thorndike, *History of Magic*, vol. 2, p. 406.

Abbas, Algazel, Averroes and Avicenna.[15] Bartholomaeus' reading therefore reflects the encyclopedic, classical and theological traditions of optics as well as the more recently accessible writings by Arab authors and commentators. So he is relatively up to date in his summaries of optical theory,[16] which are particularly provided in chapters on the sense of sight (III. 17) and the properties of the eyes (V. 5–9). Bartholomaeus also considers disorders of the eyes and their cure (VII. 15–19), light and shadow (VIII. 40–45), the rainbow (XI. 5) and the relation of light to colour (XIX. 8).[17]

At the beginning of his account of sight, Bartholomaeus sets out the prerequisites of vision in the manner of Alhacen.[18] There needs to be a healthy eye, a facing object, a moderate distance, a place for the object not too far from the line of vision, solidity in the object, perceptible size, clarity in the intervening space, illumination and time for the image to pass to the eye. The three forms of vision are described (direct, reflected and refracted), with some emphasis on phenomena of refraction. He also follows Alhacen in explaining how the eye sees distinctly 'whenne diuers maner spaces of diuers clernes and thiknes be put bitwene the sight and the thing that is isene':[19] only those rays which fall on to the eye at a perpendicular angle are effective. Rays between the eye and the visible object assume the form of a pyramid with its apex in the eye and its base on the object: 'All the lynes that buth idrawe fro al the parties of the thing that is seen maketh a piramis, ischape as a toppe. And the point therof in the blak of the yghe and the brod end on the thing that is isene'.[20]

On the vexed question of whether rays proceed from the eye or to the eye, Bartholomaeus, like Bacon, entertains both extra-

15  Cf. Seymour et al., *Bartholomaeus*, ch. 3.
16  Bartholomaeus preceded Roger Bacon in citing Alhacen. See Lindberg, *Theories of Vision*, p. 253, n. 8.
17  Bartholomaeus, *De proprietatibis rerum*, trans Trevisa; ed. Seymour et al., vol. 1, p. xv. Subsequent page and line references are to volume 1 of this edition.
18  See above, p. 55.
19  Bartholomaeus, *De proprietatibus rerum*, III. 17; ed. Seymour et al., p. 109, lines 20–2. Thorns and yoghs have been modernized.
20  Ibid., III. 17; ed. Seymour et al., p. 109, line 34–p. 110, line 1.

mission and intromission theories.[21] On the one hand, the eye does not see except through those *species* which travel in straight lines to the centre of the eye in pyramidal form. But there is another pyramid, composed of emergent rays: 'noght onliche the liknes of that thing cometh to the eihe in aschildewise but also the liknes of the sight strecchith to the thing and is isprad vppon suche a schilde in the same place'.[22] Bartholomaeus goes on to argue that since light must shine on an object before it can be seen, 'nedus it nedith to haueth a piram, a scheld, othir a toppe, of light'.[23] The base of each pyramid is on the object, its point in the eye. Only when the eye registers three sets of *species* from these three pyramids can the act of vision be completed.

In the chapter on light, a distinction is made between *lux* and *lumen*. *Lux* is the primal light that came into existence on the first day of creation: it is the source and origin of *lumen*, or irradiation: '*lumen* is a stremynge out of light, but *lux* is the substancial welle vppon the whiche *lumen* is i-oned'.[24] Bartholomaeus discusses at length how light can be a corporeal substance since it is, as biblical and patristic authorities assert, the informing agent of creation. The arguments are reminiscent of those in Grosseteste's *De luce*, a contemporary composition Bartholomaeus appears not to have known.[25] He writes on the three-dimensional propagation of light: 'light is most meuable, for hit meoueth hitself withoute cesinge, and gendrith light in lynes forthright and in roundenes al aboute, and meueth and scedith itself into alle parties aboute'.[26] Bartholomaeus repeats that there is an intimate link between light and perception, one being a condition of the other, and he notes that

---

21    Lindberg, *Theories of Vision*, p. 253, n. 26, notes that Bartholomaeus' attempt
      to reconcile these theories 'anticipates, in a number of respects, Bacon's later
      synthesis'.
22    Bartholomaeus, *De proprietatibus rerum*, III. 17; ed. Seymour et al., p. 110,
      lines 23–6.
23    Ibid., III. 17; ed. Seymour et al., p. 111, lines 3–4.
24    Ibid., VIII. 28; ed. Seymour et al., p. 507, lines 2–3.
25    Seymour et al., *Bartholomaeus*, p. 114.
26    Bartholomaeus, *De proprietatibus rerum*, VIII. 28; ed. Seymour, et al., p. 510,
      lines 23–6.

certain bodies are more receptive to light than others (VIII. 42). In an earlier chapter, devoted to the relation of light and colour, he describes how colour multiplies itself in the space between eye and object, using light as its necessary vehicle (XIX. 8).

Bartholomaeus' interest in optics was not unusual: by the mid-thirteenth century, encyclopedias had begun to register the research and scholarly interest that the subject was generating. Confirmation is provided by *Speculum naturale* (completed *c.*1250), the first part of Vincent of Beauvais' *Speculum maius*, which survives in over fifty copies. Vincent was a Dominican who made use of *De proprietatibus rerum*,[27] and indeed the *speculum* title itself may be taken as an indication of the extent to which Vincent regarded optical phenomena as a means of articulating epistemological concerns in figurative language.[28] The first two chapters of *Speculum naturale* contain much information about vision and light, and are informed by recent debates and theories.[29] Vincent's interests lie less in physics than in theology and so he draws on the tradition of light metaphysics on to which Grosseteste had, a few years before, grafted new ideas about the science of sight. So we find Vincent citing pseudo-Dionysius as well as more recent exponents of light metaphysics, such as Hugh of St Victor.[30]

Vincent begins with the familiar proposition that God is light, and that nothing is illuminated except that which is created and

27 Seymour et al., *Bartholomaeus*, p. 14.
28 Grabes, *Mutable Glass*, pp. 42–3; cf. Paulmier-Foucart, 'Oeuvre encyclo-pédique', pp. 206–7.
29 On the content and composition of *Speculum maius*, see esp. Paulmier-Foucart with Duchenne, *Vincent de Beauvais*; also Collison, *Encyclopedias*, pp. 60–3; Lemoine, 'Oeuvre encyclopédique'; Parkes, 'Influence of the Concepts of *Ordinatio* and *Compilatio*', pp. 128–9; Ullman, 'Project for a New Edition', pp. 313–24; and Young, '*Speculum majus*', pp. 4–13. On Vincent's treatment of science, see French and Cunningham, *Before Science*, pp. 173–6; and Ullman, 'Project for a New Edition', p. 324.
30 On the lasting influence of pseudo-Dionysius, see French and Cunning-ham, *Before Science*, pp. 218–24; Gersh, *From Iamblichus to Eriugena*, pp. 23–4; and Luscombe, 'Some Examples'.

formed by him.[31] By 'illumination' Vincent intends both physical light and the illumination of the soul of man:

> For the light of the father, invisible in itself, going out in manifestation, deriving from the true good and proceeding to us, comes upon our emptiness and pouring upon us fills us according to our individual virtue and capacity; and when it has filled us it changes us, that we should not be divided from the father but in the same similitude and image look to him. He fills man, illuminates him, and converts him, making changes by light.[32]

Spiritual illumination of this sort is transmitted through the angelic hierarchies who communicate to each other and to the human recipient the fire of love (*ignis caritatis*), the flame of which strives to ascend to God. But the interior soul of man is accessible only to God himself, the angels performing a ministerial function. An analogy is drawn with the effect of light on a window. God can shine through to the soul like rays of sun into a room provided that there is a means to do so: 'An angel is said to give understanding to man, just as light is said to be given to the house of him who makes a window when the house is not penetrated or illuminated by light.'[33]

Vincent summarizes two alternative theories about the creation of light. The first maintains that light was part of the work of the first day of creation and is therefore not identical with the light of the sun. The second argues that the light of the first day was essentially of the same nature as diurnal illumination (II. 32, col. 99). In either case terrestrial light was created to make vision pos-

31   Bk. I, ch. 34, col. 43, in *Bibliotheca mundi*, vol. 1. Subsequent references are to this volume.

32   'Lux enim patris invisibilis in se, procedens in nos, et exiens in manifestationem vacuos invenit, et manes a vero bono; et infundens se nobis, replet nos secundum uniuscuiusque nostrum virtutem et capacitem, et cum repleverit nos convertit, ut non dissideamus a patre, sed in eadem similitudine et imagine respiciamus ad ipsum. Replet quidem illuminando, convertit lumina faciendo.' Ibid., I. 35, cols. 43–4.

33   'Angelus dicitur dare intellectum homini: sicut dicitur dare lumen domui suae, qui fenestram facit, cum eam sua luce non penetret vel illustret.' Ibid., I. 73, col. 68.

sible and, striking a more empirical note, Vincent continues: 'there are four things which obtain in vision, namely a visible object, an observer, light through which an observer sees the visible object, and a medium'.[34] Light takes primacy among these preconditions because by its nature it is most noble. Visible objects can be classified according to their participation in light: 'Moreover there are three types of visible object, namely the luminous, which gives light, the opaque which receives light on its surface but not in its depth, and the transparent which can allow light to enter into all of its parts.'[35] The more anything participates in light the closer it approaches the divine and beautiful, for God is light. For this reason, water is more noble than earth, air than water, and fire than air (II. 35, cols. 100–1).

At once a spiritual substance, an aesthetic category and the material of creation, light captured Vincent's imagination and compelled his admiration. He describes it as a fountain, having the properties of expansion, propagation and multiplication (II. 35, col. 100); it is the most subtle and simple of substances, the motivating principle of life (II. 36, cols. 101–2); it is the first form from which all other forms proceed and its activity mirrors the propagation of God's goodness and beauty. The spatial mechanism involved is like that described by Grosseteste in his *De luce*:

> it is the best of all forms [...] among all forms light communicates itself and its beauty to the utmost extent, for one point or flash of light fills the space of the entire world. Therefore between bodies the sum of goodness exists. In this therefore it is similar to the spirit, namely God, who is everywhere, and to the soul, which fills all the body.[36]

34  'quatuor sunt quae in visione concurrunt, scilicet visibile, visivum, et lux per quam vivum videt visibile, et medium'. Ibid., II. 33, col. 99.
35  'Sunt autem tria genera corporum visibilium, scilicet luminosum, quod dat lumen, et opacum quod in superficie, non in profunditate lumen recipit, et diaphanum, quod secundum omnem sui partem lux subintrare potest.' Loc. cit.
36  'ipsa est omnium corporum optima [...] inter omnia corpora lux se, et suam pulchritudinem maxime communicat: unus enim lucis punctus, vel ictus subito totius mundi spacium replet. Igitur inter corpora summe bona

As noted, Vincent's sources are largely theological. In addition to pseudo-Dionysius and Hugh of St Victor, he refers to Peter Comestor, Peter Lombard, Augustine and Ambrose.[37] But he turns also to scientific authorities, among whom Aristotle is a favourite. On occasion he uses Avicenna and *De visu*, which is presumably Euclid's work of that name, and he is familiar with optical debates. For example, he rehearses views for and against the emission of light from the eye, considering such a possibility as an adjunct to, rather than a refutation of, the emission of light from the object. He also explores the rival claims of light as a corporeal or abstract quality. Appealing to experiential evidence, he shows how the behaviour of *species* indicates that light is neither abstract nor miscible:

> two lights can exist at the same time in the same part of the air, as is evident with different lighted candles whose flames have the same *species*, which remain at the same time in their own part of the air, neither is one *species* mixed with its neighbour through the nature of the air, as is stated in the science of *perspectiva*. Otherwise everything would be seen in confusion and nothing distinctly.[38]

On the other hand, if light is corporeal it has three dimensions. But then so do the objects of perception. Therefore, if light is a body, there will be two bodies simultaneously in the same place, which is impossible ('si lux est corpus [...] erunt duo corpora simul in eodem loco, quod esse not potest'). The impasse is solved by returning to the capacity of light as an informing agent of creation: when there is light, matter is not so much created as a form produced by the luminous body ('Cum autem sit lux, materia non tantum creatur, sed forma gignitur a corpore luminoso', II. 40, col. 105). It does not follow from this position that earthly light is a

---

   est. In hoc etiam spiritui simillima est, scilicet Deo, qui ubique est, et
   animae, quae totum corpus replet'. Ibid., II. 38, col. 103.
37   Ibid., Prol. 8, 10, 12, 18, cols. 6–7, 8–9 and 14–15.
38   'duae autem luces in eadem aeris parte simul sunt: ut patet in diversis
   candelis ascensis, quarum luces cum sint eiusdem speciei, simul in eadem
   parte manent, nec admiscetur ad invicem naturae aeris, ut in perspectiva
   dicitur. Alioquin omnia confuse viderentur, et nulla distincte' Ibid., II. 39,
   col. 104.

spiritual substance, for spiritual substances have no measurable dimensions; whereas visible light, both in its propagation and in the forms which it produces, does possess dimension (II. 42, col. 106).

As Vincent explains elsewhere, there are distinctions to be made among different kinds of light: *lux* is the spiritual, creative, divine, immeasurable substance, *lumen* its earthly counterpart, the subject of optical researches, but there are other kinds of light too:

> *lux* exists in its own nature, but *lumen* in the recipient subject. Moreover, a ray is emitted along a straight line. Truly a radiant object such as a polished body is one having no light of its own but reflected rays. *Splendor* is the reflection of *lumen* resulting from the reflection of rays.[39]

Not only *splendor*, but colour also, lies on the surface of the object. Light transmits the colour unless it is able to penetrate the surface, as it does the sea. Colour can be affected by distance, as when clouds or mist intervene between the rays of the sun and an observer (II. 60, cols. 117–18). Vincent describes the following experiment to show how light is the essential cause of colour:

> if a little red wine is poured into a clear glass, the sun shining through the wine will produce whiteness in the bottom of the glass, which whiteness is among all colours the most similar to light. Truly if a lot of wine is poured in there will be no whiteness in the bottom because then the light cannot enter because it is multiplied in depth.[40]

39  'lux est in propria natura, lumen autem in subiecto recipiente. Porro radius exitus luminis, secundum lineam rectam. Radiosum vero est, scilicet corpus politum, in se lumen non habens, radios tamen reflectens. Splendior autem est ipsa luminis reflexio a reflexione radiorum procedens.' Ibid., II. 52, col. 113.

40  'si parum de vino rubeo infundatur in vitro puro: Sol penetrans vinum, generabit albedinem in fundo vitri, quae inter omnes colores similior est luci. Si vero multum infundatur non erit in fundo vitri, quia tunc lux non potest intrare, ut multiplicetur in fundo.' Ibid., II. 43, col. 106.

Vincent's homely example acts also as a microcosm of creation, according to Grosseteste's account: through the progressive multi-plication of light through the spheres until it condenses into the central sphere of greatest density and opacity, the earth.


## From Encyclopedia to Sermon


The optical content of thirteenth-century encyclopedias reveals in abbreviated form the process of assimilation in which Grosseteste played such an active part: although Bartholomaeus and Vincent make different emphases, both draw on long-standing traditions of light and vision as metonymic of spiritual life, while incorporating new thinking on the science of *perspectiva*. The same amalgam, especially as found in encyclopedic writings, was to prove effective when transposed to another genre, the sermon exemplum.

Mention has already been made of the extent to which light, in the Christian and neoplatonic traditions, had been used as an index of spiritual illumination. In devotional writing, under the influence especially of St Augustine, it had long been the practice, following biblical precedent, to draw similar comparisons between the outer eye of the body and various kinds of 'inner eye'.[41] As indicated in the previous chapter, Grosseteste brought new complexity and sophistication to the practice of using the physical phenomena of light and vision as indices for spiritual states. He did so both by promoting his fascination with the science of

41    The metaphor is traced to Plato by Curtius, *European Literature*, pp. 136–7. On the history of the metaphor see Kolve, 'Chaucer and the Visual Arts', pp. 301–3; Lindberg, 'Introduction' to *Bacon's Philosophy of Nature*, pp. xxv–xlii; and Neaman, 'Sight and Insight'. For discussions of Augustine's theories of light and vision see Jolivet, 'Doctrine augustinienne'; Mahler, 'Medieval Image Style', 283–6; and Nash, *Light of the Mind*. See also Javelet, *Image et ressemblance*, vol. 1, pp. 376–90; and Zinn, 'Personification Allegory', pp. 198–208.

optics, and by regarding the material and spiritual forms of light and vision not as compartmentalized, but as essentially the same. Thus, for him, the derivation of corporeal light from spiritual light conferred a special status upon optical phenomena: they could actually reveal the workings of the spiritual world. He wrote in his commentary on Aristotle's *Analytica posteriora*:

> I say therefore that it is spiritual light that is extended from intelligible things, and it is the eye of the mind which is situated at the bodily eye and which sees visible bodily things. Therefore intelligible things very receptive to this spiritual light are very visible to the interior eye, and those things that can by their nature assimilate it are very receptive to this great light. And so the spirit of the mind, which similarly is a most perfect spiritual irradiation, perceives things receptive to this great light, and this certain perception is the more perfect.[42]

The approach illustrated here gives visual analogies a new importance and significance and, with the rise of *perspectiva*, a new relevance. All things considered, the more accessible components of the science must have seemed particularly suitable for inclusion in homiletic writings:[43] they had theological sanction, were topical, and allowed the preacher to appeal directly to the visual experience of his listeners.[44]

---

42 'Dico ergo quod est lux spiritualis que superfunditur rebus intelligibilibus, et oculus mentis qui se habet ad oculum interiorem et ad res intelligibiles, sicut se habet sol corporalis ad oculum corporalem et ad res corporales visibiles. Res igitur intelligibiles magis receptibiles huius lucis spiritualis magis visibiles sunt oculo interiori, et magis sunt huius lucis receptibiles que nature huius lucis magis assimilantur. Res itaque huius lucis magis receptibiles ab acie mentis, que similiter est irradiatio spiritualis perfectius penetrantiur, et hec penetratio perfectior est certitudo maior.' Grosseteste, *Aristotelis peripatheticorum principis posteriorum analecticorum*, bk. I, ch. 17, f. 26r. See further Eastwood, 'Mediaeval Empiricism', pp. 308–9; and cf. McEvoy, 'Paradigma', pp. 102–5. For the general development of analogies between the inner and outer eye in the Franciscan tradition, see Gilson, *Philosophy of St Bonaventure*, chs. 9, 11 and 12.

43 Erickson, *Medieval Vision*, p. 82.

44 Owst, *Literature and Pulpit*, pp. 190–2 and 194–5; and his *Preaching in Medieval England*, p. 349. On the extent to which sermons might draw on the mutual

It is then as moralized examples that optical material appears in homiletic writing, particularly sermons, of the thirteenth and fourteenth centuries.[45] Such exempla customarily had their place in the major section of the sermon, the *dilatatio* or development, where they would be framed by appropriate biblical allusions to light and perception.[46] The great preachers of this period, though by no means the only preachers, were the Dominicans and Franciscans.[47] Resolved as they were to evangelize, the friars had need of some means whereby religious truth could be conveyed in palatable form. The abstract conceptions of theology, if unrelieved by illustration or anecdote, would not hold a congregation. Under this stimulus the exemplum became for the first time in the thirteenth century a fully-fledged homiletic genre.[48] The sermons in which exempla featured were delivered both in Latin and the vernacular, depending on circumstance, and therefore reached a wide public. Dominicans and Franciscans preached to other clerics in their own churches and at the universities (*ad clerum*); at court;

knowledge and experience of preacher and audience, see Haskins, 'University of Paris'.

45   For discussion of the exemplum as a distinct literary genre, see Berlioz, 'Introduction à la recherche', pp. 18–20; Bremond, le Goff and Schmitt, *L'"Exemplum"*, pp. 27–42; Mosher, *Exemplum*, pp. 1 and 6; Owst, *Literature and Pulpit*, pp. 151–2; and Welter, *L'Exemplum*, p. 1. See also d'Avray, *Preaching of the Friars*, pp. 66–72; Davy, *Sermons universitaires*, p. 34; Heffernan, 'Sermon Literature', pp. 183–4; Howie, *Studies in the Use of Exempla*, ch. 1; and Schmitt (ed.), *Prêcher d'exemples*, pp. 9–24.

46   On the place of exempla within sermons, as recommended in the treatises on preaching, see esp. Charland, *Artes praedicandi*, pp. 143–4, 194–5, 209–11, 282, 293 and 314–16. See also Coleman, *Medieval Readers and Writers*, pp. 174–84; Crane, 'Mediaeval Sermon-Books'; Delcorno, *L'Exemplum*, pp. 3–13; Gilson, 'Michel Menot', pp. 132–4; Lecoy de la Marche, *Chaire française*, pp. 298–307; and Wenzel, 'Medieval Sermons', p. 26. On the flexibility of exempla (and other teaching aids) in the process of sermon composition, see d'Avray, *Preaching of the Friars*, pp. 128–31; and cf. Fletcher, *Preaching, Politics and Poetry*, pp. 252–60.

47   See Courtenay, *Schools and Scholars*, pp. 61–9; and Humphreys, *Book Provisions*, pp. 18–66 and 99–118.

48   On the (largely unchanged) uses and functions of exempla a century later, see Spencer, *English Preaching*, pp. 78–88.

and extensively in the open air in churchyards and at preaching crosses throughout the country (*ad populum*), where the congregation would be largely illiterate.[49]

It is no coincidence that, almost without exception, the men who took a scholarly interest in optics were also associated with the two orders in which preaching played such a large part.[50] Grosseteste was influential in the early phases of the Franciscan movement at Oxford;[51] Bacon, Pecham and Bartholomaeus Anglicus were Franciscan friars; Witelo's patron, William of Moerbeke and Vincent of Beauvais were Dominicans. Their studies brought them into direct and indirect contact: for example, Grosseteste, Bacon, Pecham and Bartholomaeus were each at various times active at the universities of Paris and Oxford from the early to mid-thirteenth century.[52] Their interest in optical studies made itself felt not only in the intellectual life of the West but also, through the Latin and vernacular sermons of the itinerant brothers, in wider social spheres.[53]

---

49    Heffernan, 'Sermon Literature', p. 177. The distinction between sermons intended for clerical and lay audiences is not necessarily clear-cut. See d'Avray, *Preaching of the Friars*, pp. 111–28.

50    Ibid., pp. 43–63.

51    McEvoy, *Philosophy of Grosseteste*, pp. 40–8, but note the more cautious estimate (of Grosseteste's overall achievement) by Southern, *Grosseteste*, pp. 296–8.

52    Glorieux, *Répertoire des maîtres*, vol. 1, pp. 119–22 and vol. 2, pp. 60–76 and 87–98; and his *Faculté des arts*, pp. 169–72, 231–2, 324–31, 338–42 and 386. See also Lindberg, *Theories of Vision*, p. 107. Witelo, Bacon and Pecham may have enjoyed some direct exchange of ideas at Paris, as almost certainly did Witelo and William of Moerbeke at the papal court in Viterbo. See Douie, *Archbishop Pecham*, pp. 4–13; Lindberg, 'Lines of Influence'; his 'Introduction' to *Opticae thesaurus*, pp. ix and xi–xiii; and Seymour et al., *Bartholomaeus*, ch. 1.

53    The exceptional library of the Augustinian friar, John Erghome (*fl*.1362–8), who was educated at Oxford, indicates the extent to which optical texts became part and parcel of convent learning. Erghome was a member of the York convent, where over 250 of his books were catalogued in 1372. See Humphreys, 'Library of John Erghome', pp. 116–19; and Humphreys (ed.), *Friars' Libraries*, esp. pp. xxiv–xxxv. To numerous items on Aristotelian natural science and the encyclopedias of Neckam and Bartholomaeus, Erghome added *Tractatus de visu*, *Perspectiva* (items 322e and f), *liber radiorum*

In all this, the scholarship and teaching of Grosseteste were crucial, since the members of both religious orders enjoyed close association with him. After their arrival in Oxford in 1221 he became well acquainted with the preaching friars, who authored many of the surviving collections of exempla, and exerted his influence over them. In 1229 or 1230 Grosseteste became lector to the Franciscans as the first of four consecutive secular masters to be appointed, a position which he held until his election to the see of Lincoln in 1235.[54] Thomas of Eccleston, the chronicler of the order, records in his *De adventu fratrum minorum* (1232–58) that under Grosseteste the brethren within a short space of time made incalculable progress both in scholastic discussions and in the subtle moralities suitable for preaching ('inaestimabilite infra breve tempus tam in questionibus quam praedicationi congruis subtilibus moralitatibus profecerunt').[55] The impact of Grosseteste's teaching was thus extensively felt.[56] It comprised three essential elements: the study of the Bible, the study of languages, and the study of mathematics and physical science. This last component centred on optics both as an illustration of mathematical law and as a study of light, the informing agent of the divine creation.[57] As Bishop of Lincoln, Grosseteste himself preached to his own clergy, as well as taking friars of both orders with him on his visitations of the

---

(item 364c), *ptholomeus de speculis libri duo* (item 455i), *tractatus de oculo* (item 526b), *tractatus de oculo morali* (item 605e), *Perspectiva alacen in libris 7* (item 640), and *Perspectiua peccham continens tres partes* (item 641). See also Coleman, *Medieval Readers and Writers*, pp. 172–4; James (ed.), *Catalogue of the Library*, p. 95; Moran, *Education and Learning*, pp. 27–8; and Smalley, *English Friars*, p. 29. On lay literacy, see Coleman, 'English Culture', pp. 33–45; and her *Medieval Readers and Writers*, pp. 172–4.

54    Little, 'Franciscan School', pp. 807–10; and note Callus, 'Oxford Career', p. 60.

55    Thomas of Eccleston, *De adventu fratrum minorum*, collatio 11; ed. Little, p. 807.

56    Crombie, *Grosseteste*, pp. 135–6; Little, 'Franciscan School', p. 814; and Russell, 'Grosseteste's Intellectual Life', p. 94.

57    Little, 'Franciscan School', p. 810. Cf. Easton, *Roger Bacon*, Appendix A.

diocese.[58] On his death in 1253 he probably left his library to the Oxford convent of Franciscans.[59]

Some 129 of Grosseteste's own lectures, exempla, and sermons have survived in the form of *dicta*, collected and arranged by him.[60] These reveal that the figurative use of vision and light was an important part of his mode of discourse. A favourite comparison is of the clerics of the church to the eyes of the body:

> The prelates and teachers of the church in the body of Christ are comparable to the eyes, as in the Psalm 'My eye is troubled with wrath' and in Canticles: 'thy eyes are as those of doves' [...] because they show the way of he laws to others and are one with the body, just like the leader of a journey.[61]

The eyes of the church are to be especially sensitive, for 'The faithful layman often does not feel the dust of a useless, ineffectual word or of a serviceable lie; you however who are the eyes of the bridegroom must carefully guard against such dust and, if you should be seriously affected, you must cleanse yourselves with tears of remorse'.[62]

---

58  Owst, *Preaching in Medieval England*, pp. 9–10. Cf. Grosseteste, *Epistolae*, no. 1237; ed. Luard, pp. 360–1, and see pp. 389–92.

59  See Green, *Franciscans*, pp. 26–7; Humphreys, *Friars' Libraries*, p. xix; Hunt, 'Library of Robert Grosseteste', p. 130; and Little, *Grey Friars in Oxford*, pp. 57–8.

60  Thomson, *Writings of Grosseteste*, pp. 214–32. The sermons are listed on pp. 160–91. Grosseteste's own *recapitulo* to the *dicta* testifies that they were delivered both to clerics and lay people (p. 214). Their usefulness to later preachers is indicated by the dates of the extant 38 MSS, the majority of which belong to the fourteenth and fifteenth centuries, and by the existence in many copies of a *tabula* giving subject-references (p. 215).

61  'Prelati et doctores ecclesie in corpore Christi comparantur oculis, ut in Psalmo: *conturbatus est in ira oculus meus* [Ps. xxx.10], et in Canticis: *oculi tui columbarum* [Cant. i. 14] [...] quia viam morum ceteris ostendunt membris suntque sicut dux itineris.' Grosseteste, *dictum* 41, in Oxford, Bodleian Library, MS. 798, f. 29; ed. Westermann, 'Comparison', p. 54; and see Thomson, *Writings of Grosseteste*, pp. 180 and 220.

62  'Laicus fidelis saepe non sentit pulverum verbi otiosi nocentis nulli, vel officiosi mendacii; vos autem qui estis oculi sponsi, pulverum talem

As the eye reflects the image of anyone who inspects it, so holy conversation should reflect the form and standard of right living to anyone who listens.[63] Clerics are not just eyes but also the source of light, for it is with the light of doctrine that the clergy illuminate others ('Cleri namque est lumine doctrinae alios illuminare').[64] They must shine, like stars, both within and without: within with the light of faith and without with the splendour of good works.[65] This light ultimately derives from God's love and in order to explain the workings of humility, one of the aspects of such love, Grosseteste introduces an exemplum, describing how light changes when it passes through coloured glass:

> The light of the sun in the sun or the ether is only light, having nothing in it except the nature of light [...] when however the light of the sun is joined to the colour existing in the transparent medium through which it passes, as namely to the colour of a glass, it necessarily incorporates itself to that colour and also draws forth with it that colour, and that colour is made into the nature of light and the light into the nature of the colour, and the ray is either golden or indigo, or red, according to what the colour is through which it passes.[66]

solicite debetis cavere, et, si vos forte contigerit, lachrymis compunctionis abluere.' Grosseteste, *Sermo ad clerum*, in *Fasciculus rerum*, vol. 2, p. 297. For another passage based on analogies between the inner and outer eye, see Grosseteste, *dictum* 119, f. 99a; ed. Westermann, 'Comparison', pp. 65–6.

63    Grosseteste, *Sermo ad clerum*, in Brown, ed., *Fasciculus rerum*, vol. 2, p. 298.
64    Grosseteste, *Sermo [...] in celebratio ordinum*, in Brown, ed., *Fasciculus rerum*, vol. 2, p. 273. For further passages on the spiritual perception of divine light, see Grosseteste, *dictum* 21 and *dictum* 72; ed Westermann, 'Comparison', pp. 56 and 60; and see Thomson, *Writings of Grosseteste*, p. 218.
65    Grosseteste, *Sermo ad sacerdotes in synodo*; ed. Brown, *Fasciculus rerum*, vol. 2, p. 269.
66    'Lux solis in sole vel in aethere sola lux est, nihil habens in se nisi naturam lucis [...] cum tamen lux solis adjungitur colori existente in perspicuo per quod transit, utpote colori vitri, incorporat se necessario illi colori et trahit secum etiam colorem illum, et fit ille color in natura luminis et lumen in natura coloris, et est radius vel croceus, vel Indicus, vel rubeus, secundum quod est color per quam transit'. Grosseteste, *Dictum de humilitate*; ed. Brown, *Fasciculus rerum*, vol. 2, pp. 288–9.

In the same way humility, in its primal state, is perfect and pure. It takes on an altered but not substantially different appearance when subject to the contingencies and limitations of particular human circumstances.[67]

## Optical Exempla

Grosseteste demonstrated in his teaching, sermons and letters the usefulness of optical exempla: they were an effective and economic form of rhetorical device, bringing together scientific, biblical and moral material in mutually illuminating ways. At the same time they had an added value of credibility and authority because of the traditional associations of light with God and vision with inner understanding, and because *perspectiva* itself enjoyed intellectual prestige. But if preachers were to follow Grosseteste's lead, they had need of convenient sources of a wide range of information. Encyclopedias themselves were of great use in this respect,[68] and it is significant that the two great compilations of the thirteenth century were the works of mendicants. Vincent composed his *Speculum maius* with fellow preachers specifically in mind. In the prologue he states that the work is intended for those at university involved in the study of arts through preaching, lecturing and disputing,[69] and more generally:

---

67 Grosseteste's emphasis on light and vision may have made a contribution to two Oxford sermons of Dominican authorship. See Smalley, 'Robert Bacon', pp. 15 and 17; and her 'Oxford University Sermons', pp. 316–19 and 325–7. The tradition of instruction begun by Grosseteste was continued by Pecham, who became a lecturer to the Franciscans at Oxford between 1270 and c.1275. See Pecham, *Tractatus de perspectiva*, ed. Lindberg, pp. 26–7.

68 d'Avray, *Preaching of the Friars*, pp. 232–4.

69 Vincent, *Liber apologeticus*, cap. 3; ed. Lusignan, pp. 118–19. See also Smits, 'Vincent of Beauvais', pp. 1 and 7.

Besides this, it is useful in another way: to teachers and to preachers and to all expositors of sacred scripture who contemplate a little for (as Augustine says of them), an ignorance of things makes figurative expressions obscure when we are ignorant of the nature of animals, or stones, or plants, or other things which are often used in the scriptures for the purposes of constructing similitudes.[70]

Although Bartholomaeus does not make his purpose so explicit, *De proprietatibus rerum* also provided a mine of information for preachers, who found its summaries of natural science suitable for moralization.[71]

Of even greater use to the homilist were collections that provided both the raw data and their moral or spiritual applications. The most remarkable such compilation using optical information is an extremely widespread Parisian work written between *c.*1276 and 1289, which is devoted exclusively to *perspectiva*:[72] the *Liber de*

---

70    'Accedit ad haec, et utilitas alia Doctoribus et Praedicatoribus cunctisque scripturarum sacrarum expositoribus minime contemplanda. *Ut enim Augustinus dicit, rerum ignorantia facit obscuras figuratas locutiones, cum scilicet, ignoramus vel animantium, vel lapidum, vel herbarum naturas, aliarumve rerum, quae ponuntur plerumque in scripturis alicuius similitudinis gratia.*' Vincent, *Liber apologeticus*, cap. 5; ed. Lusignan, pp. 120–1. The reference is to Augustine, *De doctrina christiana*, II. 59.

71    Seymour et al., *Bartholomaeus*, p. 13. Bartholomaeus lectured to the Franciscan convent at Paris until 1231, when he left for Germany. See Lindberg, *Theories of Vision*, p. 108; and Seymour et al., *Bartholomaeus*, p. 10. Preaching probably formed an important part of his activities at Paris. See Plassman, 'Bartholomaeus Anglicus', pp. 98, 104 and 106–7; and also Michaud-Quantin, 'Petites Encyclopédies', p. 587; Owst, *Literature and Pulpit*, p. 154; Se Boyar, 'Bartholomaeus Anglicus', pp. 177–8; and Welter, *L'Exemplum*, pp. 336–8. *De proprietatibus rerum* is one of the main sources of a collection of sermon anecdotes by Nicole Bozon, compiled in Anglo–French *c.*1320, ed. Smith and Meyer, *Contes moralisés*, in which see pp. vi–ix. English version by J. R. [i.e. John Rose] as *Metaphors of Brother Bozon*.

72    At Paris some 30 years earlier, when there was strong official resistance to Aristotelian science, Franciscan sermons were already beginning to show a fondness for optical analogies. See Davy, *Sermons universitaires*, pp. 78–9 and 351.

*oculo morali* of Peter of Limoges (1230–1306).[73] Peter was born in the district of Limoges and became canon of Evreux, refusing subsequent opportunities for higher office.[74] He became well known as a philosopher, mathematician, astrologer and preacher and was a member of the Sorbonne, to which he donated over 120 volumes.[75] It is possible, though unproved, that he is the same man as the Petrus Lemovicensis described as *decanus* of the faculty of medicine between 1267 and 1270.[76]

While at Paris, Peter made collections both of *distinctiones*, alphabetical lists of subjects useful to preachers, and of sermons by his fellow clerics.[77] The normal theatres of the Parisian preachers were the church, the royal chapel and occasionally the open air. Their sermons were delivered sometimes in Latin and sometimes in French.[78] Although the audience would therefore seem to have been relatively small and well educated, Parisian sermons of the thirteenth century were copied and distributed on a large scale and, through the medium of the friars, they were extremely influential

73   Clark, 'Optics for Preachers'; Schleusener-Eichholz, 'Naturwissenschaft und Allegorese' (I am grateful to the authors of these articles for sending offprints); Denery, *Seeing and Being Seen*, ch. 3; Spettman, 'Das Schriftchen *De oculo morali*'; Welter, *L'Exemplum*, pp. 177–80. Such is the extent of the scientific detail in Peter's work that d'Avray is unsure whether it is a preaching aid or a scientific treatise, although she favours the former (*Preaching of the Friars*, p. 279).

74   Newhauser, 'Nature's Moral Eye', pp. 127–30; Schleusener-Eichholz, 'Naturwissenschaft und Allegorese', 261–2; and Spettman, 'Das Schriftchen *De oculo morali*', p. 321.

75   Some of these have been discussed by Birkenmajer, 'Pierre de Limoges', pp. 26–30, who records two inscriptions indicating that Peter possessed optical texts (pp. 23–4). See further Delisle, *Cabinet des manuscrits*, vol. 2, pp. 167–9; Mabille, 'Pierre de Limoges'; Thorndike, 'Peter of Limoges'; and Welter, *L'Exemplum*, p. 129.

76   Glorieux, *Répertoire*, p. 364. For documentation, see Denifle and Chatelain (eds.), *Chartularium universitatis Parisiensis*, vol.1, items 416 and 433, pp. 468 and 488.

77   Lecoy de la Marche, *Chaire française*, pp. 102–10 and 331–5.

78   Ibid., pp. 226–9 and 233–337.

throughout Europe.[79] This is borne out by the large number of surviving manuscripts of De oculo morali itself: 158 at the latest count, of which forty-six exist in English libraries.[80] Lecoy de la Marche identified the Parisian preacher with a Petrus Lemovicensis who was charged by the Pope with a mission to Henry III in 1259, and who visited London a second time, in 1262.[81] If the identification is correct, then it may be that Peter's appearance at the English court helped to promote the popularity of moralized optics in this country.

The preface of De oculo morali states the rationale of the book in terms often used to justify the study of scientific data:

> If we should wish diligently to meditate on the law of God, we should most certainly take account of those things which are frequently told of in holy scripture appertaining to vision and the eye in comparison with other things. From which it is certain that a study of the eye and of those things that relate to it is most useful to the acquiring of a fuller acquaintance of divine wisdom.[82]

79   d'Avray, Preaching of the Friars, pp. 2–8, 98–9, 132–51, 160–3 and 273–81; Pelster, 'Oxford Collection', p. 168; and Pelster and Little, 'Sermons and Preachers', p. 150.
80   Schleusener-Eichholz, 'Naturwissenschaft und Allegorese', pp. 258–60; and cf. Newhauser, 'Nature's Moral Eye', pp. 132–4. On the influence of De oculo morali, see Clark, 'Optics for Preachers', pp. 331 and 343; and Welter, L'Exemplum, p. 180. For a Franciscan treatise and sermon on light written in Paris before 1294, see Squadrani (ed.), 'Tractatus de luce'.
81   Lecoy de la Marche, Chaire française, pp. 105–6. For documents, see Shirley (ed.), Royal and Other Historical Letters, vol. 2, letters 582 and 592, pp. 221–2 and 235–6; and Rymer and Sanderson (eds), Foedera, vol. 1, pt. 1, p. 381.
82   'Si diligenter volumus in lege domini meditari facillime perpendimus ea que pertinent ad visionem et oculum pro ceteris frequentius in sacris eloquias recitari. Ex quo patet considerationem de oculo et de his que ad ipsum spectant esse perutilem ad habendum divine sapientie noticiam pleniorem.' Peter of Limoges, De oculo morali, prol., ptd. A. Sorg. I have collated this edition with others published at Venice in 1496. A modern edition, by Richard Newhauser, is in preparation.

The work is divided into fifteen chapters of varying length which follow a pattern designed to implement the above statement of intent. An item of optical knowledge is described, often in some detail and with reference to the appropriate authority; it is then given a spiritual or moral interpretation which in turn is supported from biblical and patristic texts. It is evident from the author's familiarity with a wide range of scientific data that he has first hand acquaintance with works on *perspectiva*.[83] Among the scientific authors named are Alhacen, Aristotle, Constantinus, Euclid, Pliny, Ptolemy, Seneca and Vitruvius.[84]

The first chapter of Peter's work illustrates the relatively specialized nature of his references and the ingenuity of his analogies. He begins by citing Constantinus and the first book of Alhacen's work on the science of *perspectiva*. Following them, he describes the structure of the eye: its four tunics (*uvea, cornea, consolidativa* and *aranea*) and three humours (*vitreus, glacialis* and *albugineus*), of which the glacial humour is the sensitive organ of vision; the eyelids, which have a protective function; and the two optic nerves leading from the brain, through which the visual spirit runs and which intersect in the form of a cross before they terminate at the pupils.[85] At the mention of the pupils, Peter introduces with an elegant similitude ('eleganti similitudine')[86] a biblical text attributed to David: Guard us, O Lord, as the pupil of your eye ('Custodi nos domine ut pupillam oculi').[87]

This biblical allusion marks the division between the purely scientific data and their spiritual significance. For Peter proceeds to explain that just as the pupil (part of the *humor glacialis*) depends on the three other humours, three tunics and eyelids, so the pupil of the soul for its keeping depends on the seven principal virtues; and as the pupils through the optic nerves lead back to intersect in the

83  Lindberg, *Catalogue*, p. 73; and see Schleusener-Eichholz, 'Naturwissenschaft und Allegorese', p. 284.
84  Ibid., pp. 262–4; and Spettman, 'Das Schriftchen *De oculo morali*', p. 312.
85  Clark, 'Optics for Preachers', pp. 332–3.
86  Peter of Limoges, *De oculo morali*, I. A. i.
87  Ibid., I. A. ii. The similtude is based on Psalm 16:8.

form of a cross, so the spiritual pupil depends on the Crucifixion. It is therefore in the spiritual sense that the words of David are to be construed, and Peter now reinforces his text with an allied one from Deuteronomy describing God's treatment of Jacob, whom he led, taught, and guarded as the pupil of his eye ('Circumduxit eum et docuit et custodivit quasi pupillam oculi sui').[88] Since man is the pupil of God's eye, man's own eye becomes an image of his spiritual eye, which should also be kept in good health: 'In this therefore is shown that since nature takes so much of the bodily eye so we are prompted to the solicitous care of the spiritual eyes; truly, if we have been neglectful of them we shall surely call ourselves afflicted.'[89] Thus, the failing of one virtue adversely affects spiritual perception.

The second chapter begins by considering the relative hardness of the tunics of the eyes, which are then likened to the *prelati* of the church who should exhibit both the hard quality of justice or discipline and the soft quality of compassion.[90] There follows a lengthy discussion of the justice dispensed by prelates, and their behaviour is a theme to which Peter returns in Chapter Six, in which are moralized thirteen marvels of the eye. The second describes how, if a finger is placed in from of the face and the eyes look beyond it, two fingers are seen (an exemplum well adapted to rhetorical gesture). This is like the moral double vision of prelates who allow individuals to hold two benefices at the same time.[91] Thus Peter's exempla move nimbly between science and larger issues. For example, the third chapter begins:

88    Deuteronomy 32:10.
89    'In hoc ergo quae natura tanta custodia vallavit [carnalem] oculum spiritualiter informamur ad sollicitatem custodiam [spiritualium] oculorum: id est ne si negligentes fuerimus tandem [dolentes] dicamus.' Peter of Limoges, *De oculo morali*, I. A. ii. On Peter's method, note Schleusener-Eichholz, 'Naturwissenschaft und Allegorese', pp. 278–80.
90    Peter of Limoges, *De oculo morali*, II. A. i. On the meaning of *prelati*, see d'Avray, *Preaching of the Friars*, p. 14, n. 5.
91    Peter of Limoges, *De oculo morali*, VI. A. ii.

The authors of the science of perspective distinguish a three-fold visions of the eye. The first is through straight lines, the second through broken lines [refraction], the third is through reflected lines. Of which the first is more perfect than the other two, the second is more certain than the third, and the third is the least certain. In a similar way, spiritually speaking, we can assign a three-fold vision within man. One is perfect, which will be in the state of glory after the last resurrection. The other is in the soul as separated from the body until the resurrection, contemplating the divine essence in heaven, and this vision is weaker than the first. The third is in this life and this vision is the weakest of all. And it exists through reflection, just as the sight which one sees in a mirror takes place through the medium of reflected lines, the one which is called by the apostle mirrored vision. 'We see,' he says, 'now through a mirror darkly but in glory face to face.'[92]

The fourth and fifth chapters of *De oculo morali* moralize respectively the *species* emanating from the visible object and the completion of the act of vision within the brain.[93] Chapter Six on the marvels of vision is subdivided into thirteen sections, dealing with such matters as perception in a misty atmosphere, binocular parallax,[94] phenomena of refraction[95] and of reflection in plane and

92  'Auctores perspective distinguunt triplicem oculi visionem. Prima est per lineas rectas. Secunda per lineas fractas. Tertia per reflexas. Quarum prima perfectior est aliis. Secunda certior quam tertia: et tertia minus certa. Modo consimili spiritualiter loquendo possumus in homine visionem triplicem assignare. Una perfecta que erit in statu glorie post resurrectionem ultimam. Alia est in anima separata a corpore usque ad resurrectionem in celo empirreo divinam essentiam contemplante et hec visio debilior est quam prima. Tertia est in hac vita: que est omnium debilissima et habet hec fieri per reflexionem sicut et visio qua aliquid videtur in speculo habet fieri mediantibus reflexis lineis, unum ab apostolo paulo vocatur visio specularis. Videmus enim nunc per speculum et in enigmate sed in gloria facie ad faciem.' Ibid., III. A. i; and see Clark, 'Optics for Preachers', pp. 340–1. The central significance to Christian thought of the closing metaphor, from I Corinthians 13:12, is explored by Bradley, 'Speculum Image', pp. 9–27.

93  Chapter titles are listed by Spettman, 'Das Schriftchen *De oculo morali*', p. 310.

94  I.e. the apparent shift in position of an object viewed first through one eye and then through the other.

95  The fifth marvel, describing how a coin lying at the bottom of a container, may be brought into view when the container is filled with water, is similar

concave mirrors, the judgement of size and the causes of variation in apparent size. Chapter Seven on the twelve properties of the eye considers its physiognomy, capabilities and weaknesses. In the eighth chapter the seven distinguishing characteristics of the eye are associated with the seven cardinal vices. The ninth and tenth chapters deal with the covetousness and punishment of the eyes and the eleventh with seven conditions necessary to vision. The final four chapters consider the seven properties of the eye, the four objects of contemplation of the spiritual eye, the three objects in which the eye delights and the sevenfold vision of God.

Close comparisons between the inner and outer eye are characteristic of these exempla.[96] Peter of Limoges is highly select-ive, if well informed, in what he moralizes, taking from the books on *perspectiva* only such items as are susceptible to moral and spiritual interpretation. If the result sometimes seems arbitrary and forced, Peter is also capable of a striking blend of physical and moral fact which hinges on the assumption that there are real and revealing analogies between physical and spiritual perception. For instance, the section in the eleventh chapter of *De oculo morali* headed 'De informatione scholarium ex septem conditionibus quas requiruntur ad humanum visum' begins with a striking transition from one world to the other:

> In order that complete vision should be accomplished these seven things are necessary. There must be a regular disposition of the organ of vision, the presence of a visible object, a moderate distance, solidity in the visual object, visual attention over a period of time, diffused light, a transparent medium. However, three things must be excluded from the disposition of the eye: the tumour or growth of pride, the dust of avarice, the hard humour of lechery.[97]

to Holcot's moralized experiment in his *Super sapientiam Salomonis*. See below, pp. 108–9.

96   On Peter of Limoges's elaboration of the relations between the inner and outer eye, and its theological antecedents, see Clark, 'Optics for Preachers', pp. 338–40; and Kamerick, *Popular Piety*, pp. 150–4.

97   'Ad hoc ut fiat visio completa ista septem sunt necessaria. Debita dis-positio organi; presentia obiecti; proportio distantie; soliditas rei visae; attentio potentie; mora temporis; diffusio luminis; medium illustrantis.

In such instances, Peter capitalizes on his audience's interest in optics, only to remind them that there are vices to which the eye is particularly susceptible and that 'true' vision depends upon pre-conditions that are both physical and moral. In this he achieves a striking congruence with the work of an English writer present in Paris when Peter wrote, and who, inspired by Grosseteste, was attempting to make further advances in the science of *perspectiva*, Roger Bacon. Peter's borrowing nicely illustrates the extent to which scientific optics had some transferable assets for the com-pilers of exempla.[98]

In the final distinction of Bacon's *Perspectiva* (the fifth book of his *Opus maius*), he attempts to show how optics might be useful for divine truth ('sit utilis divine veritati').[99] He notes that scripture includes many references to the eye and vision. To understand fully its literal and spiritual meanings what is necessary is the science of *perspectiva* ('necessaria est hec scientia perspective').[100] He illustrates his point by using the same text as that used by Peter of Limoges in the first chapter of *De oculo morali*, 'Custodi nos domine ut pupillam oculi'. The meaning of this prayer cannot be compre-hended, argues Bacon, unless one knows how the preservation of the pupil is physically effected. There follows an account of its physiology and its principal parts which are associated, as in Peter's work, with the seven principal virtues. Bacon then elaborates by showing that the structure of the eye also mirrors the seven gifts of the spirit, the seven petitions of the *Pater noster*, the eight beatitudes and the twelve apostles.[101]

　　　Debitam autem dispositionem oculi auferunt ista tria: tumor seu promi-nentia superbie; pulvis avaricie; humor concretis luxurie.' Peter of Limoges, *De oculo morali*, XI. Further passages are printed by Clark, 'Optics for Preachers', and by Parronchi, *'Dolce' prospettiva*, pp. 521–6, who is primarily concerned with the influence on art of Peter's work.

98　　Peter of Limoges and Roger Bacon were exact contemporaries and Bacon was probably living in Paris from 1257. See Easton, *Roger Bacon*, pp. 138–9, and note Schleusener-Eichholz, 'Naturwissenschaft und Allegorese', p. 278.

99　　Cf. Hackett, 'Epilogue'.

100　Bacon, *Perspectiva*, pars 3, dist. 3, cap. 1; ed. and trans. Lindberg, pp. 322–3.

101　Ibid., pars 3, dist. 3, cap. 1; ed. and trans. Lindberg, pp. 322–5.

In the following chapter, Bacon observes that the eight conditions required for vision also have spiritual applications. For instance, just as objects can properly be perceived only at a moderate distance, so a the individual person must preserve an appropriate distance from God, neither too near nor too far: 'for remoteness from God through infidelity and a multitude of sins destroys spiritual vision, as do the presumption of excessive familiarity with the divine, and the [overly bold] investigation of divine majesty'.[102] These remarks are echoed in the eleventh chapter of *De oculo morali*, and the correlation is even closer in the case of Bacon's final observation. Talking of the three forms of vision, Peter adopts an identical array of material and order of presentation in showing their qualitative difference, the three-fold spiritual perception of man, and the application of I. Corinthians 13:12.[103]

*De oculo morali*, in its turn, would seem to have been influential on other compositions, such as the *Oculus sacerdotis* by William of Pagula, written in the 1320s as a manual for parish priests. William divided his work into three parts, the *pars oculi*, *dextera pars* and *sinistra pars*, covering respectively confessional practice, morals and dogma. The last two divisions follow Peter of Limoges's moral analysis of the eye, in which the right eye is the eye of action and morals and the left eye that of knowledge and speculation. Thus the somewhat puzzling title and divisions of *Oculus sacerdotis* become more intelligible when seen in relation to *De oculo morali*. It is likely that William of Pagula, in naming and structuring his work in these ways, recognized a second allegiance to another author of optical works, John Pecham. As Archbishop of Canterbury, he devised the Constitutions calling for improvements to be made in the education of parish priests, but he was also well known as the

---

102  Ibid., pars 3, dist. 3, cap. 2; ed. and trans. Lindberg, pp. 326–7.
103  Ibid., pars 3, dist. 3, cap. 2; ed. and trans. Lindberg, pp. 328–9. Bacon uses reflection and refraction as the basis for spiritual analogy also in pars 3, dist. 3, cap. 3 and 4; ed. and trans. Lindberg, pp. 330–5.

author of a widespread introduction to optical theory, influenced by Bacon's *Perspectiva*, his *Perspectiva communis*.[104]

The notion of organizing a manual for parish priests around 'the moralized eye' was sustained both in a supplement to the *Oculus sacerdotis* which appeared *c*.1330-40, entitled *Cilium oculi*, and in a revision made in 1385 by John de Burgo, the *Pupilla oculi*.[105] Pecham's double influence as church reformer and optical scholar itself paralleled the impact of Grosseteste's ideas for clerical reform on *La Lumière as Lais* by Pierre de Pechkam (1267), where they were in part rendered in terms of the metaphysics of light associated with 'Lincolniensis'.[106]

Most collections of exempla were much wider in scope than *De oculo morali*, but even in more general compilations *perspectiva* can feature as an important component of the overall scheme. *Lumen anime*, for instance, uses an eclectic range of scientific data to illustrate moral and dogmatic themes. It exists in three separately composed but interrelated versions, the combined manuscripts of which total in excess of 190. The first version was the work of a Master General of the Dominican Order, Berengar of Landorra (d.1330), and was probably undertaken at the behest of Pope John XXII. The second version appeared in about 1332, and the third before 1357.[107] The alphabetical index reveals the considerable extent to which such terms as *cecitas, color, lumen, lux, oculus, speculum* and *visus* are key words, associated with both the physical and spiritual worlds. Thus, light and heat are effective only in susceptible bodies in the same way that divine knowledge and love take their effect only in individuals disposed to receive them through holy works and virtuous living.[108] Just as opaque bodies

---

104 Lindberg, 'Introduction' to *Bacon and the Origins of* Perspectiva, pp. xcv–xcvi.
105 Boyle, '*Oculus sacerdotis*', pp. 83–4, 94–5 and 105–6; Owst, *Preaching in Medieval England*, pp. 296–9; and Pantin, *English Church*, pp. 189–202 and 213–14.
106 Hessenauer, 'Impact of Grosseteste's Pastoral Care', pp. 389–90.
107 Rouse and Rouse, 'Texts Called *Lumen anime*'; Thorndike, *History of Magic*, vol. 3, pp. 546–60; and his *Science and Thought*, pp. 14–15.
108 Berengar, *Lumen anime*, ch. 48C ('Actio luminis et coloris'). Elsewhere, (ch. 9J: 'Colores sunt principium videndi') virtues are likened to colours, which

reflect light better than thin, translucent or transparent ones, so Mary reflects more of God's light than the celestial stars.[109] The optical similitudes can be considerably more elaborate.[110]

A convenient sampler of the optical exempla circulating in England during the second half of the fourteenth century is provided by the *Summa praedicantium* of the English Dominican, John Bromyard (written *c*.1348).[111] His work is comprehensive, lengthy and detailed, and it was a widely known compilation, often found in the libraries of parish churches.[112] In *Summa praedicantium* are accumulated many of the components of the moral and spiritual interpretations of *perspectiva* which have been noted in the works of earlier writers. In Bromyard's work there are analogies between the inner and outer eyes; a systematic use of biblical and patristic texts on vision; brief similitudes from optical theory; and elaborate comparisons based on a more detailed knowledge of the subject. Bromyard sometimes uses optical material to explain the work of the friars: 'just as in seeing, in order that the act should be correct and virtuous, first a healthy organ of vision, secondly a clear medium, and thirdly a proportionate object are required, so in visiting and admonishing [...] the eye of a healthy and just intention is needed'.[113] Without a healthy and just intention an individual is worthy of reproach if, extracting a stalk from his brother's eye, he fails to see the beam in his own eye.[114] Defective vision can also be caused by external bodies or inner infirmities:

exist in light and which are the principal cause of seeing. On the status of this edition, see Rouse and Rouse, 'Text Called *Lumen anime*', pp. 50–2.

109   Berengar, *Lumen anime*, ch. 7Q: 'Luminis proprietatibus'.

110   Ibid., ch. 6K: 'Speculum concavum'.

111   Owst, *Preaching in Medieval England*, pp. 303–5. Cf. his remarks in *Literature and Pulpit*, p. 224 and n. 1; and also Boyle, 'Date of the *Summa praedicantium*'.

112   Savage, *Old English Libraries*, p. 132.

113   'in vidente ad hoc: quod actus eius sit rectus, et virtuosus requiruntur. Primo instrumentum sanum. Secundo medium clarum. Tertio obiectum proportionatum: ita in visitante et accusante requiruntur [...] oculus, id est, intentio sana, et iusta'. Bromyard, *Summa praedicantium*, pt. 2, f. 449v.

114   Ibid., pt. 2, f. 339v (b).

just as the light of the bodily eye can be impeded by an opaque body placed over it, or as one can be entirely blinded when captured by enemies, as was Sampson (Judges 16), or through infirmities affecting the eyes, so spiritually can the vision of the soul be impeded by things which form themselves around it through cares of the world and by those which form around others through the acceptance of duties.[115]

Spiritual comparisons can also be drawn with the objects and act of vision. As the appearance of water delights the bodily eye, so spiritually the observer is reminded that man is as water and like water dissolves in the earth.[116] In the act of vision, the eye leads the body and others, and so should the eye of the mind spiritually lead the whole man and lead others by word and example.[117]

At a somewhat more complex level, Bromyard introduces an observation on refraction and the apparent bending of a straight stick when placed in water:

truly that a double medium impedes vision is evident through the example of the straight stick which in the medium of air and water the eye sees as curved and oblique, because although in truth the air necessarily unites the medium to one sight of it, on the other hand the air prevents a sight of it since in truth it cannot unite with the water. So in the foregoing the necessary medium of living the truth in acts and judgements is the reason, or law of God [...] However, the law understood by a man either evil or led to evil, and mixed with subtleties and crafty precautions, is a disordered medium which bends straightness and perverts justice and equality.[118]

---

115 'sicut lumen oculorum corporalium potest impediri per corpora opaca superposita, vel omnino excecari potest quis ab hostibus captus sicut Samson Iudic. 16 vel per infirmitates oculis supervenientes: ita spiritualiter potest visus impediri animae in his, quae circa seipsum facienda sunt per terrenorum solicitudinem, et in his, quae circa alios sunt per numerum acceptionem.' Ibid., pt. 2, f. 427v (b). See also pt. 2, f. 429v, where the visual impediments of elongation, transposition and interposition are treated.
116 Ibid., pt. 2, f. 427r (a).
117 Ibid., pt. 2, f. 427v (a).
118 'quod videlicet visum impedit duplex medium patet per exemplum de baculo recto, qui visus per medium aeris, et aquae videtur curvus et obliquus: quia licet ad ipsius visionem unum debitum concurrat medium aer videlicet, aliud tamen non debitum concurrens aqua videlicet ipsius

And the visual pyramid appears in an unfamiliar context:

> just as all that is seen by the bodily eye is seen under a pyramidal form, of which the apex is in the eye and the base on the visible object, so also what is spiritually seen in the eyes of the faithful, such as loving and believing, is seen under the same form. Of which one angle of the pyramid is the Creator in the eye of the faithful, truly another angle, which we must see, is the creature in which we perceive need so that we sinners might heal, have compassion, and offer correction in order that we might follow the saints.[119]

It would be misleading to suggest that exempla collections, which proliferated in the late thirteenth and fourteenth centuries,[120] always incorporated sections on scientific optics. Most of the collections that are general in scope, or based on narrative, make only passing reference to the phenomena of visual perception.[121]

visionem impedit. Sic in praeposito debitum medium vivendi veritatem in agendis, et iudicandis est ratio seu lex Dei [...] Lex autem male intellecta, vel ad malum ducta, et subtilibus, et malitiosis cautelis mixta est medio deordinato, quod causam rectam curvat, iudiciumque pervertit et aequitatem.' Ibid., pt. 2, f. 448r (a).

119  'sicut omne quod videtur oculis corporalibus videtur sub forma piramidali, cuius conus est in oculis, et basis in re visa; ita etiam quod videtur spiritualiter in oculis fidei, ut amandum, credendum, sub praedicta forma videtur. Cuius formae unus angulus est creator in oculus fidei; alius vero angulus quae videre debemus, est ipsa creatura, in qua videre debemus indigentes, ut subveniamus, peccatores, ut compatiamur, et corrigamus, sanctos ut sequamur.' Ibid., pt. 2, f. 429r (b).

120  Mosher, *Exemplum*, pp. 12–16; and Pfander, 'Mediaeval Friars'.

121  Although the English Franciscan author of the *Liber exemplorum* (1275–9) knew Bacon at Paris, he does not appear to have shared Bacon's enthusiasm for optics. The *Tabula exemplorum*, another Franciscan collection from later in the same century, draws extensively on *De proprietatibus rerum*, but not for the entries concerned with vision. In Bozon's fables, where the subject of vision occurs its treatment derives from the traditional attributes of animals as found in Pliny and Physiologus and not from perspectivist writings. Bozon, *Contes moralisés*, nos. 44, 64, 76, 110, 111, 132 and 133; ed. Toulmin–Smith and Meyer, pp. 60–1, 87, 95–6, 126–8, 157–8 and 160–2. For further instances of the treatment of vision in narrative compilations see de Besançon, *Alphabetum narrationum*, tales 79, 140, 268,

Nevertheless, as we have seen, *perspectiva* could and did make inroads into homiletic discourse and there are indications that, in the England of the second half of the fourteenth century, it had become one of its well-established features. This may be attributed to the abiding, direct influence of Grosseteste, the continuing promotion of his ideas through the work of the friars, the unusually wide circulation of *De oculo morali*, and the prominence given to optical material in some more general collections of exempla.

In subsequent chapters, due account will be taken of Chaucer's debt to the optical content of encyclopedias and exempla. It will also become clear that he encountered useful material of a similar kind in other kinds of religious writing, such as Robert Holcot's commentary on Wisdom. Holcot (*fl.*1332–49) was a Dominican friar who lectured at Oxford and Northampton and whose commentary, written about 1333, was possessed by 'Every well-stocked library'.[122] It takes the form of a series of lectures, and among Holcot's sources are Vincent of Beauvais, Grosseteste and Euclid.[123] Holcot, as Smalley has observed, thinks 'in terms of sight rather than of sound',[124] and regularly describes in vivid detail instructive paintings or pictures.[125] His visual interests also show in the exempla to which he resorts in the course of his lectures.[126] For instance, he draws a moral from the ability of a man, placed in the bottom of a well at midday, to see the stars:

> he who is in a deep well around midday sees the stars, whereas he who stays in the light, on the surface of the earth, sees no star. In the same way he who is placed in the depths of humiliation, tribulation and difficulty, longs for heaven and cries to God; whereas truly he who remains in the

583, 776 and 777; ed. Banks, vol. 1, pp. 61, 97–8 and 187; and vol. 2, pp. 389 and 518.
122 Smalley, 'Robert Holcot', p. 10; and see Coleman, *Medieval Readers and Writers*, pp. 263–7.
123 Smalley, 'Robert Holcot', pp. 34 and 48.
124 Ibid., p. 5.
125 Ibid., pp. 65–82.
126 Ibid., p. 63.

light of the world and in the full glare of mundane conversation and
wantonness, cannot do so.[127]

He goes on to describe an experiment, previously used by Peter of
Limoges, in which a penny is placed at the bottom of a bowl, just
out of sight.[128] When water is added, the coin becomes visible.
Once again, external sight has spiritual application: the penny desig-
nates eternal life, which is hidden to those distanced from God
by earthly pride and pleasure. If tried by sickness, tribulation or
persecution, however, then they remember God and heaven. The
exemplum originates in that durable encyclopedia by Alexander
Neckam (1157–1217), *De naturis rerum*, which represents one of the
earliest English attempts to moralize the phenomena of sight.[129] In
his turn, Holcot was quarried by other homilists for their own
exempla.[130] The extent to which the moralizing of optical data was
a widespread practice is evidenced by its appearance in texts by
Lollards, in spite of their professed hostility to the friars.[131]

The preceding account of optical material found in medieval
encyclopedias and exempla is little more than a preliminary
survey,[132] but it is nevertheless possible to draw some tentative
conclusions. By the second half of the fourteenth century, the use

127   'ille qui est in profundo puteo circa meridiem videt stellas, ubi ille qui stat in
      superficie terrae in lumine nullam videt stellam. Eodem modo ille qui
      ponitur in profundo humilitationis, tribulationis et angustie suspirat ad
      coelem, et clamat ad Deum: qui vero stat in lumine mundi et claritate
      mundanae conversationis et lascivie stellas videre non potest.' Holcot, *Super
      sapientiam*, lectio 27. Smalley, 'Robert Holcot', p. 13, calls this edition 'the
      latest and most convenient to use'. The experiment referred to here is found
      also in Bacon and Pliny. See Lindberg, 'Bacon on Light, Vision', pp. 271–2.
128   Holcot, *Super sapientiam*, lectio 27, p. 97.
129   Neckam, *De naturis rerum*, bk. 2, ch. 153; ed. Wright, p. 235.
130   Smalley, *English Friars*, p. 35.
131   Hudson, 'Wycliffite Prose', p. 262; and Phillips, 'Wyclif and the Optics of
      the Eucharist'. For Wycliffe's optical interests, see Wyclif, *De actibus anime*,
      pars 1, cap.1; ed. Dziewicki, pp. 14–18.
132   The place to start further researches would be Schneyer, *Repertorium der
      lateinischen Sermones*.

of optics in homiletic discourse, especially sermons, was widespread and well established. Together with encyclopedias, exempla formed an important secondary route by means of which optical ideas travelled and gained currency. It follows that a working knowledge of the rudiments of optical theory was not confined to the cognoscenti: through various kinds of reading and listening, wider sections of society were aware of the processes, effects and significance of visual phenomena. Encyclopedias and exempla derive their optical content from scholarly writings and, with those more specialized texts, form an appropriate structure of ideas within which to place and interpret Chaucer's representations of the visual world. Of course, they form a context not only for the reception of his writings, but also for their production. The next chapter will begin to examine Chaucer's own susceptibility to *perspectiva* as represented by the kinds of text discussed above.

# 4 Chaucer and *Perspectiva*

There was no such thing as 'space' for medieval people.[1]

A danger in tracing the development and dissemination of optical ideas in terms of a chronological progression of cause and effect is that it tends to foreground the synthetic nature of *perspectiva*. In the second half of the fourteenth century, a range of optical texts and their derivatives represented space as at once material and metaphysical, both a product of visual experience and a spiritual entity. But beneath the apparently harmonious surface lay fault lines and internal contradictions. For example, as already noted, the very vehicle on which Alhacen's ideas depended – the natural philosophy of Aristotle – was initially denied entry to the university curriculum at Paris; the reception of Witelo's recension of Alhacen's writings was eased by the addition of a dedication stressing the neoplatonic traditions of light; and disputes about the nature of perception continued to stir controversy, as in scholastic circles at Oxford.

We should therefore be careful not to presume that, when Chaucer wrote, *perspectiva* was a serene discipline within which conflicts had been harmonized. On the contrary, its component parts were relatively unstable and open to question and in some respects offered radically different accounts of the production and meaning of space. *Perspectiva* invited debate, as the following discussion of two of Chaucer's tales makes clear, and that may help to explain why we find Chaucer engaged in a complex and long-lived series of negotiations with space as he encountered it in scientific writings, encyclopedias, homiletic literature, narrative

1    Camille, 'Signs of the City', p. 9.

sources and – no doubt – in his social existence. In so doing, to use Lefebvre's term, he developed *representational* modes that provide alternative accounts of space, modes that challenge and appropriate received ideas. A central element in that strategy, one that combined key features of optical writing and narrative, was the human body, the site at which the objective and subjective worlds meet, the place at which visual experience is interpreted and space analysed, reconstituted, modelled and produced often at variance with, or in defiance of, prevailing structures.

The present chapter engages in some preliminary examinations of that process, in relation to the Squire's Tale and Reeve's Tale. It therefore functions as a point of transition between the optical traditions already considered and Chaucer's writings, between considering how space was constructed according to optical principles and how optical space might be construed as a key element in Chaucer's larger narrative designs. It is also a prelude to the more sustained analysis of his treatment of space, and allied optical topics, that dominates the remainder of this book. The present aim is to begin an exploration of Chaucer's familiarity with texts on *perspectiva* such as those already discussed in the form of scientific treatises, encyclopedias and sermon exempla. The process of doing so introduces another means – vernacular literature – by which he became aware of optical ideas. The internal evidence suggests that Chaucer had a developing familiarity with optical writings of various kinds. But the chapter begins with a critique of four recent studies that have already argued for the direct influence of *perspectiva* upon his poetry. Although not necessarily concerned with Chaucer's spatial designs, they elaborate his indebtedness to optical thought.[2]

---

2    I have left out of account here Biernoff, *Sight and Embodiment*, since it makes no mention of Chaucer. Her ideas are, however, relevant to other discussions and are duly noted. See also Yager, 'Visual Perception', which emphasizes the influence of Boethian and Platonic notions of perception.

Other Studies


*Chaucer's Measuring Eye*, by Linda Tarte Holley, appeared in 1990, and its opening chapters contain a number of interesting observations about the relationship between Chaucer's writings and *perspectiva*.[3] Holley is aware of the importance of medieval optics as an intellectual context for Chaucer's work, its close affiliation with theories of cognition, its distinction between the conceptual work of the mind and the perceptual work of the eye, the self-conscious relativity of judgement it introduced into visual experience and its insistence on the limited capacity of sight and its proneness to deception. In looking at the spatial content of Chaucer's poetry she draws attention to the key function of the gaze, and to the extent to which Chaucer deliberately defines and designs space within his narratives (and allows his characters to do so) according to optical principles.

Unfortunately, Holley's method and argument do a disservice to her insights. Although she vows to eschew the use of models from other disciplines, she develops an elaborate analogical mode of analysis in which the perspective devices found in medieval painting are regarded as equivalent to rhetorical and stylistic devices (e.g. the periodic sentence),[4] and in which the framing devices found in the visual arts find their exact counterparts in narrative frames. She does so without evincing much awareness of the long-standing and unresolved debates concerning inter-art comparisons.[5] The result is a confusion of categories and especially an unnerving disregard for the differences between literal and metaphorical statements.[6] Her argument is not helped by some serious misapprehensions about the nature and content of *perspectiva* itself. For example, there is virtually no mention of the

3    The following remarks are based upon the introduction and chs 1–2. Discussion of specific narratives is reserved for the relevant chapters, below.
4    Holley, *Chaucer's Measuring Eye*, pp. 13 and 47ff.
5    Ibid., p. 10.
6    Ibid., e.g. pp. 5, 47 and 69.

central figure of Alhacen, although he is named by Chaucer,[7] and instead an over-reliance on Grosseteste, Bacon, Pecham and secondary studies. The result is an eccentric account of what optical scientists regarded as their objects of study. Holley emphasizes concepts of motion, force, measurement and the frame, although none of these is central to *perspectiva*.

Motion was indeed of interest to Chaucer's contemporaries, and it is taken into account in optical writings, but as a subsidiary interest.[8] The apparent movement of fixed objects, relative to a moving observer, was sometimes covered,[9] but for the most part writers developed their theories on the assumption that both the viewer and the field of vision are static.[10] The action of light, moreover, was regarded as so fast as to be imperceptible, and therefore not a promising topic for the study of terrestrial motion,[11] and the process of interpreting visual evidence virtually intuitive.[12] 'Force' is a word Holley regards as cognate with *virtus*, as used by the optical writers, and *vertu*, as used by Chaucer (GP, 4), ignoring its more usual equivalence with 'innate power' or, depending upon context and date of use, its tendency to indicate something more akin to 'inherent quality' (*OED* II. 11).[13]

The inexactness and oddness of her optical terminology extend also to *measurement*. Again, the science of measurements had eloquent adherents, but optics was not generally regarded as one of its instruments. William of Alnwick, whom Holley quotes out of Crombie, extols the beauty of measurement *per se*, not the part

---

7    Ibid., pp. 41–2.
8    Ibid., p. 7; see Weisheipl, 'Interpretation of Aristotle's Physics'.
9    Holley, *Chaucer's Measuring Eye*, p. 16. See, for example, Alhacen, *De aspectibus*, II. 3. 178–87; ed. Smith, pp. 194–9. When Holley discusses Roger Bacon on motion (p. 63) she turns to *Opus maius*, bk. 2 (not about optics).
10   A movement far more significant was that of the eyeball. See Alhacen, *De aspectibus*, I. 7. 15; ed. Smith, pp. 71–2.
11   Ibid., II. 3. 60–1; ed. Smith, pp. 121–3. Cf. Richard Swineshead, as summarized in Thorndike, *History of Magic*, vol. 3, pp. 382–3; and see Sylla, 'Mathematical Physics'; and Tachau, 'Problem of the *Species in Medio*', pp. 437–9.
12   Cf. Alhacen, *De aspectibus*, II. 3. 26; ed. Smith, pp. 103–4.
13   Holley, *Chaucer's Measuring Eye*, p. 49.

played in measurement by *perspectiva*.[14] True, optical writers were
concerned with how the eye gauges distance, but their emphasis
falls on the relative evaluation of the size of objects and the spaces
between them, such judgements being based on prior knowledge
and not with the aim of establishing absolute dimensions.[15] Finally,
the application of optical theory to framed space is not as direct
and immediate as Holley imagines.[16] Alhacen, for example, does
not regard space as framed except in isolated and special cases.
Instead, it is the product of an interaction between a usually static
observer and a field of vision restricted only by the capacity of the
eye to receive images as it looks, judges, scans, estimates, remem-
bers, compares.[17] Only much later, and gradually, did practising
artists recognize that medieval optical writings could be adapted to
provide the key to painting the world as if seen through a window
(Fig. 2.3).

This last point opens up what is probably the most serious
defect in Holley's account of medieval optics: its lack of historical
awareness. She extrapolates from studies of Renaissance art and
the development of artificial perspective in Italy, such as those by
William M. Ivins, Samuel Y. Edgerton Jr. and John White, the well
established notion that medieval *perspectiva* (especially as expressed
in the theories of Alhacen) was the foundation of artificial per-
spective as used by Ghiberti, Alberti and others. She asserts that
the same scientific influences were at work on Giotto and the early
practitioners of pragmatic perspective (a hypothesis that remains
unproved); assumes that Giottesque art was dominant in Chaucer's
England (although a key article in this area, unnoticed by Holley,
calls its influence at best 'episodic');[18] then concludes that 'optics
influenced Chaucer'. While that may be true, the case is not helped
by specious argument in which the findings of one historical

14   Ibid., pp. 25–6.
15   Cf. ibid., p. 9.
16   Ibid., p. 34.
17   E.g. Alhacen, *De aspectibus*, II. 3. 164 and 167; ed. Smith, pp. 185–6 and
     188.
18   Holley, *Chaucer's Measuring Eye*, pp. 37–8. See Pächt, 'Giottesque Episode'.

discipline are transposed retrospectively by circuitous routes to another culture and artistic medium.[19]

Norman Klassen's *Chaucer on Love, Knowledge and Sight* (1995) is altogether less audacious in its claims, more circumspect in its method and more thorough in its scholarship.[20] Klassen regards sight as the third term which mediates between love and knowledge: just as sight is vital to the experience of erotic love, so it is also a means of obtaining and representing knowledge (particularly spiritual knowledge). To understand the complexities of the tripartite relationship as it affects Chaucer's writing, Klassen rightly insists on taking account of the treatment of sight in a wide range of earlier and contemporary texts. The authors he covers in some detail include St John, St Augustine, pseudo-Dionysius, Boethius, St Bernard, Guillaume de Deguileville, Grosseteste, Alhacen, Richard Rolle, Julian of Norwich and the author of *The Cloud of Unknowing*. From the ensuing discussions he is able to show how the topic of sight occupied a crucial position at the centre of a nexus of issue concerning epistemology, cognition, aesthetics, mysticism and optics.

For the later fourteenth century, Klassen identifies a number of symptoms that indicate the extensive interest given to visual perception. For example, he detects behind the affective passion for dazzling sights and bright colours 'a growing pleasure in understanding the phenomena', including the part played by sight.[21] Again, he finds in philosophical writings on cognition that vision had become coterminous with a new kind of knowledge which was the product of human enquiry into the way things work, including the mind as it processes information from the sensible world.[22] Further, enthusiasm for vision in mystical thought 'continues un-

---

19   See Holley, *Chaucer's Measuring Eye*, pp. 35–6, where Bacon and Pecham become responsible for the discovery of pictorial perspective, and it is implied that their writings influenced Giotto's work in the Scrovegni chapel at Padua. Cf. pp. 40 and 50–63.

20   Again, my comments are limited to the opening chapters (pp. 1–74), with further discussion reserved for individual narratives, below.

21   Klassen, *Chaucer on Love*, p. 24.

22   Ibid., pp. 33–4.

abated and positively flourishes in late medieval writings in the vernacular'.[23] In addition to these new developments, sight continued to occupy its traditional place as a means of describing and evaluating the spiritual world.[24] Within this context, optics occupied an important place. For Ockham, for whom knowing is primarily 'seeing',[25] the close link between epistemology and vision underscores the importance of optical thought in late medieval intellectual life – a conclusion reached also by Tachau.[26] While paying some attention to the evidence of sermons and encyclopedias,[27] Klassen stresses the contributions of Grosseteste and Alhacen.

Klassen's overriding interest is in the evolution of theories which account for the relationship between subject and object. For this reason, his material ranges across those areas of thought (epistemology, aesthetics, mysticism) much wider than those circumscribed by the discipline of optics. His interest in optics is likewise affected by his dominant concern: in his summary of Alhacen's theories, he stresses that author's preoccupation with seeing objects in depth, but otherwise the phenomenon of space *per se* is not a pressing interest. Thus the relevance of his study to the present one is as an endorsement of the keen interest expressed in sight by Chaucer's contemporaries, and the substantial and persuasive evidence he provides of its various manifestations.

*Species, Phantasms and Images* by Carolyn P. Collette (2001) is a thoughtful attempt at marrying optics and Chaucer, if marred by a somewhat insecure grasp of the scientific material. For Collette, *perspectiva* is, in any case, subordinate to faculty psychology, which is the main cultural context she invokes. The operation of *fantasye* within a number of Canterbury Tales is her particular focus. She plots the derivation of mental images from visual experience, and to that extent optical writings enter her frame of reference, as

23   Ibid., p. 34. Cf. p. 53.
24   Ibid., p. 62.
25   Ibid., p. 66, quoting Courtenay.
26   Tachau, *Vision and Certitude*, p. xv.
27   E.g. Klassen, *Chaucer on Love*, pp. 52 and 54.

background.[28] Helpfully, she draws attention to a feature of a number of Chaucer's narratives often overlooked because it is taken for granted – the centrality of sight, and of the related processes of imagining and understanding (including spiritual insight). This feature she places within a late medieval scholastic context, noting that writers such as Wyclif and Ockham had comparable interests. Her sources on *fantasye* include Avicenna, Albertus Magnus and Aquinas, and for a synthetic treatment of faculty psychology and optics she turns to Bacon and Vincent of Beauvais. As a result, she gives undue prominence to the multiplication of *species* as the dominant theory of sight, whereas it was actually one among several and, at that, hotly contested. Indeed, in quoting from Vincent a description of the after-image, she mistakenly takes it as evidence of his indebtedness to the theory of multiplication, although the passage derives from Alhacen, who does not entertain the theory subsequently championed by Bacon (p. 14).[29] In all this there is a mixing of different types of text (scientific treatise, encyclopedic digest) without due differentiation of their functions and authorial expertise. Finally, Trevisa is credited with authorship of *De proprietatibus rerum* when he was its translator. The end result is a somewhat loose and vague account of medieval optics, but it nevertheless makes the point that it is a viable framework within which to examine Chaucer's writings, albeit from a standpoint that does not directly concern his representation of space.

Finally, Suzanne Conklin Akbari devotes two chapters to Chaucer in her *Seeing through the Veil: Optical Theory and Medieval Allegory* (2004). Since the bulk of her study focuses on a literary mode that enjoyed its zenith in the thirteenth century, Akbari rightly accentuates the neoplatonic optical theory then current. She fully acknowledges the later supremacy of Aristotelian optics, represented in university curricula by Alhacen and others, but gives it less emphasis precisely because it is less useful: although concerned with the psychology of perception, its priority is the

28   Collette, *Species, Phantasms and Images*, p. ix.
29   Ibid., p. 14.

world 'out there' of surfaces, of illusion, of Euclidean geometry. However, Chaucer is an uneasy and 'vestigial' allegorist, more interested in possibilities of meaning than in establishing hierarchies of interpretation. His modes of mimesis do not generally mix well with neoplatonic optics. As the present book argues, they are better explained in the context of the Aristotelian optics dominant in the fourteenth century.

## Chaucer's Receptivity

A priori, there is every reason for thinking that Chaucer would have been susceptible to *perspectiva* in its various manifestations, for he was receptive to Latin science, encylopedias and homiletic writing. As far as we know, he did not attend Oxford or Cambridge, the natural habitats of Alhacen's *De aspectibus* and similar works. But Chaucer's contact with university culture is clear from the Miller's Tale and Reeve's Tale, with their careful evocations of scholarly milieux,[30] and scholar friends like Ralph Strode might have been able to lend him optical texts.[31]

His interest in Latin texts generally is shown by the extensive use he makes of them in his own writings. Among classical works he knew, if in fragmentary redactions, are Statius' *Thebaid,* Juvenal's *Satires,* Cicero's *Somnium Scipionis* with the commentary of Macrobius, and – more extensively – Virgil's *Aeneid* and Ovid's *Metamorphoses,* the second of which he supplemented with the *Ovide moralisée.*[32] Notable medieval Latin works that influenced Chaucer

---

30  See Bennett, *Chaucer at Oxford,* chs. 2 and 4; Orme, 'Chaucer and Education', pp. 234–8; and Pearsall, *Life of Geoffrey Chaucer,* pp. 29–34.
31  Bennett, *Chaucer at Oxford,* pp. 63–5; and Courtenay, *Schools and Scholars,* pp. 378–80.
32  See the sketch by Pratt, 'Karl Young's Work'; and Bennett, *Chaucer's 'Book of Fame',* ch. 1; Friend, 'Chaucer's Version of the *Aeneid';* and Harbert, 'Chaucer and the Latin Classics'.

include Boethius' *Consolatio Philosophiae*,[33] Bernard Silvestris' *De mundi universitate*,[34] Alan of Lille's *De planctu Naturae* and *Anticlaudianus*, Geoffrey of Vinsauf's *Poetria nova*, Joseph of Exeter's *Frigii Daretis Ylias*, and the *Disticha Catonis*.[35] Chaucer also adapted material from a number of Latin religious works, as occasion demanded, such as Jerome's *Epistola adversus Jovinianum*,[36] Robert Holcot's *Super sapientiam Salomonis*,[37] and texts related to the *Summa* of St Raymund of Pennaforte and the *Summa vitiorum* of Guilielmus Peraldus.[38]

The range of Latin texts known to Chaucer, as well as the subtle uses to which he puts them, suggest that his working knowledge of the language was of a high order,[39] even if he shows a tendency to mistranslate and, as for example with the Clerk's Tale and *Boece*, to rely heavily on French versions of the Latin original.[40] The conclusion to be drawn is that Chaucer would have had no hesitation in tackling a medieval Latin text on optics. If the language of scientific treatises was of a technical nature, the syntax, which takes pains to avoid ambiguity, is often less difficult than that of more literary works. Ample proof of Chaucer's appetite for

33  Jefferson, *Chaucer and the 'Consolation of Philosophy'*.
34  Two of Chaucer's borrowings from Bernard are discussed by Loomis, 'Saturn in Chaucer's Knight's Tale'.
35  See Bennett, *'Parlement of Foules'*; Dronke and Mann, 'Chaucer and the Medieval Latin Poets', pp. 154–72; and Root, 'Chaucer's Dares'.
36  Dronke and Mann, 'Chaucer and the Medieval Latin Poets', pp. 177–82; and Hanna and Lawler, 'Wife of Bath's Prologue', pp. 360–7.
37  Petersen, *Sources of the Nonne Prestes Tale*, pp. 98–118; and Pratt, 'Some Latin Sources'.
38  Petersen, *Sources of the Parson's Tale*, whose views are modified by Kellogg, 'St Augustine and the *Parson's Tale*'; and by Pfander, 'Some Medieval Manuals of Religious Instruction'. See also Hazelton, 'Chaucer's Parson's Tale'; and Newhauser, 'Parson's Tale', pp. 542–601.
39  Dronke and Mann, 'Chaucer and the Medieval Latin Poets', p. 169; and Pratt, 'Some Latin Sources', pp. 554–5.
40  Dedeck-Héry, *'Boèce de Chaucer'*; his 'Jean de Meun et Chaucer'; Farrell and Goodwin, 'Clerk's Tale'; Harbert, 'Chaucer and the Latin Classics', pp. 145–7; Jefferson, *Chaucer and the 'Consolation of Philosophy'*, pp. 1–25; and Severs, *Literary Relationships*, ch. 10.

Latin science is provided by his own *Treatise on the Astrolabe*, deriving from a Latin version of an Arabic work on the subject and from John of Sacrobosco's *De sphaera*.[41] Thus, if nothing shows conclusively that Chaucer mastered *perspectiva* in its undiluted form, there is no reason in principle why he should not have done so.

We are on surer ground when considering Chaucer's familiarity with encyclopedias. In a series of articles, Pauline Aiken demonstrated that he made extensive use of the *Speculum maius* of Vincent of Beauvais, turning to it time and again as a convenient compilation of scientific lore, and mining the 'Estoryal Myrour' (*LGW*, G307) for narratives.[42] It is the basis for the account of Arcite's illness in the Knight's Tale;[43] the display of alchemical learning in the Canon's Yeoman's Tale;[44] the professional practices of the Doctour of Physik;[45] dame Pertelote's medical knowledge;[46] the Summoner's skin disease;[47] and the demonology of the Friar's Tale.[48] It is not clear whether or not Chaucer also used the other great encyclopedia of the period, the *De proprietatibus rerum* of

---

41 The full text, with diagrams, of Chaucer's treatise, together with a facsimile and translation of his major source, the *Compositio et operatio astrolabi* of Messahalla, are printed in Gunther, *Early Science in Oxford*, vol. 5. See also Manzalaoui, 'Chaucer and Science', p. 229; Pintelon, 'Introduction' to *Chaucer's Treatise on the Astrolabe*, pp. 10–11; and, for the type of scientific compilation from which Chaucer's *Astrolabe* is derived, Masi, 'Chaucer, Messahalla and Bodleian Selden Supra 78'.

42 I.e. the final part of Vincent's work: see Aiken, 'Chaucer's *Legend of Cleopatra*'; her 'Vincent of Beauvais and Chaucer's Monk's Tale'; and Wimsatt, 'Vincent of Beauvais'.

43 Vincent is 'The probable source of the poet's remarkably accurate knowledge of medicine': Aiken, 'Arcite's Illness', p. 361.

44 Chaucer 'shows a general familiarity with the material contained in the *Speculum Naturale* and *practically no other alchemical knowledge*' (author's emphasis): Aiken, 'Vincent of Beauvais and Chaucer's Knowledge', p. 388.

45 Aiken, 'Vincent of Beauvais and the "Houres"', pp. 22–4.

46 Aiken, 'Vincent of Beauvais and Dame Pertelote's Knowledge'.

47 Aiken, 'Summoner's Malady'.

48 Aiken, 'Vincent of Beauvais and the Green Yeoman's Lecture'.

Bartholomaeus.[49] The Latin text had been available since the mid-thirteenth century and a French translation by Corbéchon since 1392. Trevisa's translation appeared in 1398.

The substance and manner of homiletic discourse, the other route by which *perspectiva* might have reached Chaucer, are deeply embedded in the content and style of his work.[50] Six of the Canterbury pilgrims – the Monk, Friar, Parson, Pardoner and Nun's Priest – could have claimed a professional acquaintance with the art of preaching. Even Oswald the Reeve, as Harry Bailly remarks, is a preacher manqué (RP, 3903),[51] and the Friar is quick to recognize that the Wife of Bath's mode of address has much in common with a sermon (FrP, 1270–7). The Pardoner's Prologue and Tale,[52] Nun's Priest's Tale,[53] and Parson's Tale[54] have all been identified as sermons, if somewhat unconvincingly in the last case. Exempla, as might be expected, occur frequently in these works, but they are also present in a wider range of material, such as the Friar's Tale,[55] Summoner's Tale[56] and Franklin's Tale.[57] Although the exemplum was not restricted to sermons – it was a rhetorical

49   Curry uses Bartholomaeus to provide a context for some of the scientific passages in Chaucer's writings: *Chaucer and the Mediaeval Sciences*, pp. 61–1, 150–1 and 307.

50   See esp. Fletcher, *Preaching, Politics and Poetry*, chs. 9–12.

51   The preaching of the Reeve and of other Canterbury pilgrims is systematically discussed by Gallick, 'A Look at Chaucer and his Preachers'.

52   Kittredge appears to have been the first to indicate that PardPT form a sermon. See his *Chaucer and his Poetry*, pp. 21–2. Critics have subsequently argued over the extent to which Chaucer's work can be anatomized along strict generic lines. See Hamel, 'Pardoner's Prologue and Tale'; Ginsberg, 'Preaching and Avarice'; Luengo, 'Audience and Exempla'; Owen, 'Pardoner's Introduction, Prologue and Tale'; and Sedgewick, 'Progress of Chaucer's Pardoner'.

53   Wheatley, 'Nun's Priest's Tale'; and Petersen, *Sources of the Nonne Prestes Tale*, pp. 95–118.

54   Newhauser, 'Parson's Tale'.

55   Mrockzkowski, 'Friar's Tale'; and Nicholson, 'Friar's Tale'.

56   Shain, 'Pulpit Rhetoric', in which PardT and MerchT are also discussed.

57   Edwards, 'Franklin's Tale'.

device in general use[58] – the contexts in which Chaucer employs it reveals that a major channel of influence, as far as he was concerned, was the medieval sermon.[59] In the case of Chaucer's awareness of optical exempla, it is possible to point to one likely source: as already noted, he was acquainted with Holcot's *Super sapientiam Salomonis*, in which the author pays a good deal of attention to the sense of sight, moralizing some of its aspects.[60]

## The Squire's Tale

The structure of textual dissemination identified for *perspectiva* matches three important components of textual influence occurring in Chaucer's work. In one or two cases (Vincent, Holcot) there are precise correlations: a text containing optical ideas is the same as a text known to have been used by Chaucer. In other instances, the proximity of optically inspired text to text used by Chaucer is more speculative (as in the case of Bartholomaeus). But both kinds of optical texts (i.e. the ones known to have been used by Chaucer, and the ones he might have consulted) can be deployed to provide a context for understanding his own, innovatory, use of optical material. The analyses that follow tend to

---

58   Its use is recommended by Geoffrey of Vinsauf, one of the narrative theorists Chaucer acknowledges (NPT, 3347): see his *Poetria nova*, II. 195; ed. Faral in his *Arts poétiques*, p. 203; trans. Nims, p. 23; and see Wenzel, 'Chaucer and the Language of Contemporary Preaching', pp. 140–1.

59   Chapman, 'Chaucer on Preachers and Preaching'. Chaucer's use, particularly in WBPT, SumT and PardT, of a manual for preachers, friars and laymen, close in type and content to the *Communiloquium* of John of Wales, a Franciscan scholar and preacher, has been demonstrated by Pratt, 'Chaucer and the Hand that Fed him'. For other types of influence affecting Chaucer through sermons, see Owst, *Literature and Pulpit*, esp. pp. 22–30 and 389, n. 2; also pp. 180, n. 4, 201, 370, 388–9, 397–8, 401, 404–5, 418, 420–1, 425 and 442.

60   See above, pp. 107–9.

confirm from internal evidence that, for his optical ideas, he had recourse to already familiar compositions, but they show that he probably used other scientific sources as well. They also raise new questions about the extent to which optical ideas travelled to Chaucer through a route not yet fully discussed: that of the European vernacular literature long known to have been the building blocks of his narratives.

The obvious place at which to start an enquiry into Chaucer's internal references to the science of optics is the passage in the Squire's Tale where he alludes directly to Alhacen and Witelo:

> And somme of hem wondred on the mirour,
> That born was up into the maister-tour,
> Hou men myghte in it swyche thynges se.
> Another answerde and seyde it myghte wel be
> Naturelly, by composiciouns
> Of anglis and of slye reflexiouns,
> And seyde that in Rome was swich oon.
> They speken of Alocen, and Vitulon,
> And Aristotle, that writen in hir lyves
> Of queynte mirours and of perspectives,
> As knowen they that han hir bookes herd. (225–35)

The properties of the mirror in question were earlier described by the stranger knight who brought it, one of four magic gifts from a monarch controlling vast territories, the 'kyng of Arabe and of Inde' (110), on the occasion of King Cambyuskan's birthday feast – the others being a flying 'steede of bras', a ring that enables its wearer to understand the speech of birds and the healing power of herbs, and a sword that is at once a mighty weapon and the healer of the wounds it inflicts. The mirror and ring are specifically intended for Cambyuskan's daughter, Canacee, although the powers of the former are described as being useful also to her father. It transcends time: in the mirror, the knight tells Camyuskan, he will be able to see 'Whan ther shal fallen any adversitee' (134) to his realm or person. Thus the mirror and the horse together provide ways of escaping the normal contingencies of time and space, and may be used to personal or political advantage. They are mysterious new technologies (the horse a form of personal air transport, the mirror a kind of surveillance machine or panopticon), the latter being one that provides the security of secret intelligence and therefore the opportunity to take pre-emptive measures. It is small wonder that Cambyuskan has the mirror and sword ceremoniously conveyed, in recognition of their importance, by 'certeine officers', to the 'heighe tour' (176–7).[61]

It is the special function of the mirror (paradoxically enough) to get under the surface of appearances, to show through a process of reflection 'openly who is youre freend or foo' (136). It operates as effectively in the erotic as in the political world, revealing the intentions of 'any maner wight' on which 'any lady bright / Hath set hire herte' (137–8), or the treason of a false lover, including the identity of his new love and 'al his subtiltee', making it so open 'that ther shal no thyng hyde' (140–1). Thus the mirror puts tremendous power (as well as responsibility) in the hands of its owner, while at the same time offering protection against personal or political enemies. In the erotic sphere it acts as a kind of insurance policy against the worst effects of 'this lusty someres tyde' (142), that is the spring and summer season of love in which the tale is set.

The stranger knight's description of the mirror's powers introduces a hint of darkness into the otherwise unruffled splendour and perfection of Cambyuskan's court. Terms such as 'adversitee', 'foo', 'fals', 'tresoun', and 'subtiltee' suggest an underlying menace. Similarly, the 'woundes [...] depe and wide' (155) that the sword can cause, and the description of its naked blade carving and biting through armour, no matter how strong, 'Were it as thikke as is a branched ook' (159), remind us that Cambyuskan's rule is founded on the codified violence of chivalry, albeit balanced by the necessity of making moral judgements about the exercise of 'grace' and the healing of the victim (160–1). But it is the final episode of this unfinished tale in which the full horror of sexual politics at court is revealed. The heart-wounded female falcon tells of the agony inflicted by a 'tercelet', whose deep-dyed treason and falseness were hidden so carefully under 'humble cheere, / And

61    Cf. Foucault, *Discipline and Punish*, pp. 195–209; and his 'Eye of Power'.

under hewe of trouthe [...] pleasance, and [...] bisy peyne' (507–9) that no one could have guessed his true nature. Like a serpent hiding under flowers, waiting his time to bite, he performed the 'cerymonyes and obeisaunces' (515) that won the falcon's heart, only to abandon her cruelly at an opportune moment. Her lover's behaviour prior to betrayal is thus described in formal terms that echo the ceremonies, observances and decorum that we have already seen at Cambyuskan's feast, suggesting that the wider world of court life may mask venom and treachery of the most heinous kind. The enormity of the tercelet's behaviour, and the innocence of his victim, are underscored by three images drawn from Christian iconography: the malevolent serpent, awaiting its opportunity to despoil innocence; the gruesome sight which first confronts Canacee in the garden, of the falcon lacerating her breast with her beak so that the red blood runs down the white, leafless, sterile trunk – which recalls 'the pelican in his piety', itself a representation of Christ sometimes seen in conjunction with the crucifixion; and the graphic image which the falcon herself uses of her betrayer, when she describes 'this god of loves ypocryte' (514) as being like those *memento mori* tombs in which the saintly effigy of the deceased lies above an horrendous sculpture of bodily corruption – thus introducing the notion of sin and divine justice.

Canacee is enabled to understand, and heal, the falcon, by virtue of the magic ring which she now wears, but the whole episode is prompted by the mirror. Canacee goes to bed early after the revels, sleeps her 'firste sleep' (367), and then awakes because she is excited by the 'queynte ryng and hire mirour' (369). The effect of that excitement is visible: 'twenty tyme she changed hir colour', and in her next sleep she has a vision because of the impact the mirror is having on her emotionally and mentally: 'right for impressioun / Of hire mirour' (370–2). There is a strong sense here of the mirror's traditional affiliations with sexuality, inwardness, reflexivity and self-consciousness. We are not told what the vision was (unless it was a vision of the mirror as object), but nevertheless it is the cause of her rising, unusually, at dawn, to walk 'in the park' (392). The suffering which she encounters is exactly what the mirror is designed to avoid, anticipate and counteract. As such it is the fulfilment of a courtly fantasy, whereby the dissimulation on which policy, faction and desire depend is stripped away to reveal true intentions, while simultaneously putting the owner of this unique instrument of insight in an all-powerful position.

Considered in this way, the mirror would seem to be fully accounted for in terms of the narrative and symbolic economy of the tale. And yet Chaucer chose to insert lines not found in his immediate source (which confines itself to the magic properties of mirrors)[62] and which, if not irrelevant, are surprising and extraneous, striking an intrusive and incongruous note by introducing into the never-never land of Tartarye a topical discussion of a scientific subject.[63] The language is technical and *au fait*, strewn with appropriate terms: the mirror's effects might be explained 'Naturelly', that is as operating according to the principles of natural science, of which optics was a branch.[64] There is reference too to the mode of analysis used in optical texts, namely the geometrical constructions of Euclidean geometry, especially prevalent in the sections concerning reflection, 'composiciouns / Of anglis and of slye refelexiouns', with a hint in the word 'slye' that these are subtle and advanced calculations (Fig. 4.1).[65] The names now adduced to lend authority to the hypothesis are those of the figures central to the development of *perspectiva* as a discipline: Aristotle, whose empirical approach to natural science was highly influential, and who himself wrote on visual phenomena in a text widespread in the middle ages (*De sensu*); Alhacen – whose name is

---

62 DiMarco, 'Squire's Tale', p. 188 (*Cléomadés*); and especially Gower, *Confessio Amantis*, V. 2031–2272; ed. Macaulay, vol. 2 , pp. 3–9. Cf. Metlitzki, *Matter of Araby*, pp. 140–56. See Chaucer, *Squire's Tale*, ed. Baker, pp. 13–14; *Roman de Renart*, lines 29391–400, ed. Raynaud and Lemaître; and Spargo, *Virgil the Necromancer*, pp. 134–5.

63 Stillwell, 'Chaucer in Tartary', pp. 184–7, finds the scientific content difficult to assimilate to a romance. Cf. Goodman, 'Chaucer's *Squire's Tale*' pp. 133–4; and Lawton, *Chaucer's Narrators*, pp. 108–10.

64 Cf. Burnley, 'Chaucer's *Termes*'.

65 E.g. Pecham, *Perspectiva communis*, II. 45; ed. Lindberg, pp. 196–210, on reflection in a spherical convex mirror.

not out of place in a tale with an oriental setting – who adopted Aristotelian theories of vision as a first step towards developing his own science of sight which, as we have seen, carried all before it; and Witelo, responsible for reworking Alhacen's ideas and transmitting them to a yet larger audience of scholars.[66] The speaker of these lines is thus on target in identifying the key authors associated with the science of optics, who wrote during their lives 'Of queynte mirours and of perspectives'. They are the authors of the texts which, with one or two others such as Bacon's *Opus maius*, stand at the pinnacle of the scholarly tradition and helped to form the university curriculum.[67] The speaker seems to be aware of that too, because the final line of the passage, 'As knowen they that han hir bookes herd', alludes to the circumstances in which specialized optical texts would have been transmitted, that is in the course of university lectures at which the master would read aloud from a particular authority and provide a running commentary.[68]

These lines might be read as a gratuitous display of one-upmanship, but what larger patterns of explanation are available? They certainly accord with a general attempt on the part of the 'peple' who swarm in the courtyard of Cambyuskan's palace to assimilate the stranger knight's gifts by debunking and demystifying their marvellous aspects.[69] They use a range of strategies: 'Diverse folk diversely they demed' (202). One is to identify precedents in the 'olde poetries' (206) of myth and legend. Thus the steed of brass is compared with Pegasus, or with the Trojan horse; the mirror may duplicate one at Rome (made famous in legends of Virgil as magician); the sword is likened to that of Achilles; and the names of Moses and Solomon are invoked as previous owners of powerful rings. Another category of explanation concerns illusion

---

66   For an early attempt by Warton (1774) to provide a scientific context for these lines, see Chaucer, *Squire's Tale*, ed. Baker, note to line 132: *mirour*.

67   Cf. DiMarco, 'Dialogue of Science and Magic', pp. 61 and 64.

68   Cf. Cobban, *Medieval English Universities*, pp. 165–7; Coleman, *Public Reading*, pp. 90–1; and Kenny and Pinborg, 'Medieval Philosophical Literature', pp. 19–20.

69   Cf. Fyler, 'Domesticating the Exotic', pp. 3–7.

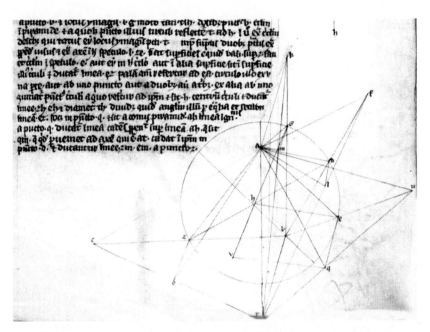

**Figure 4.1.** 'composiciouns / Of anglis and of slye reflexiouns': reflection from the surface of a spherical mirror according to Alhacen, *De aspectibus*. From London, British Library, MS Sloane 306, f. 126 (detail), 14th cent. [By permission of the British Library.]

and trickery: one speaker whispers to his fellow that the horse is
probably an automaton of the sort made to amuse princes – 'An
apparence ymaad by som magyk, / As jogelours pleyen at thise
feestes grete' (218–19). The gifts are also 'explained' by reference
to the technologies of metalwork ('sondry hardyng of metal'), and
to medical lore (243–7).

All categories of explanation are represented as limited and
inadequate, however persuasive they may seem to particular indi-
viduals. The horse of brass strikes fear into the heart of the
onlooker sensitized by the story of the Trojan horse, to the point
at which he declares that the authorities should be warned of the
danger – but of course he is wrong, and looks foolish; the tricks of
jongleurs are by definition impenetrable, occult to all but adepts,
so the truth of that explanation cannot be easily tested; and
technology itself, far from dispelling amazement, itself has a
tendency to instil wonder: the manufacturing of glass from 'fern-
asshen', for example, seems almost like an alchemical trans-
formation since 'nys glas nat lyk asshen of fern' (255).

It is significant that the discussion thus circles back to the
mirror, as if to emphasize its distinctiveness among the four gifts.
And however wondrous the making of glass, it is soon dismissed
as an old and familiar wonder, and we are left with the idea of a
mirror whose magical effects might be explained not through a
process that further mystifies, but 'Naturelly', through 'perspec-
tives'. This hypothesis does not fit into any of the other categories
of explanation: it is qualitatively different, drawing its terms from a
theoretical and experimental science which, while difficult, is not
occult and that is new, not old. Furthermore, the optical hypo-
thesis is not offered in such a way as to cast doubt on its validity,
as happens elsewhere.[70]

For the Squire tends to adopt a dismissive or ambivalent tone
in reporting the other explanations of the gifts' magical powers,
except when he treads on the narrowly circumscribed, sure ground
of his own limited experience. As a connoisseur of horses he is

70   Cf. Crane, *Gender and Romance*, pp. 138–40; DiMarco, 'Dialogue of Science
     and Magic', pp. 55–8; and his 'Squire's Tale' pp. 174–5.

quick to admire the lively (if artificial) eye of the steed of brass, which he compares with an Apulian courser, or a 'steede of Lumbardye' (193); but he is generally disdainful of the 'peple' who swarm like bees around the horse as it stands in the courtyard (as opposed to those at the feast who sit in the hall).[71] Indeed, he seems to hold them responsible for a kind of banality that overtakes the narrative once the stranger knight has finished his presentation. The wonderful horse cannot move because they 'kan nat the craft' (185) and instead they, a generalized 'prees that swarmeth to and fro' attempt to reduce it to their own fluctuating and diverse preconceptions as they gape ('gauren') at the marvel of a heavy, static, inanimate and massive horse that can supposedly fly effortlessly through the air.[72] The futility of their opinions is evidenced by their diversity – 'As many heddes, as manye wittes ther been' (202) – and by his condescending attitude towards their 'fantasies', suggesting that their explanations arise from personal obsessions and delusions and lack substance, and from ignorance: they 'jangle and trete', rehearsing 'sondry doutes [...] /As lewed peple demeth comunly / Of thynges that been maad moore subtilly / Than they kan in hir lewednesse comprehende' (220).

But the Squire is not a reliable narrator: his own area of expertise is strictly limited; his attack on the wonder of the credulous is undermined by the appeal of his own fantastical tale; the explanations he reports are clearly well-informed, interesting and plausible, rather than worthy of contempt; and he even avows that he is out of his depth in trying to understand some of the technical explanations that are proffered (246).[73] Such considera-

---

71   Kahrl, 'Chaucer's Squire's Tale', p. 203, where Witelo is incorrectly termed the *translator* of Alhacen (repeating the error of Stillwell, 'Chaucer in Tartary', p. 186).

72   On the connotations of *gauren* see Yager, 'Visual Perception', pp. 53–5.

73   Haller, 'Chaucer's Squire's Tale', p. 290; and Peterson, 'Finished Fragment', pp. 68–9. Pearsall, 'Squire as Story-Teller', pp. 87–8, argues that the Squire's attitude is actually anti-intellectual. See also his *Canterbury Tales*, pp. 139–40. On the Squire's lack of control as a narrator see Berger, 'F-Fragment', pp. 90–3; on his clumsy self-consciousness, artfully manipulated by Chaucer, see McCall, 'Squire in Wonderland'; on his fascination

tions encourage us to ignore the Squire's tone as being grounded in a false or uncertain sense of superiority, and to evaluate the various hypotheses on their own terms. As if to add additional force to the optical theory, the 'background noise' of the Squire's hauteur is not audible in these lines, and the passage is strangely devoid of colour from any narrative voice. It is especially difficult to attribute a speaker to the last line, 'As knowen they that han hire bookes herd'. Is this a courtier of Tartarye? Does the Squire include himself among the cognoscenti? Does Chaucer?

If Chaucer makes his narrator somewhat less than authoritative and confident in reporting the various explanations of the gifts' magical powers, that only helps to indicate the extent to which the passage is less about the ignorance of the people (some of whom are extremely knowledgeable) as against the expertise of the narrator, and more about knowledge itself, especially its aspirational quality, the process of acquiring and possessing it and the power that knowledge confers. That knowledge is a desirable commodity is clear from the entire passage, in which individual members of the 'peple' presume to know how the magic gifts exert their power, thereby gaining some vestiges of identity and attention. In positing their various theories they demonstrate a key mechanism by means of which knowledge is acquired. For example, the 'Rehersynge of [...] olde poetries' (206), which the Squire derides with unwitting irony, indicates that the challenge of novel information is met by accommodating it in an existing knowledge base, by using schemata that the individual already has access to, be they narrative or technical.[74] That the possession of knowledge itself gives access to power is clear from the competitive edge which marks the rival theories, with one speaker

for rhetorical form, at the excuse of meaningful content, see Haller, 'Chaucer's Squire's Tale', pp. 285–95; on his inadequate treatment of the narrative see Pearsall, 'Squire as Story-Teller', pp. 82–92 and the subsequent reconsideration in his *Canterbury Tales*, pp. 140–4. The tendency of these studies is challenged by Lawton, *Chaucer's Narrators*, pp. 110–23, although he recognizes the instability of the narrative voice.

74   Cf. Alhacen, *De aspectibus*, II. 4. 29; ed. Smith, pp. 238–9.

claiming that another 'lyeth' (217), and by the Squire's derision of
most of the explanations as half-baked.

But how are rival claims to knowledge to be evaluated, and
how is a distinction to be made between true and false knowledge?
False knowledge manifests itself as 'wonder'. Thus tides, floods,
spiders' webs, mists – that is, natural marvels analogous to the
magic gifts – are regarded with wonder until their causes as natural
phenomena are known.[75] This suggests, first, that the root of
popular wonder is ignorance and, second, that apparently mys-
terious phenomena can be rationally explained, at which point
'wonder' evaporates and is exposed as chimerical.[76] And there is
another implication: that knowledge is hierarchical in both an
absolute and social sense. Clearly, some forms of knowledge are
better than others because they provide a more complete explana-
tory framework. The corollary is that those who possess superior
knowledge (a state to which the Squire only aspires) are in an
advantageous position, for knowledge confers power and may
therefore be turned to personal, social or political advantage.

In this epistemology the mirror, 'heigh in the maister-tour',
occupies an important place as an emblem of exceptional know-
ledge, and one which 'reflects', at least to some, the new and
powerful science of *perspectiva*, evidently known only to an élite,
those who 'han hire bokes herd'. But the Squire's Tale evinces an
interest in the processes and structures of knowledge beyond the
passage in which the stranger knight's gifts are being debated.
We may note, in the first instance, a basic correlation between
hierarchies of knowledge and hierarchies of power. The most
knowledgeable individual is the king who is the donor of the gifts,
who demonstrates thereby access to magical lore and its prac-
titioners; their chief recipient, king Cambyuskan, acquires enough

75  McCall, 'Squire in Wonderland', pp. 103–5, on the treatment of wonder in
    the tale at this juncture. Goodman, 'Chaucer's Squire's Tale', pp. 130–1,
    finds a context for that treatment in other composite romances.
76  Cf. Edwards, *Ratio and Invention*, pp. 136–45, who relates the topics of
    wonder and natural science in SqT to Roger Bacon's theories of empirical
    experiment, noting the imaginative appeal of science to Chaucer.

knowledge to control the power of the horse, sword and mirror himself, although he is not privy to the secrets of their manu-facture. Canacee, who also has access to the mirror, and the ring for her exclusive use, is the king's daughter and of correspondingly lower, dependent status.[77] At the other extreme, those who are both denied the use of the gifts, and who entertain ill-informed explanations of their properties, are merely a mass of people indistinguishable one from another except in the falsity of their theories.

The possession of power through knowledge is in turn expressed through the control of spaces, spaces which are further configured according to gender.[78] The gift-giver commands vast territories: he is 'kyng of Arabe and of Inde'; Cambyuskan, as one recipient, the kingdom of Tartarye. Both, as male rulers, exert their political power in territorial terms, dominating in the public arena of the castle hall. Canacee, as the other recipient, and as Cambyuskan's daughter, enjoys dominance in the chamber and park, her domains being more the private, erotic, emotional, compassionate, healing.[79] Those who are curious about the gifts' powers but powerless to use or understand them are represented in the courtyard, outside of the main theatre of activities, the hall; and the tercelet, who is unaware even of the existence of the gifts, but who is to benefit from them, occupies a marginal place: on a sterile tree in a verdant park (which might be half garden, half wilderness) outside of Cambyuskan's castle. Of course, the exercise of power can take forms that are positive or negative, beneficial or detrimental. The sword both cuts and heals, and much depends on the character and intentions of the individual who wields the power. Cambyuskan wages war on 'Russye' (10), which causes the death of 'many a doughty man' (11); but Canacee accepts and

---

77   The hierarchy of power suggested here accords with the tale's subjugation of female to male power as explored by Lynch, 'East Meets West', pp. 530–42.

78   Cf. Foucault, 'Questions on Geography', p. 69; and Sharon-Zisser, 'Squire's Tale', pp. 379–83.

79   Cf. Crane, *Gender and Romance*, pp. 68–73.

adopts the tercelet, offering it redemption by enfolding it in her personal, bodily space. Thus the Squire's Tale ends, if abruptly, with an example of the beneficial exercise of the new powers which one of the gifts has brought to Canacee. Although it is explicitly an adventure of the ring it is also implicitly, as we have seen, an adventure of the mirror.

The Squire's Tale contains some key elements that also occur together in other narratives by Chaucer: an interest in the dispositions of narrative space; an understanding of the differences between male and female space; a basic correlation between space and power; power expressed as a function of knowledge; and the whole nexus attached to a topic of optical interest. On the other hand, there is little attempt to construct space according to optical principles, and it may be that Chaucer had yet to register and develop the full implications of *perspectiva* for his narrative art.[80] As it is, the optical content of the Squire's Tale, made memorable by the 'mirror in the master tower', remains somewhat unassimilated, as if Chaucer was aware of its potential but was unable in this narrative to realize its true significance. Part of its attraction may have been as a figure for the authorial imperative to see into the hidden spaces of the narrative, and the hearts and minds of its protagonists. Indeed, we might think of the Squire's Tale as an experimental or exploratory work in which Chaucer, a sometime squire, worked out certain formulae of which the key terms were (as we might call them) knowledge, power, gender, space, public, private. The catalytic nature of optical theory was only partially effective and the experiment was, of course, doomed to failure (as the unfinished state of the poem witnesses). For there is a fundamental contradiction between what the mirror promises (to remove doubt from our perception of others) and what, among other things, *perspectiva* offers (an understanding of the ways in which, willy nilly, visual perception is plagued by error).

---

80   Chaucer, *Squire's Tale*, ed. Baker, pp. 23–5, for problems in dating the tale.

# The Reeve's Tale

By way of comparison and contrast, The Reeve's Tale – written late in Chaucer's career – is a complete work in which spatial structures are thoroughly integrated with the governing themes. Again, it may include a direct reference to optical theory, which it represents as both an academic and a disputatious subject. But the hierarchy of expertise, in which only the élite know about *perspectiva*, has gone, to be replaced by a sense that the vital information and its terms of reference are more generally accessible. Thus, there is no longer any basis for exercising power through exclusive knowledge, and so the control of space has to effected by other means: native wit, physical force and the manipulation of things in order to create disorientation. There is also a strong emphasis on the causes and consequences of visual error and the misreading of space – interests on Chaucer's part that are demonstrably close to those of writers on *perspectiva* in its various kinds.

The lynch-pin of the narrative is Symkyn's speech on space midway through the action. By unhitching the clerks' horse, Symkyn's wife – acting on her husband's directions – has caused Aleyn and John to blunder around in the fens in pursuit of an animal which has scented the presence of wild mares. Having caught the wayward Bayard, after a good deal of time and strenuous effort, they have returned to the mill late in the day, weary and wet and in need of a night's lodging, to be confronted by a smug adversary. Their plan, to invigilate Symkyn's milling so that he could not steal their corn, has failed because of the distraction of the horse, and Symkyn has taken due advantage of their absence. The whole episode appears to endorse his contention that 'wit' is not the sole preserve of intellectuals. The miller now rubs salt in the wound by addressing the students in terms more suitable to a Cambridge college than a Trumpington mill:

Myn hous is streit, but ye han lerned art;
Ye konne by argumentes make a place
A myle brood of twenty foot of space.
Lat se now if this place may suffise,
Or make it rowm with speche, as is youre gise. (4122–6)

These teasing words allude to the malleability of space, and the extent to which it is as much a mental as a physical construct (a tenet to which, in practice, the all too materialist Symkyn does not adhere). They also locate the discourse on space, central to the study of *perspectiva*, within a university setting.[81] At the same time the topic is evidently one of sufficient notoriety to be not entirely incongruous in the mouth of a miller. The nub of Symkyn's position is the essential difference between physical space and imaginary space – a position which, given the present circumstances, allows him the luxury of heavy irony. His own house is confined, *streit*, but Aleyn and John have studied in the arts faculty at Cambridge, and so have become artful, 'lerned art'. They know how, merely by force of argument – what Symkyn earlier calls 'sleighte in hir philosophye' (4050) – to enlarge a small area 'twenty foot of space' into an area a mile broad. Indeed, they have demonstrated as much by finding themselves in the fens instead of the mill as a result of a misconceived plan. Symkyn now challenges them to acknowledge the absurdity of their attitude and behaviour by accepting his terms, his victory of matter over mind, rather than attempting, yet again, to better him by cunning clerkly means ('make it rowm with speche, as is youre gise'). Unfortunately for him, the clerks have indeed learnt their lesson and, far from behaving as before according to the terms of a preconceived but impractical plan, they size up the situation in the bedchamber and manipulate it to achieve a form of redress that goes far beyond the miller's immediate concerns. For it is he who misunderstands the nature of space, and especially the extent to which its literal and symbolic codes are interactive. Thus his heavy-handed irony is itself ironic, and the last laugh is on him.

81    Cf. Camille, 'Signs of the City', p. 9; Frank, 'Reeve's Tale', pp. 63–4; Grant, 'Place and Space'; and Woods, 'Symkyn's Place'.

I have argued elsewhere that Symkyn's speech on space has wider applications than to the immediate narrative context.[82] The contest between the miller and the clerks is emblematic of a struggle that embraces a broad range of connected issues. At the beginning of the tale the baleful effects of Symkyn's influence are being felt socially and economically as he tries by nefarious means to extend his 'territory'. His desire for social advancement is expressed through his marriage to the bastard daughter of the Trumpington parson. Both he and his wife affect an aura of defensive superiority – she parading at church with haughty manners, he ready to strike a jealous blow at anyone who besmirches her reputation (3942–68). The sexual profligacy, social ambition and corruption of the priest, which enabled their union and sustain their aspirations, are described in vituperative terms, and add further to the sense that Symkyn's belief in his own importance is illicit and an overstepping of boundaries (3977–86). In commercial terms Symkyn exerts a large monopoly, taking 'Greet sokene [...] of al the lond aboute', and turning the illness of the manciple at the clerk's hall to his advantage, stealing corn 'outrageously', and blatantly denying it (3987–4001). Thus there is much more at stake in the bedchamber scene than the mere enactment of personal revenge on the part of Aleyn and John. The promiscuity of Symkyn's family is exposed; his daughter and wife, their reputations disparaged, can no longer be the basis for overweening social ambition; with the return of the clerk's stolen corn in the form of a cake – a voluntary act on the part of Symkyn's daughter, and therefore all the more humiliating to him – his thieving has been evidenced and annulled; and in all this the superiority of the clerks' wit has been demonstrated. By the end of the tale, the 'proud and gay' Symkyn (3926), left humiliated and sprawling on the floor of his own bedchamber instead of swaggering at church, is a much reduced person whose power and influence have been seriously curtailed. His illegitimate construction of social space lies in ruins.

---

82    Brown, 'Containment of Symkyn'; and see also Williams, 'Competing Spaces'.

The integration of spatial design with thematic priorities is more pronounced and more successful in the Reeve's Tale than in the Squire's Tale. Chaucer chose to enact the contest over space in its metaphoric sense (social, economic, sexual, intellectual) as a struggle to control the space of a mill, and especially its bed-chamber. He invented that struggle in optical terms unknown to the closest narrative analogue, *Le Meunier et les II clers*, making full use of the disorienting effects of sleepiness, darkness, poor light and over-reliance on touch. In doing so he showed just how close his interests were to those of the optical treatises and their derivatives. In the Squire's Tale, Alhacen and Witelo were names to be conjured with. In the Reeve's Tale, *perspectiva* has become internalized as part of Chaucer's imaginal, and it is possible to identify analogues not only from advanced scientific treatises but also from encyclopedias.

Some examples will suffice to prove the point. In the course of the violence that ensues when Aleyn inadvertently reveals to Symkyn that he has slept with his daughter, the miller's wife takes hold of a staff, intending to hit the student. But light in the room is bad:

> And by the wal a staf she foond anon,
> And saugh a litel shymeryng of a light,
> For at an hole in shoon the moone bright,
> And by that light she saugh hem bothe two,
> But sikerly she nyste who was who,
> But as she saugh a whit thyng in her ye.
> And whan she gan this white thyng espye,
> She wende the clerk hadde wered a volupeer,
> And with the staf she drow ay neer and neer,
> And wende han hit this Aleyn at the fulle,
> And smoot the millere on the pyled skulle (4296–306).

A remarkable feature of this passage is the balance it strikes between describing the key physical circumstances, and relating those to an individual's mistaken perception of them. The light is adequate for Symkyn's wife to distinguish two figures, but not strong enough for her to tell who is who. The light shining on Symkyn's

skull, well 'vernysshed' with drink, as we have previously learnt
(4149), provides a focus of visual attention but, interestingly, it is
described in terms of its optical identity as a 'white thyng in her
eye' which her faculty of judgement now wrongly identifies as the
clerk's nightcap. This careful description of visual error does not
derive from a literary source: it is Chaucer's invention, and the
likelihood is that his account was informed by optical texts.[83]

As previously noted, Alhacen devotes a section of his treatise
to the cause of visual error and among them are errors caused by
physical circumstances, errors of recognition and errors of inter-
pretation. Under the first category he observes that objects such as
Symkyn's gleaming head are are particularly difficult to identify, for
'a visible object that is intensely luminous or shining or a polished
body upon which intense light shines will not be correctly per-
ceived by sight'.[84] Luminous though the miller's head may be, the
general gloom causes problems recognized by the author of *De
aspectibus*: 'Extremely faint light causes an error. For the tiny parts
of a body are invisible to sight'.[85] This in turn can lead to errors of
recognition. At twilight it is difficult to identify forms like animals,
clothing or trees[86] and, as Symkyn's wife discovers:

> Sight errs in recognition when the light in the seen object falls outside the
> moderate range. This happens, for example, when sight perceives an indi-
> vidual in the faint light of dawn or in an obscure place so that it fails to
> ascertain the individual's form. If the individual is a man and the beholder
> is accustomed to see a particular person in that place, he may take the seen
> individual to be that particular person, without this being so. Or, if he
> does not immediately ascertain the form of this individual on account of
> the faint light, he may assimilate the form itself to another man whom he
> knows [...] This kind of visual error frequently occurs when the object is

83   Cf. Grennen, 'Calculating Reeve', pp. 255–9; and Yager, '"Whit Thyng"'.
84   'visum fortiter luminosum et lucidum aut visum tersum super quod oritur
     fortis lux non comprehendetur a visu vera comprehensione'. Alhacen, *De
     aspectibus*, III. 3 .8; ed. Smith, pp. 287–8.
85   'Lux multum debilis errorem facit. Abscondit enim visui particulas
     corporis'. Ibid., III. 5. 8; ed. Smith, p. 295.
86   Ibid., III. 6. 11; ed. Smith, p. 298.

seen in the faint light of dawn or in the darkness of night, i.e. where no strong light exists.[87]

Under the third category, errors of interpretation, Alhacen observes that weak light can trick the eye, and provides the example of a white wall, on which the darker areas are mistakenly identified as gaps.[88] Witelo, extending and elaborating Alhacen's work, describes the kind of visual confusion faced by Symkyn's wife as she attempts to discern the difference between her husband and Aleyn:

> For from a deficiency of light an error occurs in the visual perception of similarity or difference in bodies of the same type of color or the same type of shape, in which some slight difference is manifested by sudden, hidden details, for then those details may not be seen in weak light, and because of this, those bodies will be judged as similar in all respects.[89]

That such matters were undergoing debate in scholarly circles is clear from Nicholas Oresme's *Quaestiones super quatuor libros meteorum*. It was compiled between 1351 and 1352 and is known to exist in fifteen manuscripts dating from 1366 to 1470.[90] Among the topics covered are the visual consequences of darkness and the effect of light reflecting from shiny objects.[91]

The misperceptions of Symkyn's wife are also explicable as those of someone who has just been awoken rudely from her sleep, as Chaucer is careful to show: Symkyn, tussling with Aleyn, falls backwards on to her

87    Alhacen, *Optics*, III. 6. 11; trans. Sabra, pp. 270–1.
88    Alhacen, *De aspectibus*, III. 7. 26; ed. Smith, p. 309.
89    'Ex paucitate enim lucis error accidit in visione similitidinis et diversitatis corporum eiusdem coloris secundum speciem vel eiusdem figure secundum speciem in quibus partialis diversitas per latentia signa discreta est, tunc enim illa in luce debili non videntur, et ob hoc inter illa corpora omnimoda iudicabitur similitudo.' Witelo, *Perspectiva*, IV. 153; ed. and trans. Kelso, pp. 328 and 584.
90    McLuskey, 'Oresme on Light', pp. 58–9 and 80.
91    Oresme, *Quaestiones*, III. 20; ed. McLuskey, pp. 266 and 270.

That wiste no thyng of this nyce stryf;
For she was falle aslepe a lite wight
With John the clerk, that waked hadde al nyght,
And with that fal out of hir sleep she breyde (4282–5).

These are ideal conditions for visual misapprehension. Vincent of
Beauvais describes a similar case:

> it happens that after sleep, in which all spirits move within to the place of
> digestion, leaving the exterior organs of sense, someone suddenly opening
> their eyes does not see well until the return of the spirit and heat from the
> interior to the exterior senses.[92]

Vincent goes on to note some of the characteristics of night vision,
which are similar to those obtaining at the end of the Reeve's Tale.
'The person in darkness sees him who is illuminated'[93] might apply
to his wife's sight of Symkyn in the light of the moon, and 'lumin-
ous or night-shining objects are visible in darkness'[94] to his shiny
pate, reflecting the light of the moon. Night vision is discussed, as
it is by Bartholomaeus,[95] who also describes what it is like to be
deprived of sight in terms that are reminiscent of Symkyn's wife
groping for a staff: 'He puttith forth the hond al aboute gropunge
and graspinge; he sekith al aboute of his way with his hond and
with his staf. Selde he doth ought sikirly'.[96]

---

92    'contigit, quod post somnum in quo spiritus omnes ad interiora moventur
      ad locum disgestionis reliquendo sensuum organa exteriora, statim aper
iens oculos non bene videt ante reditum spirituum et caloris ab interioribus ad
      exteriora organa sensuum.' Vincent, *Speculum naturale*, XXV. 34, col. 1797.
93    'Ille qui est in obscuro videt eum qui est in splendido.' Loc. cit.
94    'corpora luminosa vel noctiluca obiecta sunt visus in tenebris'. Ibid., XXV.
      39, col. 1800.
95    Ibid., XXV. 35, col. 1798. See Bartholomaeus, *De proprietatibus rerum* V. 6;
      ed. Seymour et al., vol. 1, p. 184, lines 3–11.
96    Bartholomaeus, *De proprietatibus rerum*, VII. 20; ed. Seymour et al., vol. 1,
      p. 365, lines 13–16.

# 5 Literary Models

To be human is not only to create distances but to attempt to cross them, to transform primal distance through intentionality, emotion, involvement, attachment.[1]

The preceding discussions of the Squire's Tale and Reeve's Tale suggest that Chaucer was in the habit of going direct to scientific sources of various kinds in order to enhance the optical content of his writing. That was no doubt the case, but it leaves out of account a key route whereby optical material reached him: through the works of certain authors whom he habitually used as models, precedents and inspiration. Three writers – Jean de Meun, Dante Alighieri and Giovanni Boccaccio – are of particular importance because of the extent to which they assimilated and transmitted optical data or used space as a key component of their narratives, either to articulate a structure of ideas or for affective purposes.

The present chapter begins by returning briefly to the Squire's Tale in order to demonstrate the extent to which its passage on optics derives from the *Roman de la Rose*. In Jean de Meun's continuation of that poem, *perspectiva* has a key role to play and in some measure provides a rationale for the entire work. Chaucer again uses some of its optical ideas for the ending of the Merchant's Tale, but the borrowing is more subtle, and he proceeds to combine it with other material taken from scientific treatises. In the *Roman* there is no direct connection between optical experience and the sense of space. For that, Dante provided Chaucer with many examples wherein a knowledge of *perspectiva* is brought to bear on the subjective apprehensions and intellectual enlightenment of the pilgrim narrator. Chaucer toyed with similar tech-

1    Soja, *Postmodern Geographies*, p. 133.

niques in the *House of Fame*, but in a comic mode that indicates a distinctive approach to narrative space. Boccaccio's contribution to Chaucer's invention of optical space is discussed in the course of Chapters Seven and Nine.

## The *Roman de la Rose*

We may detect in Chaucer's lines on optics in the Squire's Tale an awareness of those authorities who dominated the science; a sense of the intellectual excitement generated by the subject, and of its topicality; recognition that it was being widely debated, even at court; that it had a reputation as a challenging subject; and that its provenance was the universities. The lines, no more than the larger narrative, do not suggest that Chaucer himself was, at the time of writing, familiar with the content of optical treatises. However, he was extremely familiar with a highly influential work of vernacular poetry that he in part translated, a work that incorporates a long debate on the new science, the *Roman de la Rose*. This poem, read by Chaucer at an early stage of his career, and a lifelong reference-point, was also known widely among his audience and helped to stimulate his interest in the literary applications of *perspectiva*.[2]

The passage from which he borrows is part of a discourse on mirrors by Nature, who is commenting on the origins of rainbows. Anyone, she says, wishing to understand them should become a disciple of Aristotle and read the *Regarz* (*De aspectibus*) of Alhacen, whose proofs can be grasped only with a knowledge of geometry (18023–43).[3] Alhacen's book also reveals how magnifying mirrors actually work. Nature and Genius agree that if Venus and Mars

---

2    Sutherland, '*Romaunt of the Rose*'; Chaucer, *Romaunt of the Rose*, ed. Suther-
     land, pp. ix–xxxv. See also Cipriani, 'Studies in the Influence of the
     *Romance of the Rose*'; Fansler, *Chaucer and 'Le Roman de la Rose*'; and Wimsatt,
     *Chaucer and the French Love Poets*, ch.1.
3    Ed. Langlois, trans. Dahlberg.

had possessed the right optical equipment it would have enabled them to detect Vulcan's net before being trapped in it (18044–129). Mirrors also cause other effects. They can diminish the size of a reflected object, alter its position, multiply it, produce phantoms or be the cause of 'granz decevances' (18210). The ignorant observer may be so convinced of the truth of what he has seen that he will make boast to others. Nature concludes her comments by saying that the explanation of optical phenomena – how rays travel, their angles of reflection, the mechanisms of the eye – 'est ailleurs escrit au livre' (18252). Given a knowledge of the science, visual illusions can be rationally explained.

The affinities between Nature's speech on optics and both the content and context of lines 205–35 of the Squire's Tale suggest that Jean's foregrounding of *perspectiva* informed Chaucer's creative ideas, as well as his choice of words.[4] As Chaucer was to do, Nature establishes a scholastic setting for the key optical works, names some of the chief authorities, and opines that the discipline of optics is far from easy. The effects produced by mirrors can be understood by means of technical explanations, what Chaucer was to call 'composiciouns / Of anglis and of slye reflexiouns':

Autre font diverses images
Apereir en divers estages,
Dreites, bellongues e enverses,
par composiciouns diverses [...]
Font les neïs dehors pareir
Touz vis, seit par eve ou par air;
E les peut l'en voeir joer
Entre l'ueil et le miroer
par les diversitez des angles,
Seit li meiens compoz ou sengles,
D'une nature ou de diverse (18173–6, 18183–9)

Others make different images appear in different situations – straight, oblong, and upside down in different arrangements [...] They even make them appear, quite alive, outside the mirror, whether in water or in air.

4    Cf. Chaucer, *Squire's Tale*, ed. Baker, p. 171, note to lines 229–30.

One can see the images play between the eye and the mirror, by means of different angles, either compound or single, of one sort or another.

The effects of mirrors and lenses can seem marvellous to the ignorant or uninitiated, but they are scientifically explicable to the cognoscenti. Referring to the deceptive effects of mirrors or of distance, Nature remarks:

> Et quant ainsinc sont deceü
> Cil qui teus choses one veü
> par miroers ou par distances,
> Qui leur ont fait demontrances,
> Si vont puis au peuple et se vantent,
> Et ne dient pas veir, ainz mentent,
> Qu'il ont les deables veüz,
> Tant sont es regarz deceüz [...]
> [...] si serait grief chose a dire
> Et mout serait fort a l'entendre,
> S'il iert qui le seüst aprendre
> A genz lais especiaument,
> Qui nou dirait generaument. (18231–8, 18274–8)

And after these people have been thus deceived, after they have seen such things in mirrors or because of distances, which have created such illusions for them, then they go to other people and boast, and their sight has been so deceived that they say, not in truth but falsely, that they have seen devils [...] it would be a burdensome thing to tell and very difficult to understand, even if someone knew how to teach it without speaking generally, especially to lay people.

The similarities between the above passages and the treatment of optics in the Squire's Tale, where the popular reception of technical explanations is also at issue, do not need labouring, but there are some significant differences. First, Jean de Meun, speaking through Nature, evinces first-hand familiarity with the science as someone of scholarly standing who has read, or at least who has access to, what is 'escrit en livre' (18252). Chaucer, through the much less authoritative Squire, seems more on the outside of the discipline, aware that it is 'herd' at university lectures, but not himself familiar with the content of the Latin treatises. At the same time, he is conscious of a key author on the university curriculum (Witelo) whom Jean does not mention; and, as already noted, he represents optics as a topic of intellectual interest in courtly, as well as scholarly, circles.

It would be a mistake to limit to this one passage the potential of the *Roman de la Rose* for influencing Chaucer's understanding of the potential uses of *perspectiva* in narrative. For Nature's mirror is one of three which together greatly increase the promise of the poem as a vehicle for conveying optical ideas. In the first place, Nature's remarks are part of a lengthy discourse on heavenly influences in which optics has its proper place. God created the universe and set it in motion (16729–822); man is controlled through the mirror of predestination (17421–98); God's instruments are the heavenly bodies that receive the divine rays (17499–526); the stars in turn influence events on earth – events which include the formation of rainbows (17875–8000 and 18535–60). So the behaviour of light rays, the subject of *perspectiva*, is an earthly extension of the principle or mechanism by which God rules the life of man. Just as the ignorant can wrongly perceive the marvellous effects of mirrors, so wilful individuals are subject to distorted forms of spiritual perception. Lovers and dreamers are particularly susceptible to self-inflicted delusions (18345–56).

Later, Jean de Meun directs attention towards a mirror which represents the idea of a divine exemplar, a common application of the mirror metaphor in the neoplatonic tradition.[5] Genius, the priest and confessor of Nature, describes an ideal park, opposed to Guillaume's walled garden, where a 'bon pasteur' (19994) looks after his chosen flock. It is a true paradise, eternally light and eternally spring, and full of living creatures. In the course of a disparaging commentary on Guillaume's garden of erotic love, Genius describes a new, life-giving fountain in the park of the good shepherd. By contrast, Guillaume's fountain of Narcissus is

5    Bradley, 'Backgrounds of the Title *Speculum*'; and Wimsatt, *Allegory and Mirror*, ch. 6. For one of the most elaborate developments of the idea prior to Jean de Meun's (*c.*1181), see Alan of Lille, *Anticlaudianus*, I. 436–510 and VI. 73–272; ed. Bossuat, trans. Sheridan.

'Tant amere et tant venimeuse' (20410) and is to be deplored. Genius claims that Amant himself was aware of its cruelty when he called it the perilous mirror. Its reflecting crystals are 'trouble et nueus' (20448) because they are lit from elsewhere. The fountain in the park, however, contains a marvellous carbuncle so pure and bright that it provides its own light, shining more strongly than the sun itself and even vanquishing night (20524–36). Those who see themselves mirrored in this fountain perceive the truth both about the park and about themselves. The rays of the carbuncle-mirror do not deceive; their effect is redemptive: 'renforcier et resjoïr / Et revigourer leur veüe / par sa bele clarté veüe' (20584–6). Love of God is thus contrasted with love of self.

The mirror of Narcissus, to which Genius refers, is a turning-point of the erotic dream-adventure written by Guillaume, in which the progress of Amant is marked by his visual experience.[6] For, having looked into the fountain where the mirror is found, he becomes vulnerable to the arrows fired by Amor, which enter through the eye and lodge in the heart. The fountain is allegedly the one where Narcissus died, and his story is briefly retold (1439–1506). Guillaume uses it as an exemplum for the religion of love: disdainful ladies should take warning from the fate of Narcissus (1507–10). After a moment's hesitation, Amant himself gazes into the water and sees there two multicoloured crystal stones illuminated by the rays of the sun. The crystals each reflect one half of the garden (1537–70).

Amant is seeing the experience and adventure of love in prospect. He is not aware of the existence of the rosebud, the later object of his quest, until he sees it reflected in the crystal stones (1615–80). To some extent, he is repeating the experience of Narcissus, who brought about his own destruction by gazing into the fountain to fall in love with his own, unattainable, self-image. The fountain is a perilous mirror, fatal to those it entraps through the attractions of love based in visual, self-reflexive, desire (1571–8). This kind of love is destructive, whether centred on self or on

6    Gunn, *Mirror of Love*, p. 111 and see 108–13. Cf. Goldberg, *Mirror and Man*, ch. 7.

another (1588–94), but nevertheless Amant is unlike Narcissus in not gazing merely at his own reflection but also at the object of his desire in prospect, represented by the topography of the garden.[7] Some commentators have argued that Amant is gazing into the eyes of his lady, figured as the reflecting crystal stones, perceiving the promise that they hold (the rosebud), wanting the beauty that they represent.[8] At the same time, the images in the crystal stones are projections of his own longings for amatory fulfilment – 'Main de fort eure m'i mirai' (1607) – which may support more recent arguments that the episode at the fountain is already informed by Guillaume's understanding of the physiological and psychological processes of visions as found in optical treatises (a matter made more explicit in Jean de Meun's part of the poem).[9]

Gunn was the first to propose that Nature's discourse on optics, apparently so peripheral, is in fact pivotal in Jean de Meun's conception of the whole *Roman*. The problem of the poem's unity has always beset its editors and critics, who have advanced divergent opinions and theories.[10] Gunn drew attention to the proper title of the poem, endorsed by both Guillaume and Jean: *Le Mirouer des amoureus* (10648–51).[11] Jean's intention, he argued, was to use his own continuation as a glass that would reflect 'the true images of love's varied dance'.[12] The mirror thus becomes 'the

7    Cf. Kessler, 'Quête amoureuse', pp. 135–6.

8    Critical opinion is divided. See Barney, *Allegories of History*, pp. 201–7; Fleming, '*Roman de la Rose*', pp. 92–7; Frappier, 'Variations sur le thème du miroir'; Freeman, 'Problems', pp. 164–7; Goldin, *Mirror of Narcissus*, pp. 52–68; Hult, 'Allegorical Fountain', revised in his *Self-Fulfilling Prophecies*, pp. 263–300; Köhler, 'Narcisse'; Lewis, *Allegory of Love*, p. 117; Robertson, *Preface to Chaucer*, p. 95. Hillman, 'Another Look', provides an overview.

9    Akbari, 'Medieval Optics', revised in her *Seeing through the Veil*, ch. 2; Fleming, 'Garden', pp. 217–20; and Knoespel, *Narcissus*, pp. 77–104.

10    Dahlberg, 'Macrobius', pp. 2–4; Guillaume de Lorris and Jean de Meun, *Romance of the Rose*, trans. Dahlberg, pp. 2–4; Guillaume de Lorris and Jean de Meun, *Roman de la Rose*, ed. Langlois, vol. 1, pp. 26–7; Faral, '*Roman de la Rose*', pp. 441–2; Lewis, *Allegory of Love*, pp. 137, 141–3 and 154.

11    Gunn, *Mirror of Love*, pp. 49–50.

12    Ibid., p. 28 and see p. 29.

allegory's grand and all-pervasive symbol'.[13] Jean elaborates the idea of the mirror both from contemporary science and from traditional neoplatonic sources in which a sequence of mirrors is used as an analogy for the divine generative process.[14] Nature's discourse on optics is important as a means of placing the mirror of Narcissus in the context of the ultimate mirror of truth which is God.[15] The passage reveals what is 'most central and profound in the poet's thought'.[16] The visions provided by the mirror of secular love are the reflections of self-deluding fantasy compared with 'the world of true and fruitful images, each of which is reflected from the stainless and ever-luminous mirror which is the Mind of God'. The symbol of the mirror is as important as that of the rose.[17]

Subsequently, Gunn's thesis was extended and modified by Eberle, who probed more deeply contemporary meanings of the word 'mirouer'. She first placed Nature's discourse in relation to scientific optics in the thirteenth century, especially as represented by the writings of Grosseteste,[18] and then developed the notion that the whole poem is deliberately designed as an optical instrument in which the experience of love is viewed from various angles.[19] Just as, for Grosseteste, optics revealed the workings of the divine light in nature, so the *Roman*, as conceived by Jean de Meun, 'imitates and reveals the operations of Nature herself'.[20] Further, the poem multiplies 'projections' of the lover's mind in the same way that optics multiplies the images of seen objects.[21] Second, the poem is a mirror in the tradition of the *Speculum*

13    Ibid., p. 266.
14    Ibid., pp. 219–22 and 301. Cf. Paré, *Les Idées et les lettres*, pp. 207–11 and 254–60; and his '*Roman de la Rose*', pp. 125–30. See also Langlois, *Origines et sources*, pp. 107–10 and 146–7.
15    See Lewis's review of Gunn's *Mirror of Love*, p. 29.
16    Gunn, *Mirror of Love*, p. 267 and see pp. 268–70.
17    Ibid., p. 273.
18    Eberle, 'Lovers' Glass', p. 250. See further Baig, 'Vision', ch. 4; Fleming, 'Garden', pp. 225–32; Klassen, *Chaucer on Love*, pp. 154–61; Stakel, *False Roses*, pp. 88–93; and Torti, *Glass of Form*, pp. 12–22.
19    Eberle, 'Lovers' Glass', pp. 244, 245 and 248.
20    Ibid., p. 249.
21    Ibid., pp. 249 and 253–4.

*stultorum* of Nigel Longchamp. Using satire, it distorts in order to reveal folly. Third, following Seneca's *Naturales quaestiones*, Jean represents his mirror as a corrective to faulty moral vision.[22] More recently, Akbari has related Jean's optical ideas to Roger Bacon's theory of the multiplication of *species*.[23]

The interpretations of Gunn, Eberle and Akbari reveal the remarkable extent to which optics penetrated the poetic outlook of Jean de Meun. If he represented reflection and the optical production of images as metaphors or the way his poetry worked, he was in effect extending an idea already current in the scientific field. For optics itself, the science of vision and light, stood as a metaphor for the way God worked, through the emanation of the divine Light which created and was reflected in earthly existence. Nature's discourse on optics in the *Roman de la Rose*, interesting and topical in itself, is supported by a deep and imaginative understanding of the subject, one that affects the entire structure and meaning of the poem. The work itself, read in this way, becomes a potent force for the transmission of ideas about optics, and about their literary applications, both in specific and general terms. As such, the *Roman* is part of a significant trend in European poetry of the thirteenth and fourteenth centuries.[24]

Beyond borrowed passages, therefore, we may detect in the Squire's Tale a more extensive and general dialogue with the *Roman*. The Squire's Tale mirror incorporates attributes from all of the mirrors in the *Roman de la Rose* – its effects may be optically explicable, it is associated with erotic love, it reveals the truth – but at the same time Chaucer eschews the notion of mirror as divine or moral exemplar, or satirical instrument, preferring instead to associate it with the exploration of knowledge, power and space. These differences are symptomatic of a process whereby Chaucer, attracted to the *Roman* as a model, precedent and pretext for using optical material, began to discard it. We may speculate that, as his interest in optical space grew, so he turned from mirrors (rooted as

22    Ibid., pp. 246–7 and 257–9.
23    Akbari, *Seeing through the Veil*, ch. 4.
24    Leyerle (ed.), 'Language of Love', p. 188.

they were in traditional symbolic meaning) towards the more value-free area of direct vision, to which Alhacen and Witelo gave priority, and which is a cornerstone in the narrative construction of optical space. That process of transition is evident in the ending of the Merchant's Tale, where Nature's speech on optics again provides a narrative context, but one which operates in concert with other kinds of optical writing. The creative mechanisms at work here are similar to those identified in the Reeve's Tale, and tend to confirm that *perspectiva* in its various manifestations had a formative effect on Chaucer's apprehension of the visual world.

## The Ending of the Merchant's Tale

The final episode of the Merchant's Tale contains three surprising events: the restoration of January's vision, the sight of his wife and squire copulating in the pear tree beneath which he stands, and his eventual acceptance of May's explanation that he has been the victim of an optical illusion. Chaucer's treatment of these incidents is not adequately accounted for in the published sources and analogues.[25] He introduced other material, which derives both from the *Roman de la Rose* and from other, more direct, sources on the science of *perspectiva*. Medieval optical texts furnish parallels both for Chaucer's treatment of visual deception in the ending of the Merchant's Tale and for the tale's general theme of inner blindness.

The idea that January may be suffering a misapprehension is partially accounted for in analogues of the Optical Illusion type.[26]

---

25    For an earlier version of the following argument, see Brown, 'Optical Theme'.
26    Beidler, 'Chaucer's Merchant's Tale'; Dempster, 'On the Sources of the Deception Story'; Thompson, 'Merchants Tale', pp.484–6 and 518–33; Watkins, 'Modern Irish Variants'; and Wentersdorf, 'Chaucer's Merchant's Tale'.

But May goes beyond precedent when she introduces the supplementary explanation that January suffers from defective vision. In so doing she changes her strategy from what might be called a traditional, magical account of what January sees, to one which has the trappings of science. The first such statement is to the effect that January has only partial sight: 'Ye han som glymsyng, and no parfit sighte' (2383). With this utterance, May's account of optical phenomena becomes increasingly technical and January begins to be persuaded. Although continuing to claim that he sees 'as wel as evere I myghte' (2384), he concedes that what he saw pass between his wife and squire may have been imagined: 'me thoughte he dide thee so' (2386). The note of certainty has gone from January's recollection of his visual experience. May is quick to press home her advantage, and pursues a three-pronged plan of deception. First, she appeals to science by suggesting that January's eyes are defective; second, she appeal to magic by claiming that her action in the tree has cured his blindness; and third, she appeals to her husband's emotions by hinting that he is ungrateful. All three tactics are exemplified, in compressed form, in the following lines:

> 'Ye maze, maze, goode sir', quod she;
> 'This thank have I for I have maad yow see.
> 'Allas,' quod she, 'that evere I was so kynde!' (2387–9)

January capitulates, and prepares to deny the existence of what has happened by suppressing the residual, still disturbing, visual memory of his wife with Damian. He apologizes to May for accusing her falsely, although there still lurks the suspicion, prompted by vivid detail, that he thought he saw the pair together, that 'Damyan hadde by thee leyn, / And that thy smok hadde leyn upon his brest' (2394–5). With astonishing speed, January moves from absolute certainty about what he saw, to thinking that he saw it, to banishing the image from his mind. His vision has been restored, but the effect of May's eloquence is such, and his devotion to her so extreme, that he might as well continue to be sightless.

To set her husband's mind completely at rest, May elaborates the scientific explanation. Just as a man waking from sleep is not always able to enjoy perfect vision until he is fully awake, so a man cured of blindness may not be able to see properly for a day or two. She suggests, menacingly, that January is likely to undergo more illusions similar to the one just experienced. He should not be too hasty in jumping to conclusions, for appearances can be deceptive (a remark that applies to May's entire argument). Finally, she warns that mental preconceptions may give rise to visual errors, an observation all too true in its application to January, whose emotions and thoughts have been so receptive to the idea that his eyes, not May, have deceived him:

> 'Ye, sire,' quod she, 'ye may wene as yow lest.
> But, sire, a man that waketh out of his sleep,
> He may nat sodeynly wel taken keep
> Upon a thyng, ne seen it parfitly,
> Til that he be adawed verraily.
> Right so a man that longe hath blynd ybe,
> Ne may nat sodeynly so wel yse,
> First whan his sighte is newe come ageyn,
> As he that hath a day or two yseyn.
> Til that youre sighte ystaled be a while,
> Ther may ful many a sighte yow bigile.
> Beth war, I prey yow, for by hevene kyng,
> Ful many a man weneth to seen a thyng,
> And it is al another than it semeth.
> He that mysconceyveth, he mysdemeth.' (2396–410)

What May says has the ring of truth, but the science of sight to which she appeals is misapplied since it is used to account for an event that was not an optical illusion at all. The scientific content of her speech, therefore, has an ambivalent status. On the one hand, it appeals to empirical evidence, and impresses and persuades January as an objective explanation, and is more effective in this respect than the magical description May earlier espoused. As we have seen from the Squire's Tale, this is not the only occasion on which Chaucer used scientific theory for an alternative description of an optical phenomenon previously accounted for in magical terms. On the other hand, May is patently abusing scientific knowledge for her own ends: science is shown not to have the status of objective, fixed, truth, but rather to vary in its veracity according to its applications and the motives of those who employ it.

There is a distinct likelihood that Nature's speech on optics from the *Roman*, one of Chaucer's favourite passages from the poem,[27] stimulated his ideas about the themes and ending of the Merchant's Tale. In Jean de Meun's poem, *perspectiva* also appears in a comic context. Nature and Genius agree that a mirror would have saved the lovers, Venus and Mars, a great deal of trouble. Venus would have been able to foresee Vulcan's arrival and could have had her excuses ready to explain Mars's presence. She might also have been able to persuade Vulcan that adultery had not happened and that what he had seen was an illusion (18105-29). When Nature goes on to explain that mirrors can also cause illusions, she associates with these the images produced in the mind's eye by mental and emotional aberrations, including those of the besotted lover (18239–46, 18357–404). The psychological state described by Nature, and its connection with mirror images, also find echoes in Chaucer's description of January as he imagines the type of woman he would like to marry: erotic images of local beauties pass through his heart like the reflections one might see from a mirror positioned in the market-place (1577–87).

Jean de Meun provided Chaucer with a model for making optics the stuff of poetry; in the story of Mars, Venus and Vulcan he supplied a plot close to that followed in the ending of the Merchant's Tale; and he suggested a link, to be followed by Chaucer, between visual deception and sexual fantasy. But the antecedents found in the *Roman* still fall short of providing a complete framework within which to consider Chaucer's use of optical material in the ending of the Merchant's Tale. Further parts of that framework are to be found in scientific writing, encyclopedias and homiletic writings.

We may find a context for May's remarks in the third book of Alhacen's *De aspectibus*, a part of his work devoted to the circumstances, causes and types of visual deception. Alhacen recognizes

27    Fansler, *Chaucer and 'Le Roman'*, p. 231.

that weak vision, such as that which supposedly affects January, is a significant cause of error:

> A weakness or aberration of the eye produces an error in [the perception of] everything that is perceived in sight through deduction [...] In [regard to] distance: If two objects face the eye, one being of an intense color and lying farther from the eye, the other being of a faint color and nearer the eye, since the perception of their distance [from the eye] depends entirely on comparing the two, weak sight will produce an inconclusive comparison [...] But since it is certain to everyone that sight has a clearer apprehension of nearer things than it does of farther things, the viewer concludes that, between these two objects, the one that is seen more distinctly is the nearer.[28]

In his elaboration of Alhacen's work, Witelo points out that a weak eye takes longer than a normal, healthy eye to register visual events,[29] and he describes the various causes of a discrepancy that may arise between what the observer expects to see and what in fact he does see. It is this sort of dislocation of actual and imagined sights that May exploits so well: 'For when an object appears to sight in some form or other than it actually is, then an error occurs in vision through recognition, since the form in the soul may be improperly applied to another object which is not congruent with it.'[30] Witelo also notes how weakness of sight can increase the margin of error, giving rise to cases of mistaken identity: 'when an eye is dazzled by a bright, strongly illuminated color, it may judge

---

28  'Visus debilitas et immoderatio errorem invehit singulis per syllogismum in visu comprehensis [...] In longitudine: Si opponantur visui duo corpora quorum unum coloris fortis et remotius aliud coloris debilis et oculo propinquius, cum non fiat comprehensio longitudinis nisi facta collatione inter aliqua, incertam faciet collationem debilitas visus [...] Et quia certum est homini quod ex propinquioribus certior fit fides visui quam ex remotioribus, concludit illud quod apparet ei certius ex hiis corporibus esse propinquius'. Alhacen, *De aspectibus*, III. 7. 250–1; ed. Smith, p. 334.

29  Witelo, *Perspectiva*, IV. 109; ed. Kelso, pp. 256–7.

30  'Cum enim res alia aut alterius speciei visui apparet quam sit in rei veritate, tunc fit error via scientie in visu, quoniam forma quiescens in anima inconvenienter alteri rei applicatur cui non convenit'. Ibid., IV. 155; ed. and trans. Kelso, pp. 330 and 586.

every [other] color it sees to be that color or a color mixed of the two. Also a disease of the eyes can sometimes cause a horse to appear as an ass, or Socrates to appear as Plato.'[31] Or, as May might add, a love-making Damian to appear as no more than a struggling man.

Chaucer's familiarity with the *Speculum maius* of Vincent of Beauvais was discussed in Chapter Three. Vincent identifies three causes of defective vision like those which, according to May, afflict January. These are: staring too long at an object of extreme whiteness or brightness, waking suddenly from sleep, and opening the eyes after a prolonged period during which they have been closed or in darkness, a circumstance close to January's as he stares, amazed, into the pear tree:

> it happens that when someone for a long time has closed his eyes or has been in darkness, and afterwards has gone into the light, he does not see well until moderately changing light has entered from without, because, to reiterate the truth, vision is completed by a visual humour that runs to the eyes through the hollow optics nerves from the interior part of the brain, which said humour draws forth moderate colour.[32]

Bartholomaeus' *De proprietatibus rerum* also contains material close to that which Chaucer used. In his seventh book, Bartholomaeus deals at some length with the causes of defective vision and blindness, and it is possible to recognize in January a syndrome that the author describes. January is over sixty when the action of the Merchant's Tale begins, he is a bon viveur, and throughout his

---

31 'Debilitas quoque visus huius erroris est causa, lesus enim visus a colore forti, cui incidit lumen forte iudicat omnem colorem visum illius coloris, vel alterius coloris ex illis duobus mixti. Et etiam propter oculorum egritudinem aliquando equus apparet asinus, et Socrates videtur Plato.' Loc. cit.; ed. and trans. Kelso, pp. 332 and 588.

32 'contigit cum aliquis diu clausos habuit vel in tenebris fuit, et postea subito ad lumen vadit, quod non bene videt, antequam ingrediatur lumen temperate immutans ab extrinseco. Quia vero iterum visus perficitur spiritu visibili, qui defertur ad oculos per nervos opticos et concavos ab interiori parte cerebri, qui scilicet spiritus secum trahit colorem temperatum.' Vincent, *Speculum naturale*, XXV. 34, col. 1797.

life he has given immoderate attention to women. On each of these three counts, according to Bartholomaeus, a man is likely to suffer partial or complete loss of vision. A declining vitality in the humours causes gradual blindness in old age: 'first here yghen wexen dymme, and thanne they haueth defaute of sight, and at the last the vertu of sight failleth and they lesith al here sight'.[33] Food and drink may affect vision intermittently: 'defaute of sight is nought contynual but it cometh and gooth, for it waxith and wayneth by diuersite of mete and of drinke'.[34] Lechery also causes the eye to suffer: 'Hechinge and smertinge of yghen comen somtyme of outward thinges, as [...] of fleischlich likinge and ofte seruyse of Venus that corrumpith and dissolueth the spiritis and the humour cristallyne'.[35]

January's reaction to blindness is one of possessive jealousy of May, 'Lest that his wyf sholde falle in som folye' (2074). Bartholomaeus warns that blindness is indeed a wretched state that causes emotional disturbance. The blind man lives in a state of anxiety, and fears desertion by his friends – a fear that in January's case is fully justified: 'Selde he doth ought sikirly; wel nyghe always he doutith and dredith [...] the blinde is wrecchid, for in house he dar nothing tristily doo, and in the way he dredith lest his felawe wole forsake him.'[36] He ends on a moral note: 'Better is to a man to be blynde and haue his ighen iput out than haue ighen and desceyued and bigiled with fikelinge and flateringe therof.'[37] The narrator of the Merchant's Tale makes the identical point as the plan of Damian and May to deceive the blind January gathers momentum:

33    Bartholomaeus, *On the Properties of Things*, VII. 20; ed. Seymour et al., vol. 1, p. 364, lines 8–12.
34    Ibid., VII. 19; p. 363, lines 19–21.
35    Ibid., VII. 25; p. 359, lines 32–3 and p. 360, lines 3–5.
36    Ibid., VII. 20; p. 365, lines 15–16, 27–9.
37    Ibid., lines 35–7.

O Januarie, what myghte it thee availle,
Thogh thou myghtest se as fer as shippes saille?
For as good is blynd deceyved be
As to be deceyved whan a man may se. (2107–10)

As I have argued above, the usefulness of optical material in pointing a moral was taken further in homiletic literature, and Chaucer is known to have consulted Robert Holcot's commentary on Wisdom.[38] In his twenty-ninth *lectio*, Holcot relates each of the seven cardinal sins to both the spiritual and physical blindness which they separately cause. He begins with pride, which blinds by its excessive splendour. The sun is compared to the display of worldly glory, which prevents the inner eye from seeing spiritual truth by its great brightness. Showy intellectuals, fortunate and rich men are likely to be affected by this sin. The rich, powerful, and ingenious ruler of Pavia comes to mind, and forcibly so as Holcot goes on to quote from a letter of Seneca to Lucilius a story similar in moral to that of the Merchant's Tale:

> his [Seneca's] wife had a certain female servant, who suddenly became blind; she ceased to see. The story sounds incredible, but it is true: she did not know that she was blind, but kept asking her attendant if she might leave the house in which she lived, saying that it was too dark. Seneca adds: what makes us smile in her case happens to the rest of us; nobody understands that he is himself greedy or covetous. The blind ask for a guide while we wander without one, saying: 'I am not self-seeking, but living in my city demands great expenses. It is not my fault that I have a choleric disposition, or that I have not settled on a definite way of life; it is due to my youth.' Why do we deceive ourselves? The evil that affects us is not external, it is within us, it is seated in our very vitals. For that reason we achieve health with all the more difficulty, because we do not know that we are sick.[39]

---

38  See above, pp. 107–9, 120 and 123.
39  'uxor sua quandam famulam habuit, quae subito facta caeca, videre desiit. Incredibilem rem tibi narro, sed veram: nescit se esse caecam, sed semper rogavit paedagogum suum ut recedat de domo in qua est. Dicit enim domum tenebrosam esse. Et subdit Seneca: Hoc enim quod in illa ridemus, nobis accidit: nemio se avarum esse intelligit, nemo cupidum. Caeci ducem quaerunt, nos sine duce eramus, et dicimus: Non ego

Just as texts with a scientific bias provide a framework for May's final speech, so the moralizing of optical data gives a context for the theme of inner blindness as it occurs in the Merchant's Tale. For Seneca's moral applies to January: the true cause of his blindness is within. When January becomes physically blind, it is but the external manifestation of internal disorders, whether intellectual, spiritual, erotic or emotional. He is never more blind than when his sight is restored and May is able to persuade him that his eyes do not see the truth. They do, but January no longer knows what the truth is. Outer and inner blindness have become as one.[40]

## Dante's *Commedia*

Jean de Meun's ostensible mode of incorporating *perspectiva* into his narrative was as witty scholastic discourse. Chaucer aped this technique in the Squire's Tale but in the Merchant's Tale opted for bricolage, assembling fragments from a number of different optical sources. The model provided by Dante was different again, for the Italian poet had assimilated optical ideas to such an extent that he made them part and parcel of his narrative, integrating them with the experience of his pilgrim narrator. Thus the process of producing space is clearly articulated, its means being movement, light, shadow and, above all, vision. The effect is to foreground a strong link between visual perception and a sense of space, while

ambitiosus sum, sed urbs mea magnas exigit impensas: non est meum vitium quod iracundus sum: quia nondum constitui certum genus vitae: adolescentia facit. Quid nos ipsos decipimus. Non est extrinsecum malum nostrum, intra nos est, in visceribus sedet. Et ideo difficulter ad sanitatem pervenimus: quia nos aegrotare nescimus.' Holcot, *Super sapientiam*, lectio 29, p. 104. See also Seneca, *Ad Lucilium epistolae morales*, epistle 50; ed. and trans. Gummere, vol. 1, pp. 330–3.

40    Cf. Brown, 'Optical Theme', pp. 241–3; and Burlin, *Chaucerian Fiction*, pp. 207–10.

at the same time showing how the bodily production of space is itself produced and predetermined by a God co-extensive with maximum spaciousness, the cosmos. According to this credo, the human production of space is perfectible, but predicated on strict and steady adherence to the virtuous life. The results of deviance are myopia, gloom and restriction. Thus, throughout Dante's work, space, visual perception and the light that enables them are saturated in symbolic value. Poor vision and claustrophobic enclosure are associated with sin and hell; visual acuity and long perspectives with spiritual awareness and aspiration.[41]

Dante was familiar with scholastic debates on the metaphysics of light and vision, especially from his knowledge of commentaries on Aristotle by Thomas Aquinas and Albertus Magnus. From them, as well as from his reading of encyclopedic texts, he developed a complementary interest in the technical aspects of *perspectiva*.[42] Within the *Commedia* he achieved a remarkable fusion of scientific optics with the symbolic uses of light, vision and space, developing a way of describing simultaneously the outer and inner eyes, so that the experience of the one is constantly enriched and changed by the gathering awareness of the other.[43] Thus, his account of the visual experience of the narrator travelling through the universe is done with scientific and observational precision – a factor which helps to make the journey credible.

Dante's journey through hell, purgatory and paradise is one towards the primal light of creation.[44] Consequently light, the prerequisite of vision, becomes in the *Commedia* progressively more intense, showing that Dante is approaching the source of spiritual truth. The first intimation that light and truth are as one occurs in

41  Boyde, *Perception and Passion*, chs. 5 and 6.
42  Gilson, *Medieval Optics*. On Dante's direct indebtedness to Bonaventure and to scientific treatises see Bundy, *Theory of Imagination*, ch. 11; Mazzeo, *Medieval Cultural Tradition*, ch. 2; Montgomery, *Reader's Eye*, chs. 1 and 2; Parronchi, 'Perspettiva dantesca'; Singleton, *Journey to Beatrice*, ch. 2; Tea, 'Witelo prospettico', pp. 24–5; and Workman, 'Science of Light'.
43  Patterson, '"Rapt with Plesaunce"', pp. 463–8.
44  Boyde, *Dante Philomythes*, pp. 207–14; Gilson, *Medieval Optics*, ch. 5; and Mazzeo, *Medieval Cultural Tradition*, ch. 3.

the opening lines of *Inferno*. As Dante makes his way through the dark wood, he discerns a hill lit by the rays of the sun (*Inf.* I. 13–18),[45] a promise of divine illumination. Before Dante and Virgil enter hell, where no light shines, 'ove non è che luca' (IV. 151),[46] they see in Limbo the virtuous pagans who, through the application of natural reason, have glimpsed divine truth. So it is that they exist in a blaze of light enclosed in a hemisphere of darkness, 'un foco / ch'emisperio di tenebre vincia' (IV. 68–9). Hell itself is a place of gloom, where the human intellect is obscured by sin.[47]

In purgatory darkness, which baffles the will with helplessness ('quella col nonpoder la voglia intriga', *Purg.* VII. 57), is defeated by the sun, which provides a bright light and a clear atmosphere.[48] The stars and the sun move over the heavens and guide the travellers on their way towards the summit of the mountain (XIII. 13–21).[49] The sun is the means whereby Dante and Virgil approach the first light, and with the sun's beams striking full in their faces Virgil explains to Dante that the sun and God's goodness are of the same nature. As the sun reflects from a bright object, so does God's goodness enhance the ardour of man's love of God (XV. 67–75). The sun serves as a symbol of God's bounty and goodness until the tenth canto of *Paradiso*, when Dante and Beatrice arrive at its sphere. Beyond the sun is the light of God himself, the formative principle of the universe, which generates the nine orders of angels who turn the celestial spheres (*Par.* XIII. 55–60).[50] As this light multiplies, so does the love it kindles in man (X. 82–90).[51] In paradise, the souls of the blessed, like Beatrice herself, participate to a greater or lesser extent in the divine light. The larger the sphere of the universe, the more it contains of God's virtue (XXVIII. 64–6). The primal light creates and illuminates the

45    Ed. and trans. Singleton.
46    Cf. Dante, *Purg.* I. 40–8.
47    Parronchi , 'Perspettiva dantesca', pp. 44–5.
48    Ibid, p. 46. Cf. Dante, *Purg.* I. 115–17, X. 22–105, XII. 19–21 and XV. 139–45.
49    See also ibid., XIX. 37–9.
50    Workman, 'Science of Light', pp. 10 and 36.
51    Singleton, *Journey to Beatrice*, p. 30.

spheres, which glow with different splendours, although the in-
forming light remains one (XXIX. 136–41).[52] Having passed beyond
the final sphere, Dante and Beatrice enter the heaven that is pure
light, intellectual light, full of love: 'al ciel ch'è pura luce: / luce
intelletüal, piena d'amore' (XXX. 39–40).[53] They are swathed in
blinding brilliance until, like a candle is given flame, Dante's sight
is restored (XXX. 58–60). He sees a splendid river of light in which
he bathes his eyes in order to be granted yet fuller perception. The
river turns into a circle of light, its whole expanse made by a ray
reflected on the summit of the Primum Mobile, 'Fassi di raggio [...]
/ reflesso al sommo del mobile primo' (XXX. 106–7). Dante finally
comprehends the eternal light itself and he realizes that it informs
all creation:

> Nel suo profondo vidi che s'interna,
>    legato con amore in un volume,
>    ciò che per l'universo si squaderna:
> sustanze e accidenti e lor costume
>    quasi conflati insieme, per tal modo
>    che ciò ch'i' dico è un semplice lume. (XXXIII. 85–90)[54]

> In its depth I saw that it contained, bound by love in one volume, that
> which is scattered in leaves through the universe, substances and accidents
> and their relations as it were fused together in such a way that what I tell
> of is a simple light.

As the last example shows, light and sight are complementary
features of the poem. It is important, however, to make a distinc-
tion between the different areas of meaning associated with these
two optical components. Light enjoys an independent existence: it
is something the source of which can be approached, expressing
the pre-existent and eternal bounty of God's love. Sight, on the
other hand, is used to monitor Dante's response to that light and
hence the gradual development of his spiritual awareness. If the
elaborate treatment of light in the *Commedia* can be identified as

52   Workman, 'Science of Light', p. 26.
53   Ibid., p. 34; and Leyerle, 'Rose-Wheel Design', pp. 299–302.
54   Workman, 'Science of Light', pp. 53–4.

belonging to the tradition of which Grosseteste is a representative, then Dante's similarly elaborate treatment of vision aligns him with the psychological study of perception represented by Alhacen.[55]

One of the ways in which Dante indicates the misapprehension of God by man is by describing incidents in the course of his pilgrimage in which his sight is deceived. In *Inferno*, the 'cieco mondo' of sin (*Inf.* IV. 13), Virgil has to remind Dante that his understanding is affected by ignorance, his sight deceived by distance:

> [...] Però che tu trascorri
>   per le tenebre troppo da la lunghi,
>   avvien che poi nel maginare abborri.
> Tu vedrai ben, se tu là ti congiungi,
>   quanto 'l senso s'inganna di lontano (XXXI. 22–6).

It is because thou piercest the dark from too far off that thou strayest in thy fancy, and if thou reach the place thou shalt see plainly how much the sense is deceived by distance.

The poet's perception of distant scenes is progressively more sure and distinct in the clearer light of purgatory. It is indicative of Dante's spiritual education that there he should be able, with the aid of his own reason rather than with the help of Virgil, to overcome deceptive sight and see an object for what it is. For example, what looks like seven golden trees, on closer inspection, become golden candlesticks, representative of the gifts of the spirit (*Purg.* XXIX. 43–50).[56]

Similar in application to the passages on deceptive vision are those which concern weak sight. As Dante's proneness to optical illusions gradually disappears, so his weak sight is gradually strengthened. In the second canto of *Purgatorio*, the angel of God approaches, growing larger and brighter as it does so. Dante

---

55    See Gilson, *Medieval Optics*, ch. 3. For Akbari, *Seeing through the Veil*, pp. 147–77, the *Commedia* maps a progression from theories of sight based on extramission to those based on intromission.

56    Cf. Dante, *Purg.* XXV. 118–20; and see Parronchi, 'Perspettiva dantesca', pp. 12 and 55–6.

cannot bear to look at such intense brightness and this inability signals his sinfulness (*Purg.* II. 13–42). When the angel next appears, Dante has only to shield his eyes from the light rather than avert them. Virgil tells him that his progress will continue so that

> Tosto sarà ch'a veder queste cose
> non ti fia grave, ma fieto diletto
> quanto natura a sentir ti dispuose. (XV. 31–3)

> Soon the seeing of these will not be hard for thee, but as great delight as nature has fitted thee to feel.

In paradise, Dante's powers of vision rapidly grow stronger.[57] He imitates Beatrice in looking directly at the sun (*Par.* I. 46–54). She herself has perfect vision (V. 1–6), with which she helps Dante. In the sphere of the sun, his spontaneous prayer of wonder causes Beatrice to smile and so give him further insights – the splendour of her smiling eyes breaking up his absorption and focusing it on a dazzling array of illuminated objects: 'lo splendor de li occhi suoi ridenti / mia mente unita in più cose divise' (X. 62–3).[58] The eagle of divine justice later explains that vision comes from God as one of the rays of the mind of which all things are full ('alcun de'raggi de la mente / di che tutte le cose son ripiene', XIX. 53–4), yet on earth its abilities are limited: there it can see the surface of the sea but not its depths, for it may be weakened by 'ombra de la carne' (XIX. 66). In paradise, there are no such impediments. Beatrice points out that the first triad of angels derive their delight primarily not from love but from the depth to which their sight or spiritual understanding penetrates truth, for

> [...] si fonda
> l'esser beato ne l'atto che vede,
> non in quel ch'ama, che poscia seconda;

---

57  Ibid., p. 58.
58  See also Dante, *Par.* XXVI. 76–8 and XXVII. 97–9. Cf. Singleton, *Journey to Beatrice*, p. 16; and Workman, 'Science of Light', p. 32.

e del vedere è misura mercede,
   che grazia partorisce e buona voglia (XXVIII. 109–13)[59]

the state of blessedness rests on the act of vision, not on that of love,
which follows after, and the measure of their vision is merit, which grace
begets and right will.

In the final stages of his ascent through the spheres, Dante's own
sight is perfected.[60] He perceives Beatrice from afar, her crown
reflecting divine light. Distance no longer dims her image: 'ché süa
effige / non discendëa a me per mezzo mista' (XXXI. 77–8). In the
final canto, Dante's sight is made pure and vision replaces speech
as a means of inner illumination (XXXIII. 53–7).

   Prior to the perfecting of Dante's sight in the closing stages
of the poem, the poet is consistently careful to make his visual
experience recognizably human, which helps to reinforce the in-
timate connections made in the poem between present and eternal
life. The perfecting of the inner eye of the spirit begins on earth.
A number of extended similes compare the visual experiences of
the pilgrim traveller with ones from everyday life. Flames which
Dante sees burning in the eighth bolgia of hell are like fireflies seen
from a distance in a valley at dusk:

Quante 'l villan ch'al pogaio si riposa,
   nel tempo che colui che 'l mondo schiara
   la faccia sua a noi tien meno ascosa,
come la mosca cede a la zanzara,
   vede lucciole giù per la vallea,
   forse colà dov'e vendemmia e ara (*Inf.* XXVI. 25–30)[61]

As many as the fire-flies which the peasant resting on the hill – in the
season when he that lights the world least hides his face from us and at the
hour when the fly gives place along to the gnat – sees along the valley
below, in the fields, perhaps, where he gathers the grapes and tills.

59   See also Dante, *Par.* XIV. 40–1 and XXXII. 73–5; also Leyerle, 'Rose-Wheel
     Design', p. 298; and Workman, 'Science of Light', p. 41.
60   Mazzeo, *Structure and Thought*, pp. 106–10.
61   See also Dante, *Inf.* XXXI. 34–8 and XXXIV. 4–15.

As they progress up the mountain of purgatory, illuminated as it is by celestial bodies, Dante and Virgil emerge from a fog which has surrounded them to perceive the sun dimly, as the earthbound traveller glimpses the sun as a disc through mountain mists. An appeal is again made to the experience of the reader (*Purg.* XVII. 1–6).[62]

In scenes such as these, a sense of space is unavoidably conveyed. As indicated in the first chapter, Muscatine has argued that two types of space, held in tension, occur in the *Commedia.* One is schematic, and is used by Dante to order the conceptual relationships of hell, purgatory and paradise. The other is produced by an accurate and consistent first-person viewpoint; consistency in direction, location and time; continuity and connection between places; and a verisimilitude of human response to experience, involving attention to the details of touching, walking, talking or casting shadows.[63]

The architectonics of hell are at once vertiginous and threaten enclosure. Dante stands on the brink of the pit, which was

> Oscura e profonda [...] e nebulosa
> tanto che, per ficcarlo viso a fondo,
> io non vi discerned alcuna cosa. (*Inf.* IV. 10–12)

> so dark and deep and full of vapours that, straining my sight to reach the bottom, I could make out nothing there.

As he and Virgil are taken through the air to the eighth circle, Dante registers the progress of their descent – 'vidi poi, ché nol vedea devanti' (XVII. 124) – by the approaching sights of the torments of the damned. He later records, as he witnesses the punishments of the counterfeiters, his ability to see down to the bottom of the pit: 'fu la mia vista più viva / giù ver'lo fondo' (XXIX. 54–5). In purgatory, as we have seen, there is more of a sense of openness as the sun and stars wheel overhead. In

---

62 See also Dante, *Purg.* V. 37–42, XXIII. 1–6 and XXIX. 70–81.
63 Muscatine, 'Locus of Action', pp. 118–19. Cf. Campbell, '"Nel mezzo del cammin"'.

paradise, the sense of physical space finally dissolves in a sense of infinite expansiveness, much as the human powers of sight are replaced by perfected vision. In Muscatine's terms, schematic and individuated space become one.

The *Commedia* is strewn with analogies, deriving from the science of optics, which explain the behaviour of light and vision. They strongly recall the optical exempla discussed above in Chapter Three. Appropriately for a cantica much concerned with light, they occur with greatest frequency in *Paradiso*.[64] The effect of Beatrice's looking at the sun on Dante is like that of a reflected ray of light (*Par.* I. 49–54).[65] They enter the sphere of the moon as water receives a ray of light and remains unbroken ('com' acqua recepe / raggio di luce permanendo unita', II. 35–6).[66] Beatrice describes an experiment using a light and three mirrors to demonstrate that differences in the reflective capacity of this sphere are not caused by alterations in its distance from the light source (II. 91–105).[67] The angelic spheres and those of the universe are mirrors of God's light (IX. 61–3). The soul of Rahab sparkles like a sunbeam in clear water, 'come raggio di sole in acqua mera' (IX. 114). The two circles of the Dominicans and Franciscans exist in relation to each other like two parallel rainbows, one born of the other (XII. 10–21).[68] Beatrice opens Dante's eyes

> [...] come a lume acuto si disonna
>      per lo spirto visivo che ricorre
>      a lo splendor che va di gonna in gonna,

64   Cf. Dante, *Purg.* XV. 16–24; and see Miller, 'Three Mirrors', pp. 263–79; Parronchi, 'Perspettiva dantesca', p. 46 and also pp. 11 and 68; and Workman, 'Science of Light', p. 20.

65   Parronchi, 'Perspettiva dantesca', p. 68; and Workman, 'Science of Light', pp. 20, 21 and 28.

66   Ibid., pp. 52–3.

67   Miller, 'Three Mirrors', p. 263; and Parronchi, 'Perspettiva dantesca', pp. 25 and 73–8.

68   Cf. Dante, *Par.* XXXIII. 115–20; and see Parronchi, 'Perspettiva dantesca', pp. 82–5; and Workman, 'Science of Light', pp. 39–40.

e lo svegliato ciò che vede aborre,
si nescïa'e la sùbita vigilia
fin che la stimativa non soccorre (XXVI. 70–5)[69]

as sleep is broken by a piercing light when the visual spirit runs to meet
the brightness that passes through film after film, and the awakened man
shrinks from what he sees, so unaware is his sudden waking till judgement
comes to his help.

The Trinity was formed like a light ray shining into glass or amber
(XXIX. 25–7); the eternal light, though reflected in many mirrors,
remains as one (XXIX. 142–5); and the effect of entering the
empyrean is like that of sudden lightning when it momentarily
deprives the eye of vision (XXX. 46–8).[70]

## The *House of Fame*

Dante owed a double allegiance to *perspectiva* – one to the tradition
of light metaphysics represented by Grosseteste, one to the
Aristotelian tradition which flowered in the writings of Alhacen.
According to the former, visual experience and the behaviour of
light are indices of, and guides to, the nature of God. According to
the latter, the subjective production of space is a function of the
bodily senses, especially sight, and is prone to error and fraught
with emotion. In combining these two traditions within a narrative
framework Dante provided Chaucer with a precedent of which he
took full advantage in *Troilus and Criseyde*, as Chapters Nine and
Ten will show.

The *Commedia* was for Chaucer a major conduit for the recep-
tion of optical theory: it incorporates within a narrative context
the metaphysics of sight, the deficiencies of human vision, the

69 Parronchi, 'Perspettiva dantesca', pp. 61–2.
70 For other optical allusions, see Dante, *Par.* III. 10–15, XIV. 97–102, XVII.
121–3, XXVIII. 4–12 and XXX. 109–14.

scientific explanation of light and perception, the moral application of optical data and the production of space. Dante is an important source for Chaucer's treatment of optical subjects, but he was not comfortable with the role of Christian apologist. The schematized moralizing of *perspectiva* was not for him: Dante always moves insistently and urgently towards a symbolic application of optical experience; Chaucer is frequently content to allow it to remain at an experiential level. If, for Chaucer, ideas of vision have a wider application, then these are kept within the confines of the narrative and its pattern of meaning; they are not generally subsumed within an overarching ideology. Or, if one is invoked, its application remains an option, rather than an imperative. Nevertheless, Chaucer was impressed by the human dimensions of the *Commedia*'s optics, and especially its linkage of vision and light with space.

In studies of the influence of Dante on Chaucer a familiar comparison is that between the descent of Chaucer's eagle in the *House of Fame* and various passages in the *Commedia*.[71] However, that episode still has much to reveal about the nature of Chaucer's spatial imagination as it operated both in response to Dante's poem and independently of it.[72] Fully consonant with the *Commedia* is Chaucer's emphasis on visual activity – a marked feature of the *House of Fame* from start to finish.[73] The dreamer's first action on leaving the temple of glass is to look 'faste aboute' (481) in an attempt to get his bearings. It is a disconcerting process in this unfamiliar landscape: operating at the outer limits of his ocular capacity he registers – as far as the eye can see – nothing but a desert, a 'large feld' of sand which, at the other extreme, is made of grains of sand as small as 'man may se' (482–7). After the cornucopia of images seen in the temple this is a terrifying place. Apart

---

71   See also Dante, *Purg.* II. 17–24; and see Bennett, *Chaucer's 'Book of Fame'*, pp. 48–58; Chaucer, *House of Fame*, ed. Havely, pp. 14–15; Dilts, 'Observations on Dante', pp. 26–8; and Praz, 'Chaucer and Italian Writers', pp. 50–1. See also Koonce, *Chaucer and the Tradition of Fame*; Looten, 'Chaucer et Dante', pp. 549–60; and Robinson, 'Chaucer and Dante', pp. 292–77.

72   Cf. Akbari, *Seeing through the Veil*, pp. 203–10.

73   Mazzeo, *Medieval Cultural Tradition*, p. 56.

from the two extremes of horizon and sand grains there are no
visual reference-points, no other sign of life: no town, house, tree,
bush, grass, cultivated land or other living creature (484, 489). In a
desperate act of devotion, the dreamer redirects his gaze and looks
heavenwards to discern, close to the sun, and again at the limits
of vision ('as hye / As kenne mighte I with myn ye', 497–8), a
mesmerizing object like a huge, soaring eagle, golden and shining
as if it were a second sun. He sees it approach, moving 'somwhat
dounward' (508), feathers glinting, then soar higher as he watches,
fascinated by 'the beaute and the wonder' (533). In its sudden
swoop, like that of a thunderbolt, the dreamer is frightened to dis-
cover that the situation is reversed, for he is now in turn the chief
focus in the eagle's field of vision 'when hyt beheld / That I a-
roume was in the feld' (539–40), the prey of a creature fabled for
acuity of sight far exceeding human capabilities.[74] He is snatched
like a lark and carried aloft, too traumatized to look anywhere.

The ebb and flow of visual activity is closely linked to the
production of space, as it is in the *Commedia*. The dreamer sees, as
far as he is able, across great distances and, closer at hand, in great
detail. He registers the disorienting effect of a featureless terrain as
he glances about, trying to find a focus. When he finds one – the
eagle – it produces a sense of the sky above, and of the narrowing
space between man and bird as the dreamer gradual perceives
more and more detail, and becomes increasingly sure of what it is
that approaches. The eagle's reciprocal gaze further reinforces the
specificity of their spatial relationship. In all this, Chaucer provides
a structure that accentuates spatial design. The episode begins
with a sharp contrast between the artificial and enclosed interior of
the temple and the wide-open space of the desert; the dreamer is
put 'out at the dores' (480) of one on order to enter the other.
Again, by splitting the episode across two books, and beginning
the second with an invocation to classical deities, Chaucer puts
the dynamism of the scene into suspended animation just at the
moment when the eagle has begun to descend. The effect is to fix
in the mind's eye, almost as if it were a manuscript illumination,

74   Minnis, *Shorter Poems*, pp. 201–2.

the vital components of the scene: a desert, the sun shining, a soli-
tary figure gazing skywards and intent on a single focus, a bright,
golden eagle wheeling and descending, the distance narrowing,
encompassing space of sky and land. Finally, having placed the
dreamer as a lost soul in a vast, empty landscape, a disorienting
place of maximum extensiveness, he shows him suddenly running
to maintain his freedom, only to be seized and imprisoned in the
bird's huge claws in another moment of abrupt transition from
one kind of space to another: 'Withyn hys sharpe nayles long, /
Me, fleynge, in a swap he hente' (542–3).

At the same time, and again in line with Dante's practices,
visual activity and the production of space are not represented
merely as reflex actions responding to external stimuli. Internal
processes of thought and feeling also have an important part to
play. The interaction of these with vision is first in evidence when
Geffrey finds himself alone in the desert, where the absence of
customary reference-points entails a sense of isolation and loneli-
ness that threatens his identity as a social being: 'no maner creature
[…] / Ne sawgh I, me to rede or wisse' (489, 491). The shock
drives him further inwards, and prompts him to assert his belief in
Christ, through prayer, while fearing that his eyes may fall victim to
error and hallucination, to 'fantome and illusion' (493).[75] Such
thoughts and emotions in turn affect the direction of his gaze, as
he turns his eyes to heaven (495). The reciprocity of thought and
vision, with an admixture of emotion, is again clear through the
process of interpretation in which the dreamer now engages. He
becomes conscious, 'war', of a visual focus 'faste by' the sun and
he thinks he knows, though he is not yet sure, what it might be:
'Me thoughte I sawgh an engle sore' (499). He is unsure because of
the distance, and because the creature appears to be much bigger
that any other eagle he has previously seen. What is more, it seems
to be made of gold, and shines as brightly as a second sun. The
unusual qualities of the supposed eagle engender fascination and
wonder, transmitted through visual experience – 'never sawe men
such a syghte' (504) – but, as it approaches, the marvellous bird

75   Cf. Doob, *Idea of the Labyrinth*, pp. 334–5.

begins to look more natural, for all its uncanny radiance, which is now provided with an explanation. The dreamer records at the end of the first book that the eagle's dazzling appearance is caused naturally, by its 'fethers bryghte' (507). The detail is repeated after the invocation, but with a subtle shift of emphasis that further dispels the initial notion that the eagle might be made of gold: its feathers shone 'as of gold' (530). Once snatched from the ground, such rational interpretation is out of the question: the dreamer's fear ('drede') is such that his senses are numb, 'al my felynge gan to dede' (553). He has had too much of a shock, 'to gret affray' (552), to record what he sees. A balanced account of visual experience, and of the thought processes involved, depend upon the relative equanimity of the perceiving subject. It was threatened, but not overcome, by the desert; now he has lost his equilibrium, and cannot estimate distance – 'How high, I can nat telle yow' (547) – because he is dazed and confused, 'astyonyd and asweved / Was every vertu in my heved' (549–50).

Without a doubt, the account of vision, space and the psychology of perception implied in Chaucer's lines has a context in the theories propounded by Alhacen. Found in his writings are such ideas as the schema, based on previous visual experience, to identify an object as yet indistinct; the visual array of recognizable forms as a basis for estimating size and distance, and for providing a place with spatial identity; the practice of comparison between memory image and seen object in order to identify unusual features, such as extraordinary size; the proneness of vision to error and illusion; and a recognition that the brightness of a distant object can make it seem larger than it really is.[76] Whether or not Chaucer had recourse to scientific texts in such cases, Dante provided him with an entirely sufficient set of optical examples. But Chaucer was not merely transcribing what he found in the *Commedia*: rather, he was absorbing the principles of its optical lessons, applying them in his own ways, resisting the allegorizing tendencies of Dante's work, reconfiguring and recombining its

76   See above, pp. 47–61.

episodes by blending them with other material – and in so doing taking possession of spatial descriptions for his own purposes.[77]

Thus, *Inferno* XIV finds Dante and Virgil encountering a barren plain that might have served as one model for Chaucer's field of sand. However, the terrain is of limited extent, being framed by a wood and a moat, and bisected by a stream. Nor do its visitors venture beyond the safe border, and while the ground may be a dry, deep sand as found in the *House of Fame*, it is far from being deserted. Instead, it is the punitive home of those who have been violent against God. There is no solitude, but herds of naked souls crying out in incessant pain as they lie, crouch or run while flakes of fire fall slowly from the sky, igniting the ground.[78]

Two episodes in *Purgatorio* are closer to what Chaucer wrote. In the second canto, in an episode previously mentioned, there is a focus on the sun, coupled with the approach of a mysterious bright light, its cause and identity gradually becoming more distinct. Like Chaucer's dreamer, Dante the pilgrim is operating at the limits of his perceptual capacity, registering visual events while self-consciously subjecting them to processes of thought and interpretation. He and Virgil are beside the sea, as the sun rises, when Dante notices a puzzling and indistinct light approaching swiftly across the water. He likens its initial appearance to that of the planet Mars glimpsed low on the horizon through dawn mists. But this light approaches with unmatchable speed, and when Dante looks again after a brief glance at his companion it has grown larger and brighter. Now he can discern more detail: a whiteness on either side and then, little by little, the shape of something else beneath. At first he is unable to say what the forms are, but then identifies wings, and a boat piloted by what Virgil recognizes as the angel of God. Its brightness becomes ever more intense as it approaches. The kneeling Dante cannot bear the dazzle and so averts his eyes, looking down.

The second episode, in *Purgatorio* IX, also involves a winged creature, one that represents the idea of a secular (Roman) empire

77    Cf. Clemen, *Chaucer's Early Poetry*, p. 91.
78    Cf. Schless, *Chaucer and Dante*, p. 45.

founded on justice. The creature appears to Dante within a pro-
phetic dream, and what he seems to see is an eagle, with feathers
of gold, poised in the sky with open wings, and about to swoop.
After wheeling awhile the eagle descends, terrible as lightning, and
snatches Dante to take him to the sphere of fire, where both burn
together. The imagined fire awakens Dante, who finds that the sun
is already two hours into the day, and that he has been brought to
the gate of purgatory. Dante's eagle is the precursor of the eagle of
divine justice that features in *Paradiso* XVIII-XX. The second eagle is
more static, appearing first as an heraldic head and neck pricked
out by lights in the sky. It then becomes a great, wheeling bird that
sings and speaks at some length to a listener considerably more
receptive and attentive than Chaucer's 'Geffrey'.

Chaucer's development of a sense of space is more deliberate
and leisurely than Dante's and, for all its borrowings, Chaucer's
episode is quite different. It retains an air of mystery; there is no
guide to provide direction and reassurance; no explanatory ideo-
logical framework systematically applied and waiting to be re-
vealed; no sense of how the field of sand might relate to a larger,
coherent structure. However excited Chaucer was by Dante's
visual world, he did not allow that excitement to distract him from
his own purposes. One of those purposes – for which the model
of the *Commedia* was eminently useful – was the creation of clearly
differentiated spaces as one means of articulating the meaning of
the poem. For the field of sand is but one of four places
representing different phases of the dreamer's experience, and
each has a carefully created and separate spatial identity: the temple
of glass is light and airy, like a Gothic edifice; the temple of Venus
claustrophobic; the whirling wicker basket labyrinthine.[79]

79    Boitani, *Chaucer and the Imaginary World of Fame*, pp. 178–9; Edwards, *Dream
      of Chaucer*, pp. 102–7; Minnis, *Shorter Poems*, pp. 191–2; Schless, *Chaucer and
      Dante*, pp. 44–50 and 52–3.

# 6 The Mind's Eye: The *Book of the Duchess*

everything that is visible is imaginable; for just as color, direction, distance, presence and existence can be observed ocularly, so they can be apprehended imaginarily.[1]

Thus far, this book has considered the extent to which optical texts dealt with spatial phenomena; it has described the spread of optical ideas through encyclopedias, exempla and vernacular literature; and it has explored Chaucer's susceptibility to those influences. But Chaucer's interest in space is more than occasional and episodic: it is fundamental to the ways in which he structures narrative, represents events and articulates ideas and emotions. To demonstrate these claims, the present and ensuing chapters offer readings of the spatial content of entire works: the *Book of the Duchess*, Knight's Tale, Miller's Tale and *Troilus and Criseyde*. From his early to his late work, Chaucer's account of the production of space is complex and subtle, with the legacy of *perspectiva* acting as a significant, informing context.

A dream vision is not the obvious place to start. If medieval optics is concerned with the perception and interpretation of forms in the material world, dream narratives dematerialize things, endow them with powerful symbolic – if often enigmatic – meaning, and disrupt spatial continuity with abrupt transitions from one place and time to another. It might be thought, therefore, that the production of space as a visual process involving the eye, the body and the external world is best examined through a more realistic genre. Dante taught Chaucer otherwise and, as the *House of Fame* has already suggested, his own dream poems reprocess and make vivid, as if to hold up for analysis,

---

1    Peter Aureol (d.1322), quoted by Tachau, *Vision and Certitude*, p. 107.

visual experience in the waking world.[2] If they promote a sense of spatial disorientation, the sense of space *per se* can actually increase as the dreamer withdraws from normal consciousness, with all its distractions and anxieties, into the liberating and focused world of dream vision. In that world, space is elastic and adaptable, deployed now to articulate the conceptual relationships of allegorical components, now to inform the hyper-realism of a particular scene. If, in the process, dream visions saturate images and events with symbolic content, that is but an intensification of the function that objects, actions and their spatial identities have in waking life.[3]

For a purely physiological account of vision and the production of space is not the one Chaucer knew. The medieval understanding of these phenomena accorded them a psychological dimension and symbolic value – properties well suited to the introspective world of the dream vision. As we have seen, Alhacen recognized that the mental processing of visual data was an integral part of the perceptual act, that the 'production of space' is in part a subjective process that takes place in the mind's eye, through recognition, memory and imagination. So we might consider the dream vision genre as providing Chaucer with an opportunity to examine the extent to which the sense of things seen, of space experienced, can be divorced from ocular perception and stable boundaries. It also provided a means of exploring the connections between the production of space and the production of personal and social identity.[4]

2    Kolve, *Chaucer and the Imagery of Narrative*, ch. 1.
3    Boitani, *Chaucer and the Imaginary World of Fame*, pp. 178–9.
4    Natter and Jones, 'Identity, Space'.

## The Story of Ceyx and Alcyone

The narrator's condition in the opening lines of the poem does not bode well for the reliability of what is to follow. He is in a state of extreme and enduring melancholy,[5] an affliction well known for its ability to induce delusory images. What the poem effects is a cure for this illness, or at least an indication of where the cure might lie. The proposed therapy requires him to turn ever more inwards, confronting aspects of his own identity, until he is 'taken out of himself' by a dream that transfers attention and sympathy to another, someone who needs his help, the man in black. This process is psychological, moral and social. The initial sense of personal alienation is reinforced by the disjunctive nature of the dream's episodes, but at the same time there is an attempt to show how the apparently discrete units of the narrative are related to each other. The recognition that they are holds forth the possibility of the emotional and social reintegration of both the dreamer and the man in black. A developing spatial awareness, of how different people and things relate one to another, is one means by which the reintegration is achieved. Vital to the making of connections is the demonstration that space is as much a conceptual, imaginary, mental construct, intimately related to the subjectivity of the individual, as it is an inalienable feature of the tangible, waking world.

At first, the narrator is in a withdrawn and isolated state, turned inwards. The location is nothing other than his 'mynde', represented as being in a state of emotional and sensual numbness: he has 'felynge in nothyng', has lost his bearings, and is 'mased', to the point of vertigo (11–15). He recognizes that it is unnatural, 'agaynes kynde', to suffer such disorientation and in so doing implies what the desirable, healthy norm might be: a state of equilibrium, of recognition of the variety of emotional and sensual experience, and of interaction with the outside world. The dynamic between psychological disorder and recuperation will drive the entire poem as it seeks ways to rediscover lost directions, to stimu-

5    Heffernan, *Melancholy Muse*, ch. 2.

late numb emotions, break the cycle of introspection, and re-establish connections between isolated individuals and the larger community of which they are a part. Awareness of spatial relations is an index and expression of that process – spatial relations under-stood not just as the relative location of human and other forms in the physical world, but also as the product of mental activity peculiar to the individual, who sees the external world, and confers meaning on it, in accordance with personal predispositions.

For the time being, however, the narrator has lost the capacity to produce space.[6] He is in a state of mental, emotional, bodily and spiritual torpor under the general influence of melancholy: 'melan-colye / And drede I have for to dye' (23–4), his depression such that he feels it has 'sleyn my spirit' (26). What has gone is liveli-ness, 'quyknesse', responsiveness to the world around him, 'lusty-hede', or vigour. He is beset by 'fantasies [...] in myn hede' (28), and all this militates against the spatial identity of the scene, which remains unknowable. There is, however, an acknowledgement of how the dreamer's condition might seem to others and of their desire to know its cause (30). Among its various characteristics it results in the loss of his ability to locate himself in relation to the external world and to order that world in relation to his own priorities. In this state, the world acts on him, he is merely a subject, a sentient being reduced to a thing by seemingly over-whelming external forces. The retrieval of a sense of personal space, and with it a reassertion of his identity, is therefore a pro-cess of negotiation between the spatial constructions made by the individual, and those made by others, within the context of the pre-existing arrangements of the physical world.

The first step towards the recovery of some personal control is the narrator's decision to read. Suddenly, we become aware of his location in space and time: 'late this other night' (45) he sat upright on his bed and asked someone to fetch a book. This simple but vivid scene contains several elements that, in different guises, will be crucial to the narrator's developing sense of expan-siveness: his body and its posture, a physical setting, an inter-

6    Edwards, *Dream of Chaucer*, pp. 70–1.

mediary. Furthermore it sets off in the reader's or audience's mind a scene that has to be imagined with some rudimentary spatial referents: we 'see', at night, a bedchamber, a sleepless figure sitting on a bed, a shadowy servant bringing a book. Our response to the *Book of the Duchess* thus replicates one about to be described by the narrator: his experience of reading. And the book chosen is not just any book, but 'a romaunce', or book of vernacular fables, designed to appeal to the imagination, to beguile the time, to provide some escape from besetting anxieties, to 'drive the night away' and perhaps effect a change in the reader's state of mind such that his sense of isolation, of space reduced to a bed in an anonymous room surrounded by darkness, might be overcome by a more expansive notion of how his existence connects with the larger world. What is more, the book has another kind of appeal to the mind's eye.[7] As well as being fictional, full of fables, it was written in rhyme by clerks and poets long ago for others to read and 'be in minde'. It is therefore a storehouse of memory, a means of passing on certain kinds of truth in fictional form. In so doing, it spans time, linking 'long ago' to the present, and tells of a past when men loved 'the lawe of kinde' (44–56). So it holds out the possibility of connecting the reader with others who might have experienced his debilitating condition, and of offering some examples of how to honour the laws of nature, as the narrator no longer can. The book he reads, and the function it performs, become emblematic of the therapeutic role of the *Book of the Duchess* itself.

The second step in the narrator's retrieval of spatial equilibrium is his response to the story he reads. In Ovid's tale he discovers a figure, Alcyone who, although from a distant past, exhibits melancholic symptoms similar to his own when she hears of her husband's disappearance in a shipwreck. The shipwreck scene (66–75) is another vignette, an episode told with extraordinary economy, offering a momentary glimpse into the awful time-and-space-bound circumstances of the tragedy: Ceyx goes 'over see', a tempest rises, the mast breaks and falls, the ship is broken, all are drowned and lost. The memorably stark objectiveness of the

7    Ibid., pp. 72–3.

description (an abbreviation of Ovid), the speed of the arbitrary event, contrast with the subjectivity of Alcyone's love and the relative stasis of her own situation.[8] The spatial disorientation of Alcyone is also comparable to that of the narrator. She faces only emptiness, absence and isolation 'at hom', which grows more and more intense as she waits for news. Looking, finding the lost visual and emotional focus that her husband provided, filling the void, reconstructing her space, now becomes a compelling activity: 'Anon she sent, both eest and weste / To seke him' (88–9). Her story inspires pity because, unlike the narrator's, it has an identifiable cause: the loss without trace of him she loved 'alderbest'. The personal expression of the narrator's sympathy who has 'such pittee and such rowthe / To rede her sorwe' (97–8) that it affects him all the next day, marks a crucial moment in his own cure. Earlier (lines 9–10) he had stated that joy and sorrow were all the same to him in his melancholic state, but now a story in a book has stimulated an emotion which drives out his existing preoccupations to replace it with empathy for someone else's predicament. Thus the temporal distance between the grieving Alcyone and the despondent narrator is bridged by an act of imaginative sympathy and the narrator's horizons enlarge so that his own self-absorbing unhappiness is placed in a larger context and thus forgotten.

But Alcyone's anguish does not abate. She enters further within herself, swooning when it becomes impossible to find Alcyone in the outside world, and is driven almost mad by sorrow (101–4). Single-minded to the point of fixation, she 'koude no reed but oon' and she too now sits, if 'doun on her knees', and weeps, prompting more pity, her action echoing the narrator's and, as in his case, signalling an attempt born of near-despair to reconstruct by different means a personal space contracted and grown almost meaningless. Her instrument is a prayer to Juno; her desire is to see Ceyx, or alternatively (which amounts to the same thing) to know where he is, or how he is, or in what manner or condition; and her chosen mode of communication 'som certeyn sweven',

8    Ovid, *Metamorphoses*, XI. 410–795; ed. and trans. Miller, vol. 2, pp. 108–11. Cf. Davenport, *Chaucer*, pp. 58–72; and Minnis, *Shorter Poems*, p. 93.

suggesting that dreams may well provide insights denied to the perceptual faculties that operate in waking life. As if to emphasize this latter point, Alcyone's body becomes limp, insentient, she hangs down her head, swoons, becomes 'cold as ston' (122). She is helped (as the narrator was) by others: women catch her, and take her to bed in a vulnerable state, 'al naked' (125). Motifs already encountered in the dreamer's account of his own condition – psychological malfunction, an inert body, a bed, intermediaries – thus recur.

Juno in turn requires an intermediary, 'hir messager', to go to Morpheus and explain that he is to make Ceyx's body speak as a simulacrum of its living self (149). The geographical directions she gives provide some impression of the vastness of the terrain that the gods command, including the 'Grete Se', but there is little sense of actual place until he comes to the 'derke valeye' (155), reminiscent of the dark night that the narrator wishes to drive away. Once there, Chaucer provides a careful description that includes spatial terms so that the dwelling-place of Morpheus seems to have substance and depth against its neutral, or non-descript, background. Thus the valley 'stant *betwixe* roches tweye' (156); a sense of height is conveyed by the well springs that run *'fro* the clyves *adoun*' (161); and the enclosed atmosphere incorporates menace and fear, for the water makes 'a dedly slepynge soun' (162), a motif that echoes the narrator's state and anticipates that of the man in black.

Spatial specificity, of a kind not found in Ovid, now comes thick and fast. The waters of the stream run *'doun ryght by* a cave / That was *under* a rokke ygrave / *Amydde* the valey, wonder *depe'* (163–5). It is a pictorial conception of a nocturnal landscape, with an attempt at spatial unity as the mind's eye is led both by both by the stream and by the descent of the 'messager' from the high point of the cliff down to a central point of the valley and towards the deep cave where Morpheus and Eclympasteyr lie. Their cave, like the valley, is shrouded in darkness: there, it is as dark 'As helle-pit overal aboute' (171), which suggests one visual model, the traditionally rocky terrain of an underground hell-cave, that

Chaucer had in mind.[9] Amid the inert, snoring, oblivious bodies, that lie in all manner of positions, the 'messager' at last rouses Morpheus with a comic mixture of shouts ('Awaketh!') and a loud alarum blast with his horn in the god's ear. Visual contact is at last established: Morpheus looks at him with 'hys oon ye' and asks drowsily 'Who clepeth ther?' (184–5).

On hearing the message from Juno, Morpheus himself becomes the go-between and carries out her request. He stands at the foot of Alcyone's bed, ventriloquizes Ceyx's voice and, calling her tenderly by name, encourages her to awake and leave her sorrowful life, offering no more consolation than the certainty of her dear husband's death and disappearance from view: 'For certes, swete, I am but ded. / Ye shul me never on lyve yse' (204–5). But he does provide the physical details she longs to know, saying when and where she will find her husband's body – 'such a tyde [...] the see besyde' (207–8) – in order that she might bury it. At these bleak facts Alcyone wakes up, looks, and sees nothing. Whether or not the dream has been consolatory remains a moot point, for her emotional condition and physical state hardly improve: '"Allas!" quod she for sorwe / And deyede within the thridde morwe' (213–14).

At least, Alcyone dies with what she wanted, namely a knowledge of the real circumstances of Ceyx's death, and there is a sense in which the *Book of the Duchess* as a whole is about the process of 'waking up' to reality, about the volition towards moments of sudden and intense realization, and of the changes (of attitude, action, thought, feeling) that follow. As the narrator discovers through his reading of the tale of Ceyx and Alcyone, one of the means whereby 'waking up' occurs is through the written word when, in moments of epiphany, the reader discovers in the text a passage that deepens understanding, or provides a solution to a problem or anxiety long endured. Of course, the impact of the text does not stop with reading, but continues in the thought and imagination of the reader, and so it is that Chaucer describes the narrator reflecting back on the narrative he has just read and

9    Edwards, *Dream of Chaucer*, pp. 75–7.

applying it to his own case. It helps us as modern-day readers, as it evidently helped Chaucer's own alter ego, to recall the sequence and meaning of a narrative in visual terms. And in this context we can begin to see one of the purposes of Chaucer's quite deliberate and emphatic use of descriptions with marked spatial character-istics: they confer distinctiveness on a scene, they are one of the ways in which he makes an episode graphic and unique, and they help to make it memorable, to 'stand out'.

The impact of the tale on Chaucer's narrator is quite extra-ordinary, because it has suddenly provided him with a perspective on his own condition. However, its effectiveness depends upon a careful reading and a well-formulated response (a heartfelt covert appeal, one suspects, of Chaucer to his readership past and pre-sent!). Thus, having 'red thys tale wel / And overloked hyt every-del' (231–2), the narrator is not only sympathetic towards Alcy-one's plight, he is also amazed: 'Me thoghte wonder yf hit were so' (233). For the narrative has given access to information otherwise unknown (though also as yet unverified): 'I had never herd speke er tho / Of noo goddes that koude make / Men to slepe' (234–6). His discovery of a narcotics of the imagination evidences the kind of connection that the written text has made between the reader and a previously unsuspected body of knowledge that has the capacity to alter beneficially his own, life-threatening condition. But the access of new knowledge is also a challenge to existing mindsets: 'I ne knew never god but oon' (237). Thus the personally reconfiguring potential of what the narrator has read is consider-able, and radical. It opens up a new opportunity, a new possibility for a 'cure', a new approach, and a new message, addressed to the gods, that might recover long-lost or neglected connections between the Christian present of the narrator and a world in which pagan forces were potent, or indeed between the different realms of experience in which these two kinds of governing power domi-nate. (The gods, it seems, may still have power over the body.) In all this the deep-seated image of Morpheus' cave dominates, the narrator vowing to bestow propitiatory gifts items that will transform his bleak rocky, monochrome dwelling-place into an opulent, soft, well-upholstered, gilded, 'chambre', and decorate his 'halls' with gold and tapestry. The undertaking is hypothetical because he does not know where the god's dwelling is – he will bestow the gifts 'Yf I wiste where were hys cave' (262) – but it hardly matters because he is making an imaginative link with Morpheus that is evidently effective: his prayer is hardly uttered when he is filled with an overpowering desire to sleep (272–5). He falls asleep on his book and dreams: 'Me mette so ynly swete a sweven' (276), a transition that indicates a further movement into the self that was initiated by melancholy, then redirected by the book.

## The Narrator's Dream

In the event it is the narrator's own room that undergoes a makeover, and it is this transformation that marks the culmination of the narrator's retrieval of a sense of personal space. It follows on from, and is a consequence of, the enlargement of emotional, intellectual and imaginative space that his reading has produced. The context in which it occurs is that of a dream so wonderful that not even Joseph would have had the skill to understand it it, or so he claims. Chaucer's audience is thereby challenged to do the work of interpretation, but now without the aid of a narrator, although they at least have the model of his reading and reflecting back on Alcyone's dream. In this respect it is significant that the process of *reading* the dream is stressed (289), and that *thoghte* is used periodically as a synonym for *dreme* (291). These terms suggest that the process in which the reader must engage – active participation in the realization of a text – is not fundamentally different from the process of dreaming. The sense data of the dream, the thoughts of the narrator, and the imagination of the reader, work together to produce a scene which is internally coherent, like the cave of Morpheus and its surrounding terrain. But in creating a sense of ambient space it far surpasses Ovid's landscape, and that is largely because it places a mediating subject at its centre.

Like Alcyone, the narrator lies in bed asleep, 'al naked', susceptible, having surrendered conscious control over what is to happen. The time is inherently hopeful, unlike that of the 'derke night' in which we formerly saw him in his bedchamber, for now it is 'in the dawenynge' and so full of the promise of light. Within his dream, he awakes a changed person, in a state of intensified sensual awareness: alert, receptive and outgoing, in contrast to the brooding, indifferent inwardness of his former self. The description of his bedchamber is correspondingly transformed into one that accentuates interior space, but not as severed from exterior space – rather, as continguous with it, the two (inside and outside) inter-penetrating. Like Morpheus, he is awakened by noise, and although an act of sight, 'loked forth' (294), prefaces the description that follows, it is sound, as well as vision, that gives what follows its sense of space. 'Smale foules a gret hep' have startled him ('affrayed me') out of sleep through the volume and sweetness of their song, effecting a somewhat less rude awakening than that achieved by the *messager* to Morpheus. Their sound is all around him, for the birds sit together *on* the *outside* of the chamber roof, *upon* the tiles, '*overal aboute*' (300), each singing in its own way but in a harmonious and integrated fashion, more like a church choir than a dawn chorus, for this is 'The most solempne servise / By noote' (302–3) ever heard. The idea of choir-song within the echoing interior of a church further enlarges the aural space,[10] and it also uses the notion of harmony to celebrate the restoration of a state of mutual accord between the narrator's inner and outer worlds. The effect on him is deeply beneficial: there was never so soothing a sound unless it had been 'a thyng of heven' (308), for it is a sound at once joyful and sweet, 'So mery a soun, so swete entewnes' (309). It fills up the space of the bedchamber: the near-outside penetrates and saturates the inside atmosphere, claiming the narrator's wholehearted attention: 'al my chambre gan to rynge / Thurgh syngynge of her armonye' (312–13). The transformation is semi-miraculous, beyond what human agency could have achieved: 'instrument nor melodye / Was nowhere herd yet half so

10    Lewis, 'Anniversary Service'; and Robertson, 'Historical Setting'.

swete, / Nor of acord half so mete' (314–16). Space here seems expansive, not restricted, and expressive of a relaxation of anxiety, and of a relieved rediscovery on the narrator's part of how it might be possible to co-exist in a reciprocal relationship with his mental and physical environment.

Gone is the dark, silent, introspective, isolated bedchamber with which the poem began. The narrator now seems joyfully re-incorporated in the world around him, aware of its space and how it is defined but not limited by the roof, the birds on it, the sky above and heaven beyond. As the light of dawn grows stronger he also becomes aware that the interior surfaces of the chamber are 'Ful wel depeynted' (322), that the windows are 'wel yglased / Ful clere' (323–4), all of which 'to beholde hyt was gret joye' (325), again signalling the extent to which he now responds instinctively and appreciatively to the evidence of his senses. And with good reason: the whole story of Troy 'Was in the glasynge ywroght thus' (237), represented by episodes that feature some of the main protagonists, while all the walls are covered in fine colours depicting 'bothe text and glose / Of al the Romaunce of the Rose' (333–4). What, exactly, is being represented here?[11] In the case of the Troy story, for example, there are characters and scenes that the narrator recognizes and names, ones that are familiar to him and which (we may presume) have had some impact on him, to which he has in the past responded and can now remember from their images – much as we saw him respond to the tale of Ceyx and Alcyone. In one sense, then, what we are given here is the inside of the poet-narrator's skull, full of words and images from those influential narratives and texts that he had most fully absorbed – one of which, as the previous chapter has shown, was instrumental in demonstrating how poetry and *perspectiva* might be combined.

The room is now flooded with light. Through the glass of each window, crossing the distance between walls and bed, the sun shines 'Upon my bed with bryghte bemes, / With many glade

11   Chaucer, *Book of the Duchess*, ed. Phillips, pp. 7–8; and Salda, 'Pages from History'.

gilde stremes' (337–8). The window might be thought of as the eye of the room, the room itself as mental space with a consciousness at its centre, receiving the impression of secular images (some pagan), and processing them through feelings, thoughts and memory within the context of an overarching Christian schema. Far from being an isolating process, it is one thoroughly integrated with and responsive to the larger world, which is beautiful, colourful and radiant: 'the welken was so fair – / Blew, bryght, clere was the ayr' (339–40). Not even a cloud disturbs the balanced climate (343). Thus the sense of profound discontentment has gone. The narrator is now well-adjusted, expansive, receptive, enlightened, attuned to his surroundings and his imagination.

Chaucer registers this loss of alienation by reconstructing the personal presence of the narrator in ways that make it co-extensive with his surrounding space, while at the same time showing how, through sound and sight, the narrator produces his own spatial world, imbuing its content with meaning. He restores to the narrator a sense of his place in relation to other components of the physical world and shows how they in turn act upon him. This exploration of influence has been implicit in the narrative from the outset and it will continue to have central importance. It helps to explain why there is so much emphasis on different kinds of *messager*, for it is only by understanding the nature of the message-bearers that connections can be re-established between components of a system that has become fragmented.

## *Messagers*

Who or what are the *messagers*, or intermediaries, charged with this all-important function? Thus far, there is the unnamed 'one' who brings the narrator a book. There is the book itself containing Ovid's story of Ceyx and Alcyone. Within that narrative, there is Alcyone's prayer to Juno, the women who put her to bed, Juno's *messager*, Morpheus and Alcyone's dream. Then there is the narrator's prayer to Morpheus, his dream, and within it the birds, and the images on his walls and windows. All act as intermediaries, effecting change by carrying information to a sensitized human subject. These *messagers*, with which the poem is full, explain in part how people (the dead Ceyx) and things (painted images) affect a receptive human subject over the distances of space and time.[12] That they do have that power is clear from their subjective impact: Ovid's tale stirs the reader's compassion, Alcyone registers the awful truth of her husband's death, the birds and images cause joy and pleasure. The mesh of connections brought about by *messagers* gradually reconstitutes and reintegrates the dismembered experiences and discontinuous scenes of the narrative, emphasizing as it does so the essential links between human beings of the past and present, and between them and their individual circumstances. According to this cultural ecology, memory and emotion, or fellow-feeling, preserved through text and image, have the power to remind individuals of their place within a larger social and intellectual system, and therefore to give them human identity, a place in the world.

Underlying the activity of *messagers* is a fundamental question of cognition: how does the recipient know that the message received and understood across space or time is an accurate version of the original? As we saw in an earlier chapter, the question was addressed by Roger Bacon through the theory of *species*. Following Alkindi, he maintained that each visible object produces an incessant stream of images, otherwise known as *species*, that are three-dimensional facsimiles of the original and capable of travelling by means of light rays across the intervening distance to a percipient eye. Bacon and other supporters of the theory demonstrated its truth by calling attention to the behaviour of light rays as they pass through coloured glass.[13] The colours are projected on to an adjacent opaque body, and these visible effects, which they eye then receives, are the *species* of the colours in the glass:

12   Lynch, "'Taking Kep'", pp. 171–8.
13   See above, pp. 64–8 and 92–3.

when we observe rays penetrating strongly-coloured glass, we sensibly observe the colour in an opaque body near the glass and the colour sensibly and by itself alters vision; and yet we know that what alters vision is the species and similitude of the colour of the glass.[14]

In the *Book of the Duchess*, the golden beams of the sun shine through scenes of the story of Troy and fall on the recumbent dreamer. It is an extraordinarily topical and subtle way for Chaucer to express the influence and importance of the story of Troy in his own memory, imagination and work.[15] Here it is, illuminating his alter ego as it was to be projected into *Troilus and Criseyde*. What Chaucer has done is simultaneously to objectify and personalize the idea of the *messager* by rendering it in terms of an illustration (light through glass) associated with the transmission of *species*, while using that to represent his reception of ancient stories. For the theory of how *species* transmit their information is analogous to the transmission of literary influence: the matter of Troy, like coloured glass, produces its own effect or *species* which, while its source is in one place, has its own sensible consequences elsewhere, on a contingent object such as a poet with a susceptible imagination.

It is conceivable that Chaucer was not alluding to the theory of *species* in this scene, but it seems unlikely; and even if he was not, some members of his audience would have placed the scene within the context of contemporary debates about optical theory. In the first place, there is a basic consanguinity with Bacon's approach and theory such that his thought, or subsequent versions of it as discussed by later writers, might well have seemed hospitable. Bacon was an integrationist who sought to reconcile and amal-

---

14 'quando aspicimus radios penetrantes vitra bene colorata, videmus in opaco iuxta colorem sensibiliter qui visum per se immutat et et sensibiliter, et tamen scimus quod est species et similitido coloris vitri.' Bacon, *De multiplicatione specierum*, I. 2; ed. and trans. Lindberg, pp. 10–11, lines 135–8 (cf. I. 1, pp. 4–5, lines 37–41); and Bacon, *Perspectiva*, pars 1, dist. 6, cap. 4; ed. and trans Lindberg, pp. 89–91, lines 272–98; and pars 1, dist. 9, cap. 1; pp. 128–31, lines 64–98.

15 Carruthers, '"Mystery of the Bedchamber"', p. 78; and Zink, 'Allegorical Poem', pp. 124–6.

gamate the inheritance of Grosseteste and Alhacen. In doing so
he tended to err on the side of inclusivity and ambiguity, as in
the long string of synonyms he attaches to the word *species*, terms
that include words and concepts familiar from Chaucer's lexicon:
virtue, form, image, similitude, phantasm, intention.[16] Nor is he
over-punctilious about the precise way in which, *messager*-like, the
*species* makes contact with the eye, opting for the loose terminology
of 'impression'. Like Alhacen, he was also interested in what hap-
pened to the *species* thereafter, and elaborated ideas to explain the
action of the imagination and the memory such that the mental
processing of the *species* is seen as an integral part of the act of
perceiving things in space. Thus there is an interactive relationship
between external forms and the perceiving subject, with the *species*
acting as a kind of sign of its point of origin which, like any other
sign, has to be interpreted on the basis of past familiarity. The
concept of the sign allows Bacon to recognize that the relationship
between word and concept is essentially the same as that between
visual *species* and what it represents. To quote Tachau: 'Like every
other entity, the uttered (or written) word is capable of generating
*species* that, in turn, multiply through the senses of hearing (and
sight) into the inner senses.'[17] The attractiveness of this notion to a
poet writing about the mental reconstruction of space (conceived
as a visual and aural phenomenon) hardly needs stressing.

Second, there were other specific applications of Bacon's
theory that make of it an intriguing and informative context for the
*Book of the Duchess* and for Chaucer's poetry more generally. For
Bacon's theory raised the question of the reliability of mental
images and, as subsequent writers responded to Bacon's thesis
(often in the course of their commentraies on the *Sentences* of Peter
Lombard), the images produced in dreaming became a test-bed of
his ideas, along with after-images, delusions, the images produced
in mirrors, optical illusions, the effect of light passing through

16    Lindberg, 'Introduction' to *Bacon's Philosophy of Nature*, pp. lv–lvi; and
      Michaud-Quantin, 'Champs semantiques'.
17    Tachau, *Vision and Certitude*, p. 19.

a coloured window and imagination itself.[18] Thus Henry of Ghent (*fl.*1276–92) proposed that the *species* produced in dreams were identical to those produced in the imagination by waking experiences, raising the problem of how true images might be differentiated from false ones.[19] In response, Duns Scotus emphasized that a *species*, as the intention of the object that produced it, had to be distinguished from its originating form, and that what he called intuitive cognition was able to separate *species* originating in an object with those that were merely hallucinatory.[20] Indeed, the intellect was capable of overcoming even the deceptiveness of ordinary vision.[21] Peter Aureol (d.1322), for his part, gave a much more prominent role to illusions, after-images, mirages, dreams and hallucinations in order to develop his theories of cognition, pointing out the permeability of physical and mental apprehensions of various phenomena, including space: 'everything that is visible is imaginable; for just as color, direction, distance, presence and existence can be observed ocularly, so they can be apprehended imaginarily'.[22]

Third, the whole question of the status of the *species* achieved notoriety and enduring controversy with their repudiation by William of Ockham (*c.*1285–1349).[23] He argued that intuitive cognition does not depend upon the presence of a visible object, or of its representation, and that therefore *species* are not necessary. For we can have true and accurate knowledge of objects even when they are not present to the eye. Furthermore, he claimed that *species* cannot be known experientially: while we are looking at a visible object we are not aware of anything passing between it and the eye. The idea that vision is completed through representations

---

18 Ibid., pp. 23, 99, 144–7, 232 n. 86 and 346; and Tachau, 'Problems of the *Species in Medio*', p. 409.
19 Tachau, *Vision and Certitude*, p. 57.
20 Ibid., pp. 64–6 and 68–75.
21 Ibid., p. 79.
22 Ibid., p. 107.
23 Ibid, ch. 5; and see Pasnau, *Theories of Cognition*, pp. 4–18 and 162–7; Stump, 'Mechanisms of Cognition'; and Tachau, 'Problem of the *Species in Medio*', pp. 394–443. Cf. Klassen, *Chaucer on Love*, pp. 58–62.

or images of the object is an unnecessary complication: all that is needed is an 'impressed quality' of the object in the sense. Ockham thereby attempted to refute the notion that visual perception was in effect a double act, requiring a secondary process inside the perceiver. He explained memory as the product of abstractive cognition working together with intuitive cognition. He conceded that objects are able to act at a distance, as when the sun is the cause of illumination or heat, but light and colour, not their *species*, are present in the medium, and so the object from which they emanate is apprehended directly.

Other Franciscans, and Dominicans equally well versed in the science of *perspectiva*, attacked Ockham's argument point by point. John of Reading drew attention to mirror images and after-images to support the notion of *species* as the transmitters of information from object to eye, where they continued to affect the imagination and the intellect, forming the basis for abstract cognition. Similar arguments were advanced by Walter Chatton and Richard Fitz-ralph. Of special interest is Robert Holcot, whose influence on Chaucer has already been noted. He too supported the per-spectivists in their attack on Ockham's views. Acknowledging that *species* has many synonyms, he regards it as 'a quality causative of the cognition of a stone when the stone is not present'.[24] For him, *species* are synonymous with 'concepts', 'intentions', 'words' or 'habit' in the sense of 'outward appearance', and are necessary to explain how complex knowledge derives from simpler perceptions. On the other hand, he regarded as untenable Bacon's view that the *species* was a natural similitude of the object. For Holcot it is immaterial and possesses a subjective status since it is processed by the imagination or memory, which could not function without them.

The *species* controversy provides evidence of an extraordinary self-consciousness, a conceptually sophisticated and reflective awareness, of the processes of seeing and interpreting. As a context for the *Book of the Duchess* (and one that merits further

24    Tachau, *Vision and Certitude*, p. 249.

exploration) it provides a paradigm for Chaucer's dealing with optical theory as it affected his conceptions and representations of space and his interest in separation, and action at a distance.[25] By one route or another he appears to have been aware of key optical ideas that he proceeds to assimilate and repossess, working with them and exploring their implications for his own work. In his dream vision, he is not content with a purely physical notion of space. He explores it also as a mental phenomenon, as an inherent component of narrative, as an aid to vivid remembering, as related to identity, as an elastic medium uniting disparate times and places, as the physical context within which community, social and cultural relationships exist, as an intensely personal entity produced by a perceiving subject, as mediated not only by sight but also by sound and other *messagers*. In all this, *perspectiva*, and the impact it had, was a catalyst, a stimulus to explore and deploy a complex phenomenon.

## Retrieving the Space of the Man in Black

In the third phase of the poem, *messagers* continue their vital function of maintaining links between individuals and groups that might otherwise be disparate.[26] The most notable instance is the narrator himself, acting as intermediary between the man in black and the world he shuns.[27] He enables the grieving man to recover or stabilize his self-definition, which is in a volatile and confused state of superfluity: he is by turns the man in black, John of Lancaster, a lyric poet, Sorrow, a lover, Christ himself, no one. The process whereby the man in black retrieves a more stable and measured sense of his identity is marked by a retrieval of his ability

25    Burnley, 'Some Terminology'.
26    Cf. Rooney, *Hunting*, pp. 143 and 153.
27    Martin, 'Mercurial Tradition'.

to produce space – a process that is mediated, and to some extent engineered, by the narrator.

The narrator is in a position to act as facilitator because of his newly rediscovered ability to produce space in ways that integrate him with his surroundings. 'Woken up' within his dream, his senses reinvigorated, he now produces space unselfconsciously and energetically, through sight, hearing, movement and mental activity. He hears 'goynge bothe up and doun' outside his chamber 'Men, hors, houndes, and other thyng' (348–9), so introducing an-other contiguous area, this time at ground level. The integration of different spatial locales, through the medium of a narrator restored to psychological health, is thus sustained. When he 'herde that, / How that they wolde on-huntynge goon' (354–5) it precipitates an absurd, dream-like, impulsive reaction, but one that links near and far. Naked as he is, he takes his horse, leaves his chamber, and never stops until he reaches the outer field, 'feld withoute' (359). The abruptness and alacrity with which the narrator quits his inward-looking chamber for the bustling hunt of the outer field indicates that solitary introspection has now been decisively re-placed by a sociable outwardness in which space is managed under the rubric of a common purpose. His sense of haste expressing eager consent to this new kind of space, the narrator speeds on until he overtakes a great crowd of hunters, trackers and hounds (360–1). The place is memorable for an atmosphere of excitement, exultation and engaging diversity in contrast to the phase prior to the dream, when the outside world was in danger of becoming undifferentiated to the point of non-existence. After his former glumness, social discourse now seems easy and natural. Joining the other hunters, he is no longer alienated but in the right place at the right time, seizing the moment, reintegrated with the activities around him: '"A Goddes half, in good tyme," quod I, / "Go we faste"' (370–1). The paradox here is that there is a corresponding diminution in self-definition: having reclaimed his spatial identity, the narrator 'loses himself' by becoming virtually indistinguishable from the other hunters.

But in the middle of the public excitement, the hunters' quarry gives them the slip, escaping secretly to an unknown place.

This suggests that there are imperceptible spaces contained within the outer envelope: the hunters' best efforts to circumscribe, invade and incorporate the hart's space are for the time being thwarted. In view of the elaborate and extended pun on *hart* and *heart*, this is an important delineation of the difference between public and private space, and between the individual's sense of what is inside and what is outside.[28] The natural tendency of the subjective consciousness, especially one in a downcast state, is to retreat from the public gaze: 'at the laste / This hert rused and staal away / Fro all the houndes a privy way' (380–2). Its behaviour, natural in the circumstances, suggests that the introspection with which the poem deals may not necessarily be permanently replaced by a more outgoing attitude, but that instead there is something fundamental and complementary about the alternate states of inner contemplation and outward participation, and it is the restoration of that balance that is the key to psychological and social health.

With the slowing down of the hunters' activities the narrator's own pace becomes more measured, moderate and free from the constraints of the hunt once the 'forloyn' has sounded, indicating that their quarry has left its pursuers well behind. Alone again, the narrator describes how 'I was go walked fro my tree' (387); he is now seemingly open to the fortuitous and less directed events 'as I wente', in the manner of a wandering dream-vision narrator. Linking the terrain of the hunt with that of the mysterious forest is the whelp that fawns at the narrator's feet. The dreamer interprets the mute but eloquent behaviour of the creature hypothetically: it 'crepte to me as lowe / Ryght as hyt hadde me yknowe' (391–2), holding down its head and holding back its ears in a way that is both subservient and affectionate. As he tries to catch the dog (395) it flees down the path into the forest, and the narrator gives chase. Thus this new *messager* has induced him to cross the threshold of another domain.[29] He follows it along a path

28  Minnis *Shorter Poems*, pp. 117–23, and see esp. Grennen, '*Hert-Huntyng*', and Prior, '*Routhe* and *Hert-Huntyng*'.
29  Friedman, 'Dreamer'; Heffernan, 'That Dog Again'; and Rowland, 'Whelp'.

(398) as he penetrates deeper into the forest, finds that 'roaming' is the natural activity of the animals that inhabit it (443), and imitates their natural, spontaneous movement 'wonder faste', following them with urgency further into the forest, 'Doun the woode' (444) as he is led by them, rather than pursuing them.[30] Suddenly further movement is arrested in a moment of monochrome stasis that contrasts with the coloured exuberance of the preceding lines. After the vitality of the forest animals there is something inert, irresolute, dejected and life-denying about the black figure who confronts him.

The person he discovers is someone who, like his own earlier self, has become desocialized, solipsistic, uttering lyrics to no one but himself, 'a compleynte to hymselve' (464). The rhyme is tuneless, 'Withoute noote, withoute song' (472).[31] Again, individual components that belong together in an integrated whole (like the birdsong, or hunt) have disintegrated, become fragmented, isolated and useless.[32] It is the insistent presence of the narrator that prompts a response recognizing the necessity of sociable behaviour (what is a lyric without an audience?). It becomes the dreamer's project to be the new *messager*, encourging the man in black once more to produce that space by a process of visual and spoken interaction that is founded in the process of 'telling' (555): 'oo thyng wol ye here? / Me thynketh in gret sorowe I yow see' (546–7).[33]

The narrator's function is not only to elicit the story of the man's sadness, 'discure me youre woo' (549), to make the private public, but to try and amend it as a listener, interlocutor and *messager* so that the isolated man in black can reconnect himself to the outside world – a process that is expansive, healing, a remedy for alienation. In achieving this end the narrator adopts a pragmatic and empirical approach, vowing that he will 'preve hyt by assay', but his genuine and avowed intention, 'by my trouth', is to

---

30   Chaucer, *Book of the Duchess*, ed. Phillips, p. 26.
31   Butterfield, 'Lyric and Elegy', esp. pp. 48–53.
32   Cf. Minnis, *Shorter Poems*, p. 132.
33   On the reconfiguration of space in the poem as a response to plague, see Smith, 'Plague, Panic Space', pp. 388–93.

restore the man in black's personal and social integrity. This entails, again, a resocializing arrangement in the course of which the narrator will harness the man in black's narrative to a particular purpose. In return for telling, the narrator will do all in his power to find a remedy, 'to make yow hool / I wol do al my power hool. / And telleth me of your sorwes smerte' (553–5). The arrangement is premissed on the belief that an act of articulation to a sympathetic listener is therapeutic in itself: 'Paraunter hyt may ese youre herte' (556). The strategy works with amazing rapidity as the narrator fulfils his function of *messager*. Hearing 'thys tale', told 'Thus pitously, as I yow telle', the narrator can hardly bear to live, such is the effect on his own heart: 'Hyt dyde myn herte so moche woo' (713).

The reduced state of the man in black, as a lone individual talking to himself, and his gradual recovery, are represented in terms of the loss and retrieval of a personal space that is at once moral and physical. For Chaucer choreographs the body language of the man in black, and of the narrator, to show how the former's narrow introversion gives way under the latter's influence to a more outgoing attitude. The narrator first finds him in diminished condition, sitting down and with his back to a huge oak tree (444–7). His enigmatic appearance and body posture are the visual signals that arouse the narrator's curiosity and make him approach as a hunter might his quarry (458). He finds sitting erect a wonderfully attractive knight – at least that is what the evidence suggests: 'By the maner me thoghte so' (453). He is pleasing in size, proportion and youth but, as we are soon to learn in greater detail, the harmonious and integrated balance of his outer appearance is not matched by his inner state.

The fact that he is 'clothed al in blak' is again stressed (457) and the narrator now 'stalked even unto hys bak, / And there [...] stood as stille as ought' (458). Closer scrutiny provides more details. Still oblivious to the narrator's presence, the man hangs down his head and with 'a dedly sorwful soun' that recalls the melancholy of the narrator and of Alcyone, as well as the sleepers in the cave of Morpheus, he utters a complaint. The narrator's empathy is immediately aroused, since the complaint is 'The moste pitee, the moste rowthe' he ever heard. He now notices the unhealthy pallor of the knight's face, as colourless as his clothes, 'pitous pale and nothyng red' (470), for the blood has fled from it instinctively, to protect the heart (490–1). The effects are so extreme that there seems to be no blood in any of the man's limbs (498–9), and at this the narrator acts: he 'stood ryght at his fet, / And grette hym' (502–3).

This social act, designed to bridge the space between them, has no immediate effect because the man in black is too self-absorbed, too inward:

> [...] he spak noght,
> But argued with his owne thoght,
> And in his wyt disputed faste
> Why and how hys lyf myght laste (503–6).

'Sorwe and hevy thoght' (509) have cut him off from social contact and exchange, to the point where sensory perception of, and response to, others, have ceased: 'he herde me noght; / For he had wel nygh lost hys mynde' (510–11). Eventually, 'at the last', he becomes aware of the presence of someone else and how he stands and what he does (515). This marks the beginning of his recuperation, because he has been stimulated to transfer attention from himself to someone 'outside'.

The growth of the man's sensory and spatial awareness acts as an index of his returning psychological health. His blindness to the presence of the narrator is now corrected as he registers it through both sound and sight in terms of posture, position, gesture and manner of speech:

> But at the last, to sayn right soth,
> He was war of me, how y stood
> Before hym and did of myn hood,
> And had ygret hym as I best koude,
> Debonayrly, and nothing lowde. (514–18)

Decorum and courtesy, a social approach appropriate to the occasion, produce the desired effect, for the man in black stirs from his deep thought, becomes aware of his discourtesy and is correspondingly apologetic (519–21). However formal, mannered and conventional this exchange, its result is to begin to include the mourning knight in a wider social space.

That space becomes ever more imbued with meaning, and with potential for further expansion, as the dialogue develops. Its foundation remains sight and sound: for example, the narrator voices the conclusion that his visual observation has led to: 'oo thyng wol ye here? / Me thynketh in gret sorowe I yow see' (546–7). But the man in black is not to be so easily encouraged out of his shell, and seems to say as much with a defensive glance: 'With that he loked on me asyde, / As who sayth, "Nay, that wol nat be"' (558–9). Gradually, though, he admits to feelings of nakedness, emptiness, a numbing sorrow that have deprived him of his sense of personal definition and social identity (577, 705), similar to that suffered by the narrator at an earlier stage. It is a positive indication of his desire to break free from this state, by explaining its origins, when he takes control of his personal space, inviting the narrator to 'Blythely [...] com sytte adoun' (749), deliberately bringing him into closer physical proximity, placing him as it were on an equal footing and acknowledging and building on their social relationship, one in which attentive listening to a narrative will be all important (750–2).

## Embodying White

The further retrieval of the knight's personal space, identity, and place in the world is achieved through an articulation and remaking of mental images. If the woman who has occasioned his suffering 'Is fro me ded and ys agoon' (479), her image remains clear, a White perceptible even in the enveloping gloom: when it is 'never so derk, / Me thynketh I se hir ever moo' (912–13). The blame for her death lies with lady Fortune, who is many ways her physical antithesis. Everything about Fortune expresses ambivalence and duplicity: even her walk (she 'goth upryght and yet she halt') and facial expression (she 'baggeth foule and loketh faire', 622–3). She is 'An ydole of false portraiture' (626) with a monster's head hidden 'As fylthe over-ystrawed with floures' (629), laughing with one eye as she weeps with the other (634) and, as the chess metaphor makes clear, capable of comprehensive control of her victims' room for manoeuvre. By contrast, White is associated with expansiveness, integrity and wholesomeness, she was entirely what she seemed, and her looks and appearance were attractive, open and honest. The powers Fortune controls seem to be one of the causes of the identity change that has overtaken the man in black, as his bowed head and sidelong glance suggest. Much of his emotional energy is devoted to affirming the durability of White's qualities of *mesure* over the transient, imbalancing, introverting effects of Fortune's.[34]

But this is no psychomachia in which two personifications battle for supremacy in the imagination of the knight. Or, to put it another way, what begins as allegory on the tribulations of Sorwe in his encounters with Fortune and White (herself a creature of Nature) gradually changes its mode to reverie as the knight reorders in his memory a sense of White's personal appearance and aura, and their subjective effects upon him. This process of retrieval itself mimics and reinforces the reconstruction of personal space in which the knight is engaged through his encounter with the dreamer.

At the outset, the knight's self-dramatizing posture of grief represents an escape from, a protection against, overpowering emotion. He takes refuge and solace in alternative roles of suffering: his plea 'whooso wol assey hymselve / Whether his hert kan have pitee / Of any sorwe, lat hym see me' (574–6) echo words attributed in medieval lyrics to Christ on the cross; while the blunt, self-enclosed statement 'y am sorwe, and sorwe ys y' (597) might have been spoken by a personification straight out of the *Roman de la Rose*. But the knight begins to shed these evasive and

34   Allen, 'Portrait of a Lady', pp. 336–42; and Chaucer, *Chaucer's Dream Poetry*, ed. Phillips and Havely, pp. 33–4.

reductive personae once he is encouraged to focus his thoughts on White. The recollection of her, her forcible impact on his imagination, and his involuntary response, drive out all that is contrived and forced.[35] In a figure that recalls the painted walls of the narrator's bedchamber, one that would not have been out of place in a scholastic discussion of *species*, he describes himself as susceptible, a *tabula rasa*, a white wall, or blank retable, receiving the lasting impression of a drawn or painted image[36] – a true portraiture to set against Fortune's false image:

> Paraunter I was therto most able,
> As a whit wal or a table,
> For hit ys redy to cacche and take
> Al that men wil theryn make,
> Whethir so men wil portreye or peynte,
> Be the werkes never so queynte. (779–84)

White catches his eye because she shines, or sheds light, more brightly than other ladies, and again this process, analogous to the qualities of the sun when compared with other planets ('fairer, clerer, and hath more lyght', 822) recalls the earlier incident. As in the case of the bedchamber, we are being asked to consider the mental space of the central subject, what has affected it, and how.

Her beautiful, radiant appearance took hold of his mind just as a white wall 'catches' a picture: 'she ful sone in my thoght / [...] so was ykaught / So sodenly' (837–9). His nature and existence are thereby changed: he abandons rational advice, taking no heed of 'counseyl', and instead gives priority to White's gaze and his own feelings, 'hir lok / And [...] myn herte' (840–1). Thus his former state of being is replaced by an intuitive vibration between two key elements of the outer and inner worlds – *lok* and *herte*. The impression is of a sudden, exciting enlargement of his personal experience and sense of 'where he belongs', but also implicit is a desire for spatial reorientation such that he will be drawn into White's orbit of attention.

35  Edwards, *Dream of Chaucer*, pp. 82ff. and 87–91.
36  Akbari, *Seeing through the Veil*, p. 191; and Chaucer, *Book of the Duchess*, ed. Phillips, note to line 780.

The eyes of White are crucial to the development of a relationship that is at once affective and spatial. For the knight's heart has itself become percipient, reacting with pleasure to 'hir eyen', their beauty seeming to epitomize White's entire appearance (841–5). This is because, as *messagers* of the heart, White's eyes convey her inward disposition: well proportioned and positioned in themselves (itself an attribute signalling moderation) the knight reads in them a litany of admirable qualities: 'Debonaire, goode, glade, and sadde' (860). The contrast with Fortune's grimace could not be more marked, and furthermore her 'look' has the power fully to engage the attention of others, as if drawing them out of themselves: 'Hyt drew and took up everydel / Al that on hir gan beholde' (864–5).

Among those who attempted to interpret the meaning of White's looks are 'fooles' who imagined that they conveyed the conventional, erotic, secret message of 'mercy' to them as aspirant lovers. The knight knows otherwise. White's looks were guileless, 'no countrefeted thyng', but an involuntary and beneficial exercise of visual power, 'pure lokyng', with no ulterior motives. Her half-open eyes were a gift of nature that expressed 'mesure', moderation and balance. Nor was her gaze directed indiscriminately: it was deliberate, controlled (874–82). It enabled her to exert power over her personal space, even though it sometimes inadvertently hurt those who came under its influence and who misinterpreted the language of her eyes (883–7).[37]

A eulogy of White's face and body follows, punctuated by imagery that develops the idea of her ambient space as one that drew him to her. Even in memory, and in his present reduced condition, she retains her light-giving quality: 'never so derk, / Me thynketh I se her ever moo' (912). But in life her effects were felt further afield: she gave light to others while leaving herself un-diminished, 'lyk to torche bryght / That every man may take of lyght / Ynogh, and hath hyt never the lesse' (963–5). Her infectious 'maner and [...] comlynesse' (966) spread far and wide through sight, for all those who saw her might, if they were

37   Galloway, 'Authority', p. 35.

receptive enough, receive a favourable visual impression of those qualities: 'every wight [...] / Myght cacche ynogh, yif that he wolde, / Yif he had eyen to beholde' (968–10). A light-catching, exemplary visual focus, her presence as 'chef myrour of al the feste' (974) dominated social occasions: she stood out even among ten thousand people. But her attractiveness was not merely that of a dazzling woman with a powerful visual image. The recuperative drive of the poem is towards personal and social reintegration, and that is expressed in spatial terms. White is an epitome of that process: she unites in a harmonious whole such qualities as 'stede-fast perseveraunce', 'esy, attempre governaunce', and 'suffraunt [...] wyt' (1007-10). Moral and psychological integrity are then linked to topographical and architectural space when the man in black asserts that 'trouthe' has taken up residence in White as a lord occupying a key property:[38]

And I dar seyn and swere it wel –
That Trouthe hymself over al and al
Had chose his maner principal
In hir that was his restyng place. (1002–5)

The immediate effect of White was to make her lover want to establish a relationship defined by increasing proximity, and mediated by sight. He had a continuing great desire to see her, and the effect of doing so was profoundly therapeutic, for it banished sorrow (1102–5). In other words, she held out the prospect of healing his emotional turmoil, of replacing his sense of isolation and separation with the unenclosed unity of 'trouthe'. The knight's present, grieving state is a yet more extreme version of the alienation he experienced as White's unrequited lover. Remember-ing it, and the happy outcome, helps now to effect some remedy. To the extent that White represents principles of integration, completeness and moderation, her memory holds out the possi-bility of re-ordering a more harmonious fashion the dislocation and fragmentation of his present existence.

38   Pouchelle, *Body and Surgery*, ch. 8.

The movement from visual desire to bodily unity follows a pattern adumbrated by the dreamer in his approach to the black knight. The knight approaches White, cautious and nervous, almost struck dumb, his bodily appearance and eloquent statement in itself, physical closeness now replacing exchanged glances:

> With sorweful herte and woundes dede,
> Softe and quakynge for pure drede
> And shame, and styntynge in my tale
> For ferde, and myn hewe al pale –
> Ful ofte I wex both pale and red –
> Bowynge to hir, I heng the hed (1211–16).

After a period of rejection, and further courtship, they enter at last into a full relationship, the knight crossing the threshold of White's gaze so that their hearts interpenetrate and become as one (1289–95).

Now, the reanimating, revitalizing presence of White has been cruelly replaced by absence, inertia, void, death. The bodily space she occupied is empty, company is bereft without her, fellowship is 'naked', social life has lost its value 'As a corowne withoute stones' (980), and the knight is left with nothing but a *species*, a memory image, something always in danger of ossifying into merely conventional description, something 'ded as stoon' (1300), like a commemorative statue. The task that now faces him, and which is to some extent enacted in dialogue with the narrator, is a re-orientation of his attitude, a change of focus, such that what White represented can be re-formed, reanimated and reincorporated into his own, continuing life.

On the other hand, the affirmation of this to the narrator, and through him to a larger audience, gives the image of White an external and iconic status: the private has been made public.[39] Eventually, the same is true of his grief, as he admits in words at last unadorned, stripped bare of rhetoric: 'She ys ded!' (1309). The narrator's sympathetic response – the most profound and radical of the poem – links internal to external, private to public, knight

39    Carruthers, '"Mystery of the Bed Chamber"', pp. 80–1.

to dreamer, poet to patron, narrator to audience, mental space to physical space. An intuitive flash of understanding, made effective by its lengthy preparation, promises the reabsorption of the isolated and melancholy mourner. Small wonder, then, that the poem ends with an abrupt widening of focus to the returning hunt, a sudden reminder of its proximity and purposeful movement, and of the relative position of the knight and narrator in time and space: the hunt

> Gan homward for to ryde
> Unto a place, was ther besyde,
> Which was from us but a lyte –
> A long castel with walles white
> Be Seynt Johan, on a ryche hil (1315–19).

There, John of Gaunt, earl of Richmond, can resume his young and still impressionable life, and project a reanimated image of Blanche who, as 'walles White', is figured again in architectural, containing, and protective terms.[40] As the castle bell strikes twelve, linking the spaces of the dream and the castle, the sense grows that he has been provided with a perspective on the death of Blanche, a way of breaking free from the time-stopping effects of excessive immersion in private and imaginative space, and with a text that enshrines a lasting but dynamic commemorative image. His job of *messager* done, the narrator awakes out of his own inner space to find himself in another place, 'lyinge in my bed', with the book of Ceyx and Alcyone, 'And of the goddes of slepyng' (1328) still in his hand. This rapid backward movement through the different locales of the poem ends only with the audience, or reader with book in hand, now having seen the result of the narrator's resolve 'to put [...] in ryme' his experience, and with the similarly self-conscious and 'awake' task of forming a response to the poem, of accommodating the imaginative space it opens up.

---

40    Ellmann, 'Blanche', pp. 103–6. Cf. Pouchelle, *Body and Surgery*, pp. 126–39.

# 7 Chivalric Space: The Knight's Tale

The Aleph's diameter was probably little more than an inch, but all space was there, actual and undiminished.[1]

Implicit in the configurations of space in the *Book of the Duchess* is an underlying difference between the space produced by the dreamer and the modes of spatial production available to the man in black. The former, essentially a private individual, is more of a free agent, creative and eclectic in his attitude, free to move in spontaneous response to external stimuli; the latter, even if cured of melancholy, is constrained by the expectations raised by his public identity. In the spatial negotiations that take place between them is an incipient awareness of the demarcations between people of different social status, between noble and bourgeois, patron and client. Thus we may differentiate space according to the social status of the producing agent, and posit that the schemata used by different individuals, the kinds of space they can imagine and make, vary accordingly. Insofar as space is a shared medium of social communication it has potential to become contentious, politicized, as rival individuals or groups jostle for its control, decorously or otherwise.

The Knight's Tale also features a preeminent aristocratic figure but he, unlike the man in black, is in full possession of the public space of his domain. He has, as it were, entered the castle to which the man in black has become marginal, and uses it as an instrument of masculine hegemony. The space thereby produced and controlled has its own political problems precisely because it excludes the kind explored with such finesse in the *Book of the Duchess*. The world of Theseus leaves precious little room for

1    Borges, 'The Aleph', p. 26.

individual initiative, private life or the feminine. When these forces do assert themselves within Athens, the result is a challenge to the basis of the duke's power. It is a challenge in which the Chaucer's audience is itself implicated, for by iconographic means he offers it the possibility of reconstructing Theseus' space according to symbolic codes alternative to those of chivalric rule. Confident and adept in dealing with challenges to his *modus operandi*, Theseus is at last confronted by a series of events governed by forces stronger than his, ones that throw into question the very basis of his vision of a world in which space symbolizes and enables absolute political control. *Perspectiva* provides a route into understanding the spatial structures of the tale, for the science of optics offered Chaucer models for representing visual perception as the basis on which the individual's perception and interpretation of space depend.

## The Dominance of Theseus

No less than in the *Book of the Duchess*, Chaucer uses space in the Knight's Tale as an attribute of those episodes that function as nuclei of meaning, as the nodes at which the themes of the narrative meet in complex conjunctions.[2] If we follow V. A. Kolve's line of reasoning, that Chaucer organizes his narratives around memorial centres of meaning,[3] then in the case of the Knight's Tale each such centre (the tower-prison, the grove and the lists) has its own distinct spatial identity. The nature of the space associated with and determined by each becomes one of the means by which those places, and their significance, are remember-ed. To take the case of the grove: it is the place to which Palamon flees to hide when he escapes from prison and where he meets by chance the disguised Arcite, now an unrecognized member of Em-elye's household, who has made the grove a place of retreat in

2    Woods, 'Up and Down'.
3    Kolve, 'Chaucer and the Visual Arts', pp. 296–8.

which to utter his desires and shed his subterfuge. It is where the emotional agitation and volatility of both knights are much in evidence: Arcite roams up and down lamenting his condition before sitting, lost in thought; Palamon sits fearfully in a bush before jumping to his feet when he recognizes Arcite. They agree to meet there the following day, when they fight like animals until interrupted by Theseus.

In different ways, each has been brought to the grove by his own will acting in response to the decrees of fate: condemned to exile, Arcite returns incognito in the hope of winning Emelye; Palamon has escaped from prison. Situated 'faste ther bisyde' (1478), a mile or two 'out of the court', and free from the artificial constraints represented by Theseus' palace, the grove is where natural emotions come to the fore, a place where their control or concealment is momentarily avoided, where individualized feelings are forcibly expressed and where even the rules of chivalry (to Theseus' great horror) are set aside. A natural space, with ill-defined borders, it nevertheless provides no real freedom for Palamon or Arcite, whose chance encounter there only exacerbates their deadly rivalry while accentuating the cruelty of the fate that holds them in its sway.[4]

Significantly, it is Theseus who brings the grove into sharper visual focus. It is on his territory, and he and a hunting party are heading straight towards it (an event itself ordained by fate) because, in a reprise of the the pun used in the *Book of the Duchess*, it is reputed to contain a 'herte' (1688–9). The directness of their route is stressed: the duke is intent on the pursuit of the animal, which is in the habit of escaping through the grove and over a brook (1692–3). Thus the grove is seen from outside, as trees in a landscape, or 'launde', a place to be searched. As they approach, Theseus glimpses the flashing swords of Palamon and Arcite (1696–700). At first they are too far away to recognize, so he spurs his horse and intervenes (1703–9). Angry at this challenge to his authority, he condemns them to death until persuaded by Emelye and others to be less harsh, and resolves that the duelling knights

4    McAlindon, 'Cosmology, Contrariety'.

should be allowed to settle their differences at a tournament. Thus, the freedom of Palamon and Arcite is not only illusory but fleeting, and their transgressions are soon contained within the political and ethical system run by Theseus.

In Chaucer's source, Boccaccio's *Teseida*, the grove is less distinct, the incident less dramatic, the spatial identity of the place less pronounced. By the time that Palemone and Arcita meet there, Arcita has already visited it many times to complain of his love. And it is not Palemone who overhears Arcita, but his servant (IV. 63–91).[5] Thus Palemone goes to the grove expecting to find Arcita, and the two embrace as long lost friends while acknowledging their rivalry in love. The discovery of the duelling knights is not made from afar, so there is no description of approach. Nor is the royal party motivated by the flight of a particular animal towards it, for they are in the 'boschetto' from the start. And it is Emilia who first sees Palemone and Arcita, as she comes to the bank of a stream. Eventually, Teseo is called and he interrupts the duel (V. 77–82). Thus, in redesigning Boccaccio, Chaucer uses space as a vector to transmit key ideas.

That may in part be because space is, in different senses of the word, a subject of the tale as Chaucer explores the nature of the control and ownership exercised by Theseus over the physical, social and ethical dimensions of his realm. Indeed, if we are to understand the organization and meaning of space in the Knight's Tale we must recognize that Theseus is the key figure: through him we see how space might be arranged and subverted under a chivalric regime. At the outset, the duke's dominance of Athens is total. The very gaze with which he first perceives the distant knights, 'Under the sonne he looketh' (1697), is redolent of regal domination. Later, before the tournament begins, he sits at a window of his palace, like a god enthroned, above his admiring citizens (2528–32). Again, his spatial control is based on male military might, vindicated by success or by the perceived rightness of his cause. If he conquers Thebes in order to avenge the depre-

5    Boccaccio, *Teseida*, ed. Marti; trans. Havely. For the version of Boccaccio's
     poem used by Chaucer, see Coleman, 'Knight's Tale'.

dations of a tyrant, Creon, taking Palamon and Arcite as prisoners, he has also conquered the 'regne of Femenye' ruled over by his wife-to-be, Hippolyta – an altogether more ambiguous claim (875– 8). Then again, the ideological principles of Theseus' control, while they might be territorially expansive and politically inclusive, are essentially public and masculine, so excluding, subduing or suppressing the private, the subjective, the feminine, or at the very least translating those categories incessantly into external action. The castle to which he brings the Theban cousins epitomizes the nature of Theseus' power: Emelye may walk in the garden, and the knights may mope in their prison, but all do so within confines determined by Theseus and controlled by him.

He expresses his dominance through action, but also through social organization, ritual and buildings. As various critics have shown, life in Athens is marked by careful attention to display, ceremony, due procedure, rules and order – principles that also find expression in architectural forms such as the duke's castle and the amphitheatre he builds.[6] From Theseus' point of view, his ability to control boundaries and limits, whether of behaviour or buildings, is essential to the maintenance and exercise of political dominance. In practice, his control of social space is a subtle, sometimes crude, but usually effective, instrument of policy. By force of arms he can expand his own territorial limits, an act that entails the destruction of others' cultural boundaries, barriers or protective walls. In the exercise of government and justice he keeps others within prescribed limits, whether they are those of prison, garden, exile or amphitheatre. Moreover, Theseus is aware of the adaptable and symbolic qualities of space, and is adept at remaking parameters to accommodate and defuse crisis.

The assurance, gusto and intelligence with which Theseus manipulates the political space of chivalry receives a check with the death of Arcite, and the closing phases of the narrative reveal that his sense of rules, limits and boundaries (of chivalry, or governance) has undergone a significant change, and that he himself is

6    See esp. Halverson, 'Aspects of Order'; and Jordan, *Chaucer and the Shape of Creation*, ch. 7.

subject to spatial manipulations beyond his grasp. Thus, one of the dynamics of the tale is the gradual erosion of masculine power through female agency, the public by the private, the rational by the emotional, and the eventual recognition that the kind of power Theseus claims to express in his ordered, ceremonial society is a false, or at the very least an incomplete, representation. And it is in prison, with the sighting of Emelye, that the contesting of Theseus' space is first broached.

## Prison and Misprisions

Chaucer undertakes his reconstruction of the space of Theseus' prison, as he found it in Boccaccio, in a variety of ways and at a variety of levels.[7] In the first instance, he reforms Boccaccio's design to suggest an altogether different kind of interior; second, the visual experience of Palamon is rendered in terms recognizable from the science of *perspectiva*; and finally, he engages the reader's imagination by drawing on a range of iconographic motifs of enclosure. In all this the production of space is ultimately Chaucer's own, but he also delegates that activity, as it were, to his protagonists and to his audience. The extent to which Chaucer is generating his own kind of narrative space is especially clear in detailed comparisons between the Knight's Tale and the *Teseida*.

Initially, Theseus' incarceration of the Theban knights seems summary and harsh, with no hope of release: 'and he ful soone hem sente / To Atthenes, to dwellen in prisoun / Perpetuelly – he nolde no raunsoun' (1022–4).[8] Palamon and Arcite are consigned to a tower and the adversity of their condition is accentuated by the placing of its description just after a reference to Theseus' glor-

7    Brown, *Chaucer at Work*, pp. 58–64.
8    Reidy, 'Education of Chaucer's Duke Theseus', pp. 399–402; and Robertson, 'Elements of Realism', pp. 229 and 247–8.

ious, laurel-crowned return to Athens to live – again perpetually,
'Terme of his lyf' – in joy and honour (1025–9). By contrast, they
live 'in a tour, in angwissh and in wo, / This Palamon and his
felawe Arcite / For everemoore; ther may no gold hem quite'
(1030-2). The verb that governs these words – 'lyveth' – is found
in the preceding lines about Theseus' well-being (1028), so that the
dependence of the knights' fate on their captor, as well as their
opposite condition, is suggested in a verbal dependence. Thus, the
misery, the long, hopeless duration of the imprisonment, and
the control of Theseus over his captives, are made clear.

These are Chaucerian innovations, designed to focus attention
on the stark nature of the knights' existence and on the nature of
the duke's power. By contrast, Boccaccio's first mention of the
imprisonment of Arcita and Palemone suggests that the two
knights were treated with special care and given a lax form of
house arrest. They are set aside from other prisoners taken at
Thebes and enjoy the privilege of living in a room within the
palace of Teseo with all their wants attended to ('faccendo lor
servire a lor piacere': II. 99). At an early stage, therefore, the likeli-
hood of there being some contact between the heroes and other
members of the royal household is established; and the possible
hardship of their situation is mollified. They live in an urban
palace, in relatively comfortable quarters complete with a balcony
and adjoining garden close enough for Emilia and the prisoners to
exchange glances.

Chaucer renders Teseo's dwelling as a medieval castle, with its
keep and 'feudal dungeon',[9] while Boccaccio's palace room, which
is part of Teseo's domestic space, becomes a distinctive, isolated
and austere tower. It rises up above the rest of the duke's castle,
seemingly impenetrable. It is emphatically the place where Pal-
amon and Arcite are incarcerated, visibly separate:

> The grete tour, that was so thikke and stroong,
> Which of the castel was the chief dongeoun,

9    Boitani, *Chaucer and Boccaccio*, p. 154; and Pugh, *Imprisonment*, pp. 112–26
     and 347–73.

(Ther as the knyghtes weren in prisoun
Of which I tolde yow and tellen shal) (1056–9).

The interior dimensions of the prison, as a physically containing
edifice, are implied when the tower later resounds to Palamon's
complaint, and the restrictions it imposes are brought out in the
poignant Chaucerian detail of his chains:

> Swich sorwe he maketh that the grete tour
> Resouneth of his youlyng and clamour.
> The pure fettres on his shynes grete
> Weren of his bittre, salte teeres wete. (1277–80)

Elsewhere, Chaucer's conception of the prison as a restrictive,
dark and hopeless place is apparent: Palamon seems destined
'In cheynes and in fettres to been deed' (1343), and dwells 'In
derknesse and horrible and strong prisoun / Thise seven yeer'
(1451–2). Within this murky, monochrome stronghold, where even
the prisoners' complexions are drained of colour, movement is
possible only with permission from the gaoler. Palamon is allowed
to climb to a vantage-point high in the tower, and there at least the
darkness is pierced by a well-protected window 'thikke of many a
barre / Of iren greet and square as any sparre' (1075–6). The
impact of the prison as a separate, imposing place is therefore
much more forcible in the Knight's Tale than in the *Teseida*, and its
qualities are further underscored by a contrast with the garden it
adjoins – a place of colour, sweet fragrance and dawning light,
where Emelye roams – prompted not by the chafing of lost liberty
but by the May season and its promise of love. The inversion of
the customary situation, whereby a tower houses the aristocratic
woman for her own protection while men enjoy outdoor freedom,
adds to the sense of crisis.[10]

   Just as the term, experience and nature of imprisonment are
more vivid in the Knight's Tale than in the *Teseida*, so too is
the crucial event more climactic. Boccaccio begins the passage on

10   Gilchrist, *Gender and Archaeology*, pp. 136–45; and her 'Medieval Bodies',
     pp. 57–8.

the knights' first sight of Emilia with a conventional description of
Spring, then focuses on the appearance of Emilia in the garden,
amusing herself there and clad in a tunic, singing songs of love ('e
'n giubba e scalza gia cantando / amorose canzon, sé diportando',
III. 8). It is not in the course of the first description of her in the
garden that Emilia is seen. Her garden wanderings are represented
as an habitual activity – 'E questa vita più giorni tenendo' (III. 9) –
until one day she is noticed. Chaucer, for his part, also begins with
a Spring setting and the appearance of Emelye, but then moves
immediately to Palamon's sight of her from the tower window. It
was on this particular day in Spring, on this unique occasion ('it fil
ones', 1034), that she caught his eye. The incident thus has a
sharper sense of expectation than its source: 'Bright was the sonne
and cleer *that* morwenynge' (1062). Unlike Emilia, Chaucer's
Emelye remains unaware of the prisoners' interest in her until they
meet in the grove – a factor that imbues the space connecting
them to her with irony as well as poignancy. Gone is the com-
plicity that accompanied the exchanged glances of Emilia and
Boccaccio's knights. Nevertheless, Chaucer's space is saturated
with the knights' emotions. If Emelye is unaware and self-
contained, they are overflowing with anguish and sensitized to any
incident that offers a hope that their existence might be bettered.
Palamon rails at the condition of his life even before he sees her:
he is 'woful' (1063), 'sorweful' (1070), 'compleynynge of his wo'
and in despair (1072–3).

The distinctiveness and complexity of Chaucer's spatial design
for Theseus' tower prison are revealed by the existence of three
sequential, integrated constructs outlined above. There is the space
of the tower as just discussed, in which the accent is on isolation,
the circumstances of confinement, enclosure and the restriction of
movement and light; then there is the sighting of Emelye by
Palamon, uniting in however fragile a way the interior of the
prison with the outside world; finally there is a retrospective
account, conducted initially by Palamon and Arcite, but extending
throughout the remainder of the tale, of what the space of 'the
prison' means.

Chaucer makes careful preparations for the second phase of his spatial design. Initially, he accentuates the distance between the knights and Emelye. He positions Palamon at the top of the tower, in a 'chambre an heigh' (1065). As in the *Teseida*, the prisoner is adjacent to the castle garden, 'evene joynant to the gardyn wal' (1060) where Emelye is. She is near, yet far, whereas in the Italian version the palace room and garden seem to be on much the same level; and they are certainly close enough for Emilia to return the knights' admiring gazes.[11] Arcita is attracted, at first, by the sound of her singing. Chaucer's heroine also sings, but she is not heard (1055). Presumably Palamon is too far away.

Thus Chaucer changes the emphasis of the incident to a contrast between the prison and the outside world, the prisoners and Emelye, to the distance between them, and to sight as the faculty that bridges the gap. His account of the latter process pays attention to the optical effects of distance in determining what the observer sees as well as how he sees it. As opposed to the generality of the preceding phase of the spatial design, which concentrated on the circumstances of imprisonment, this phase is described in 'real time', mapping Palamon's visual response as it happens and in ways attentive to the psychology of perception. If it was Chaucer (or the Knight as narrator) who produced the space of the first phase, it is Palamon who produces the space of the second, just as it will be the audience's interpretative responsibility to produce the space of the third.

Palamon's elevation provides him with a panorama of Athens: he 'al the noble citee seigh', including the garden, 'ful of braunches grene' where the bright Emelye, 'Emelye the shene' roams up and down (1066–9). In Alhacen's terms, this is an ordered array of contiguous forms (*corpora ordinata continuata*) connecting the viewer to his visual field and so enabling the accurate perception of objects within it, and of relative distances. As yet, Palamon's visual activity is of a general kind: he is merely scanning the scene below without any particular attention to detail, giving it what Alhacen calls 'perception at first glance' (*comprehensio per intuitionem*) prepara-

11    Kolve, *Chaucer and the Imagery of Narrative*, pl. 37.

tory to full contemplation of specific details.[12] The 'sorweful' Palamon is perhaps too preoccupied to do otherwise: he paces up and down in his high prison chamber, 'romynge to and fro' – an activity that, in mimicking Emelye's movements, only makes it seem more likely that the two of them are destined to be matched. Ruing his miserable existence, 'aventure or cas' does indeed intervene (1070–4). Just at this crucial point, Chaucer inserts his description of the heavily protected window, 'thikke of many a barre / Of iren greet and square as any sparre' (1075–6). The sudden, emphatic intrusion of this screen (a barred frame, possibly in the form of a grid) certainly adds to the pitiful nature of the knight's condition, prevented as he is from attaining his freedom. But it also accentuates the contrast between the exterior and interior worlds while at the same time enabling them to enter into a relationship, however tentative. Light penetrates the dark prison, Palamon's gaze takes in the outdoor scene. More, the prison bars, by marking the point of transition from foreground to far distance, increase the sense of space separating Palamon from Emelye. Thus the window becomes the eye of the room, a sensitized receptor, in a way comparable to the window of the dreamer's bedchamber in the *Book of the Duchess*, and to the mirror in the master-tower of the Squire's Tale.

It is 'thurgh' the window that Palamon's eye is, inevitably, caught by the appearance of Emelye. The random scanning ceases as his attention is held by a bright light. So forceful is her effect that he blinks and cries out as if 'stongen [...] unto the herte' (1079). While acknowledging the presence here of conventional ways of describing 'love at first sight', we must also recognize that Palamon's experience has closer analogues in optical science.[13] For it is not Emelye's eyes, shooting out 'Cupid's arrows' in the traditional fashion, but rather her brightness (exaggerated though that may be) that enables Palamon to see her and fall in love. As

12  Alhacen, *De aspectibus* II. 4. 5; ed. Smith, p. 219. Cf. ibid., vol. 1, pp. lxx–lxxii.
13  Cline, 'Hearts and Eyes'; Collette, *Species, Phantasms and Images*, pp. 34–44; and Donaldson-Evans, 'Love's Fatal Glance', pp. 202–5.

we have noted, it was Alhacen's achievement to supplant with experimental proof the Platonic theory of eye-emitting rays.[14] He drew attention to the fact that very bright light is painful to the eye, and that a brightly lit object leaves an after-image – evidence that light and illuminated colours have an effect in the eye. He therefore proposed that in vision the eye receives light from external sources. Light and colour, Alhacen insists, are what the eye is sensitive to: the eye senses the light and colours which exist on the surface of the visible object. Palamon's eye, in the clear morning sunlight, is attracted by the greenness of the garden and the brightness of Emelye: 'Therewithal he bleynte, and cride "A!"' (1078). Her recurrent association with the words *brighte* and *sheene* continue to remind us that she is, both literally and figuratively, a source of light, a woman whose form has a forcible impact on susceptible males. The sudden and painful sight of her leaves an optical and mental after-image in the dark tower, that is at once the vestige of a material reality and the trace of an ideal of love towards which Palamon strives.

The sense of crisis, of a fragile link thrown momentarily between two disparate worlds, is simply absent from Chaucer's source. It is true that Arcita, in the *Teseida*, looks from a window to see Emilia. But it is a deliberate, not a casual, act, prompted by the sound of her voice. And rather than stand on one side of the window, he puts his head through it, so that the framing effect is absent. Absent too is the contrast between the dark, restricting, high interior and the bright, ground-level world outside (III. 11-12). Palemone joins Arcita at the window and together they gaze at Emilia and sigh until she returns their stares. Concerned as he is to regain a classical ambience, Boccaccio uses the incident as an excuse for a relatively leisured conversation between the two knights in which they allude, like well-read students, to Apollo and Daphne. Meanwhile, they gaze at Emilia's eyes, in which they perceive Cupid fitting and releasing arrows in their direction as she gazes back at them. The momentous impact of the event is further diluted by several repetitions of a similar scenario in the course of

14    See above, pp. 50–5.

which Emilia becomes ever more self-conscious and coquettish (III. 28 and 38–42).

In the *Teseida* space is homogeneous, unproblematic, enveloping, uniting the knights and the woman and indeed the reader, who sees Emilia from their point of view. Chaucer, though, insists on a sharp dislocation between what Palamon sees and what his audience sees of Emelye. The description of Emelye in the castle garden that precedes Palamon's sighting is done as if were from the privileged viewpoint of someone who was able to observe her at close quarters, complete with rose-coloured complexion and blonde hair 'broyded in a tresse / Bihynde hir bak, a yerde long, I gesse' (1049–50), but Palamon's point of view is quite different. He does not see Emelye in any detail, and instead immediately transforms her vision into something preconceived: an unknown woman, seen from afar for the first time, and in an unfamiliar place, is instantly changed into an incarnation of Venus. From this juxtaposition of 'Emelyes' there emerges the sense, much more than in Boccaccio, that optical experience, and the spatial constructions that accompany it, are in the eye of the beholder, and distinctive to it. The impression is reinforced when Arcite looks at Emelye, is affected in a similar way, but chooses to see her not as a goddess but as a woman of flesh and blood. Thus their differences are exposed, and the basis for their quarrel is laid.

Palamon's sharply individuated reception of the image of Emelye is fully in accord with Alhacen's optical psychology, according to which the forms of the outside world are judged in accordance with past experience and models of interpretation.[15] Furthermore, if the initial perception is not then modified with a closer examination the particularities of the object will not be registered and there is likely to be misidentification:

> vision that depends on previous knowledge, or defining features, or minimal visual scrutiny is not truly determinate. For perception of a visible

---

15    Cf. Witelo, *Perspectiva*, IV. 10; ed. and trans. Kelso, pp. 83 and 400.

Chaucer and the Making of Optical Space

object through previous knowledge or through defining features only
involves the object as a whole according to its general nature.[16]

Thus in Palamon's case the rapidity of the visual event, and the
sudden triggering of predilections, lead to a kind of distortion of
what the reader has seen Emelye to be. Palamon's margin for error
is only worsened by the distance that separates him from her.
Moderate distance is critical to accurate perception, and the deter-
mination of what is moderate varies with the type of object seen:
'the distances at which sight perceives a visible object correctly are
limited, none of them having been too great or too small in extent;
and for each visible object there is a corresponding range of dis-
tances'.[17] Otherwise, errors of recognition will ensue:

> And it is in the nature of recognition to assimilate an object that is
> currently in view to an object that has been seen before according to an
> acquired form, and from this assimilation sight apprehends what any thing
> is. Moreover, recognition is differentiated according to recognition of the
> individual, or of the universal, or of both, so every error in recognition will
> occur in either or both of these categories [...] For instance, there will be
> an error of recognition in the case of distance. If a known person is seen
> from a great distance, he may appear to be another person known to the
> viewer so that when he sees Peter the viewer sometimes assumes he has
> seen Martin, since it is unquestionable that both are known to him.[18]

16   'visio que est per cognitionem precedentem, et per signa, et per modicam
     intuitionem non est comprehensio certificata. Quoniam comprehensio rei
     vise per cognitionem precedentem et per signa non est nisi circa totali-
     tatem et universalitatem rei vise in grosso'. Alhacen, *De aspectibus*, II. 4.
     29; ed. Smith, pp. 238–9.
17   'remotiones ex quibus visus comprehendit rem visam vera compre-
     hensione sunt ad aliquem terminum, et nulla earum erat maxima nec in
     remotione nec in propinquitate; et in unoquoque visibilium sunt secun-
     dum illud visibile'. Ibid, III. 3. 6; ed. Smith, p. 286.
18   'Et proprium est scientie communicare rem visui presentem cum re prius
     visa in forma recepta, et ex hac communicatione adquiritur diffinitio rei
     cuiuscumque. Diversificatur autem scientia in scientia individui et
     universalis, aut utriusque, et omnis error scientie erit error in aliquo
     istorum aut in utroque [...] Error enim scientie in longitudine erit. Si a
     longitudine magna videatur homo notus, apparebit fortisan esse alius
     videnti notus, unde aliquando videns Petrum visum dicit esse Martinum,

Palamon, we might say, has assimilated the image of Emelye to that of Venus.

The episode in the tower prison fractures the unity of Theseus' world. First, it suggests that female identity, far from being a single phenomenon, 'femenye', that can be subdued by superior male force, is in fact volatile, multivalent and resurgent, and as much the creation of men as of women themselves.[19] For a number of different 'Emelyes' have now stepped forward, each occupying a different space in the eye of the observer, and turning the garden into a heterotopia.[20] There is the quiescent sister of the vanquished queen of the Amazons, Hippolyta, now Theseus' wife; there is the mysterious woman who wanders, half Virgin, half romance heroine, in the castle garden; there is the deified creature of Palamon's fantasy; and there is the fleshly woman, to be won by force, seen by Arcite. Second, it has become clear that the absolute control of individual space, even if that takes the form of imprisonment, is no easy matter. It is not just that, through the power of sight, Palamon and Arcite 'escape' their immediate surroundings, but that their perception of those surroundings is radically transformed by their vision of Emelye. The restrictive space of the tower now becomes a topic of intense speculation, meditation and discussion as the knights move from a response based primarily on their immediate physical circumstances to one which asks: 'What does imprisonment mean?' This questioning (which is often a self-questioning) distinguishes the third kind of space associated with the tower, one that illustrates the process whereby space is produced according to symbolic codes. However extreme and anguished their state of existence, Palamon and Arcite repossess the idea of imprisonment in ways that are profoundly personal and private, and which therefore run counter to the chivalric schemata that Theseus commands and that appear to be his sole mode of spatial production. Consequently, Palamon and

---

cum constet utrumque ei esse notum.' Ibid. III. 6. 2 and 4–5; ed Smith, pp. 296–7.

19    Crane, 'Medieval Romance', pp. 50–4.
20    Foucault, 'Of Other Spaces', pp. 25–6.

Arcite can from henceforth express their desire for Emelye only by challenging, contesting and breaking Theseus' spatial boundaries which are, perforce, political and public ones. Exiled, Arcite returns in disguise to become Emelye's page; frustrated by long imprisonment, Palamon drugs the gaoler and escapes. Both flout the duke's enforcement of separation and distance in order to enjoy the greatest possible closeness to Emelye.

The symbolic associations of the tower prison are well established and there is no point in rehearsing them again in detail.[21] Instead, what I wish to stress are their range and variety, the extent to which the audience is involved in producing this symbolic order of space and – again – the degree to which Chaucer's practice differs from Boccaccio's. Significantly, it is possible to divide the figurative connotations of imprisonment into those posited by Palamon and Arcite and those additionally available to readers or listeners, but not to the two heroes. The knights' perceptions are themselves by no means uniform: each urges a different kind of symbolic construction, depending on their individual proclivities and experiences.

Arcite's first response to the crisis brought on by their new-found rivalry in love is to counsel resignation because, like it or not, they are the victims of adverse Fortune: 'taak al in pacience / Oure prisoun, for it may noon oother be. / Fortune hath yeven us this adversitee' (1084–6). Kolve has shown how the juxtaposition of prison and garden echoes the iconographic design of the house of Fortune, and there is plenty of textual evidence (especially the repeated emphasis on *aventure* and *cas*) to corroborate Arcite's claim.[22] The vagaries of Fortune affect both knights, but as a conception of how human action is constrained by immutable forces it is particularly associated with Arcite.[23] Fortune also plays her part in the *Teseida*, but her less extensive power begins to be felt after the prison scene, and Boccaccio then stresses other

21   Blodgett, 'Chaucerian *Pryvetee*', pp. 485–9; Boffey, 'Chaucerian Prisoners',
     pp. 84–6 and 94; Kolve, *Chaucer and the Imagery of Narrative*, pp. 85–105.
22   Ibid., pp. 86–9. Cf. Whitehead, *Castles of the Mind*, ch. 9.
23   E.g. 1285–90 and 1489–90.

aspects of the iconography of Fortune – such as her reins (III. 75), and her simultaneous giving and taking (VI. 1) – in order to express the changeable and inscrutable nature of the knights' destiny. Chaucer embodies the idea of Fortune in the tower prison.

Once released from the confines of the tower, Arcite does not lose his sense of enclosure. On the contrary, it intensifies: exiled, out of sight of Emelye, separated from his rival who still has the means to see her, he declares: 'Now is my prisoun worse than biforn' (1224). His life has become a veritable 'helle', a place well known for its dungeon-like qualities.[24] This paradoxical definition of release and freedom (albeit in exile) as a different kind of prison also extends to Theseus' tower, which Arcite now sees as 'paradys', by contrast with his own state, because it enables 'the sighte of her'. It is a topography that readers of Middle English literature recognize from *Piers Plowman* with its 'tour on a toft' representing heaven, and 'dongeon in a dark vale' signifying hell. Arcite's reappraisal of the space he occupies, and that represented by the tower prison, is a good example of the way in which space is susceptible to rapid fluctuations of meaning as circumstances change, as human priorities alter; of how its significance can be quite specifically determined by individual perceptions; and how its symbolic value can clash with that favoured by another.

For Arcite's belief that Palamon dwells 'in blisse' (1230) is a misprision to rival Palamon's own perception of Emelye as Venus. Far from being in paradise, Palamon is afflicted by a debilitating emotion that is an extreme form of the psychological constraint that both knights share. Theseus later refers to their general state as one caused by the 'laas' or snare of erotic love (1817)[25] and the 'prison of love' is a motif found in the *Teseida* (e.g. III. 23). While Arcite is aware of its potential for conflict with other, more rational, systems of 'lawe' governing human society (1165–8), it is Palamon, much more than Arcite, who experiences what it is like to be locked in to the emotion of jealousy. It is, after all, an

24  Kolve, *Chaucer and the Imagery of Narrtive*, pp. 149–53.
25  Joseph, 'Chaucerian "Game"-"Earnest"', pp. 84–8; and Van, 'Imprisoning and Ensnarement', pp. 9–12.

attribute of the goddess Palamon serves (1928–30).[26] Arcite's freedom, and ability as 'a lord' to find ways of winning Emelye, have the appearance of a great advantage from Palamon's point of view. He, though, must 'sterve here in a cage' (1294), his heart held and consumed by the 'fyr of jalousie' (1299), a feeling both figured and aggravated by the walls and bars that hold him.

As in the case of Fortune, hell, and Love, jealousy as a prison is a traditional image with an established iconography. Like Fortune and Love, jealousy (or Jalousie) plays a prominent part in a work Chaucer began to translate, the *Roman de la Rose*, in which, as guardian of the rose, Jalousie keeps Bel Aceuil locked in an adamantine tower.[27] Thus Chaucer might be seen as drawing again on a received symbolism of 'prison space' in order to thicken the meaning of what the knights endure. But they are not solely responsible for generating the multivalent significance of imprisonment. The reconstruction of that space in symbolic terms is as much the work of the poem's audience who are given, as it were, an interactive role in this respect. Not only is it a case of recognizing, on the basis of prior knowledge of the *Rose* and other texts, the different dimensions of meaning that the tower-prison will accommodate, and of acknowledging that one knight is prone to a particular kind of interpretation, but also of evaluating the whole range of possible meanings. When the narrator asks 'Who hath the worse, Arcite or Palamoun?' (1348) he is in effect inviting his listeners to discriminate between different kinds of imprisonment and inviting each person to construct the prison space of the narrative, within the given parameters, as she or he sees fit.

Thus far there is a collusive quality to the process, as the reader collaborates with the knights to produce meanings that they themselves initiate and recognize. But the tower prison allows of another interpretation that, while it may be rooted in the utterances of Palamon and Arcite, goes beyond what either conceives. There is an element of this in the echoes of the *Rose*, but it is far greater in the allusions to the *Consolatio Philosopiaey*,

26   Cf. 1839–40, 2626–35, 2732, 2783–5.
27   Brown, 'Prison of Theseus'.

which Chaucer also translated. Palamon and Arcite do not know it, but their situation mirrors that of Boethius, even down to some of the physical details of their imprisonment.[28] As political prisoners enduring a harsh regime they experience one day a vision of woman who changes their entire outlook. Of course, the ironies are manifest: far from providing philosophical resignation to their plight in the manner of Lady Philosophy, Emelye only exacerbates their state of imprisonment. Nevertheless, each knight does subsequently make an effort by force of thought, and in Boethian terms, to escape the worst effects of incarceration – Arcite by urging patience to counter the depredations of Fortune, Palamon by speculating on the futility of human existence. But they both stop far short of the radical reconstruction of prison space urged on Boethius by Lady Philosophy. Towers of the mind have their uses, she says, as stable bastions of reason, places to withdraw to in a world in a world of 'fleetynge errour' (*Boece*, I. Prosa 3, 62–71):

> But we that ben heghe above, syker fro alle tumolte and wood noyse, warnstoryd and enclosed in swich a palys whider as that chaterynge or anoyinge folye ne may nat atayne, we scorne swych ravyneres and henteres of foulest thynges. (I. Prosa 3, 76–81)

Now the tower of reason is hardly the kind of tower in which Palamon and Arcite are imprisoned, for it is there that they come to know the vicissitudes of life in an extreme form. Nevertheless, their experience does lead in the direction of philosophical speculation, towards an effort of re-definition whereby they might master their circumstances instead of being mastered by them. And if neither Palamon nor Arcite achieves sufficient detachment in order to turn the state of imprisonment to his own existential advantage, an audience receptive to the poem's philosophical allusions might well recognize the possibility of doing so, of escaping the oppressive contingencies of the human condition on what Boethius called 'fetheres of philosophye'. That kind of

---

28    Chaucer, *Boece*, I. Prosa 1, 85; I. Metrum 2, 29–32; I. Prosa 2, 29–30; and I. Prosa 5, 69–70.

imaginative involvement illustrates one way in which Chaucer's narrative poetry can engage the reader in the process of making the meaning of a key space. Boccaccio's representation of imprisonment is more limited, less suggestive of alternative meanings, less open to audience involvement.

## Theseus Circumscribed

The renegotiation of the space of the tower prison, whether undertaken by the two Theban knights or by the reader, occurs in circumstances defined by Theseus and on his territory, but without reference to him. It therefore has the potential to clash with the duke's own intentions and edicts. The rapid recalibrations of 'what the prison means', in the aftermath of Emelye's appearance in the garden, suggest that, while Theseus might impose the form of imprisonment and its primary meaning (punishment), he has no control over chance events or over the workings of others' imaginations. Some of those imaginings prompt Arcite to return from exile, and Palamon to escape from prison, in direct defiance of the spatial restrictions imposed by their captor. As we have seen, this leads to the episode in the grove, where the precepts of chivalric conduct are similarly flouted.

Far from posing a serious threat to Theseus' power, the incident is quickly absorbed and dealt with according to the precedents at his disposal. At first inclined to the summary judgement of execution, he is persuaded by Hippolyta and Emelye to be more lenient and so he decides to use the knights' dispute as an excuse for a judicial tournament at which the prize will be the woman they both love. In the course of making his decision, Theseus reflects humorously on his own personal history as a lover. What is impressive about the duke's response is not just its power over life and death, but its flexibility, its readiness to have second thoughts, to accommodate a female point of view. Nor is this the only occasion on which Theseus has cause to stop one course of action, reflect, compromise, and adjust his actions accordingly. Returning to Athens with Hippolyta as *his* trophy, his way is blocked by a line of grieving women. Initially angry at this interruption to his triumphal procession, he quickly redirects his ire at the tyrant of Thebes, Creon, who has dishonoured the dead bodies of their sons, and leaves forthwith on an avenging mission. Creon's anti-chivalric behaviour, a breaking of the bounds of accepted norms of conduct in war, is duly punished by the destruction of his city. Theseus' soldiers tear down the buildings, and leave the city walls 'wyde', reducing to ineffective rubble one of the features that defined the topographical and chivalric space occupied by Creon. In the process, Theseus extends his own sphere of influence and raises his profile as a conqueror yet further. Again, before the tournament begins he decrees that, to prevent loss of life, the combatants will use blunted weapons.

The efficiency, responsiveness, adaptability and intelligence of Theseus' chivalric project only make it the more difficult to challenge.[29] At mid-point in the narrative, it appears to be a highly effective political system, able to reposition its parameters, absorb crisis and counteract threats to its principles or design. It is able to do this by superior force, by ensuring consensus and acquiescence in Greece, by public displays of power and by vigilance. Yet the potential threat, whether from chance events, women or private imaginings, is ever-present. Thus the chivalric order that Theseus controls is at once successful and pervasive but flawed and limited. And in using the control of space as an instrument of policy he demonstrates both the extent of his power and its inherent limitations. For, whatever else it might be capable of, space is not susceptible to absolute control by the most powerful members of society; it is a subtle medium which others, too, can manipulate, and contest.

Nowhere else in the narrative is the elusive ambiguity of space better demonstrated than in the amphitheatre. Its building by Theseus on the site of the grove is, first and foremost, an act of

29   Cf. Scheps, 'Chaucer's Theseus', pp. 25–30.

reappropriation, a superimposition of chivalric form on a place characterized by its wildness and lack of boundaries. Theseus, the ruler of Athenian territory, identifies the space of the grove as incontestably his, governed by his rules and ordinances. In so doing, he obliterates the possibility that Palamon and Arcite might be able to settle their dispute privately and outside of chivalric norms. Their competition for Emelye will be a public one in which the knight who is seen to dominate the space of the tournament will be able henceforth to possess and dominate the woman. It is to be a replication in miniature of the opening connection between conquest and the subjection of 'femenye'. So the amphitheatre, even as it is announced, is pregnant with meaning. More, the very ground on which it arises is itself significant: 'here in this place', that is on the spot where Palamon and Arcite have been found up to their ankles in blood, fighting like animals, concealed until discovered. The place is given identity, and the second major stage of the knights' conflict is given a monumental form to match that of the tower-prison, both in its encircling design and its closed gates (2594-7).

The building of the 'theatre' is a deliberate, decisive and knowing act, quite unlike what happens in the *Teseida*. There, the tournament takes place in an amphitheatre that already exists as part of Boccaccio's classical scenery (VII. 1 and 10); it is not spirited into existence for a special occasion in the manner of a medieval tourney.[30] Nor does the Italian counterpart incorporate oratories to Venus, Mars and Diana. Instead, the temples are placed at indeterminate points in the vicinity of Athens, while the prayers offered there journey even further away, to Thrace and Mount Cithaeron. But in the Knight's Tale there is a conflation of these disparate elements such that the place of combat becomes a force-field for the aspirations, emotions and destinies of the three protagonists, their oratories ranged at precise intervals on the outer wall. In other respects, too, the design is expressive of Theseus' political ideology, the whole scheme an attempt to reassert both its

30   Crow and Olson, *Chaucer Life-Records*, p. 472; and Rickert, *Chaucer's World*, pp. 211–14.

principles and its practice. From Boccaccio he borrows the concentric design, which enables the duke to direct the gaze of his subjects towards the central arena and what he intends as a spectacular resolution of the Thebans' quarrel. Its shape also emphasizes the presumed perfection of his mode of social and divine inclusivity, while the tiered arrangement of the seating allows each 'degree' its due visual share of the drama, within a strict hierarchic arrangement. One of its most interesting features, again not found in Boccaccio, is the emphasis placed on the contribution made by artists and craftsmen to the production of this particular space. Theseus spares no expense to employ the best carvers and painters to produce a public place through which he can articulate his power and wisdom in a symbolic display, while encouraging his subjects' compliance by containing them within a congenial area of his own devising. The artisans fulfil his wishes in ways altogether more acquiescent than Chaucer appears to have been in reproducing the kinds of spaces favoured by his aristocratic patrons.

For, as others have noted, the design of the theatre mimics that of the zodiac and therefore indicates that there may be powers and influences beyond Theseus' ken likely to take an interest in determining the outcome of the tournament.[31] In other words, the amphitheatre as an expression of Theseus' conception of the issues at stake in Palamon's rivalry with Arcite, is put in parentheses. It becomes a site not just of their contest, but of the contesting of Theseus' political vision. He may direct the public gaze towards the Theban knights, but his own activities are in turn scrutinized by superior beings, as when the watchful Venus expresses her sorrow at the outcome of the tournament so that her tears (presumably in the form of rain) fall into the lists (2664–6). Part of the contesting of his world view takes the form of a demonstration – or exposé – of the means whereby a powerful ruler confers symbolic value on the space under his control. Such is Theseus' self-belief, or presumption, that he does not acknowledge that the

31    Pearson, 'Ordering the World', pp. 12–19. Cf. Wheatley, *Pivot of the Four Quarters*, pp. 411–19.

symbolic value of space, insofar as it is produced by human agency, is notoriously provisional, partial and difficult to control. It might be said that, in describing the making of the lists, Chaucer's topic is not so much the symbolic value of space (as it was in his earlier dealings with the tower prison) but the very *process* by which political space is produced and given social significance, only to become the focus of competing claims to power.

As a theatrical production witnessing to the legitimacy and effectiveness of Theseus' rule the tournament fails: its dénouement disappoints and causes widespread disillusionment. For the ending of the plot is not the one that Theseus scripted. Arcite demonstrates superior force of arms, but he fails to win Emelye: he is unhorsed by a 'furye' sent by Saturn and fatally wounded at the moment of victory as he is the in the act of claiming his 'space' in Athenian society by exchanging glances with Emelye (the first time in Chaucer's narrative that this crucial connection, so common in Boccaccio, is made).[32] This climactic incident is heralded by a moment of spatial expansiveness: Arcite rides in victory the length of the 'large place', 'Loking upward upon this Emelye' high in the tiered seats and she returns his gaze with 'a freendlich ye' (2680). Yet the only space that the glorious Martian victor can now look forward to is much smaller: that final and most intimate of personal spaces, the grave, where he will be 'Allone, withouten any compaignye' (2779). The tragedy is a graphic revelation of the flaws and limitations in Theseus' design. In the first place, the symmetry of the amphitheatre belies the imbalance and volatility that exists among the gods whose oratories it includes. Their desires and intentions often conflict, as evidenced by the quarrel that breaks out between Mars and Venus. While the inclusion of the oratories, and the piety they encourage, might propitiate the deities, human agency cannot control the squabbles of the pantheon. Second, Theseus' design completely ignores the determining force behind events in the lists and beforehand: Saturn, god of prisons (2457), whose orbit describes an arc wider than that

---

32    Baldwin, "'Gates Pure and Shining and Serene'".

of Venus, Mars or the Moon, and who is therefore in a position to control their motions as well as those of mere mortals.

The death of Arcite cannot be accommodated by Theseus as easily as the fight in the grove or the grieving of the Athenian widows. Having confounded his best-laid plans it throws Athenian society into a crisis that finds expression in rituals of effacement. The buildings of Athens are hung high with black cloths as the funeral cortège passes through the streets below and the grove itself (or what remains of it) is destroyed. Both acts signal a questioning of identity and direction, and if they attempt to exert control over significant spaces, it is a kind of control that replaces distinctive characteristics with their attempted erasure – the very opposite of the previous process, whereby the grove was made significant and became the occasion for making the amphitheatre.[33] Now, with Arcite inexplicably dead, the emphasis is on producing a space that is no more than that – void of distinguishing features, and in the case of the grove a wasteland which, with its atmosphere of mourning and desecration and its burning timber, recalls the smouldering ruin of Thebes. It is as if the principles of Theseus' rule have imploded, however tenaciously he might cling to the outward forms of ceremony.

The lines connecting city with grove, civilized with untamed, boundary with transgression, public resolution with private conflict, lover with desired woman, humans with gods, have ceased to be clear and have become instead causes of profound introspection. Some of the old certainties have gone. The death of Arcite has opened up a fissure between Theseus' conception of power, and the powers to which he is in turn subject. A mood of despair settles upon Athenian society. Egeus, Theseus' father, attempts a rational explanation for what has happened, but it is woefully inadequate. Instead it is the women who best express the emotional perplexity of the moment: 'Why woldestow be deed [...] / And haddest gold ynough, and Emelye?' (2835–6). Theseus' reaction is equally confused: he tears down the grove where Palamon and Arcite fought, thus placing himself in conflict with

33    Cf. Lynch, 'Partitioned Fictions', pp. 109–12.

the local gods who live there, contesting their control of that space, making them 'ronnen up and doun, / Disherited of hire habitacioun, / In which they woneden in reste and pees' (2925–7). Nor is it easy to have much more confidence in Theseus' philosophical attempt to reconcile the disastrous events of the narrative with a benevolent deity, Jupiter (previously unmentioned), several years after the crucial events. The man whose microcosm failed, and who took an almost vengeful and vindictive attitude to the gods of the grove, now announces the importance of recognizing that everything has its allotted time and space, its boundaries which should not be wilfully transgressed.[34]

One is left with a kind of consolation somewhat different from the one Theseus intends: that neither he, nor anyone else within his society, controls, or even understands, the full significance of space. That is the preserve of a God absent from the Knight's Tale, and perhaps not conspicuously present in Chaucer's England who, we are told at the end of *Troilus*, is 'uncircumscript, and al may circumscribe'. The consolation also has a less theological tendency: that space cannot be appropriated by the politician, the administrator, by male power, because it is adaptable, subject to alternative constructions, of the private, the pious, the female, the heartfelt, which may in turn lead to some redress: to a reappraisal and revision of existing structures and their modes of control and representation. For the final outcome of the crisis is a marriage, that is at once personal and political, between Palamon and Emelye, Athens and Thebes. The political map has been redrawn as Theseus struggles to express an altogether more complex understanding of the principles that govern his politics of space, and of his own incarceration in what he acknowledges to be the 'prisoun of this lyf'.

---

34    Cf. Smith, 'Plague, Panic Space', pp. 393–405.

# 8 Urban Space: The Miller's Tale

> Space is nature's way of preventing everything from happening in the
> same place.[1]

At the end of the Knight's Tale, Theseus appears to reassert his
world-view with vigour and authority. To describe the loving force
that, according to his account, makes for an ordered universe, he
uses the familiar image of a chain of love that connects, separates
and contains a hierarchy of categories. The elements, for example,
must exist 'In certeyn boundes, that they may nat flee' (2993).
Limitations are temporal as well as spatial: 'al that is engendred',
whether human beings, trees or rocks, have their allotted span,
'Over the whiche day they may not pace' (2998). Earthly things are
but fleeting reflections, images, 'speces' (3013), that have no lasting
duration. The progenitor and manager of this order of existence is
a paradoxical figure, a 'Moevere' who is nevertheless 'stable [...]
and eterne' (3004). To refuse patient acceptance of what is
ordained is tantamount to challenging the godhead: 'whoso
gruccheth ought, he dooth folye, / And *rebel* is to hym that al may
gye' (3045–6); it is, to use another loaded word, 'wilfulnesse'
(3057). In terms of the events that have given rise to Theseus'
public meditation, those who have despaired or lost faith or
questioned the meaning of life in the wake of Arcite's death fall
into the category of wilful rebels, for Arcite dies at the allotted
time and in a manner that could have been worse, say in old age
with his prowess forgotten. As it is, according to Theseus, he has
died in an admirable way, 'with duetee and honour' (3060), and in
so doing has escaped the greatest constraint of all, having gone
'Out of this foule prisoun of this lyf' (3061).

1    Dear, 'Postmodern Bloodlines', p. 49

The politics of space in late-fourteenth century Oxford seems a world away from that of ancient Athens, however medievalized the Greek city is in Chaucer's account. From the grandiose, international and cosmic dimensions of the Knight's Tale we move abruptly to the domestic preoccupations of John, a carpenter with a pretty wife and a student lodger. In the event, the business of producing, controlling and contesting space is as problematic in a carpenter's house as it is in a duke's castle. We might have expected as much from the precipitate nature of the Miller's interruption: no sooner has Theseus argued for the inviolate design of neoplatonic hierarchies as the foundation for his own world view than the Miller issues a challenge both to that, and to the decorous progression of the tale-telling, by insisting that he will speak, instead of the Monk, in order to 'quite' the Knight. But the content of his tale does not just have the effect of levelling differences: while pointing to basic similarities between the spatial structures and politics of Athens and Oxford, it also develops a critique of the chivalric scheme by insisting on space as primarily a material and optical, not a symbolic, commodity. Seen from this angle, space enables the expression of sexual allure and the satisfaction of personal desire; but if allowed to become a vehicle for imaginary meanings then the perpetrator is likely to experience a rude shock of disillusionment. In this respect, the Miller's Tale renews the attack on Theseus' spatial principles, but from a social standpoint quite different from the aristocratic milieu within which their shortcomings have already been exposed.[2] Given the Oxford setting of the tale, and the key role of Nicholas the clerk, it is hardly surprising to find that the attack on symbolic space may be construed as a critique levelled from the standpoint of Oxford scholars in pursuit of a *perspectiva* based on empirical, not metaphysical, principles.

As many have noted, the Miller's Tale has a parodic and symbiotic relationship with the preceding tale, and the treatment of space is no exception. Thus the Miller's narrative likewise includes an apparently dominant male, supposedly in charge of the archi-

2    Patterson, *Chaucer and the Subject of History*, ch. 5.

tectural structure that contains his household members. His dwelling sometimes bears a marked resemblance to a prison (3634), especially for Alisoun his wife, whom he holds 'narwe in cage' (3224). Here jealousy is a significant factor (3294), as it was for Palamon and Arcite. John's control of Alisoun and of his house is subverted by two rival lovers, who echo those of the preceding tale, as well as by the connivance of his wife. Again, no less than in the Knight's Tale, the production of space is closely linked to the motives and propensities of the producer, and the political 'game' tends to be won by whoever is most adept at the manipulation of space, who is not necessarily the person nominally in control of it. Nicholas, while fully aware of the symbolic potential of space, uses that knowledge only to misdirect John; Alisoun, devoid of Nicholas's imagination, produces space as it were inadvertently, through the existence of her powerful, sexual aura. In fact it is in her, not John as the supposed controller of domestic space, that all of the male protagonists anchor their spatial structures, whether real or make-believe. The tale thus offers a re-gendering of the predominantly male space found in the Knight's Tale. Again, the physical enjoyment of Alisoun is achieved through quasi-theatrical devices that bear comparison with the directorial energies of Theseus. Given the emphasis on space as a feature of the physical, rather than the mental, world, as a means to an end, the descriptive devices used to suggest space tend to be located in the physical circumstances of the tale: interior rooms, the street outside, sound, Alisoun's body. The transgression of spatial boundaries through apertures, bodily orifices, holes, windows and doors, then becomes a covert way of mocking Theseus' claims to the inviolability of separate spatial categories.

Of course, the transgression that gives rise to all of the others is that of old John in marrying a young wife. To that extent, the Miller's Tale might be considered a grotesque endorsement of Theseus' credo: overstep the prescribed boundaries and – especially for a person of some status and authority (John is a 'riche gnof') – the results will be thoroughly demeaning and salutary. But the tale is not easily reduced to so simple a message, for it also runs against the grain of the Knight's Tale by endorsing the notion that the deliberate – even exuberant – breaking of boundaries is permissible and necessary, as long as the perpetrator knows what he or she is doing. John and Absolon do not, Nicholas mostly does, and Alisoun never puts a foot (or any other part of her anatomy) wrong.

## The Monday Nocturne

The tendency of the Knight's Tale is to represent wilful acts of spatial transgression (unless they are justified by moral right) as disastrous, and Theseus' eventual response to the conundrum of Arcite's death is a reassertion of the sanctity of boundaries, one that well suits his political philosophy. But the Miller's interruption of the Host's measured scheme for a hierarchical sequence of tale-tellers enacts within the pilgrimage framework the very rebelliousness that the Knight deplores. In the Miller's Tale, no boundaries are sacred, and their transgression is comic rather than tragic. The Miller presents an alternative world in which there is much moving and precious little stability, where the restless, dynamic interpenetration of separate spaces is fundamental to its nature.[3] Its difference may be illustrated by an extraordinary sequence of nocturnal sounds and silences that fill the air in the environs of John's house on the fateful Monday (3638–56). First, a few brief words, fully intelligible only to those aware of the situation, are exchanged at Nicholas's instigation. 'Now, *pater noster*, clom!', he says; and to acknowledge the need for quiet John and Alisoun in turn repeat 'Clom!' or 'Hush!' Having thus been instructed by Nicholas, the 'visionary' who has foretold a repeat of Noah's flood, to say his paternoster, John does his 'devocioun', sits still, and prays silently, all the while listening for a sound that will not come, that of the rain. At length, exhausted by the work of making ladders and hauling tubs and provisions into the roof

3    Hertog, *Chaucer's Fabliaux*, pp. 190–3.

beams John, 'for wery bisynesse', falls asleep as the curfew bell
sounds 'or litel moore'.[4] It is replaced by new noises, for in his
deep sleep John 'groneth soore, / And eft he routeth'. Under
cover of these welcome signals, Alisoun and Nicholas creep
silently, 'stalketh' and go 'softe adoun', their respective ladders,
their excitement at the success of the ruse, and their sexual energy,
barely contained. Speech, which might in any case disturb John,
sleeping above their heads, is not necessary: they fully understand
each other's needs and desires, and so quickly, 'Withouten wordes
mo', they climb into the carpenter's bed. There they engage in
'revel', bodily pleasure, play and relief, a 'bisynesse of myrthe and
of solas' that contrasts comically with the serious hard work of the
carpenter that has helped them achieve their aims. Similarly, the
muted sounds of sexual activity, here described as 'melodye',
counterpoint the groans and snores of John. And thus they con-
tinue unabated until the early hours when a second bell rings, the
'belle of laudes', signalling daybreak, and another kind of music
becomes audible: 'freres in the chauncel gonne synge'.

Dialogue – silence – silent prayer – listening for rain – the
curfew bell – John's groaning and snoring – silent descent of the
ladders – sexual harmony – the lauds bell – friars singing – each of
these sounds and silences indicates a stage reached in an accelerat-
ing progress towards the culmination of Nicholas's plot. Together,
they articulate a sequence of chronological events rendered not in
visual terms but (as is appropriate to the gathering darkness) as
auditory and tactile. Yet each sound, act of listening, or silent
movement, originates at a different place and suggests its own,
distinctive space. In the manner of musical notes, one supplants,
mixes with, or replaces another, so indicating not so much a
hierarchy of separate spaces according to the Thesean model, but
an overlaying or intermingling of one with another, in accordance
with the mingling of bodies enjoyed by Absolon and Nicholas.
The scoring of sounds and silences within a rhythm of time (not
unlike the psaltery music that Nicholas plays with such address at

4    Andrew Butcher kindly provided me with a helpful note on curfew bells in
     Canterbury and Oxford.

an earlier moment of sexual arousal and expansiveness) is not merely an extended euphemism for harmonious and joyful sexual union. Rather, the erotic is used metonymically, with the merging of bodily spaces indicating the larger forms of spatial interpenetration that are everywhere apparent, resonant.

## The Manipulations of Nicholas

Some of that more general merging or appropriation of spaces is the result of Nicholas's deliberate agency. Within the passage just discussed he adopts a commanding tone indicative of the authoritative role he has assumed within John's household. He cues the action with 'Now', instructs John in the words he is to utter, and then demands silence. John, entirely persuaded by the ruse of the flood, has ceded his own control of domestic space to his lodger. The effect is to have contained himself in tub of his own contriving while Alisoun and Nicholas usurp the space of his house and even that most intimate of places, his bed.[5] That Nicholas has a well-developed awareness of space as a projection of the individual, and as an instrument of power, is clear from the outset. Self-effacing or 'privee', with an outward angelic appearance that belies his capacity for machinations, he is not easily susceptible to the spatial manipulations of others because, on the face of it, he is himself so difficult to 'read' or position.[6] Instead, his true personality is expressed through the ways in which he ordains, fills and controls the space of his *chambre* – the first place, within the larger dimensions of John's *hostelrye*, that Chaucer describes.[7] Its contents, intrinsically so expressive of the clerk's predilections, are carefully arranged. The room – unusually for an Oxford student at this time – is his alone, occupied by an indi-

5     Kolve, *Chaucer and the Imagery of Narrative*, pp. 211–14.
6     Blodgett, 'Chaucerian *Pryvetee*', pp. 483–4.
7     Kolve, *Chaucer and the Imagery of Narrative*, p. 165.

vidual whose apparently 'sweete' nature (3206, 3219) is caught by
the fragrance of the 'herbes swoote' filling it, although the 'lycorys'
and 'cetewale', a gingery spice, with which his disposition is also
linked, suggest characteristics that are altogether more zestful and
astringent (3205–7). Within the room, a secular treatise on astro-
nomy (Ptolemy's *Almagest*), other books 'great and small', an astro-
labe for calculating the position of the stars, and 'augrym stones',
used for mathematical calculations, that 'layen faire apart', presum-
ably in readiness for use, are all placed on shelves at the head of his
bed (3208–11). Elsewhere is a cupboard covered with a coarse red
cloth, and 'al above' a 'gay sautrie' (3212–13). When Nicholas plays
his psaltery at night the music fills the room as he makes 'melodie
/ So swetely that all the chambre rong' (3214–15).

The neat, well-organized nature of Nicholas's bedchamber
indicates a certain self-consciousness about spatial arrangements.
Its contents, sounds and smell identify it as a three-dimensional
location alive with Nicholas's interests, talents and nature and one
of their remarkable features is a pronounced secular, rational and
pseudo-scientific bias. Nicholas's 'fantasye' is to use the means at
his disposal, the 'interrogaciouns' and 'conclusiouns' of astronomy,
to predict the weather and other events. This in turn entails
plotting configurations of space and time. His adroitness at doing
so is well illustrated by events in the carpenter's house.[8] Thus we
might say that the space Nicholas produces is of an intellectual
kind, 'subtile and ful queynte' (3275), based on knowledge and the
power it confers over other, less knowledgeable individuals, and
over the physical world. It takes the form of a *chambre* that be-
comes the nerve-centre of his operation to dupe John, and its
opening gambit is to use the room *as* a space inhabited by some-
one with access to the arcane knowledge of prophecy, one that has
fallen mysteriously silent (3439). So when Robin, John's servant,
looks 'ful depe' into the room through a cat-hole at the bottom of
the door, he eventually sees in the twilight, as it were in per-
spective, the very image of a learned clerk engulfed in a religious
revelation, gaping upwards:

8     Goodall, '"Alone"'; and his 'Being Alone', pp. 7–10.

And at that hole he looked in ful depe,
And at the laste he hadde of hym a sight.
This Nicholas sat evere capyng upright,
As he had kiked on the newe moone. (3442–5)

The general situation described here, in which a partially
illuminated room with an aperture is used as a kind of laboratory,
or 'camera obscura' to conduct optical experiments, is familiar
from Alhacen. He is fascinated by the 'lights that enter through
holes, slits and doors into dusty chambers',[9] because they provide
opportunities to demonstrate that light travels in straight lines. The
light of the moon or stars is as useful in this respect as daylight or
direct sunlight.[10] In one case the experimenter is enjoined to 'place
one eye at the circumference of the perpendicular hole',[11] and in
other practical demonstrations is required to squint through a
variety of small openings in the walls of darkened rooms in order
to register visual effects (including optical illusions) and make ob-
servations that confirm the tenets of Alhacen's theories (Fig. 8.1).[12]

There is a further context for Nicholas's practices in Peter
Aureol's lectures on the *Sentences* of Peter Lombard (1316–18) in
which he addressed the *species* controversy referred to in Chapter
Six, above.[13] He argued that, since *species* by their nature act as
intermediaries between the object and the eye, there can be no
certainty that the image received by the observer is an identical
replica of the object that generated it. Visual error, far from being
the exception and explicable by reference to 'normal' conditions,
in fact epitomizes the entire visual process. There is thus a key dif-
ference between what appears in the eye and what actually exists.
Aureol underpinned his argument with evidence from after-images,

9     Alhacen, *De aspectibus*, I. 3. [1]; trans. Sabra, p. 13.
10    Ibid., I. 3. [4]; trans. Sabra, p. 14.
11    Ibid., I. 3. [53]; trans. Sabra, p. 31.
12    Cf. Ibid., I. 3. [109]; trans. Sabra, p. 43.
13    The present paragraph is based on Denery, *Seeing and Being Seen*, ch. 4.
      See also Tachau, *Vision and Certitude*, ch. 4; and Smith 'Introduction' to
      *Alhacen's Theory of Visual Perception*, vol. 1, pp. xcvi–xcix.

**Figure 8.1.** Looking into a room through an aperture at an optical illusion. The viewer to the left looks into the room (*domus*) through an aperture (*foramen*) at two walls, set up one behind the other. The text inside the room reads: *Apparet mihi parietes esse coniunctos, et quandoque apparet quod sint unus* ('It looks to me as though the walls are joined, and sometimes it looks as though they are one.'). Alhacen, *De aspectibus,* from Paris, Bibliothèque Nationale MS Lat 7319, f. 63 (detail), late 13th/14th cent. [Bibliothèque nationale de France.]

dreams, mirages, illusions, hallucinations, reflection and refraction – all of which produce apparent images. While conceding that, in most cases, the existing object and its appearance are likely to coincide, that does not contradict the notion that we perceive appearances, not things. It follows that the world of appearances, though usually a faithful register of the objective world, is inherently deceptive and, furthermore, we have no way of knowing if what we see is correct or not. For Aureol, error is not subsidiary but central to the experience of visual perception – a principle which 'hende' Nicholas adroitly exploits.

The gusto with which Nicholas pursues his stratagem, as well as the secular nature of his own enthusiasms, suggest that the symbolic spaces of religion are, for him, signs without substance, to be manipulated and improvised *ad lib* in gleeful pursuit of his own ends. Not so John who, as we shall see below, takes such matters seriously. Knowing that space is individuated, Nicholas readjusts and reconfigures the mechanisms of sexual affection and piety whereby John produces the space of his personal world. He does so first in the manner of a philosopher stunned by a sudden, privileged insight into the workings of 'Goddes privetee', then as a clerk charged with scripting a dramatic narrative (the second Noah play) featuring a carpenter taken from the town guild. Building on John's knowledge of a famous episode in the mystery cycles, the 'sorwe of Noe with his felaweshipe', which featured the legendary intransigence of Noah's wife, Nicholas proceeds to conjure a vivid and appealing scenario (second flood, premonition granted to those favoured by God, salvation by boat), to describe the key spaces (inundated city, John's house, tubs in the beams, the survivors floating out safe and dry), script the dialogue (3577), and instruct John in the building of his set. He is thus a producer of space in the theatrical sense, readjusting the spatial arrangements of the biblical ark to suit the requirements of the revised plot (3538–62).[14] Or, to put it another way, he contrives first an optical illusion (the perspective device) and then links it to a means of duping John's 'inner eye'.

14    Brown, *Chaucer at Work*, pp. 93–5.

# The Narrowness of John

John willingly accedes, becoming an actor on a domestic stage over which he has lost control, playing a double role as latter-day Noah and deceived husband. The extent to which, in spite of his jealous possessiveness, he has in fact lost control of the domestic situation, is indicated by the number of times that, in quick succession, he is 'sent on his way' by his lodger and wife once he has internalized Nicholas's supposed vision. 'Go, God thee speede!' (3592), 'Go now thy wey' (3596), 'Go, save oure lyf' (3600), and 'Go, deere spouse, and help to save oure lyf' (3610) are all imperatives with which John willingly complies, and in doing so witnesses to the fact that he has now become the creature of others' control, bound to do their bidding. That John should prove so susceptible is due in part to the doubleness with which he apprehends space. It is for him as a carpenter at once tangible, physical, defined by material boundaries and objects, and conceptual, regulated by his doting love for Alisoun and by his religious sensibilities.

If Nicholas's defining physical space is his relatively capacious room, through which he exerts control over the rest of the house as if it were the set of a play directed by him, John's defining space is narrow, restricted, and best represented by the tub or kimelin in which he allows himself to be confined. Unlike Nicholas's spaces, which are permeable, interactive and sociable, John's are isolating, anti-social and self-centred. Paradoxically, they are the consequence of social transgression as much as of personal limitation: old John has married a young and attractive wife, whereas (as the Miller reminds us) men should find partners 'after hire estaat' (3229). The result is that John, rather than Alisoun, is 'in the snare' (3231), entrapped by his own behaviour. John's retentiveness and possessiveness are also imaged by the very space over which he believes he exerts control: the 'cage' in which his jealousy confines Alisoun is embodied in the house itself, shown as dark, silent and prison-like on the fateful Monday night when John shuts the doors 'withoute candel-lyght' and 'dressed alle thyng as it sholde be' (3635).

Of course, the space that John produces is affected also by other aspects of his personality. He is a 'sely', as well as an old and jealous, husband, and this conditions the ways in which he responds to the apparent crisis that besets his lodger. He tends to think in stereotypes, and in the most black-and-white of terms, about the dangers of mental exertion. First, it is the silence of Nicholas, the lack of sound from his room, that first arouses, and then sustains, suspicion. The space normally associated with Nicholas, filled as it is with his possessions, sounds and smells, suddenly seems empty, silent. John speculates, without any evidence, that Nicholas might have died (3427) and Robin his knave, who knocks at the student's door like a madman, cannot hear a thing (3439). Thus John becomes aware, 'hath greet merveyle' (3423), that the space in one part of the house has mysteriously changed its nature, though he remains unaware of its true cause.

It is significant that the location of Nicholas's bedchamber, as well as the barrier between it and the rest of the house, is emphasized in order to stress the elevated, separate nature of the intellect that inhabits it, as well as its difference from the mentality of John. Robin is told to go *up* (3431), is described as going *up* (3434), and stands knocking and crying *at* the bedroom door. Having looked *through* the cat-hole, he goes *down* to report what he has seen. Of course, John has a ready explanation for Nicholas's plight, one that moralizes 'up' and 'down' to the student's disadvantage while placing John momentarily in a superior position. He asserts that, in spite of appearances, Nicholas has been brought low by pride, 'falle, with his astromye' (3451) in an attempt to penetrate the forbidden space of 'Goddes pryvetee' (3454). Better the myopia (and complacency) of ignorance, especially that of a 'lewed man' who knows nothing but his creed (3455). As if in proof of John's interpretation, Nicholas's supposed predicament falls neatly into a narrative pattern: John cites the well-known case of 'another clerk' who was so concerned 'to prye / Upon the sterres' in order to knowe the future that he did not look where he was going and so 'was in a marle-pit yfalle' (3460). The same exemplum had been used by Nicholas of Autrecourt (*c.*1330) to assert not the misleading nature of philosophical enquiry, but the deceptiveness of vision.[15] Ironically, it is John who is being led by the nose, who quickly accepts Nicholas's outlandish version of future events, and who suffers a spectacular and painful fall from the height of the beams to the 'celle' of the floor.[16] But for the time being John is confident in decrying high-falutin' intellectual endeavour and in emphasizing the importance of practical, down-to-earth remedies. He calls for a staff, 'that I may underspore / Whil hat thou, Robyn, hevest up the dore' (3465–6). John sees this action as a levering of Nicholas by force out of his intellectual space: 'He shall out of his studiying, as I gesse' (3467).[17]

The practical banality of John's contesting of Nicholas's space is no preparation for the alacrity with which he falls for his lodger's stratagem. For John's practical attitude is yoked to a highly sug-gestible religious imagination. Both of these traits are captured in his contribution to the Monday nocturne. He is exhausted by the day's work, lies awkwardly in his tub, and snores; but he also groans 'for travayl of his spirit'. The nature of John's piety has often been described as superstition, but it may be indicative of a certain kind of religiosity current when Chaucer wrote, and here rendered risible by a clerk whose own religious beliefs appear to be nugatory.[18] In the eyes of some believers, certain meditative practices had the power to transform the everyday into the sacred space of biblical narrative in which the devout could, by force of imagination, become vicariously involved in a re-enactment of, or a witnessing of, key biblical events. It was a form of affective piety essentially dramatic in conception and fed by those same mystery plays on which Nicholas now draws so readily and effectively.

Initially, John thinks that Nicholas is 'in despeir' (3474), a spiritually corrosive form of melancholy, and he favours a prac-tical, physical remedy: he 'hente hym by the sholdres myghtily, / And shook hym harde, and cride spitously' (3475–6). He wants to

15    Denery, *Seeing and Being Seen*, pp. 2–3.
16    Holley, *Chaucer's Measuring Eye*, pp. 95–8.
17    Gallacher, 'Perception and Reality', pp. 41–3.
18    Fletcher, *Preaching, Politics and Poetry*, pp. 239–48; and Vaughan, 'Chaucer's Imaginative One-Day Flood'.

knock some humility into Nicholas, to make him relinquish his presumption in searching out God's 'pryvetee', 'looke adoun', wake up and think on Christ's passion – this to win him back from what appears to him as a state of spiritual truancy. These are not the actions and attitudes of a man who is merely superstitious, though they may be those of a person schooled in a particular kind of popular religious devotion. Even John's next actions – in which he makes the sign of the cross to protect his lodger from 'elves and fro wightes' (3479), recites a night-spell on the 'foure halves' of the house and invokes the 'white pater-noster' and 'Seinte Petres soster' alongside Jesus and St Benedict – may be more mainstream than is usually realized,[19] as he attempts to include Nicholas in a protective space, defined by the outer walls of the house, governed by saints. But the terms that best describe the nature of John's belief are *affecioun, ymagynacioun* and *impressioun* (3611–3), words that express the very lineaments of affective piety as it stirred emotion, provoked vivid images, and altered understanding and sensibility. Within this context, John sees, verifies with his own eyes, the evidence first reported by Robin – that Nicholas has experienced a religious vision. Thus it is that John, made suggestible by his religious proclivities and the visual illusion devised by Nicholas, is encouraged to see in his mind's eye (thanks to Nicholas's brilliant evocation) scenes that are wholly hallucinatory, but no less convincing for that: a second Flood that inundates his domestic space, with real-life protagonists including his own beloved wife in the role of victim. To save her, says Nicholas (appealing as well to his practical side) John will have to make a hole 'an heigh' in the gable on the garden side, over the stable, so that the three of them float free. To this dramatic simulacrum John reacts with a great intensity of emotion: he 'bigynneth quake' (3614) as his imagination takes over and begins to condition his subsequent behaviour. Weeping and sighing in ways not dissimilar to Margery Kempe's expressions of piety in the next century, John too is swept away by fervour: he 'wepeth, weyleth, maketh sory cheere; / He siketh with ful many a sory swough'. Yet the outcome

19   Watson, 'Christian Ideologies', pp. 82–4.

is anticlimactic and banal: 'He gooth and geteth hym a knedyng trogh' (3618–20).

Thus John's religiosity, whatever its context and implications for Chaucer's more immediate audience, is not only exploited by Nicholas (along with the carpenter's practical streak, and his besotted love for Alisoun) – it is also kept firmly in place by being represented as ridiculous, as ultimately a 'fantasye' (3840), an act of self-deception. The same is true of John's behaviour in his tub. In his sleep he 'groneth soore' for 'travaille of his goost', but the suffering of his spirit is debunked both by the bizarre place in which it happens and by a more pointed bathos: the groaning is accompanied by snoring caused by an uncomfortable position – 'eft he routeth, for his hed myslay'. If John's piety is kept within strict limits, or reduced to absurdity, it is also subject to restrictions that John, the maker of compartments, himself creates, or at least accepts – and this in spite of the way in which his brand of piety encourages the crossing of boundaries, through playing roles in biblical pageants. It is as if John has lost control or recognition of boundaries, crossing them inadvertently (in marrying Alisoun, in falling for Nicholas's ruse), or policing them when it is pointless to do so (as in shutting up the cage of his house when Alisoun has, to all intents and purposes, already flown). In this respect he is, again, a parodic version of Theseus who, while he once overestimated the bounds of his power, soon reinstated his belief in the nature of boundaries and their usefulness as articles of faith, policy, control. John, though, all too easily allows himself to be boxed in by spaces of his own making. The tub is a case in point, but he is also ready to swear, no less than three times (3508–12), that he will not betray Nicholas's vision of a new apocalypse which, if only it had wider currency than his own overheated imagination, might have been exposed for the fiction it is.

## Alisoun's Aura

If Nicholas is the knowing breaker of boundaries between spaces
that are at once optical and mental, and John is the victim of
knowing too little about such boundaries and the consequences of
their transgression, where does that leave Alisoun? Is she merely
compliant, or does she too produce a distinctive space? It cannot
be domestic space, for that is John's territory, however inade-
quately controlled. Nor, unlike Nicholas, does she have a desig-
nated room within it. It is certainly not the tub, or any other
containing device, real or figurative, that her husband devises, and
indeed her general restlessness, like that of a colt in a *trave*, or trap,
suggests her impatience with any space of another person's inven-
tion, unless it suits her own purposes. But nor is her distinctive
space found in the world beyond John's house, say in the parish
church, which she visits on 'an haliday', only to return to domes-
ticity. However, there is a clue in the way in which Alisoun readies
herself for such outings: she pays a great deal of attention to her
personal appearance, grooming herself in order to be admired by
washing her forehead until it shines 'as bright as any day' (3310).
Her defining space is, then, her own body, which she prepares and
attires in ways that will attract visual attention.

In fact, Alisoun's body has such a powerful sexual aura that
its effect is felt far and wide – in church, where Absolon pays
special attention to her while 'sensing' the wives of the parish; and
within her house, where John is driven to jealousy and Nicholas to
acts of sexual harassment. She thus magnetizes three men, for
whom she is a lodestar and desired focus both of their eyesight
and daydreams.[20] So much is apparent in the infamous description
of her physical appearance, in which the conventional rhetoric of
female body parts ordered decorously from top to toe is dropped
in favour of a spatial arrangement driven as it were by the
tumescent gaze of the male narrator. Prepositions abound as he
dwells caressingly on her clothes, the pleasures that might lie be-

20    Josipovici, *Touch*, pp. 10–14.

neath, the prospect for sexual intimacy, in ways that make a fetish of the items, their materials and textures: a 'barmclooth [...] / *Upon* hir lendes', 'smok [...] broyden al *bifoore* / And eek *bihynde, on* hir coler *aboute,* / Of col-blak silk, *withinne* and eek *withoute', 'by* hir girdel heeng a purs of lether, / Tasseled with silk and perled with latoun', 'A brooch [...] *upon* hir lowe coler', 'Hir shoes [...] laced *on* hir legges hye' (3235–67).

There is a spatial coherence and assurance to Alisoun's world and her place within it that is not matched even by Nicholas's, for whom space is ambivalent, potentially unstable, in need of conscious, intellectual control. Indeed, the interlocked parts of his invented spaces collapse like stage sets when, dropping the script, he 'ad libs' by imitating Alisoun's action at the shot-window, feels the searing coulter, inadvertently shouts 'Water!', and so causes John to cut loose from the beams and come crashing to the floor. Alisoun though, while accepting and playing with gusto her part within Nicholas's play, does not produce space through the invention of ingenious ploys, but through the instinctive use of her body. She simply *is* Alisoun, she is what men desire to get, restive within her cage, but sure-footed in escaping it, moving with consummate ease through the mesh of male gazes, accommodating with her 'likerous ye' the likes of Nicholas, rejecting with her 'nether ye' the likes of Absolon.

So if we consider the question of who exerts the most effective power over the space of John's household, then Alisoun is a leading contender. It is not just that she is central to the imagined spaces of three men, but that she acts with spontaneous and effective self-assurance in negotiating the spaces within which her admirers seek to contain her. She is beyond John's control, wrests herself from Nicholas's grasp, and deals with Absolon with unforgettable aplomb. In all cases, it is first and foremost her body that is both the desired object of male possession, and the medium through which she demonstrates the superiority of her command of space, a command that is intuitive and immediate, not premeditated as in the cases of all three men.

In any event, her horizons are altogether more undefined and free than the narrow domesticity of John's life, the intellectual complexities of Nicholas's scholastic mentality and the networks of urban society in which Absolon moves. While not ostensibly exceeding such male-dominated boundaries, she nevertheless dominates those spaces from the inside, and extends her influence beyond them.[21] Many commentators have noted, in her portrait, the high density of allusions to the appearance, smells, textures, sounds and tastes of animals, trees and plants. And, like a child of nature, 'wylde and yong' (3225), Alisoun needs open spaces. She may wear a belt, but it is round the waist of a body 'gent and smal' as 'any wezele' (3234). She is as lively and playful 'As any kyde or calf' (3260) and skittish or 'Wynsynge [...] as is a joly colt' (3263). So it is hardly surprising that, initially at least, she resists instinctively the forced transgression of her personal space. When Nicholas, his actions a testimony to the power of her body over men, grabs Alisoun 'by the queynte' (3276) and 'heeld hire harde by the hauchebones' (3279), she springs away like a colt held in a frame to be shod, 'as a colt dooth in the trave / And with hir heed she wryed faste awey' (3282–3).

Alisoun is not to be won by force. Her eventual compliance is entirely voluntary, once she decides to take advantage of the possibility for an erotic adventure as provided by Nicholas. The mutual nature of their affair is indicated by the extent of Alisoun's complicity in the plot to dupe John. She and Nicholas agree on the devising of a trick, the two of them now acting in accordance with each other's desires. By contrast, the would-be pairings of Alisoun with John or Alisoun with Absolon entail some measure of continuing enforcement, coercion or rejection. But the joint objective of Alisoun and Nicholas is to be in each other's bodily space in the most intimate way imaginable, whereby 'She sholde slepen in his arm al nyght' (3406) not merely because Nicholas wishes to, but because Alisoun does too: 'this was his desir and hire also' (3407). To achieve their aims, as well as to further demonstrate the extent of this reciprocity, Alisoun temporarily occupies the 'knowledge space' that is normally the sole preserve of Nicholas. When John, having spoken at length to his visionary lodger, tells Alisoun his 'pryvetee', she is already several steps ahead; 'she was war, and knew it bet than he' (3604). And she dissembles, acting the part that Nicholas has devised, by pretending to be distressed at John's news of an impending disaster: she 'ferde as she wolde deye' (3606).

Of course, the force that has breached Alisoun's personal space is sexual desire – in part that of Nicholas for her, but more especially hers for him. The same force penetrates social boundaries, as shown by John's marriage to a young wife (which also ignores taboo, with near fatal consequences for John), or Alisoun's liaison with an intellectual, or the narrator's own comment at the end of his portrait: she is 'a prymerole, a piggesnye, / For any lord to leggen in his bedde' (3268–9). Conversely, the boundaries between different kinds of social space may be invoked to contain unsanctioned behaviour. Fearing bodily violation by Nicholas, Alisoun threatens to go public: 'Lat be, Nicholas, / Or I wol crie "out, harrow" and "alas"!' (3285–6).

That Alisoun knows where to draw the line, as well as when to cross it, is further shown by her vigilant control of the border of Absolon's space, which meets with hers at the infamous shot-window.[22] First, she sends him on his way – 'Go fro the wyndow, Jakke fool' (3708) – much as she and Nicholas had earlier sent John on his way. On the second occasion, she is more threatening: 'Go forth thy wey, or I wol caste a ston' (3712). On the third occasion she agrees to offer Absolon a kiss in return for his departure, and then proceeds to take complete control of the space he has unadvisedly chosen to enter, even if liminally. Quick-witted, acting fast, she undoes the window 'in haste' (3728), urging speed, as if recognizing that her mode of action will help to create confusion in the drooling Absolon, and conceal the nature of the trick. She returns to imperatives that, this time, Absolon can hardly resist: 'Have do [...] come of, and speed the faste' (3727). Again, she invokes the notion of a 'neighbourhood watch' in order to keep Absolon's behaviour within strict limits. He is to be quick, 'Lest that oure neighebores thee espie' (3729). The joyful moment that

22    Brown, "'Shot Wyndowe'".

follows, Absolon's mouth lingering 'Ful savourly' on 'hir naked ers' (3734–5) is evidence enough that physical volition has outstripped cognition and that, in the independent management of her body space, Alisoun knows no equal.

## Absolon as *Flâneur*

Absolon, by contrast, has no fixed abode, but is forever trying to appropriate, unsuccessfully, the space of others – of John, to become his wife's lover; of Nicholas, if only he were in the student's place; even of Alisoun herself, by dressing so effeminately. In all cases, Absolon misjudges his role and the possibilities of success. If anything his space is outside, beyond the walls of John's house, in the shifting scenes of Oxford life. As we shall see, Absolon's activities link one scene with another, but when he attempts to bridge the gap between street and house he introduces a discordant, interruptive note into the nocturne that, until then, had expressed the interpenetration of personal and public spaces as achieved, evident: Absolon 'cougheth with a semy soun' (3697) at the bower window.

   Absolon is a curiously postmodern creature. He exists as a pastiche of various social roles and attitudes and seems to be made up of fragments of other people's life-styles. His posturing and incessant movement suggest instability, or an inabilty to command a personal sphere that has any real significance or impact (except through pretence and conceit). As if in restless pursuit of himself, or his true identity, he flits from one occupation to another, as parish clerk, surgeon, barber, lawyer, dancer, musician, reveller, ladies' man, actor. He appears to move easily over cultural boundaries, shuttling back and forth from one place to another, glimpsed now here, now there, but he is often in a marginal role, or in the process of entering or leaving, or being directed or steered in a certain direction.[23] For example, he 'Gooth with a sencer', moving in a predatory or feline way among the women of the church (3340, 3346–7), later 'forth he gooth' (3355) to John's house to station himself at the bower wall, and 'rometh' there again on a later occasion (3694), standing 'stille' as if he has reached the limits of his territory, only to be told to 'Go fro the wyndow' by Alisoun (3708). At the same time, he recoils from certain features of bodily boundaries (such as farting) and his speech, which is 'dangerous', standoffish or affected, creates further self-protective barriers. Clearly, Absolon will in practice have more trouble in negotiating the borderland between male and female body space than Nicholas, who has no such inhibitions of deed or word. For all these reasons, one tends to think of Absolon as a peripheral character, whereas in point of fact Chaucer pays more descriptive attention to him than to any other protagonist. Absolon's contribution to the spatial design of the Miller's Tale is of corresponding importance.

Absolon's contradictory urges, to both cross boundaries and keep his distance, are caught in his pseudo-courtly behaviour. He may be keen on 'sensyng' the wives of the parish, but he does so in a place – a church – where he can hardly enact his supposed desires and in a way that expresses a hankering for intimacy, but without physical contact, that is by a kind of looking that apes that of many a lovestruck squire: 'many a lovely look on hem he caste' (3342). Such is the constrained intensity of his ardour for one woman that the habitual functions of religious space are transmogrified into sexual tokens. He refuses an offering from Alisoun because he has 'swich a love-longynge' for her (3349). Of course, the juxtaposition of secular and religious frames of reference is a commonplace of courtly narratives (as we saw in the Knight's Tale), but the extent to which Absolon appropriates the sacred in the service of the erotic is shocking, or perhaps an indication of a marked lack of discrimination, an indication that – unlike his rival, Nicholas – he is unaware of where borders are, of how to strike a

23    On walking as a manipulation of spatial organization, see de Certeau, *Practice of Everyday Life*, ch. 7 (esp. pp. 97–102).

balance between them, and how best to break through those that stand in the way. Thus it is that his language at the shot-window, mixing piety with sensuality, is absurd and incongruous rather than sexually exciting. He calls to Alisoun in terms borrowed from the Song of Songs, a biblical work that is at once erotic and spiritual, but in ways that suggest nothing so much as an infantile craving for oral satisfaction. She is his 'hony-comb' (3698), 'sweete cynamome' (3699), and he longs for her 'as dooth a lamb after the tete' (3704). As the hoped-for culmination approaches, Absolon's religious fervour becomes increasingly indecorous. He asks for a kiss 'For Jhesus love, and for the love of me' (3717). This is a religiosity far more shallow, unthinking and unfeeling than John's.

The mingling of different social spaces through the activities of this individual devoted to 'play', in the sense both of role-playing and recreation (3686), is illustrated not only by his behaviour in the parish church and at the shot-window. He goes also to the abbey of Oseney not for devotions but for pleasure, 'With compaignye, hym to disporte and pleye' (3659), and there speaks by chance to a monk – 'axed upon cas a cloisterer' (3661) – who gives him news of John's activities. In Absolon's world, religion has become secularized as well as sexualized and this, together with his networking abilities, help to sustain his pretensions and reputation as a lover, pretensions of which he is not easily disabused. But they are not those of a romeo confident of success (as Nicholas is) but of one who is in love with love, who fears disappointment, whose real focus is himself (as his appearance and preening demonstrate). He strikes the attitude of the unrequited lover, is 'for love alwey so wo bigon' (3658), and an actual disappointment is less an intimation of personal inadequacy than an affirmation that he is following the hallowed path of many another spurned lover. At Alisoun's second refusal he declares histrionically: 'Allas [...] and weylawey, / That trewe love was evere so yvel biset' (3714–15). Thus he plays the part of a lover, and goes through the motions in a self-admiring way, while at the same time ensuring failure through his chosen mode of enactment. It is a strategy, conscious or not, that further maintains his ambivalent, self-contradictory or marginal status.

Recognizing the extent to which Absolon cannot maintain this precarious state or, to put it another way, recognizing the extent to which Absolon deceives himself, is one of the pleasures of the tale. At one level, it surfaces as ludicrous idiocy, as when he swears to be Alisoun's 'page' (3376), or accuses her of neglect (3701–2), as if his head has been turned, quixotically, by romantic fictions. But it is also evident in his wrong reasoning and wilful misinterpretation of would-be symbols. He hears from the Oseney monk that John has not been seen at the abbey 'Syn Saterday' and so is probably at the 'grange' collecting timber or else 'at his hous' (3664–70). Since Absolon has not seen John 'stirynge / Aboute his dore' (3673–4) all day he concludes (wrongly) that the carpenter must indeed be at the grange and that time is therefore ripe for a tryst at the shot-window. Much as he misconstrues the visual signs he proceeds to misconstrue bodily and psychological symptoms. His itching mouth is taken as a 'signe of kissing' (3683) and his dream – 'Al nyght me mette eek I was at a feeste' (3684) – of an appetite soon to be satisfied. Of course, the premonitions come true, but not in the form of the 'Som maner confort' (3681) that Absolon imagines.

The moment of fulfilled disillusionment is delightful and complex in the extent to which it identifies Absolon as a self-contradictory creature of borders who must, at last, command his own space. The lack of visibility – 'Derk was the nyght as pich, or as the cole' (3731) – is important for the success of Alisoun's trick, but it also concentrates attention on the sense of touch, and texture, and especially on the tactile encounter between the two bodies, one allegedly eager to join with the other in a token of sexual attachment, the other just as determined to deliver a decisive rebuff. Absolon is all anticipation, wiping his mouth, the organ on which so much predilection and fantasy have been focused, 'ful drie' (3730). There is nothing romantic about Alisoun's rejoinder: 'at the wyndow out she putte hir hole' (3732), and as Absolon kisses it 'Ful savourly' (3735) a mesh of intersecting contradictory impulses lies exposed. Absolon, squeamish of body and mouth, has kissed Alisoun's arse; the place to which he was drawn, the shot-window low on John's bower wall, now becomes the place from which he instinctively withdraws: 'Abak he stirte' (3736); as realization dawns, Absolon the romeo becomes Absolon the barber, thinking it 'amys, / For wel he wiste a womman hath no berd' (3736–7); and most of all, Absolon the extravagant poseur as lover of Alisoun is cured of his delusion, 'heeled of his maladie' (3757), vowing now to despise paramours (3758), his nice manners forgotten in an access of rage, biting his lips for anger (3745), wiping them now not in delectation but disgust, trying to cleanse them with whatever comes immediately to hand: 'With dust, with sand, with straw, with clooth, with chippes' (3748), rather than the cardomon and liquorice with which he sweetened his breath before visiting John's house. He is now intent on another reversal, on revenge, a curse for a kiss (3754–7).

Volatile, mercurial, Absolon gets his come-uppance not only on account of his character and demeanour but also because he occupies the wrong space at the wrong time. This is one of his besetting problems throughout the wooing of Alisoun, for Nicholas is 'near' and he is 'far'. His chances of success are therefore remote. The narrator spells out his predicament in the form of a proverb, its air of received wisdom underlining the hopelessness of Absolon's case before the details of the case are laid bare: 'Alwey the nye slye / Maketh the ferre leeve to be looth' (3392–3). Anticipating Absolon's later state of mind, 'wood or wroth', he applies the proverbs to the narrative situation. Absolon is a loser because he is simply too far away, because he cannot readily be seen by Alisoun, and because his rival is nearer, filling her visual frame and blocking the light between her and Absolon: 'By cause that he fer was from hire sight, / This nye Nicholas stood in his light' (3395–6). Thus the spatial design of the narrative, and especially the presence of Nicholas within the household where Alisoun lives, Absolon's restriction to church and street, and the habitual lines of sight which these arrangements enable or prevent, are highly significant for the development of subsequent events. And it hardly helps Absolon's case that Nicholas is *hende*, meaning 'near at hand', and therefore convenient, but also ingenious, or adept at turning a situation to his own advantage. As we have seen, he is a consummate manipulator of domestic space. The result is that, as Absolon reaches his moment of greatest physical intimacy with Alisoun he has never been, as far as she is concerned, further away as an object of sexual or emotional attachment.

Absolon reconfigures his spatial priorities with great alacrity, quickly shrugging off the role of paramour with which he has long been associated. In the process the street outside John's house, with its detritus, and the neighbourhood, with its smithy 'over the strete' (3760), assume a distinctiveness that they have not had before. For Absolon is no longer the *flâneur* and socialite; he has become instead focused, decisive, an interventionist concerned to assert his own dignity and reclaim his self-respect rather than remain the lovelorn fop.[24] The spur is an event so shameful that it reveals in an instant a dominant, if demeaning, trait: he cries like a beaten child (3759). But then he 'grows up', recognizes that he should have 'ybleynt', or turned away, when Alisoun told him to, establishes a more secure grip on the immediate social space, turns his familiarity with it to his advantage, and strikes a triumphant blow that (while intended for Alisoun) is grievously painful and humiliating to Nicholas. The change in Absolon's orientation is marked by alienation from Alisoun, and by anger, but also by a turning inwards – 'to hymself he seyde, "I shal thee quyte"' (3746) – and by a sense that his relationship with Oxford itself is at issue: 'me were levere than al this toun [...] / Of this despit awroken for to be' (3751–2). There is a further indication of Absolon's shifting relationship with it in his encounter with the smithy, Gervays. He goes purposefully, if stealthily, 'A softe paas [...] over the streete' (3760), knocks quietly, gains entrance without trouble, identifies what he needs – 'That hoote kultour in the chymenee heere' (3776) – and leaves quietly resolute 'out at the dore' to return to the 'carpenteris wal' (3786–7). Absolon's change of orientation is marked by his purposeful and practical attitude towards the space he enters. Aware of Absolon's reputation, Gervays suspects that 'Som gay gerl' (3769) is the cause of the parish clerk's chagrin. Little does he suspect that, hot coulter notwithstanding, Absolon's heat in these matters is now entirely 'coold and al yqueynt' (3754).

24    Wilson, 'Invisible *Flâneur*', pp. 61–3.

The Drama of Urban Space

It is at times like this, when an individual is able, largely of his own volition, to renegotiate his relationship to his surroundings, that we realize that urban space is quite different from space dominated in a hierarchical and authoritarian manner by an aristocratic household. In contrast to the Athens of the Knight's Tale, Oxford is made up of a series of social networks, each with its own node or distinctive place, their interlinking allowing individuals to move from one node to another. In the process, they encounter different sets of values, use different strategies for responding to them, and in so doing create identities that may be relatively simple or quite complex and which can be, as in Absolon's case, in a state of change. And they have some room for manoeuvre and choice, that ranges from living compliantly within the existing structure of networks, to challenging some part of it.[25] In the Miller's Tale, the central node is of course John's house – the one place in the narrative with which all of the protagonists are linked. In its environs are the street and smithy, and those shadowy but important figures, the 'neighbours'. Other places exist in a kind of gravitational field around this central locale. Each has distinctive features, affiliations and associates. Reasonably near is the parish church, an outlet for Alisoun and indeed for other women. The university is not seen, but its influence is felt through the presence of Nicholas, his bookish interests and the mention of other clerks. Further afield is the abbey at Oseney, linked to John through his work and associated with 'cloisterers'. Absolon, as we have seen, traverses a circuit defined by John's house, the abbey and the parish church. His role as a link-man and his movements – quick, abruptly curtailed, preplanned or impetuous – do much to weave together the various threads that make up the fabric of Oxford society. Other places, of less significance to the narrative, have a vaguer or more generalized existence: the drinking places Absolon

25  Soja, *Postmodern Geographies*, pp. 149–52; Cf. Strohm, 'Three London Itineraries', pp. 11–15.

frequents, the chancel where the friars sing, the grange that services Oseney abbey, London as a timely destination for John's inconvenient servants.

However disparate its parts, town and hinterland have a unitary existence in which all the nodes are dynamically inter-related and overlaid, as the Monday nocturne suggested. Their interpenetrating takes two main forms, and an intermediary one. The first main form is that of habitual, voluntary, sanctioned actions by individuals moving between two or more nodes. It depends upon the integration of different social spaces. In this category would come the relationship between the carpenter's house and Oseney abbey, as mediated by John, or between his house and the parish church, as mediated by Alisoun. Absolon's mediation of all three places is ambiguous, and falls into the intermediate category. As we have seen, he sexualizes pious space in the parish church, is emphatically refused entry to Alisoun's space, and at Oseney is also marginalized. Absolon makes his enquiry of the monk 'Ful prively' (3662), but his informant 'drough hym apart out of the chirche' (3663) to speak. This manoeuvre may be articulating the difference between what utterances are appropriate to a church (pious ones) and what appropriate to the world outside (gossip), but it certainly demarcates two different kinds of space, in one of which, at least, Absolon has at best a tenuous status. Nicholas's night with Alisoun also falls into the intermediate category. Although the Monday nocturne suggests a momentary equilibrium, post-coital calm and harmony, its ele-ments are fissiparous, and it is not long before cacophony replaces harmony, instigated by Absolon's muted, polite cough, and tapping at the shuttered window.

Paradoxically, the consensual mingling of body space cele-brated at the heart of the poem exists within, and to some extent because of, the third category of spatial relations – unknown or suppressed in Theseus' world – that is contestive and coercive, whose boundaries are wilfully, sometimes cunningly, attacked, transgressed, crossed, with or without the connivance of those in the opposing territory and sometimes without their knowledge. The narrative is full of audacious and exciting moments of penetration: John and his servant break down the door to Nicholas's room; Nicholas (he would have John believe) has peered into God's 'privitee' to foresee a second Flood; Nicholas imagines John breaking out of the gable on his house to float free in his tub, followed by Alisoun and Nicholas; Nicholas joyfully penetrates Alisoun's body; in thrusting her arse out of the shot-window, Alisoun assaults Absolon's bodily boundaries; Absolon violates Nicholas's body with the hot coulter; the neighbours rush in to John's house, formerly so impenetrable.

At such moments, the Miller's Tale presents itself as a theatre of spaces, in which interiors are used to trick John, enjoy Alisoun and exclude Absolon, and exteriors to achieve some redress.[26] But it is also a drama of interactive identities, as mediated and expressed in and by space. We might consider, in conclusion, the melding of interior and exterior at the end of the tale. It is an episode that also concerns the identity of John and the manipulation of social and visual perception. The house remains dark and shuttered, expressive of John's obsessive hold on Alisoun. Unknown to him as he lies snoring, confined to his tub in the beams, his wife has been freed, and has freed herself, of the marital cage of jealousy. With the antics at the shot-window, and especially Nicholas's cry 'for wo' of 'Water!' the integrity of the closed, hushed, house is lost. Once John wakes at Nicholas's shout, his mind turns to the biblical episode that has imaginatively shaped his actions, 'Nowelis Flood'. He sits up, cuts the securing rope with an axe and hurtles the long distance to the floor: 'doun gooth al; he foond neither to selle, / Ne breed ne ale, til he came to the celle / Upon the floor, and ther aswowne he lay' (3821–3).

John's fall, metaphoric as well as literal, is enough to bring him to his senses as the extent of his folly stands revealed – in a word, to engineer a change in his perception of himself, and of his lodger, if not his wife, that would amount to a change or adjustment to his own identity. But it is not to be, at least not in these terms, for the resourceful Nicholas and Alisoun orchestrate an invasion of the neighbours by shouting 'Out!' and 'Harrow!' in the

26  Woods, 'Private and Public Space'.

street. Suddenly the house, previously so closed, private and exclusive, is opened to public view, and with it John's mental state is held up for scrutiny and ridicule. The neighbours run in to 'gauren' on John, 'pale and wan' (3827–8), his arm broken, trying now to stand, but borne down by Nicholas and Alisoun. The neighbours 'laughen at his fantasye' of the Flood, as retold by his lodger and wife. They stare and gape, 'kiken and cape', into the roof, as if to verify the details with their own eyes (3840–1).

No one will listen to John's version of events: 'For what so that this carpenter answerde, / It was for noght; no man his reson herde' (3843–4). Reasonable as his protests may be, he is gainsaid, 'sworn adoun' with 'othes grete', much as he was physically 'bore adoun' by Nicholas and Alisoun. As a result, he is taken for mad throughout the town, 'holde wood in al the toun' (3846). Even the most subtle and influential opinion formers of all, kindred spirits of Nicholas, the fraternal clerks, believe it and openly assert it: 'For every clerk anonright heeld with oother. / They seyde, "The man is wood, my leeve brother"' (3847–8). No matter that what they, and the neighbours, think is not true. They believe it to be true, and so to all intents and purposes it is. What passes for truth in this close-knit world is the generally accepted perception, the reputation, of John as mad. His identity has truly changed, and Nicholas has successfully perpetrated another of his optical illusions.

# 9 Trojan Space: *Troilus and Criseyde* (Part I)

It [the body] is a concrete physical space of flesh and bone, of chemistries and electricities; it is a highly mediated space, a space transformed by cultural interpretations and representations; it is a lived space, a volatile space of conscious and unconscious desires and motivations – a body/self, a subject, an identity: it is, in sum, a social space, a complexity involving the workings of power and knowledge *and* the workings of the body's lived unpredictabilities.[1]

Trojan space melds the psychological space explored by Chaucer in his dream visions, the political and ideological space of aristocratic governance and the intimate space of domestic and sexual activity within an urban setting. But *Troilus* is more than a summation of what the preceding chapters have discussed, for there are other kinds of complexity. One stems from the range of techniques used by Chaucer to create a sense of Troy as a substantial and dynamic, if embattled, society. For example, the spread of rumour and the regard for reputation,[2] or the encircling and menacing presence of sworn enemies, make their own distinctive contributions to the spatial identity of the city, supplementing the careful delineation of rooms, buildings and streets. Then again, within and across the walls of Troy, different kinds of space tessellate – domestic, political, military, sexual, religious – each tending to conflict with the others.[3] Furthermore, there is a network of connections between the spaces within Troy (effected, say, by Pandarus' to-ing and fro-ing) as well as between the physical, emotional and spiritual aspects of the narrative through dreams, prophecy,

---

1    Hooper, 'Bodies, Cities, Texts', quoted in Soja, *Thirdspace*, p. 114.
2    Turner, 'Greater London', pp. 34–5.
3    Foucault, 'Of Other Spaces', p. 22.

prayer and metaphor. Thus a mesh of linking lines itself helps to thicken the spatial distinctiveness of this narrative.[4]

Apart from noting the intricacy and extent of Chaucer's spatial design we should also note an underlying pattern. The spaces mentioned above exist at the beginning of the poem in a relatively disconnected state. By the middle of the poem the experiences of Troilus and Criseyde, and the mediating activities of Pandarus, have effected a synthesis both of previously disparate spaces within Troy and of the emotional, physical and spiritual spheres. With Criseyde's departure there is a gradual, then accelerating, disintegration of that synthesis before Troilus achieves in the afterlife a new understanding of the ways in which parts of his experience relate to the whole. To use Mark Lambert's terms, the movement of the first half of the poems is centripetal, that of the second half centrifugal.[5]

What, in all this, is the place of optical space? As previous chapters have shown, vision is the meeting place of objective stimuli and subjective apprehensions. Thus the gaze is a highly economical and effective way with which to articulate and bridge different kinds of space, and Chaucer gives some prominence to scenes that incorporate key visual events. But we may also detect at the heart of Chaucer's poem a debate about the very nature of optical space. On the one hand is the kind generated in Troy by light, colour and sight – one that is essentially the same as that described by Alhacen as a product of the individual and fraught with error and misconception. In literary terms it is the visual world of Boccaccio. On the other hand is the all-encompassing space described in the closing stanzas of the poem and reflected in Troilus' extraordinary understanding of his past as he sees it from a new perspective in the afterlife. The optical space here is essentially that described by Grosseteste, for whom illumination, in generating space and enabling sight, was the informing principle of God's creation. Its major literary embodiment is Dante.

4    Boitani, *English Medieval Narrative*, pp. 222–3.
5    Lambert, '*Troilus*, Books I-III', pp. 120–1.

In what follows I begin with a discussion of those aspects of Trojan space that are at root abstract and conceptual but which nevertheless impact on the apprehension and structure of physical space: emotion, personal belief and the planetary gods. I then consider the city of Troy as the place which holds these and other types of space in tension. The final subsection deals with the interplay between architectural and subjective 'interiors'. The following chapter continues the analysis of *Troilus* by looking at the connections between different kinds of space, the forces of disintegration, the function of the gaze and the contribution made by optical theory to the spatial themes of the narrative.

## Emotion and Personal Belief

Space in *Troilus* is malleable and permeable: it is a mental and emotional construct as much as a physical circumstance; it carries symbolic meaning; and it has metaphysical implications. The interplay between subjective and objective worlds in turn invokes a wider and more public frame of reference – the belief space of Trojan culture.

It is not just a case of recognizing that heaven is skywards and hell under ground – rather that the story of Troilus and Criseyde is contained within a larger narrative whose protagonists are the gods, working in their own ways to determine events on earth. Troilus and Criseyde, as well as other members of their society, are deeply implicated in an invisible drama which profoundly affects their ability to control their own spaces: these have already been pre-empted, as it were, by the likes of Juno and Mars. Of course, the Trojans have a well-developed religious consciousness and are well aware of their place within the larger scheme of things. Some – members of the priestly caste like Calkas and Cassandra – claim special knowledge of the patterning of future events; others, such as Pandarus, try to take advantage of the ways in which heavenly

influences work for or against human intentions; yet others of a
more pious inclination, like Troilus, are even more acutely aware of
the ways in which the stars, or ideas of heaven and hell, impinge
on the thoughts, feelings and actions of daily life and attempt
through prayer to communicate with, or even negotiate with, the
higher powers. In various ways, then, decision, choice, action,
imagination, are conditioned by a sense of the spaces that lie
beyond immediate perception.

As an initial example we might take the experience of Troilus
when, full of foreboding about Criseyde's departure (even though
she has been gone for just one day), he dreams that he is alone in
a horrible place, or in an alien space, 'amonges alle / His enemys'
(V. 251–2). Wrenched awake with a sudden start, feeling a tremor
about his heart and quaking for fear, in a semiconscious state he
seemes to be falling 'depe' from high above before entering the
grim waking reality of his room and weeping. The dream might be
adequately explained in psychological terms as imaging the sudden
change in his emotional condition, with intimations of worse to
come: bereft of Criseyde, he fears falling out of her favour, losing
his high place in her affections. But, by this stage in the narrative,
high ('o-lofte') and low (or 'depe') have accumulated other sym-
bolic freight. As is well known, Fortune, the executive officer of
the fate determined by the gods, is traditionally represented as a
blind woman turning a wheel on which are positioned individuals
in various stages of ascent and decline. Those at the bottom fall off
into the murky depths below. So at one level Troilus' dream is
registering his changed position on Fortune's ever-moving wheel
as it turns, dislodging him from its zenith. There is forewarning of
this process, and of the callousness of Fortune's behaviour, at the
beginning of the previous book: 'whan a wight is from hire whiel
ythrowe, / Than laugheth she' (IV. 6–7). It is now Diomede's turn
to be 'sette up' by Fortune on her wheel (IV. 11). Troilus, for his
part, is well aware of the irresistible force controlling his life, and
in despair asks Fortune why, in spite of his efforts to honour her,
she should so mistreat him as to make him 'out of honour falle /
Into miserie' (IV. 271–2).

What Troilus falls into from the nadir of Fortune's wheel is the misery of a personal hell, and here again the mythography of a pagan hades interacts with Troilus' sense of spatial dislocation. The narrator reports that, once Criseyde is resolved to leave Troy, it is impossible to imagine, understand or describe the cruel pains then endured by Troilus 'That passen every torment down in helle' (IV. 1698). Traditionally a place of division and pain, his hell is also a place of isolation: he writes to Criseyde 'youre absence is an helle' (V. 1396). His experience is virtually indistinguishable from its mythic counterpart. Once Troilus returns from surrendering Criseyde he takes to his bed 'and walwith ther and torneth / In furie, as doth he Ixion in helle' (V. 211–12). So the physical contortions of Troilus, which are an expression of the emotional pain he suffers, mimic those of Ixion, whose punishment in hell was to be lashed to a turning wheel. The reference just anticipates Troilus' dream of falling, helping to focus its allusiveness both on falling down into hell, and on the turning of Fortune's own wheel. Troilus, it seems, is rapidly losing control to produce and control space according to his own physical and emotional imperatives.

In *Troilus*, hell is not just a useful myth pillaged for imagery that represents psychological states; it is a real enough place in the mindsets of Trojans and Greeks alike.[6] Diomede describes with some relish the vengeance that the Greeks will wreak on their enemies, claiming it will surpass and shame the tortures known to the gods of the lower world, the Manes, who are responsible for inflicting retribution as the pains of hell (V. 890–6). Earlier, Troilus himself alludes to the topography of the underworld in describing its river of fire – 'Flegitoun, the fery flood of helle' (III. 1600) – from which, figuratively speaking, Pandarus has rescued Troilus by enabling him to enjoy Criseyde. Criseyde, too, knows about hell. The place at which she stops listening to the bloody story of Thebes, marked appropriately by 'thise letters rede', is, somewhat ominously, where Amphiorax 'fil thorugh the grounde to helle' (II. 105). She, like Troilus, comes to know something of such a fall

6    Barney, 'Troilus Bound', pp. 456–7; and Windeatt, 'Chaucer and the *Filostrato*', pp. 171–3.

when it takes the form of a sudden emotional void opening up as if the ground were about to swallow her. Once her exchange for Antenor has become generally known, she is visited by her female friends, who try to comfort her. She weeps, but not for the reason they adduce – rather because of the 'bittre peyne' endured by her spirit as she remembers 'fro heven into which helle / She fallen was' since she last saw Troilus (IV. 712–3). Later, she declares that her eternal dwelling-place should be 'Stix, the put of helle' (IV. 1540) – although Styx is another river of hell, rather than a pit – if she should ever be faithless to Troilus. But Criseyde is no Alceste, even if Troilus would think her so as he defends her against Cassandra's prophecy of her betrayal: Alceste's fidelity was such that she chose to die and go to hell in order to save her husband's life (V. 1527–33). Troilus has his own model for enduring the afterlife, declaring to Pandarus that Criseyde's 'darte' is so embedded in his soul that it will be there for ever, even beyond death, when he will 'down with Proserpyne [...] wone in pyne', eternally complaining of their 'twynned state' (IV. 473–6) – separation and exile being conditions that Proserpine, the queen of hell, herself endured.

What of heaven? Like hell, it is known to the living imaginatively and intellectually through legends and myths; or intuitively and vicariously through intense emotion. But whatever their intimations of the afterlife, Troilus and Criseyde are aware of heaven and hell as spaces both physical and metaphysical to be entered by their spirits at the moment of death. After her female comforters have left, Criseyde again recalls a myth in order to counteract the unpleasant realities of her new existence. She and Troilus may be separating, but she bequeathes 'Myn herte and ek the woful goost therinne' to complain eternally with Troilus' spirit so that they should 'nevere twynne' but be together without pain 'in the feld of pite [...] / That highte Elisos', like Orpheus and Eurydice (IV. 785–91). Elysium would seem an appropriate destination for someone whose face, soon to look cadaverous, was 'lik of Paradys the ymage' (IV. 864). When Troilus mistakenly believes her to be dead, he prepares to follow so that his spirit might be with her either in heaven or hell, 'low or hye' (IV. 1199). She wakes just in time to prevent his suicide, but her own body has been hovering on the brink of extinction, her spirit on the verge of transition from body to afterlife, 'alwey o poynt to pace' (IV. 1153) and only just induced to return to her 'woful herte' by Troilus as it 'flikered ay o-lofte' between this world and the next (IV. 1219–22).

Of course, Troilus' own spirit soon becomes fully aware of the nature of the heavenly afterlife. At death he is freed from bodily encumbrance and misery as a 'lighte goost' going blissfully through a universe characterized by its vast spaciousness and capacity to contain. Chaucer is here drawing on a complex set of models that include the apotheosis of Arcita in the *Teseida* (XI. 1–3) and Dante's vision from paradise of the 'little threshing-floor' that constitutes our world (*Par.* XXXI. 133–59), as well as episodes in Macrobius and Boethius.[7] Moving vertically through the elemental spheres that surround the terrestrial globe, Troilus reaches the 'holoughnesse of the eighthe spere' where he enjoys complete comprehension, 'ful avysement', of the heavens, both by seeing the 'erratik steres' and by hearing the sound of celestial melodies (V. 1807–13). His ability to register the space around him, and its distinguishing features, by sensory means, is thus not impaired by death – rather it is perfected, as it had been for Dante, and from his vantage-point, with the benefit of his new percipience, he realizes a new and radically different relationship between earth and heaven. Earth, not hell, is now 'down' and, viewed from above, it is relatively insignificant, a 'litel spot' surrounded by sea, a wretched place of vanity compared with the pure happiness he now knows 'in hevene above'. Narrowing his focus yet more, Troilus 'lokyng down' sees the very place where he was slain. The *contemptus mundi* theme now extends even to those who weep copiously for his death: Troilus laughs at their woe, damning all 'blynde lust' that is motivated by the fleeting satisfactions of lives that will not recognize the necessity to 'al oure herte on heven caste'. The insight over, Troilus' spirit journeys to his due place within the heavens, accompanied by the divine guide of souls: 'forth he wente [...] / Ther as Mercurye sorted hym to dwelle' (V. 1826–7).

7    Boitani, 'What Dante Meant', pp. 127–30.

Before concluding the poem, however, Chaucer draws out the analogy with Christian structures of belief. No less than Troilus, 'yonge, fresshe folkes' should despise worldly vanity and transient values and focus upwards on as god that looks like them: 'of youre herte up casteth the visage / To thilke God that after his ymage / Yow made' (V. 1838–40). The allusion to an elevated god whose image is that of a human being would perhaps have recalled the figure of Christ on the cross that appeared as an object of devotion on the raised rood screens of medieval churches – the more so when Chaucer refers in the next stanza to 'hym the which that right for love / Upon a crois oure soules for to beye / First starf' (V. 1842–4). And he directs his audience's eyes yet further upwards, for Christ also, like Troilus, 'roos and sit in heuen above'.

## The Planetary Gods

Whatever one might think of Chaucer's attempt to infiltrate a pagan story with Christian ideas, there is no escaping the importance he attaches to religious mindsets. Spiritual attitudes are fundamental to the way in which his characters see and interpret the physical world. If there are indeed spaces which the spirit enters beyond death, then the spaces of the present world are correspondingly provisional, contingent and deceptive, at best a model for a higher reality. Such presumptions underlie the attitudes of service and fidelity adopted by Troilus and Criseyde towards the gods that exert most influence on their lives (or so they think). To some extent, Troilus' loyalties are divided between war and love which, given the tempestuous liaison of Venus and Mars, may go some way towards explaining why he can effect only a temporary reconciliation between these two contradictory forces. As he draws ever closer to intimacy with Criseyde he faces the challenge of excelling both as a military hero (thereby winning Criseyde's admiration and respect) and as a lover. Thus 'By day, he was in Martes heigh servyse' but at night he lies considering 'how that he myghte serve / His lady best' (III. 437–41). In the latter case, Troilus' service readily translates into devotion to Venus, whom he places at the pinnacle of the pantheon he addresses just prior to entering Criseyde's bedchamber, asking that she should inspire him 'As wys as I the serve, / And evere bet and bet shal, til I sterve' (III. 713–14).

Criseyde, for her part, later acknowledges the significant effect that Venus has in guiding and shaping their relationship. She asks the goddess not to let her die before she has acquitted herself well in proving worthy of Troilus' love (IV. 1661–3). Spoken just before they go their separate ways, and in less fervent tones than those used by Troilus, her words sound relatively hollow, as if she is aware that there are forces other than those governed by Venus that will determine the outcome of events. Subsequently faced with the emotionally harrowing consequences of Criseyde's departure, Troilus too develops a more ambiguous attitude towards the erotic influences that have been shaping his life. He appears exasperated at what the service of Venus actually entails: abject subservience, unquestioning devotion, pain, humiliation, fear of betrayal. Acknowledging that he has been attacked ('wereyed') by love on all sides, he declares that it is pointless for Cupid to desire victory because he, Troilus, is already in thrall: 'I am thyn and holly at thi wille' (V. 587). Internecine strife is irrelevant and Troilus, having felt the dreadful anger of an aggrieved and mighty god, pleads for mercy, vowing 'lyve and dye I wol in thy byleve' if only Cupid will send Criseyde soon – that is, exert his power to reanimate the deserted spaces from which Troilus feels so alienated.

This is not mere piety, nor the projection of religious aspirations on to purely imaginary constructs. In Troy, the power of the gods is a fact of existence: from their separate but linked domain they direct human events and control both space and time. For Troilus' anxiety about Cupid's vindictiveness is well-founded: the god's violent intervention at the temple of Palladion comes in direct and immediate response to Troilus' professed contempt for lovers. The knight's self-congratulatory glance, and pleasure in his own rhetoric of denigration, provokes in its turn a contemptuous and angry glare, and a desire for revenge: 'the God of Love gan loken rowe / Right for despit, and shop for to ben wroken' (I. 206–7). Without further ado he hits his victim full square with one of his legendary arrows. Thus Troilus' life is instantaneously changed: he is stopped in his tracks, transfixed by the sight of Criseyde, and the temple in which he had been freely roaming suddenly narrows to the distance that separates them and which he now yearns to bridge.

Familiar as they may be with the sometimes painful principles according to which the gods operate, Troilus and Criseyde tend to be more aware of the power of Cupid and Venus, and less so of the influence wielded by other gods – even though their power to reconfigure space is even more impressive and extensive. Thus Calkas reminds the Greeks that fire will transform Troy to 'asshen dede' because Phoebus and Neptune, who made the walls of the city, have not received recompense from King Laomedon. They too are angry and bent on revenge (IV. 113–26). Troilus wrestles with the notion that human events, such as his loss of Criseyde, are not just the effects of a sequence of causes but are fated to happen by pre-ordained patterns. He attributes this process to 'forsight of divine perveyaunce', the superior perception of a god who arranges outcomes in advance according to the merits of the case: 'God seeth every thyng [...] / And hem disponyth [...] / In hire merites' (IV. 963–5). The result of such speculation is not resignation to the benign governance of an inscrutable deity but rather despair and helplessness, as when Troilus, falsely believing Criseyde to be dead, and wrongly interpreting the pattern of events, berates Jove: 'Fy on youre myght and werkes so dyverse!' (IV. 1195), vowing to perpetuate his union with Criseyde by committing suicide rather than accept separation by divine dictat.

There is no avoiding the fraught relationship between these two worlds whose spaces and narratives interpenetrate: the one superior, mysterious, vengeful, all-powerful, divine, independent; the other inferior, subject, timebound, dependent, mortal, rebellious. Gradually and inexorably the workings of destiny assert their presence behind and beyond human intentions and desires. It is a process to which Chaucer's audience is itself privy, knowing in advance the dénouement of the Trojan story and privileged also in its access to the inner recesses of Troilus' and Criseyde's feelings and beliefs. The latter are put severely to the test by the 'fatal destyne' that Jove has 'in disposicioun' and which spells the re-positioning of Criseyde in the Greek camp and enduring pain for the abandoned Troilus: 'Criseyde moste out of the town, / And Troilus shal dwellen forth in pyne' (V. 5–6). The turn of events, his melancholy and worrying dreams, exert a baleful effect until Troilus becomes convinced that he is close to death. He perceives a confirmatory sign – the recurrent shrieking of an owl – that he is about to make the transition from one world for another and so calls on Mercury to fetch and guide him (V. 316–22).

Similarly, in Criseyde's case, the veil between the human world and that of the planetary gods becomes more translucent and she also seems to lose some of her own volition to become caught up in the subtle mechanisms of stellar influence. After Diomede's second visit, as Criseyde's affections change, the pro-cess is figured by movements from one space to another that are both celestial and terrestrial. Chaucer describes in delicate terms the approach of nightfall: Venus as evening star appears just as the sun, Phoebus, sets; the moon prepares to rise in Leo and the others stars of the zodiac, here called Signifer, become visible. The dance-like sequence is both natural and inevitable, and in this soft, inviting, crepuscular atmosphere it seems pointless for Criseyde to resist the tendencies of her emotions. The extent to which she is involved in, or responds to, prevailing conditions, is caught in her own movement into her father's brightly lit tent, which mirrors the appearance and movements of the stars: 'Signifer his candels sheweth brighte / Whan that Criseyde unto hire bedde wente / Inwith hire fadres faire brighte tente' (V. 1020–2). It is as if one space has been completely subsumed by the other.

## The Contested City

The preceding two sections have identified some of the features of subjective space in *Troilus and Criseyde*: the expansion and contraction of emotion, the ascent and descent of religious aspiration. In doing so, it has proved impossible to divorce subjective space from physical space. The distance across which Troilus desires Criseyde is an outward manifestation of inner intentions, and the visible presence of the planets provides a focus for thoughts directed at the gods. In effect emotion and belief represent two spatial extremes: on the one hand the all-encompassing space of the heavens, on the other the world of the lovers contracted to the span of a bed or a heart. The larger contains the smaller but so do other, intermediary, worlds such as the political and the military. Indeed, it is possible to represent the power structure of the poem according to the design of that Ptolemaic universe through which Troilus moves at the end of the poem. Beyond its outer rim is the Christian god, below that the planetary gods, then the realm of military events, then one of politics, then a sexual world, then a personal one. Each sphere, we might say, has a controlling or decisive intelligence, such as Pandarus in the sexual sphere, Christ in the Christian or Hector in the military. Each sphere exerts influence over those below it, and is in turn affected by those above. Such a model – which Chaucer encourages his audience to consider – is helpful in a number of ways. First, it accentuates the extent to which the most intimate of private, internal spaces – precisely because they are small and 'at the centre' – are suffused by the complex effects of larger spheres of influence. Second, it highlights the ways in which certain individuals are defined and restricted by the sphere in which they move. Finally, by way of contrast, it reveals the extraordinary nature of Troilus' life and death: in different ways and at different times he knows all of these levels of experience (with the exception of the Christian) at first hand, and also recognizes that such a structure does exist.

However, the model has shortcomings as an account of spa-
tial design. By being a conceptual schema of the force-fields that
govern events in Troy, it pays scant attention to the details and cir-
cumstances of key events; it is an over-generalized account of
power and influence (for example, it can not easily accommodate
domestic space); it is a hierarchical arrangement of forces that in
practice act in ways anything but deferential towards each other; it
suggests too readily a 'trickle down' process of cause and effect
when in practice the causes of particular events are complex and,
to those most involved, often inscrutable; it represents space as a
contingency of human experience that is finally transcended; and it
appears to differentiate between different kinds of space. The last
point is the crux of the matter. As far as the narrative is concerned,
there is only one spatial medium in which everyone and every-
thing, from hell to heaven, from Troilus to Phoebus, exist. Indeed,
the very pervasiveness of three-dimensional space is one means
whereby the essential continuity of the human and divine is estab-
lished. True, the narrative space of *Troilus* is subdivided such that
different areas have different functions and uses – areas marked
by stars, or man-made boundaries – but there are no absolute
divisions: there is always the possibility of crossing from one space
to another. Furthermore, there is a chronic instability in those
spaces that do exist as well-defined areas: they are subject to
counter-claims, to competing interests. Similar observations might
be made of the space of a number of Chaucer's narratives, but his
Trojan story incorporates a set of interlocked circumstances that
makes the whole issue of spatial control both fraught and promi-
nent: the gods' vow to secure the destruction of the city; its state
of siege; the wooing of Criseyde. Each circumstance has Troy as
its focus of interest and so it is the city, and not a nest of spheres,
that models more adequately the spatial complexity of the narr-
ative; Troy is the theatre where the drama of space is enacted.[8]
    A rough classification of the different kinds of space within
Troy yields a number of varieties: emotional, religious, political,
military, domestic, sexual, social, private, public. Each is super-

8    Cf. Zumthor, *Mesure du monde*, pp. 111–41.

imposed upon the other, and sometimes the categories coalesce, but on other occasions they vie with each other for prominence. So although these categories may, at any one time, appear to be in equilibrium, the potential for conflict is ever-present. Given the prevailing conditions – divine hostility, siege, love affair – crises are inevitable. Specific examples of contested space come readily to mind: the lovers railing against the light of 'cruel day' as it intrudes in their chamber and signals the end of their night of joy (III. 1688–1701); the violent and bloody skirmish that makes the Trojans flee back to their city (IV. 43–9); Calkas' claim over Criseyde, entailing her departure from Troy, a claim buttressed by the prediction that 'fire and flaumbe' will soon turn the city to 'asshen dede' (IV. 106–19); the public clamour against Hector's resistance to the exchange of Criseyde for Antenor (IV. 176–96) and Troilus' extreme reaction to the news (IV. 218–43); the demands of political responsibility, curtailing Pandarus' 'libertee' and freedom of movement when he needs to succour Troilus (V. 281–7).

Contested space is registered at the personal level as emotional disruption, alienation, threat and coercion. 'Smoky reyn' closes in on the night Pandarus succeeds in contriving Criseyde's stay at his house – a rain that produces 'verray feere' on the part of Criseyde and her women (III. 624–30). Calkas later asserts that the Greeks' control of Trojan space is well-nigh complete: their enemies are 'fetered in prisoun' (IV. 106). When Criseyde registers the full impact of her impending separation from Troilus she feels keenly both woe and 'hire constreynte' (IV. 741). Troilus for his part knows the constraint of forced trust as he reluctantly accepts her departure and, against his better judgement, agrees to believe in her return: 'he gan his herte wreste / To trusten hire' (III. 1427–8). As soon as they hear news of the parliament's decision, he and Criseyde endure sharp alienation from their surroundings and even Pandarus registers a sense of dislocation: Criesyde's 'wo-bygon' appearance is so extreme that he can hardly bear to stay in their house, 'As he that pite felt on every syde' (IV. 824). A far cry, this, from his ebullient entry into Criseyde's space at the start of Book Two. But on second thoughts that earlier scene does contain the seeds of Criseyde's desolation: he disrupts the communal reading, in a paved parlour, of the story of the siege of Thebes; disturbs Criseyde's equanimity with news of Troilus' interest in her; and causes her in defence (even if only in play) to imagine a different kind of existence in a different kind of space – as a religious recluse in a cave, reading saints' lives rather than romances.

The forms in which various agencies produce, inhabit and contest space are often architectural and topographical, and so the drama of space within Troy is enacted at a series of locations that combine to create the impression of a multi-functional city striated with personal and public fault-lines. The locations are themselves carefully differentiated and often depicted with considerable detail – details that reflect Chaucer's close familiarity with the appearance and workings of that new Troy where he lived, while offering his audience imagined spaces with which they could readily identify. For example, there are distinct areas for religious activity, for ritual acts of celebration, propitiation and prayer, which are further embodiments of the belief space of Trojan culture. At the temple of Palladion religious practice has become social event, and the devotional purposes of the occasion seem obscure as Troilus and his followers move through the crowd, he looking now here, now there. Yet the temple does become a site of sudden conversion once Cupid acts, and for that reason it is sanctified in his mind as the place where he first saw Criseyde, standing still, alone, behind other people, in her own space, 'in litel brede', near a door – as if to indicate her propensity for leaving options open.

## The Topography of Troy

What helps to establish Troy as a coherent city with a distinctive topography is the notion of there being contiguous exterior space, which in turn suggests a continuum beyond the walls of a single house. Buildings are clustered, abut streets, have outsides as well as interiors. Streets are particularly important in providing a sense of continuity between one part of Troy and another and one part of the narrative and another. The street down which Troilus rides in desolation at Criseyde's departure is the one from which, in happier times, Criseyde hears a tumultuous shout, then sees from her window Troilus ride in victory from the gate of Dardanus en route to his own palace while her own household members rush out to join in the public spectacle. Visible from her window, across the street, is another house, to which Pandarus draws attention by asking Criseyde who lives there (his real motive being to direct her gaze into the street in which Troilus is shortly to appear for a second time).[9]

The streets of Troy are social arteries that enable the coming and going to houses, to parliament, to temples, the visiting, meetings, forays and returns that characterize life in the city, but the city is also given identity by the river Symois, running straight 'as an arwe clere' down to the sea (IV. 1548). Streets and river are crossed by the encircling, protective and gated battlements of Troy, the 'walles of the towne' on which Troilus and Pandarus await Criseyde's return and where Troilus puts his head out over the parapet in order to see better (V. 1145). A warden guards the nearby gate and at dusk he calls in the people outside who are grazing their animals (V. 1177–80). Dotted over the landscapes are the hedges, trees and groves that Troilus scans eagerly for signs of movement. In the same direction lies the 'valeye fer with-oute' where he bids adieu to Criseyde and reluctantly delivers her into the hands of Diomede. Visible yet further is the Greek 'oost' and its tents (V. 667), from which on one occasion a consoling breeze blows to soothe the deserted Troilus (V. 673–9). Among the temporary structures of the Greek encampment the 'tent of Calkas' is the chief focus of interest (cf. V. 841–7). From there Criseyde can see Troy all of a piece, with its 'toures heigh and ek the halles' (V. 730). From an even wider perspective, Troilus sees that the contested space of Troy is itself bordered by that same sea into which the river Symois flows, across which the Greeks have journeyed. In some respects Chaucer provides a cartography of the city such that

9    Camille, 'Signs of the City', p. 27.

its position and prominent features, as if marked in relief, are
mapped to help understand the physical geography of the narrative
and the scale of its setting: thus the Greek camp is a half-day's ride
from Troy, Sarpedoun's house a mile from Troilus' palace.[10]

What makes the map precious and poignant is that it records
the nature and existence of a city that no longer exists, but which
embodied for Chaucer's audience the foundational myth of Lon-
don itself.[11] Chaucer was representing an originary past, decked out
in contemporary dress, architecture, military strategy and mores, at
the very moment when that point of origin was about to be
effaced. Yet without the fall of Troy there would have been no
voyage of Aeneas, no founding of Rome, no Brutus, no Britain,
no Troynovaunt. The ambiguity of the Trojan past contributes
to the bitter-sweet flavour to the narrative: for his audience the
destruction of that city on which their own was supposedly
modelled was a necessary disaster as well as an admonition. In
*Troilus and Criseyde* the precarious nature of urban space is accentu-
ated through references to a siege that threatens not only its walls,
streets and buildings but also the very fabric of its culture: its
citizens, institutions and ideals. The siege, and its known outcome,
produce within the protagonists a self-consciousness about the
identity of Troy, about its destiny, about the meaning of the spaces
contained within its walls[12] – a meaning which changes with the
fortunes of war: peace provides liberty of movement and freedom
of communication as enjoyed by bees flying to and from a hive (IV.
1352–8). That Troy will be destroyed is axiomatic, so the dwindling
spaces of Troilus' life, the premature desolation he perceives, are
indicative of a wider and more complex civic devastation soon to
follow. Such ideas would have been particularly resonant in the
aftermath of the 1381 invasion of London – an event characterized
by Chaucer's friend, John Gower, as the fall of 'new Troy'.[13]

---

10    Klassen, *Chaucer on Love*, pp. 177–8.
11    Zumthor, 'Espace de la cité', pp. 23–4.
12    Cf. Steinberg, '"We Do Usen Here No Wommen for to Selle"', pp. 261–5.
13    Gower, *Vox Clamantis*, I. 13; ed. Macaulay, trans. Stockton. Cf. Federico,
      'Fourteenth-Century Erotics of Politics', revised in her *New Troy*, ch. 1.

Criseyde's departure is itself predicated on the fall of the city: that is what her father has foreseen, and why he now wants her domiciled in the Greek camp. The sense of impending doom intensifies in the closing books. The narrator begins the fourth by reminding his audience of the firm grasp in which the Greeks now hold the Trojans, 'Liggyng in oost [...] stronge aboute Troie town' (IV. 29–30). Troilus is aware that Calkas' prophecy has become Greek propaganda and virtually an article of faith, one that is likely to influence even Criseyde herself: Calkas will tell her that 'this cite nys but lorn, / And that th'assege nevere shal aryse', for which reason the Greeks have sworn to maintain it 'Til we be slayn and down oure walles torn' (IV. 1479–82) – an outcome of which Diomede is in little doubt (V. 904–10). Later, bemoaning his fate to Pandarus, Troilus' version of his own ending is curiously similar to that of Troy as he envisages the loss of identity that comes with annihilation and the chief organ of inner space, the heart, reduced to 'poudre' in an urn after the 'fir and flaumbe' of his funeral pyre, in which 'my body brennen shal to glede' (V. 302–15).

## Interiors

As well as being a tangible setting for the unfolding tragedy, the city also exists as an idea in the minds of its residents, as evidenced by linguistic usage. The effect is to strengthen the bonds that unite the protagonists to the city and its distinctive spaces, for they speak as if familiar with them. It is a place invested with value, visible on all sides: Pandarus claims that he would not bring a harmful letter to Criseyde 'for the citee which that stondeth yon-dre' (II. 1146) and Troilus prepares to leave it 'in wo' as he readies himself for suicide (IV. 1205). Troilus alludes to the sacred spaces of the city when he vows to Pandarus that, if necessary, he will swear on all the gods 'in all the temples of this town' not to betray to others his liaison with Criseyde (III. 383). The siege is ever-

present as a condition making Troy's continued existence precar-
ious, though it seems not to trouble Pandarus unduly when he
playfully suggests that his house might be undermined before
Criseyde's women would wake up (III. 767). For him, it is also a
place of varied social experiences, 'ful of lordes al aboute' (V. 400),
any one of whom might provide a diversion for Troilus during
Criseyde's absence. Thus the way in which Troy is internalized,
and represented, varies with each individual. The wily Diomede
knows that the very process of internalizing will have to stop if he
is to win Criseyde. For her, Troy and Troilus are inextricably
linked, and in view of the unavoidable 'jupartie' Troy now faces he
recommends 'Lat Troie and Troian fro youre herte pace!' (V. 912).

   This will be no easy matter, for city and siege are embedded in
the very metaphors with which Criseyde and others describe their
experiences. Criseyde, ever anxious about the progress of the war,
calls Hector 'the townes wal' (II. 154). As she begins to fall for
Troilus his 'manhod and his pyne' cause love to mine her heart (II.
676–7). Subsequently the same force 'opned hire the gate' to joy (III.
469). Troilus, in turn, becomes to her 'a wal / Of stiel and sheld
from every displesaunce' (III. 479–80) but not before he has over-
come a debilitating moment when his intensity of feeling is such
that he swoons, his feelings having 'fled [...] out of towne' (III.
1091). Once news of her departure breaks, Pandarus thinks that no
one ever saw 'ruyne / Straunger than this' (IV. 387–8) and, as
noted above, it brings Troilus to the brink of ashen annihilation.[14]

   While the spaces of Troy may be internalized through meta-
phor, there is also a broader, complex rapport, or interactive rela-
tionship, between person and architectural surroundings.[15] Cris-
eyde enters one of the smallest spaces of her palace, a *closet*, in
order to be alone and 't'avise hire bettre' in responding to Troilus'
letter (II. 1215), yet the outcome is not further personal enclosure
or greater constraint or self-control but a developing sense of
openness and liberation: 'she 'gan hir herte unfettre / Out of
desdaynes prison' (II. 1216–17). In outlining his plan for meeting

14    Sprung, 'Townes Wal', pp. 135–8.
15    Cf. Lambert, '*Troilus*, Books I–III, p. 120.

Criseyde at the house of Deiphebus, Pandarus appeals to Troilus' 'verray hertes privetee' (II. 1397) as if there were a basic congruity between it and the private space of the *chaumbre* in which they speak. When Troilus finally accepts that Criseyde can not 'dwelle' in Troy, it triggers an extreme and violent inner dislocation – 'his soule out of his herte rente' (IV. 1700) – that is reflected in his own abrupt departure: 'Withouten more out of the chaumbre he wente' (IV. 1701). This movement is expressive not only of Troilus' despair but also of his crossing the threshold of one phase of his personal narrative as he enters another: he is leaving 'interiors', a *chaumbre* that is the place of sexual and emotional warmth and intimacy, and will henceforth be on the outside of Criseyde's life. Troilus' disorientation is caught in his abject behaviour within his own *chaumbre*, clutching at air once Criseyde has departed. The night before he lay in her arms, but now he weeps alone, obliged to 'graspe aboute', finding 'in this place [...] naught t'enbrace' but a pillow (V. 223–24). Even the city itself becomes an image of exclusion, isolation and separation, its walls a seemingly insurmountable barrier to the retrieval of Criseyde. As the warden of the gate calls the herdsmen 'withoute the yates' to drive their beasts into the darkening city, or stay outside for the night, so too Troilus is driven yet further inwards into his dark misery: 'And fer withinne the nyght, with many a teere, / This Troilus gan homward for to ride' (V. 1181–2).

The more complex the space, the more complex the competing claims on it, and nowhere is this more true than in the case of domestic space, which is the dominant setting for much of the narrative. There are no fewer than four significant and substantial households: those of Criseyde, Pandarus, Troilus and Deiphebus. Each is subdivided such that different actions can be located within different rooms and open spaces.[16] Criseyde's palace has a first-floor *chambre* with a window and, near it, a cedar tree (II. 919); a *closet* with a seat and window opening on to the street; paved *parlour*, *hall* with steps down to a sizeable garden, furnished with

16   Smyser, 'Domestic Background'. Cf. Barron, 'Centres of Conspicuous Consumption'.

wide, sanded walkways that are railed and shaded, and benches (II. 818–23); and gates (presumably from a courtyard) that open on to the street. Pandarus' house has a *closet, myddel chambre, my chambre, outer hous, stewe* with window (III. 601) and trapdoor (III. 759), *goter,* and *pryve wente* (III. 787). Of Troilus' palace we learn little other than it has a *chambre* containing a bed but with room for a guest to sleep on a *paillet* (III. 229). The house of Deiphebus, however, is more fully described: there is a place to dine, a small *chambre* containing the bed that Troilus uses (II. 1646), a staircase down to an *erber grene,* and a *grete chaumbre.*

Some of these domestic spaces have highly specific and restricted applications, such as the *goter, pryve wente* and *stewe* by which Troilus gains access to Criseyde in Pandarus' *closet.* Others are more flexible, more open to a variety of related uses. The *chaumbre,* for example, is repeatedly a place of retreat, of freedom from public scrutiny, a place to sit and rest, but also one marked by an intensification of subjective and sexual experiences, of privacy, of introspection and reconsideration, of recent events; it can be a place of private conversation (V. 512–16) or abject abandonment to prevailing emotions (IV. 729–34, V. 197–205) – a kind of safety-valve that in Troilus' case can lead to bedridden inertia (II. 1305–7). Closets provide an even smaller space where the personalized atmosphere of the *chaumbre* is further intensified by solitude and personal reflection. Thus Troilus, at last alone, retreats to his *chaumbre* after his life-changing experience at the temple of Palladion and meditates in his mind's eye on the image of Criseyde. Criseyde withdraws to her *closet* to sit 'stylle as any ston' and consider the pros and cons of Pandarus' news (II. 598–609), or to concentrate singlemindedly on writing a letter to Troilus. Pandarus provides a *closet* for her first night with Troilus.

As in the case of the temples, the private space of the household is, on closer inspection, multifunctional, a site for competing claims and, indeed, the very place where the conflicts inherent in the production of space are most keenly felt by those enmeshed in them. Thus Criseyde, alone in her *closet,* tries to evaluate the relative merits of maintaining her independence and surrendering to Troilus. Troilus, alone in his *chaumbre,* cannot reconcile his desire for physical intimacy with the politics of separation. On such occasions, the intensity of his soul-searching is akin to that of the temple, and so domestic space is appropriated, as it were, as an outlet for religious *Angst*. Similarly, during the episode at the house of Deiphebus, there is a sustained tension (engineered by Pandarus) between the political domain – the influential friends of Deiphebus are rallying to Criseyde's defence against the supposed slanders of Poliphete – and the sexual: the whole device is a cover to bring Troilus and Criseyde together in the same bedchamber.

The last example illustrates a further level of complication. We have already seen that domestic space has affinities with subjective experience and psychological states; and that it is partitioned into connecting rooms, such as the *chaumbre*, which are multi-functional and therefore contested spaces. In addition, domestic space generally, and especially the more accessible and shared variety, is highly deceptive to the untutored eye. Thus Helen, Deiphebus, Hector and Criseyde, dining together at Deiphebus' house, have been hoodwinked into thinking that Troilus lies alone in his host's *chaumbre* because he is unwell; the women who visit Criseyde to commiserate over her departure sit with her sociably, unaware that her crying is on account of her separation not from Troy, but from Troilus; Criseyde believes that she and her women are staying overnight at Pandarus' house to shelter from the rain; and so on. In such circumstances, those privy to the subplot may seek more private spaces, such as a garden (II. 1114), or *chaumbre*, or they may resort to whispering, say in the convivial space of a hall, where meals are served, and where there is a good chance of being overheard. Alternatively, decorum and unspoken codes of discretion may prompt others 'fer awey to stonde' to enable a private conversation (II. 216). On one occasion, the complicity of Pandarus and Criseyde in the secrets of the night, secrets concealed by the artful manipulation of interior spaces, gives rise to a jocular exchange between them (III. 1555–68), but the abiding impression is of a domestic space that is undependable, fraught with danger and insecurity, however protective its walls might appear. Deiphebus, safe in his own house, helps the progress of Trolius' love affair 'unwiste of it hymselve' (II. 1399), thanks to the manipulations of Pandarus.

If Troilus is relatively passive and ineffectual in the manipulation of spaces bounded by architecture, Pandarus is a past master. Not for nothing does the narrator invoke 'Janus, god of entree', the two-faced guardian of doors, as Pandarus embarks on his mission to win Criseyde's heart. From the outset his schemes depend upon the manoeuvring of people in and out of rooms: he promises Troilus that he will 'come into a certeyn place' where he will be able to plead with Criseyde (II. 1364). That place is a *chaumbre* in the house of Deiphebus, which Pandarus appropriates as, to all intents and purposes, a stage-set, paying attention, as a theatrical producer would, to the plotting, timing, blocking, scripting and acting of a supposedly ill Troilus (II. 1513–35). Unknown to others who gather at Deiphebus' house, they perform their own roles to perfection, guided and cued by Pandarus (II. 1716–29).[17]

The episode is a kind of rehearsal for the *coup de théâtre* he creates at his own house.[18] There, having persuaded Criseyde and her women to shelter overnight from the heavy rain, he appears to invent on the spur of the moment a bright idea as to where she should sleep: 'By god, right in my litel closet yonder' where she will not be disturbed by the noise of the rain or thunder (III. 663). Showing her the layout of the sleeping arrangements, and reassuring her as to security, he observes that her women will sleep 'in this myddel chambre that ye se [...] wel and softe' (III. 666–7). He himself has guaranteed their collective safety as 'wardein of youre wommen everichone' by announcing his intention to sleep 'nat [...] far asonder [...] in that outer house allone' (III. 660–5). Once the guests have retired – Criseyde in the closet, her women within calling distance just outside its open door, 'at this closet dore withoute / Right overthwart' (III. 684–5) – anyone still stirring is told to go to bed. But if there is no more skipping or tramping about for other members of the household (nomore to skippen nor to traunce', V. 690) it is just the time for Pandarus

17 Turner, *'Troilus and Criseyde'*, pp. 248–53.
18 Brody, 'Making a Play'.

ngage in 'Th'olde daunce' (V. 695) in which he is such an
ert. He unpins the door to the *stuwe* in which Troilus waits and
ches in secret, and enters it to encourage him in his enterprise,
fore undoing a trapdoor that leads into Criseyde's room. For-
nately, the wind roars so violently that no one can hear any other
oise, and so Criseyde's women sleep soundly. Nevertheless,
Pandarus takes the precaution of shutting 'softely' (III. 749) the
connecting door between them and the closet. As he returns
'pryvely', or stealthily, Criseyde awakes in a fright, asking 'Who
goth there?' (V. 752). It is hardly surprising that she is taken aback
to see Troilus and Pandarus appearing in her room out of thin air;
she asks: 'which wey be ye comen, benedicite?' (III. 757).

Pandarus may be highly skilled in managing the people and
domestic spaces of this world, but he is not so good at perceiving
the extent to which they are interpenetrated by those of the other.
Troilus is more sensitive to such contingencies, as is shown in their
debate on the meaning of dreams (V. 316–85). Criseyde, for her
part, does not have the religious proclivities of Troilus, nor the
means to control a range of spaces (her own included) in the man-
ner of Pandarus. Her forte is to make the most of the situations in
which she finds herself, and to that extent her production of space
may be termed diplomatic, although its horizons are limited to her
immediate acquaintances and family. For example, she becomes
active in negotiating with Troilus the whys and wherefores of her
departure from Troy, taking the initiative by calling a halt to their
lamentations (IV. 1254–60). Again, the scenarios she sketches for
her return tend to depend upon a judgement about the possibility
of peace, or the manipulation of her father's difficult position as a
traitor in the Greek camp who still has extensive connections with
Troy (IV. 1390–3). In the event, Criseyde is unwilling or unable to
act, and so fails to turn her changed circumstances to the kind of
advantage she describes to Troilus, opting instead – if gradually – to
make the most of Diomede's overtures. Thus, her account of being
reunited with Troilus turns out to be one of those 'fantasies' of the
sort she accuses him of harbouring in imagining that she will never
return (V. 1615).

# 10 The 'covered quality of things': *Troilus* (Part II)

the centres of our fate [are located in] the spaces of our intimacy.[1]

The previous chapter identified some of the components of Troy's spatial identity. The present chapter continues that discussion by examining how those components are linked to create a coherent model of social space, first through the agency of Pandarus and then by means of the gaze – the most subtle, effective and pervasive instrument in bridging the distance between subjective experience and the objective world. To an unusual extent it is Troilus who registers both the diversity of the components that constitute the spatial world of Troy and the possibility of their being connected in a unified whole. But, given the volatile political and military situation that world is fragile and insecure, and his awareness of integration is replaced by an acute sense of fragmentation and alienation once Criseyde leaves Troy. His experience in turn indicates that *Troilus and Criseyde* incorporates, and is to some extent driven by, a profound and sustained meditation on the nature of optical space. Its terms and concepts are as determined by Boccaccio and Dante, Alhacen and Grosseteste – on the one hand a visual world in which objects, visual fields, distance and others are perceived and interpreted (sometimes mistakenly) by means of certain psychological processes; on the other hand a visual world in which such matters are at best an index of the principles according to which God – himself co-extensive with universal space – operates in human affairs.

1    Bachelard, *Poetics of Space*, p. 28.

# Links and Networks

Pandarus is adept at crossing thresholds, and at enabling others to do so. His activities also make him, quite literally, a go-between, as he traverses the space between one place and another. In his to-ing and fro-ing he travels twice from his own house to Criseyde's palace, once from there to Troilus' palace, once from Troilus' palace to the house of Deiphebus, and four times to Troilus' palace either from his own house or from the parliament. His journeys are more distinct and deliberate in the first half of the poem than the second, but collectively they are highly effective in conveying an impression of Troy not just as a topographical entity but also as an integrated yet diverse social unit.

Chaucer accentuates the speed and directness of Pandarus' earlier journeys, as if joining with straight lines the key places, plotting the distances between them. This may be a reflection of Pandarus' own philosophy of planning, culled by Chaucer from Geoffrey of Vinsauf.[2] Appropriately enough for this manipulator of interiors, the analogy is with building a house. It requires forethought, patience, a sense of timing, a close coupling of intention and effect: the successful builder of 'plots' will 'bide a stounde, / And sende his hertes line out fro withinne / Aldirfirst his purpos for to wynne' (I. 1067–9). Furthermore, there are various ways of achieving the same end, according to the predilections of different individuals. As the narrator remarks elsewhere: 'every wight which that to Rome wente / Halt nat o path, or alwey o manere' (II. 36–7). Once his mind is made up, Pandarus' style is direct and decisive: having first calculated, 'caste', the favourable disposition of those crucial lines of influence stemming from the moon, he 'took his way ful soone / Unto his neces palays ther biside' (II. 75–6). Thereafter, the groundplan of Pandarus' design gradually becomes evident as he himself develops the lines of connection between Troilus and Criseyde.

2    McGerr, 'Medieval Concepts of Literary Closure', pp. 168–9.

At Criseyde's palace, the burden of his song concerns the way in which narrative, however subtle its art, has as its 'entencioun' a certain ending (II. 258) – in this case, Troilus' desire for Criseyde – and the perception of this 'goodly aventure' (281) in her personal destiny. In other words, he gradually outlines the sequence of intention, cause and effect in which Criseyde is to play her part. For Troilus, too, the progress of the affair is mapped in linear terms as a series of paced events (1349). As the pace of events quickens, so the speed and directness of Pandarus' mediation increase. With his plan for Deiphebus' dinner party beginning to materialize he moves without stopping from one place to another, linking them in a web of deceit as he catches the moment of opportunity. Having persuaded Deiphebus of the urgency of the case he goes without stopping – 'took his leve, and nevere gan to fyne' (1460) – directly to his niece's house, as 'streyght as lyne' (1461). Once there he turns his evident speed – 'O verray God, so have I ronne!' (1464) – to his advantage, using it as an indicator of the crisis that allegedly faces her as the victim of Poliphete's supposed slanders. From there he goes to visit Troilus – 'up anon [...] and forth gan for to wende'– who, by contrast, is 'stille as ston', awaiting the outcome (1492–4). Pandarus here seems to be imparting energy, galvanizing the inert lover or the domesticated Criseyde, who has just risen from table, with a new kind of motivating focus and concern. His energy is contagious, infecting even the narrator, who wants to flee 'prolixitee' and go straight to the outcome: 'faste go / Right to th'effect, withouten tales mo' (1565–6)

As events gather momentum, Pandarus moves ever more frequently between the lovers, ready ('prest') and 'diligent' as he 'shof ay on' and 'to and fro was sent' (III. 485–7), urging them to a place and time of culmination. By developing secret but dependable lines of communication he is also establishing a sense of security such that Criseyde eventually has few qualms about receiving Troilus, given his 'prive comyng and the siker place' (921). Nevertheless, she confesses herself in a dilemma, 'At dulcarnoun' (933), about how to act. This is not such an insurmountable problem for Pandarus, who has applied himself diligently to the conundrum of bringing the lovers together in the same bed.

*Dulcarnoun* is, after all, a geometrical problem expressed in the shape of a two-horned pattern of intersecting lines, as devised by Euclid. It is a diagrammatic analogy of the lines Pandarus has been drawing between various points in Troy as a way of solving the puzzle of how best to bring Troilus and Criseyde together in the same bed – a puzzle he is about to solve.

Thereafter, the structure he has so laboriously put into place becomes less prominent. Now fully serviceable, it is activated as and when necessary. Eventually, another great plotter of lines of influence, cause and effect, Calkas, disrupts and fractures Pandarus' schema with his own solution to where Criseyde should be. While no dynamic go-between, Calkas also acts decisively and directly when the conjunction of events and auspices makes it appropriate to do so. He urges the exchange 'ful soone', 'ful ofte', and the ambassadors go to Troy 'streight' (IV. 135–40). His is the more powerful network because of his authority as a priest whose plans are laid with all the force of astrology and prophecy behind them. As Pandarus himself knows, Troilus and Criseyde's amorous connections, seemingly so secure, hang by a thread, the 'wire' of worldly joy that all too often breaks.


## The Gaze


The plotting of Pandarus exploits lines of connection between people and places in Troy; his movements back and forth, and those of others, establish a complex network of links; news, talk, and letters help to sustain social interchange; subliminal events, birdsong, prophecy, dreams, prayer and direct action from on high identify channels of communication between this world and that of the gods. Chaucer thereby builds up a dense mesh of interconnections that does much to give substance to Troy, its inhabitants' place within it, and the events both human and divine in which they are involved. But of all the lines that link person to

person, and person to place, that of the gaze is by far the most
subtle.[3] Another kind of 'hertes line', connecting the innermost
recesses of the individual with the surrounding world, it crosses
effortlessly (but often with emotional consequence) the bodily
border between objective appearance and subjective experience.[4]
Considered for its contribution to the spatial design of the nar-
rative, the gaze is a special case, for not only is it a link connecting
one bodily object with another, it is also constitutive *of* space. In
the act of looking the observer registers the presence of space,
measured especially as distance between eye and object, but also as
a visual field, and his or her place within it. Indeed it might be
argued that the gaze is the most powerful and effective spatial link
of all, being both intimate and instrumental, able to penetrate the
heart of another, or span great distances. It is a bridge-building
device common to all human participants. At the same time there
are great variations in how individuals see, what they think they
see, and how they interpret what they think they see. Vision is also
a kind of net that collects images to project on to the screen of
memory. Finally, we may note that although the gaze is under the
control of the individual, it also works in an involuntary way, can
be distracted, and can be manipulated by others, including the likes
of the gods, and Pandarus.

The scene Chaucer models to drive the rest of the narrative
follows Boccaccio (*Filostrato* I. 18–28) and has as its armature a
mesh of gazes.[5] As Troilus leads his young knights up and down in
the 'large temple on every side' (I. 185) his gaze is indiscriminate,
darting hither and yon, 'Byholding ay the ladies of the town, /
Now here, now there' (186–7) because his affection is not fixed on
any one in particular. He then takes delight in watching, 'gan to
wayten', for lovelorn behaviour in any members of his company,
one sign of which is visual fixation, were one to 'lete his eighen
baiten / On any womman that he koude espye' (190–3). Such

3   Stanbury, 'Voyeur and the Private Life'.
4   Windeatt, 'Gesture in Chaucer', pp. 146–53.
5   Stanbury, 'Lover's Gaze', pp. 229–3; and her 'Visualizing', pp. 474–7. Cf
    Burrow, *Gestures and Looks*, pp. 126–30.

obsession, likely to be disdained by the woman in question, Troilus dismisses contemptuously as foolishness and a loss of discernment: 'O veray fooles, nyce and blynde be ye' (202). The look of conceit and self-admiration that follows as he raises his eyebrow – 'he gan caste up the browe, / Ascaunces, "Loo!, is this naught wisely spoken?"' (204–5) – inadvertently attracts the attention and wrath of the god of Love, who 'gan loken rowe', and unleashes an arrow at Troilus, the arrow being traditionally (though not explicitly here) indicative of the transfixing of a lover's gaze, the image of its object of admiration entering through the eye to lodge in the heart. Now it is Troilus who is revealed as 'blynde' in the pride he has displayed, thinking himself impervious to love. And it is a gaze that is to humble him: 'with a look his herte wex a-fere' (229).

For the time being, Troilus continues his aimless 'lokynge', glancing indiscriminately at this lady or at that, no matter whether she be from Troy or not. Then, as it were by chance, 'upon cas', his gaze pierces a crowd of people and penetrates a long way until it meets the figure of Criseyde, and stops: 'thorugh a route / His eye percede, and so depe it wente, / Til on Criseyde it smot, and ther it stente' (I. 271–3). Troilus is astonished, stopped in his tracks, and begins to look more carefully: 'gan hir bet biholde in thrifty wise' (275). The emotional supercharge is tremendous, his heart spreading and rising as he sighs, softly, and attempts to conceal his discomfiture. In a trice he has become one of the lovers he formerly despised, fascinated by what he sees, and not least by Criseyde's way of looking at him as he had looked when he raised his eyebrow – 'Ascaunces' – as if she now says '"may I nat stonden here?"' (292), although her expression soon brightens.

Criseyde's overall 'look', which includes both her way of looking and her general appearance, prompts such desire and 'affeccioun' in Troilus that he vividly internalizes her image, which 'in his herte botme gan to stiken', not unlike an arrow, but one that imprints 'Of his his fixe and depe impressioun' (I. 297–8). So affected is Troilus that he now hardly knows where to direct his gaze, 'Unnethes wiste he how to loke or wynke' (301). The transformation in the nature of Troilus' gaze could not be greater: formerly random and presumptuous as he 'poured up and doun'

(299) it is now focused, careful and self-effacing. What he has discovered is the affective power of lines of sight, having been 'unwar that Love hadde his dwellynge / Withinne the subtile stremes of hir yen' (304–5). Such is the impact of Criseyde's gaze that he thinks he feels the spirit in his heart die 'Right with hire look' (307). He is now incapable of doing more than stand still 'to biholde', keep silent and from a distance – in order to retain the appearance of composure – sometimes 'On other thing his look [...] caste' but always reverting to Criseyde, 'eft on hire' (314–15). The service over, he returns to his palace devastated by the sight of Criseyde, 'Right with hire look thorugh-shoten and thorugh-darted' (325), again recalling the effects of Cupid's arrow, and as if in anticipation of the figure with helm 'tohewen' and shield 'todasshed' and embedded with 'many an arwe' penetrating 'horn and nerf and rynde' (II. 638–42) when Criseyde gazes at Troilus passing through the street beneath her window.

The temple scene is a virtuoso display of the ways in which sight lines and space interact. The sheer variety of terms used to denote the act of vision – *byholding, wayten, baiten, espye, loken, percede, smote, wynke, poured, caste* – itself signals that there is here a close attention to different kinds of gaze, their uses and effects, especially as embodied in Troilus' behaviour. His casual, impertinent glances give way to a single stare in which his eye seems to be emitting a powerful ray that is weapon-like in its capacity to pierce and strike. Paradoxically, in finding its target in the figure of Criseyde, Troilus' own eyes are made vulnerable to her looks, to the extent that he surrenders his easy domination of the space of the temple and now stands subservient to Criseyde in a space defined by her presence, by his visual access to her in the form of repeated, furtive glances, darted in her direction, and by her looking at him. This reconfiguration of space, brought about by a realignment of Troilus' gaze, is marked by contraction and intensification. The significant space is no longer primarily the 'large temple' but a corridor of exchanged looks within it; and at the same time there is a tremendous increase in the affective content of the scene. Also, as Troilus discovers once he leaves the 'service', the spatialized event rapidly assumes a deep associative and personal value as a unique conjunction: it becomes that person with that appearance in that place at that time. When, eventually, he and Criseyde enjoy the intimacy of sexual love, Troilus can hardly believe his eyes, and pays tribute to Criseyde's, those 'humble nettes' that first ensnared him (III. 1355).

## The Parts and the Whole

Troilus' sight of Criseyde reveals his former smugness as a false consciousness. Then, he appeared sure of his opinions about love and was secure in his social demeanour; afterwards, he is acutely aware of his need for Criseyde, the distance that separates them, the division between his private torment and public face. Not until Criseyde is won does Troilus rid himself of his sense of alienation, or feel fully integrated with her, his inner self and society at large – an integration he identifies as a truer consciousness than any he has known before. With Criseyde's departure, Troilus experiences a fragmentation of the elements that, all too briefly, constituted his new-found world. It is only after death that his spirit achieves, once more, an even fuller awareness of the ways in which the parts of his experience relate to the whole.

Criseyde is more pragmatic, able to adjust to a particular set of circumstances allowed by fate, not to be so anxious about the larger picture. Whereas Troilus experiences with a shock a sudden dislocation of inner space, in which he idolizes Criseyde, and outer space, in which he is devoid of her, Criseyde is already aware of the disjunction between her subjective self and her public identity as the daughter of a traitor. She manages the interface between these two orders of existence much more successfully than does Troilus, eliding or negotiating their differences subtly and practically, as occasion demands or allows. Thus Troilus' worlds of inner and outer are much more likely to polarize, Criseyde's more likely to find an accommodation.

Judged from Troilus' point of view, the earlier part of the narrative is centripetal as he tends towards his 'lode-sterre' (V. 232), Criseyde; the later part of his life is centrifugal, as her loss disorientates him, producing extreme behaviour and an over-whelming sense of alienation and division as the wholeness of his experience becomes atomized and dismembered. The terms in which Troilus' personal trajectory is represented are spatial, and indeed his sense of space, and of belonging, varies according to the condition in which he finds himself. His progress, or regress, takes full account of the larger spatial elements of the narrative, and the lines that connect them, but – once plunged into crisis – many of those links become fragile, brittle and broken.

It is Pandarus who points out the perils of fragmentation: it has a disabling effect on the achievement of such goals as the winning of Criseyde, for 'he that departed is in everi place / Is nowher hol' (I. 960–1). As we have seen, Pandarus' project is to unite the disparate spaces of Troy as a framework for Troilus' union with Criseyde. He does so within the context of a society that is itself factionalized – a factor he turns to his advantage at the house of Deiphebus where, for the first time, he brings Troilus and Criseyde together in the same small room. There, Criseyde agrees to receive Troilus into her service, promising him that she will not hold back in bestowing gladness upon him, and so healing him of his disorder: 'Now beth al hool' (III. 168).

The wholeness that Troilus eventually knows is unusually complete in that it incorporates physical, emotional and transcendent features. In the aftermath of the episode at Deiphebus' house, and in anticipation of even better things to come, Troilus' soul fills with 'joie or feste', chasing out the 'olde wo' that made his heart quail, a misery that is now diminished and reduced to nothing, 'for joie wasten and tomelte, his grievous sighs 'fledde' His soul too is 'ful of joie' as if responding to a burgeoning May after a dead and dry winter (III. 344–57). When the moment comes to embrace Criseyde, the fulfilling act of holding her – 'He hire in armes faste to hym hente' (1187) – and the sheer joy of touching her, release a prayer to love that is all about connectedness: 'thow holy bond of thynges' (1261). As previously mentioned, Troilus

feels that he has found his place within a larger scheme of things –
'me bistowed in so heigh a place' (1271) – a scheme of love that is
extremely capacious: 'thilke boundes may no blisse pace' (1273).
The feelings of integration and expansiveness are so intense that
he is transported to another level of reality, and is hardly able to
believe his eyes or feelings: 'may it be / That it be soth, that ye ben
in this place?' (1347–8). Criseyde kisses him in confirmation, but
'where his spirit was, for joie he nyste' (1351).

However transported his spirit may be, both lovers are at
pains to assert the extent to which they have achieved a complete-
ness of physical and emotional union, and both want to preserve
and repeat the experience of intimacy. For Criseyde, Troilus is 'so
depe in-with my herte grave' that she will be unable to forget him,
and she asks Troilus not to let any 'fantasie' creep into his brain,
but keep her 'as faste in mynde / As I have yow' (III. 1503–7). For
her own part, she encloses, 'shette', Troilus' qualities, and her
recollection of their meeting, in her heart as if it were a room
(1548–51). When next they meet, they again express physically
their mutual desire to give what the other needs: 'ech of hem gan
otheres lust obeye' (1690).

Troilus' sense of being at one with Criseyde, 'Whos I am al
[...] / And that I thus am hires' (III. 1607–8), develops into a more
general awareness of being at one with the universe itself. This
sensation he describes as a 'newe qualitee' (1654), which he is at
first unable to define, but which he later identifies as part and
parcel of the cosmic scheme. It has a social dimension, too, and
finds expression in extrovert activities, in his full and harmonious
integration with the public sphere. Leading a life 'In suffisuance, in
blisse, and in singynges' he 'spendeth, jousteth, maketh festeynges;
/ He yeveth frely ofte, and chaungeth wede', surrounding himself
with the 'fresshest and the beste' people he can find (1716–22).
Such behaviour in turn enlarges his reputation, which reaches even
to the skies: 'swich a vois of hym was and a stevene, / Thorugh-
out the world, of honour and largesse, / That it up rong unto the
yate of hevene' (1723–5). This is the outer manifestation of his
inner condition of 'gladness' by means of which his personal and
social space are dilated. And there is now continuity between his

inner state and its outer expression such that he enjoys a state of 'ese' (1728) after his long period of distress.

As if to signal his novel state of connectedness, Troilus takes Pandarus by the hand, and leads him into his garden to explain in a Boethian hymn that his new-found liberation, and insight into the integrating nature of love at personal, social and universal levels, paradoxically depends upon constraint, on mutually accepted restrictions. For love is a kind of 'governaunce' with its own laws, capable of joining people together 'with an holsom alliaunce' – quite unlike the prevailing relationship of Greeks and Trojans – knitting together 'lawe of compaignye' and making couples dwell in virtue. Love even constrains the elements, restricting (say) the sea in its capacity to flood the land; and if love did not, letting go 'his bridel', then the result would be sudden fragmentation, disunity: 'Al that now loveth asondre sholde lepe' (III. 1763). Similarly god the creator, 'auctour [...] of kynde', ensures that love circles and binds the human heart, so that there is no escape from its encompassing power (1765–8).

Again, the practical impact of Troilus' revelation is considerable: he propagates the war (of all things) with renewed vigour, his 'hardynesse and myght' increased by love, and by the desire to win Criseyde's gratitude and admiration. Loving her has been a life-changing event: she has 'altered his spirit so with-inne' (III. 1772–8). At times of truce he goes hawking and hunting and this activity too is all of a piece with loving Criseyde. When he returns to town, she is ready to salute him 'from her wyndow down, / As fresshe as faukoun comen out of muwe' (1783–4). At this stage in the narrative, Troilus appears able to roam freely over, to command as his, the different spaces of Troy whatever their designation. Even those of domestic and public life seem to have lost their sense of difference: the window is no longer a point of separation between interior and exterior, closet and street, introspection and sociability, but a means of mutual communication.[6] Artificial divisions of the social order, and the divisive effects of sin, are likewise set at nought. Troilus, although of 'blood roial',

6    Cf. Dobbs, 'Seeing through Windows', pp. 407–18.

does not stand on ceremony by allowing his pride to make him haughty, and the benefits are widely felt: 'Benigne he was to ech in general, / For which he gat hym thank in every place' (1802–3). Love directs him to flee not only pride but also envy, anger, greed and all other vices. Thus, after his 'disese' he achieves a degree of holisitic equanimity in 'lust and in quiete [...] with Criseyde' (1816–20) that he has not known before and the extent of which he did not anticipate.

## Separation

The threat of division, absence, fragmentation, is felt even as the lovers achieve their greatest intensity of mutual bliss. At the end of their first night together, the onset of day is going to 'make dis-severeaunce' (III. 1424), and cannot be resisted. It is only with the utmost reluctance that Troilus leaves Criseyde, his heart registering the pain of separation: 'Now fele I that myn herte moot a-two' (1475). But part they must, and so the rhythm of the affair is set: again they meet, make love as passionately as before, and with deep regret, when time dictates, 'twynne' (1711) – a term that is to become a key word in the index of their history. Indeed, as the narrator makes clear at the beginning of Book Four, their separation is henceforth his predominant topic, construed as 'how Criseyde Troilus forsook' (IV. 15); or, in the terms of the present discussion, how the spaces that their love coalesces, or bridges, again become sharply differentiated, distinct and isolated one from the other. The key factor in his change of tack is, of course, that same war in which Troilus engages with such gusto. The siege of the Greeks, 'Liggyng in oost [...] stronge about Troie town' (29–30) exerts such a powerful military and political pressure on Troy that no-one within its walls, no matter how well protected or covert their private lives, can escape the consequences.

The immediate effect on Troilus of the decision to exchange Criseyde for Antenor is his denaturing, a loss of identity and presence. He ceases to flourish and be expansive; he is not now in the springtime of his love, but the winter, about to be stripped of his happiness and reduced to the very essentials of his existence. Lying 'byraft of eche welfare' he is 'ibounden in the blake bark of care' as in the winter leaves are 'birafte / Ech after other, til the tree be bare, / So that ther nys but bark and braunche ilafte' (IV. 225–9). His anguish of impending loss finds expression in a severe dislocation between his body and the space of his *chaumbre*. Now, it seems, bereft even of his human, civilized, chivalric, characteristics, but nevertheless acting within the logic of images (of his wounded heart) he behaves uncontrollably, like a 'wylde bole [...] idarted to the herte', springing 'Now her, now ther' (239–40). Driven almost mad by grief, the *chaumbre* is for Troilus no longer an inner sanctum for quiet reflection, or a refuge from the torments of unrequited love, but a place in which he vents extreme anger and frustration at losing Criseyde. That loss is at the same time a loss of control over himself, his personal space, and its integration with the wider world. The *chaumbre* becomes a self-imposed torture chamber. Like a maddened, wounded bull he rampages round the room, beating his breast with his fists and 'His hed to the wal, his body to the grounde, / Ful ofte he swapte' (244–5).

The agent Troilus suspects as responsible for this turn of events is the arbitrary goddess Fortune, who is herself divided between well and woe, beauty and ugliness, past and future. He asks her 'Shal thus Creiseyde aweye for that thow wilt?' (IV. 264) and sees Criseyde's departure in terms of further deprivation, loss and division. He is bereft of joy and would sacrifice his life, which is now an encumbrance, rather than continue to exist in a half-dead state. Such effects are typical of Fortune's behaviour, who delights through changeful violence 'To reve a wight that most is to hym deere' (285). The consequence is that body and spirit are now at odds – the latter, 'that errest to and fro', having lost its direction, its lines of connection, its purpose. Troilus wonders why, in its state of alienation, his fugitive soul, 'lurkynge in this wo', won't try to achieve some redress, drastic though that might be, by leaving his body and breaking his heart, in order to follow Criseyde for, as he says, 'Thi righte place is now no lenger here' (303–8). His spirit has a natural inclination towards her and, in a rhetorical address, he asks that she should receive 'whan myn herte dieth, / My spirit, which that so unto yow hieth' (319–20). In the interim of this self-dramatizing scenario other bodily organs will atrophy, and especially his eyes with their lines of sight, which can no longer engage with those of Criseyde: 'youre disporte / Was al to sen Criseydes eyen brighte' (309–10). Cut off from the light that enables them to work properly – 'she is queynt that wont was yow to lighte' (313) – they can do little now but weep themselves to blindness, 'wepen out your sighte' (312). Since the 'vertu' that empowered them is 'aweye', Troilus' eyes are redundant, dysfunctional.

It is in just this state of imagined severance – 'Delyvere now the world [...] / Of me' (IV. 515–16) – and with blinding tears, that distil 'As licour out of a lambyc ful faste', that Pandarus now encounters Troilus. Even his own gaze signals the extent to which the protagonists of this drama have become isolated and despondent: 'to the ground his eyen doun he caste' (519–22). But it is not long before the practically-minded Pandarus proposes a recuperative strategy: if separation is the order of the day, the way in which Fortune is tending, then Troilus should seize the moment and himself instigate a forceful separation of Criseyde from Troy, by abducting her: 'Go ravysshe here? [...] / And other lat here out of towne fare, / Or hold here stille' (530–2). But the proactive control of space was never Troilus' forte, and the proposal meets with a reply that is itself divided between desire and reason, prompting more tears (572–5), his love increasing even as hope diminishes and cares mount and the *ese* of love yields to 'litel reste' (581).

Criseyde is no less riven, burning 'in love and drede', not knowing what to do for the best, when she hears the news from parliament (IV. 678–9). Like Troilus, she experiences dislocation; her body may be with the women who come to comfort her, but her mind is at a distance: 'She herde hem right as though she thennes were', and 'Although the body sat among hem there / Hire advertence is alwey elleswhere' (695–8). She seems to have crossed the divide between heaven and hell, fallen over the brink

(712–13), and wonders what will be in store for her and Troilus should she 'twynne' from him (757–8). In an echo of Troilus' Boethian speech, she imagines herself devoid of him, deprived of her life-sustaining element, and asks: 'How sholde a fissh withouten water dure? / What is Criseyde worth, from Troilus?' A plant or creature cannot survive without its natural nourishment (765–8).

When the lovers do meet again they are so conscious of the forces driving them apart that they are initially unable to speak, 'So gan the peyne hire hertes for to twiste' (IV. 1129). But when Criseyde swoons, and Troilus believes her dead, the mood of resignation turns to defiance as he draws his sword to follow her apparent example: 'Ther shal no deth me fro my lady twynne' (1197). Once revived, Criseyde counsels acceptance of their fate in the expectation that 'the twynnyng of us tweyne' can be ameliorated by acknowledging that pain is all part of the experience of love (1303–6). However much he might appear to accept Criseyde's optimism in the likelihood of her return, the prospect of their parting is for Troilus a devastating, violent wrench: with 'his soule out of his herte rente' he leaves the *chaumbre* (1700–1).

From this point onwards Troilus and Criseyde become increasingly lost in their own, now separate, worlds, and experience a steadily accelerating isolation and disintegration of self, relationship and surroundings. Criseyde is so jolted by the trauma of their parting that she is unable to concentrate, hearing only 'a word or two' of Diomede's overtures, being 'with sorwe oppressed so / That, in effect, she naught hise tales herde / But here and ther' (V. 177–9). Troilus, for his part, does not seem able to sustain a complete image of Criseyde, but thinks instead of different parts of her body, as though it had been dismembered. Even these are now known only by their absence, and by their lack of identifiable location: 'Wher is hire white brest. Wher is it, where? / [...] Wher ben hire armes and hire eyen cleere [...]?' (219–20). She has become insubstantial, no more than a memory to which Troilus desperately clings; although he may 'graspe aboute' in 'this place', his *chaumbre*, he finds nothing to embrace but a pillow (223–4). The immediate material world is all too tangible and present, but its forms are not the ones Troilus craves. He tries to imagine Criseyde's location – the space she occupies, its reference-points – now that their respective locations are emptied of unified meaning. She, though out of sight, remains his 'lode sterre', as he, too, was her guiding light. Just as he is surrounded by emptiness, so from her perspective (he imagines) there is nothing where he once was. He asks: 'Who seth yow now [...] / Who sit right now or stant in youre presence? / [...] Now I am gon, whom yeve ye audience / Who spekith for me right now in myn absence?' (232–6). His answer, 'no wight', is poignantly wrong for, line by line, reader or audience have supplied the repeated answer: Diomede.

## Fragmentation

Nothingness, the absence of form, focus and stability, becomes for Troilus an *idée fixe*. He imagines the annihilation of his own sensory awareness, now so useless, when 'my body brennen shal to glede' (V. 303), with nothing but sword, helm and shield left as relics. He is impervious to the social pleasures of a visit to Sarpedoun's house: there may be such a fair company of ladies dancing such as 'was nevere isene with ie', but it is of no avail to Troilus, who cannot see them as a source of distraction and comfort. He wants only a highly particularized object of attention, his faithful or 'pietous' heart busily searching out Criseyde, 'Now this, now that, so faste ymagenynge' (451–5). The images spun in his own brain take precedence over the visual world, the attractive appearance of the ladies causing him sorrow because he sees in them only the absence of Criseyde, even forbidding them to play music – 'this was his fantasye' – because 'she that of his herte berth the keye / Was absent' (460–2). He is desocialized, talking to himself, but as if addressing Criseyde to welcome her back: 'How have ye faren syn that ye were here?' (466). Troilus' disorientation – 'al this nat but a maze' (468) – verges on madness.

The break-up of Troilus' mental and emotional integrity through the crippling absence of Criseyde is further explored by means of his restless wanderings in Troy. On these occasions, the familiar spaces that formerly interpenetrated and that he knew, could access and enjoy, become spaces that are sharply distinct from each other, and from which he is estranged or barred. He is now more sensitive to marks of division, of exclusion, of walls and barriers, and of his own isolation and distance from Criseyde, than he ever was before.[7] His inability to enjoy life in her absence, to 'have [...] feste', prompts Troilus to suggest to Pandarus that, by way of compensation, they should 'sen hire paleys atte leeste' (V. 524–5). He finds an excuse for them 'in town forto go' without his entourage and so rides to Criseyde's house. But it provides cold comfort: it is no longer welcoming and animated by the light and warmth of her presence; instead, the sight of 'hire dores spered alle' makes Troilus think that 'his sorwful herte braste a-two' (530–1). Looking more closely, 'whan he was war and gan biholde', he sees 'How shet was every wyndow of the place' (534) – those self-same windows that had been such an important means of contact between him and Criseyde. His heart now turns as cold as frost and, with his face a corresponding 'dedlich pale' (536), he hurries on without a word and so quickly that no one else is able to see his expression. An exile in his own city, Troilus' act of pilgrimage has been rendered meaningless because it was to a 'shryne, of which the seynt is oute', leaving him only the external shell and its 'colde dores' to kiss and venerate (551–3). Troilus is enacting not so much 'the therapy of distance' as the trauma of a separation which no pilgrimage can heal.[8] Indeed, he characterizes the entire house as 'desolat', 'empty' and 'disconcolat', a dark space, a lantern de-void of light, that is the epitome of his own desolation.[9]

Increasingly aware that his affair with Criseyde is under threat, Troilus is sensitive to the other places in Troy that he associates

---

7    Lynch, 'Partitioned Fictions', pp. 119–22. On London as an essentially fragmented city, see Turner, 'Greater London', pp. 25–9.
8    Jospivoci, *Touch*, pp. 65–71.
9    Edwards, 'Desolate Palace', pp. 412–16. Cf. Boccaccio, *Filostrato*, V. 53–4.

with her. Henceforth, as he rides up and down, 'every thyng com hym to remembraunce / As he rood forby places of the town / In which he whilom hadde al his pleasaunce' (V. 562–4). What distinguishes these visual events is Troilus' sense of distance from the places he sees. The intimacy he formerly enjoyed in relation to them is now beyond reach, in the past, detached from his present experience, *yonder*. Thus it is '*yonder*' that he last saw Criseyde dance, in '*that* temple' exchanged glances, '*yonder*' heard her laugh, '*yonder*' saw her play happily, '*yonder*' asked him to love her well, '*yonder*' was looked at by her 'so goodly', at '*that* corner in the *yonder* house' heard her sing, in '*that yonder* place' was first taken 'unto her grace' (565–81). The visual component of these memories only increases the pathos: whereas Troilus was involved in those lines of sight that established a spatial, emotional and sexual relationship with Criseyde, the same sights now place him in the position of an external observer. In the prayer to Cupid that follows, Troilus acknowledges that the 'processe' in which he is engaged is one of remembering the key elements in the progress of their love, from which it might be possible to construct a coherent history.[10] At the same time, it is an involuntary process – Troilus cannot prevent the memories flooding back – and one that others will have to compose into a cogent narrative: 'Men myght a book make' (585). As matters stand, he is able only to register, subjectively, a rich variety of disconnected episodes and his distance from them. His spatial relationship with the city has undergone a profound change.

The restlessness, spatial discomfort and gruelling sense of separation from the person he loves continue unabated. The scene shifts to the gate of Troy from which Criseyde rode so far away, 'a ful good paas'. Troilus goes back and forth, 'up and down ther made he many a wente', lamenting her departure, hoping to see her again 'com into Troie' (V. 605–9). Now the far-off features of the landscape, as well as those of the town, articulate his memories, his emotional distance from Criseyde and his exile from happiness: 'to the yonder hille I gan hire gyde [...] and ther I took of hire my leve! [...] yond I saugh hire to hire fader ride [...] hider

10    Schibanoff, 'Prudence and Artificial Memory'.

hom I com whan it was eve [...] here I dwelle out caste from ioie'. The sole remedy is having Criseyde near, restoring her to her rightful place so that he might 'sen hire eft in Troie' (610–15). In this dislocating condition of seeing Criseyde without the spaces to which he had access, when he was used to seeing her within them, Troilus believes that he too has become objectified. He looks as if through the eyes of others to see himself 'defet, and pale', imagining their commenting on his condition, wondering about the causes and feeling sorry for his own impending death. His psychological disorder, or 'fantasie', is a symptom of 'malencolie' (617–27), and it makes him return, compulsively, to the edge of the city to await Criseyde's return. He walks 'Upon the walles faste', looking at the Greek encampment, and talking to himself (though in Pandarus' presence), uttering words of comfort and hope that seem to make nothing of the distance between him and Criseyde, for it is bridged by a fragrant and soothing wind:[11]

> Lo, yonder is myne owne lady free,
> Or ellis yonder, ther tho tentes be,
> And thennes comth this eyr that is so soote
> That in my soule I fele it doth my boote. (669–72)

Troilus attributes the cause of the wind to 'my ladys depe sikes soore', proving the case by observing that 'Of al this town, save onliche in this space' is there wind that sounds so painful, as if saying mournfully '"Allas! Whi twynned be we tweyne"'. Thus rhetorical exaggeration takes on the status of empirical evidence, and metaphor is made literal, in Troilus' deluded mind. The entirely fanciful nature of Troilus' 'explanation' is a measure of his state but it is also an attempt, however futile, to restore 'this space', a mutually recognized channel of communication between himself and Criseyde, a channel now blocked by the walls of Troy.

    An interactive spatial relationship with Criseyde is unlikely to be restored. While she might gaze at the place where Troilus lives, just as Troilus gazes at the Greek camp, they do not see each

---

11   Cf. Boccaccio, *Filostrato,* VII. 2.

other. Fragile lines of sight, extended over long distances, cannot easily be reciprocated. The space between them has become, in every sense, too great to bridge, too much dissolved in the public, military and political domains and no longer able to sustain emotional intensity or sexual intimacy. As far as the latter are concerned, Diomede is much better placed than Troilus. Nor is Troilus helped by the way in which Criseyde now regards Troy. From her tent she can see the whole city as it were in perspective, complete in itself and – if she has taken any notice at all of her father's prognosis – doomed to destruction. Thus, as she looks, her gaze is affected by great sadness, both for the loss of Troilus, who is gradually receding from her mind, and for the inevitable loss of the city she once knew. It is regretfully, 'Ful rewfully', that she looks upon Troy, 'Biheld the toures heigh and ek the halles', and laments her lost yesterdays. For she knew 'pleasance and [...] ioie, / The which that now al torned into galle is, / [...] ofte withinne yonder walles!' (V. 731–3).[12] She might deliberately remind herself of her avowed 'entencioun' to return but the images of the city and of Troilus, so intertwined with each other, are slipping away: 'bothe Troilus and Troie town / Shal knotteles thorugh-out hire herte slide' (767–9).

On Troilus' side it is not long before visual obsession and mental derangement result in optical illusion. At dawn on the tenth day he and Pandarus take up their positions 'on the walles of the town [...] / To loke if they kan sen aught of Criseyde' (V. 1112–13). They stand there until noon, imagining that everyone 'That com fro fer' is she, until, viewed more closely, 'thei koude knowen hym aright' (116–17), hope and disappointment rising and falling accordingly. They have no better luck in the afternoon, so Troilus decides that Criseyde will come 'neigh even', and goes with Pandarus to the gate, to persuade the porter to keep it open should she arrive late. The day 'goth faste' and evening falls, Troilus straining to see as far as he can into the gathering gloom: 'He loketh forth by hegge, by tre, by greve, / And fer his hed over the wal he leyde' (1144–5). Seeing nothing, he becomes convinced

12    Cf. Boccaccio, *Filostrato*, VII. 14–15.

that Criseyde in her wisdom has decided to 'riden pryvely [...] / By nyghte into the town' (1150–4), to avoid public recognition. And then, as if in confirmation, he sees her, exclaiming to his friend: 'Pandarus, now woltow trowen me? / Have here my trouthe, I se hire! Yond she is! / Heve up thyn eyen, man! Maistow nat se?' But expectation has outrun reality: Pandarus sees only too plainly what the object is, and the extent of Troilus' delusion: 'Al wronge, by god! What saistow, man? Where art? / That I se yond nys but a fare-cart' (1156–62), a cart for conveying merchandise – merchandise being what, in effect, Criseyde became in the bartering process between Greeks and Trojans. Disconsolate, Troilus goes home, to return 'on the morwe unto the yate' (1192), his restlessness becoming more frantic: 'up and down, by west and ek by este, / Upon the walles made he many a wente'. It is all for nothing because, like it or not, he is blind: 'hope alwey hym blente' (1193–5).

Criseyde's long absence now aggravates Troilus' physical, psychological and social dismembering: neither eating nor drinking 'for his malencolye', he flees the company of others (V. 1215–17), is disfigured enough to be unrecognizable, and is so lean, wan and feeble that – in an echo of the iconography of Saturn, the god of melancholy – he walks with a crutch. This is anger turned self-destructive: 'with his ire he thus hymselve shente' (1223). Letters are to little avail. They allow him to describe to Criseyde, warily, something of his parlous condition, his 'unresty sorwes soore' (1355). In one of her replies, Criseyde alleges that his turmoil, 'youre unreste', grieves her and she counsels submission to the will of the gods (1603–6) but makes it clear that she herself is in such disarray and dislocation – 'yet in swich disjoynte / I stonde' (1618–19) – that planning for their reunion is fraught with problems. Re-establishing a continuum of space between them is well-nigh impossible across the nomansland that now intervenes and, reluctantly at first, Troilus recognizes the change that has overcome Criseyde. Her letter is 'al straunge', alienating and, once the brooch on Diomede's captured cloak proves her infidelity, he imputes their loss of integrity to her. She has broken her faith, her promise, her love and her truth – moral qualities central both to the continuation of their relationship and to the chivalric ethic by which

Troilus lives. Criseyde's actions strike at the very heart of his moral code, his sense of himself and of his position in relation to the rest of society. Promises themselves, the very foundation of chivalric society, are called into question: 'Who shal now trowe on ony othes mo?' (1681). Criseyde has sacrificed what was once so precious, her reputation, her 'name of trouthe' (1686–7) and is diminished thereby. The distance between them is now acute, definite, final: 'clene out of youre mynde / Ye han me cast' (1695–6) and yet, with no hope of bridging it, Troilus cannot stop himself from loving her.

Troilus' sense of integrity and wholeness is eventually restored, but on another level of existence, and one where truth is upheld, faith maintained, promises kept and love sustained. It is a world, or universe, conceived of as an integrated spatial system, one that contains all space within the uncircumscribed embrace of God himself. It is the final vindication of Troilus' Boethian vision, in which each component occupies its appropriate place, benefiting its contingent parts by keeping within bounds, the whole infused with love in a kind of metaphysical ecology. Troilus' privileged access to these transcendent spaces is the direct outcome of his sensitivity to the nature of love as experienced with Criseyde. Against the odds he maintained his truth, his love, his promise, his faith. And though tempted to break out of sexual and social bounds by abducting her, he allowed Criseyde to find her own destiny, painful though the outcome was.


## Optical Contexts


What are the appropriate optical contexts within which to place the spatial content of *Troilus*? In the first place there are a number of broad affiliations with the tradition represented by Alhacen, Witelo and Bacon – as in the repeated emphasis on the gaze as both active and passive,[13] and on space as a product of visual activity, or in Chaucer's linking of the interpretation of visual data with the psychological condition of the viewer. At a more detailed level it is entirely feasible to continue the procedure adopted in previous chapters and find analogies, within the writings of *perspectiva* for (say) Troilus' mistaking a *fare-cart* for Criseyde in the difficulties attendant upon clear perception over long distances in failing light – causes of visual deception also found in the writings of the optical moralists.[14] It would be appropriate also to recognize the extent of Chaucer's indebtedness to Boccaccio's handling of optical space, both in general matters and specific detail. Such contexts confirm again the extent to which Chaucer's writings are imbued with details deriving from the optical inheritance studied in this book.

But perhaps a more effective way of construing the complexities of Chaucer's spatial design is as the result of the conflux of two optical traditions. One, essentially Aristotelian and Arabic and best represented by Alhacen, is a natural science that accentuates the processes and phenomena of vision (including visual error) and the psychology of perception in its response to a physical world constituted of light, objects and space. It is a tradition entirely appropriate to the pagan mentalities of Troy. The other tradition is Platonic, more easily assimilated to Christian thought, and is best represented by Grosseteste. It takes a symbolic view of the visual world and its constituent parts, regarding them as ephemeral and insubstantial but nevertheless indicative of a higher truth. Objects, light, vision and space itself are held to be radically deceptive and transient, at best signs of a higher, enduringly stable, reality. Troilus, a denizen of the pagan world and deeply implicated in its operating principles, nevertheless achieves after death a fundamental realignment of his way of apprehending reality – moving in effect from Aristotle to Plato (or Boethius), from Alhacen to Grosseteste, from Boccaccio to Dante.

13    Stanbury, 'Lover's Gaze', pp. 223–9; and Moore, 'Troilus's Mirror'. And cf. Klassen, 'Optical Allusions'.

14    Holcot, *Super sapientiam*, lectio 157; ed. Ryterus, p. 523.

As noted in Chapter Five, the same kind of double allegiance is found also in Dante, whose work stimulated Chaucer's, but in *Troilus* the reconciliation between the competing claims of the two traditions is more tentative. Their existence, side by side, is intimated in the narrator's hymn to Venus at the beginning of Book Three, when he refers to 'thilke covered qualitee / Of thynges' (III. 31–2). Henceforth, the double focus of Troilus' experience – both to the earthly and the transcendent, the surface and the depth – becomes increasingly apparent. Troilus' own prayer to love, uttered at the very moment of his most intense physical enjoyment of Criseyde, expresses the elation of self-discovery, but also captures a tension between the physical and the metaphysical – one also caught in Criseyde's increasing impatience with Troilus' devotions. As previously noted, what Troilus experiences here is a sense of space beyond the everyday, and of his place within a wider scheme of things. Intense though his pleasure in Criseyde's body might be as he caresses it, and kisses her, the prayer queries the nature of sense perception to ask if it is a sufficient 'hevene' in itself, or also a route of access to another kind of bliss. Rendered in optical terms, the question is whether (as according to Alhacen) space is a human construct, a response to the world of surfaces, or whether (following Grosseteste) it is an expression of God's creativity. Latent here also is an indication of the different aptitudes appropriate to the two kinds of space. 'Alhacen space' requires active production, an incessant process of human mediation as signals stream from the physical world to the eye and brain of the beholder. 'Grosseteste space' is predicated upon a kind of spiritual receptivity, passive acceptance and wonder, as when Troilus states 'I kan namore, but laude and reverence' (1273).

Troy, of course, is a deceptive and covert world in more senses than one, the appearance of things belying their reality. Troilus masks his emotions; the affair is conducted in secret; domestic space, seemingly so open, conceals furtive liaisons; the private is hidden within the public – as when Troilus must dissemble a cheerful expression to 'blind' the king and others so they do not suspect his affair with Criseyde (IV. 648); the women visiting Criseyde misconceive the cause of her sorrow; Troilus refuses to recognize Criseyde's infidelity until confronted by the brooch he gave her on Diomede's captured tunic; and so on. For Pandarus, such duplicity is in the nature of an existence governed by Fortune. Appearance, including spaces, are there to be manipulated to personal advantage because, according to his lights, space is no more nor less than a medium in which to live and to control if at all possible. Thus he advises Criseyde, weeping 'pitously', to 'Aris up hastily' so that Troilus does not find her 'bywopen' (911–17).

But Troilus cannot tolerate this looking-glass world, and is often uncomfortable, if complicit, in the deceptive roles in which he is cast by Pandarus. He wants to believe in, and has strong intimations of, a coherent structure that lies beyond the visible while at the same time being related to it, a liberating openness beyond earthly constraints. Teasing out the relationship between mundane and divine space can be a ticklish business, but a cornerstone of Troilus' emergent credo is the ideal perceptiveness of God. He sees everything in past, present and future and therefore cannot be deceived: 'God seth al biforn – / Ne God may nat deceyved ben' (IV. 974–5). By contrast, a seer like Calkas has severely restricted foresight, however much he may be 'in sleght as Argus eyed' (1459), impervious to the blinding effects of women's ways, or a canny manipulator of Trojan space. But from God nothing, 'no cause', is hidden (1654), and given that this kind of deity is the object of Troilus' aspiration it is small wonder that with the departure of Criseyde, when he inhabits a world of surfaces, deserted shrines, shut doors, closed windows, blank walls and empty landscapes, he lives in a kind of hell.

# 11 Retrospect

Ther saugh I Colle tregetour
Upon a table of sycamour
Pleye an uncouth thyng to telle –
Y saugh him carien a wynd-melle
Under a walsh-note shale.[1]

In Chaucer's writings, the magical properties of space do not go unnoticed, for space is susceptible to sudden transformation and is a vehicle for optical illusions. The linkage between magic and space is relatively direct in the Squire's Tale and is developed at some length in the Franklin's Tale, where the clerk of Orleans conjures elaborate pageants out of thin air and makes the threatening rocks disappear. By and large, spatial manipulations designed to deceive get short shrift in Chaucer's writings: the vanishing rocks are the result of trickery with tides. It may be that Chaucer recognized space as a phenomenon sufficiently changeable and deceptive in itself and in scant need of further interference by those with ulterior motives. Nevertheless, the magic of space held for him a certain fascination. 'Hende Nicholas' is one individual whose spatial manipulations win the day and Chaucer himself, no less than 'Colle tregetour', was a kind of magician of narrative, exploiting the protean and malleable nature of space to contract a scene, expand it, charge it with significance or use it to show 'the ability of the human mind to encompass the world'.[2]

Chaucer's prestidigitations with space sometimes border on the fantastical[3] but the preceding chapters have been at pains to

---

1    Chaucer, *House of Fame*, 1277–81
2    Andrew, 'Games', p. 171.
3    Boitani, *Chaucer and the Imaginary World of Fame*, pp. 178–9.

show that, even in a dream vision like the *Book of the Duchess*, he owes a debt to scientific ideas that were available to him in a range of writings. Taken together, those writings constitute a cultural context that thickens our understanding both of Chaucer's practices and of the reception of his works. The writings range from theological and philosophical tracts (Grosseteste, Bacon) to specialized treatises (Alhacen, Witelo), more accessible expositions (Bartholomaeus, Vincent), homiletic compilations (Peter of Limoges, Robert Holcot) and literary texts (Jean de Meun, Dante, Boccaccio). Chaucer's engagement with the optical content of such works is now direct, now indirect, now close, now distant but, as we have seen, each kind of writing is capable of furnishing close analogues for passages in his own works. He was alive to the scientific, encyclopedic, homiletic and literary expressions of the optical tradition; he transmuted it for use in his own narratives; they evidence a recurrent interest in space as an optical and psychological phenomenon; and his engagement with the politics of space was ubiquitous and far-reaching.

What were the creative benefits to Chaucer of his interest in optical space? First of all, it fed his interest in scientific accounts of human experience. Second, it opened up new possibilities for describing the interaction of human subjects with the surrounding world: the idea that space was mediated through an individual's eye could be readily translated into narrative by placing a protagonist at the centre of a complex process of ocular stimulus and psychological response – a response as often as not fraught with error. Third, it encouraged him to explore the effects of juxtaposing two kinds of space – broadly speaking the mimetic, or optical, and the symbolic, or iconographic – thus presenting his audience with a challenging collision between the world of surfaces constantly made anew by individual observers and the world of received meanings reinforced by authorities of one sort or another. Finally, the science of *perspectiva* and its progeny allowed him to offset traditional ideas of light, vision and space as essentially metaphysical qualities (as they are in Boethius) with notions that insisted on their primary existence as features of the material world.

The nature of Chaucer's response to optical space is highly distinctive; he is not a passive recipient of predigested ideas. Although there are literary precedents for his interest in *perspectiva*, he rejects or radically modifies the poeticized science of the *Roman de la Rose*, the progressive dynamic between human vision and divine revelation found in the *Divina Commedia* and Boccaccio's attempts to reinstate the visual density and volume of the pagan past. It might also be argued that he rejects, or at least offers a critique of, an account of space that would explain it merely in terms of visual activity. Taking his cue from the optical treatises themselves, he shows the extent to which human vision is fallible, and susceptible to illusion and error.[4] Again, as *Troilus* suggested, he exploits other contradictions within the optical tradition, questioning the adequacy of theories that pay too much attention to the workings of the eye to the detriment of other considerations. To give Alhacen his due, the psychology of perception is a key part of his account of the perception of space, but Chaucer considerably expands the role of the interpreting subject. Typically, she or he is affected in the construction of space not just by visual stimuli but also by mental preconceptions, emotional states and belief systems, as well as by other sensual data – especially those deriving from hearing and touch.

In this respect, it would be possible to describe Chaucer as complying with a Lefebvrian account of space. Lefebvre, too, acknowledges that a purely visual account of space has severe limitations and pitfalls, not least because it plays into the hands of those who use space as an expression of power and instrument of control. Dominant groups create visual representations of that space (maps, buildings) to consolidate and reinforce their ascendancy. However, those living under their sway can resist such politically motivated representations. Through a process of negotiation between spatial practice, representations of space, and daily living, the individual produces *representational* space that counters the status quo. Writers are particularly adept at indicating possible strategies for doing so. So, in the Knight's Tale, Chaucer may be

4    Cf. Yager, 'Visual Perception', ch. 5.

thought of as describing social practice in chivalric society, pro-
viding an account of a representation of space (the amphitheatre
built by Theseus) and in producing representational space, show-
ing how social practice and its representation are countered – by
Palamon and Arcite (in evading prison) and by the gods.

One of the ways in which that countering takes place is
through an emphasis on the experience of the individual subject
who, while forcefully affected by visual incidents, produces space
using other means as well. Some of those means are his or her
mental processes, especially prejudices and preconceptions, which
mediate and individualize visual perception. As we have seen in
*Troilus*, as well as the Knight's Tale, other means are belief systems
which give the seen world a particular orientation and frame of
reference. Above all, there is the human body (an emphasis made
in different ways in the Miller's Tale and *Book of the Duchess*) both
as the site of subjective interpretation and as an object in space. It
exists in an ever-changing relationship with its surroundings –
surroundings known visually but also by the other senses (espec-
ially hearing, smell and touch) and possessed by means of move-
ment and gesture.

What this amounts to is the possibility (perhaps a necessity in
terms of the individual's sense of identity) of appropriation; that is,
of producing one's own space out of the complex and continuing
interactions of given spatial constructs, their representations and
social practice. We have seen such appropriations at work, notably
in the Knight's Tale and *Troilus*. It follows that the recognition,
crossing and transgression of boundaries is an eloquent notation of
the interplay between one kind of space and another – personal,
public, domestic, political, sexual and so on. In the process of
finding a way into and through different kinds of space, individuals
and social groups establish networks that take them from one kind
of space to another. The Miller's Tale and *Troilus* furnish some
examples from the literary sphere. In consequence, the meaning of
any one space is likely to be complex. In the case of a building, its
space may have an 'official' function and meaning but one which is
contested, subverted or appropriated by individuals or groups.
Thus, at the temple of Palladion, the space defined by the building

is at once religious, social, public, private, sexual and a node in a network of social relations peculiar to Troy.

The intertwining and superimposition of different kinds of space in a single locale make their interpretation difficult but, as Lefebvre insists, space has a history and so we can decipher at least some spatial codes and symbols by paying close attention to their cultural contexts. Except in the broadest of terms, and drawing his frame of reference from Panofsky, Lefebvre has little to say about medieval notions of space, let alone its representational aspects. It is to be hoped, therefore, that the present book does something to explore in detail some representational versions of late medieval English space while providing it with a set of historical referents in optical science. In the process, the versatility and usefulness of Lefebvre's ideas have become apparent, as also the scale of the project that he envisaged.

It is one thing to historicize Chaucer's spatial practices by referring to optical treatises but other contexts, beyond the scope of the present study, beg for consideration. I offer the following lines of enquiry as possible supplements to my own approach, or as alternative ways of providing an account of Chaucer's spatial practices. For instance, it would be instructive to place Chaucer's account of feudal space in the Knight's Tale alongside a treatise on chivalric rule, or read his delineation of urban life in the Miller's Tale together with a topographical analysis of late medieval Oxford. To do so might help to highlight the extent to which Chaucer's fictional accounts of space are not direct transcriptions from treatises or social practice – any more than they are direct transcripts from texts on *perspectiva* – but, instead, spatial constructs sufficiently familiar to ensure recognition, sufficiently different to be a vehicle for his own priorities.

Nor is it viable to pretend that any one context provides a golden key to unlock all the subtleties of Chaucer's spatial designs. As was clear in the *Book of the Duchess*, the spatial content of his descriptions is sometimes linked to processes of memory-making.[5]

5    Cf. Yates, *Art of Memory*, pp. 101–2.

The spatial organization of memory images, including their dispos-
ition according to an architectonic order, is inbuilt in memory
systems used in the Middle Ages.[6] One of Troilus' responses to the
dismembering effects of the experience of losing Criseyde is a
deliberate re-membering and in the course of this process space –
anchored in and around architectural constructs – plays an im-
portant part.[7] Similarly, it has been argued that the Knight's Tale is
organized around key locations that embed images designed to be
retained in the memory as a means of unlocking narrative sequence
and thematic content;[8] and the *House of Fame* deploys architectural
space to 'house' memory images in due order.[9] What remains
under-explored is the precise function of the spatial components
within Chaucer's memorial descriptions. Traditionally, the relative
position of places was regarded as crucial for the ordered remem-
bering of ideas and events. But in Chaucer's descriptions space
itself is used as a feature both of place and of the disposition of
elements within it. The technique has the effect of making the
place and its content 'stand out' as significant and worthy of
mental retention but the emphasis also falls on optical process, the
subjective experience of vision, and its intimate connections with
thought, feeling and preconception.

A more recent development also likely to have influenced
Chaucer's spatial designs was the advent of an affective piety
linked, as it often was, to narrative. In a work such as Nicholas
Love's *Meditations on the Blessed Life of Jesus Christ* the reader is
enjoined to become vicariously involved in the life and passion of
Christ. Love's account of the wedding at Cana, for example, in-
cludes a vivid evocation of domestic space seen through the eyes
of Christ's anxious mother as she discovers that the wine has run
out and moves from chamber to hall to whisper in the ear of
Christ, whose lowly position in the seating plan is carefully noted.

6    Carruthers, *Book of Memory*, pp. 27–8; Howard, *Idea*, pp. 146–7.
7    Nolan, 'Chaucer's Poetics of Dwelling'; Schibanoff, 'Prudence and
     Artificial Memory'.
8    Carruthers, 'Seeing Things'.
9    Buckmaster, 'Meditation and Memory'.

In this type of meditation a two-fold process is at work. On the one hand, the narrative moment is being constructed in spatial terms that derive from the practical experience of everyday life. On the other hand, the spatial arrangements of the real world, whether they are those of seating plans, hospitality, interior architecture or human bodies, are given dignity, validity and worth because they are represented as being essentially the same as those found in the biblical narrative.[10] The whole thrust of the Franciscan project is to break down the boundaries between the two and sanction the experience, drama and visual intensity of the one in terms of the other. Mary's experience can be ours and our experience can, by imaginative extension, provide insight into hers. Within this narrative tradition, space is adopted as a personally meaningful construct, drenched in the emotive immediacy of the individual's inward life.

Although Love's *Mirror* did not appear until 1410, earlier translations of parts of the text, as well as other works of Franciscan piety, circulated in England during the fourteenth century.[11] The movement also found a receptive audience among lay proponents of the 'mixed life', who endeavoured to seek spiritual values within the everyday demands of their secular activities.[12] So it is perhaps not entirely accidental that, in Chaucer's writings, moments of enhanced spatial awareness coincide with pious practices. Palamon's devout response to the experience of seeing Emelye – praying on his knees to Venus (245) – is condemned by Arcite as 'affeccioun of hoolynesse' but it links to Palamon's much greater awareness of the spatial dimensions of his vision of Emelye. John's access of piety, in the Miller's Tale, is linked to his sense that Nicholas has been overstepping the bounds of human space in order to pry into the mysteries of God. Another notorious

10   Love, *Mirror*, ed. Sargent, pp. 81–2.
11   Ibid., pp. xii–xvii; Despres, *Ghostly Sights*, ch. 2; Keiser, 'Middle English Passion Narratives'; Salter, *Nicholas Love's 'Myrrour'*, pp. 97–114; and Sargent, 'Bonaventura English'.
12   Beckwith, Christ's Body, pp. 52–5; Carey, 'Devout Literate Laypeople'; Hughes, *Pastors and Visionaries*.

case is Troilus' insistence on praying at length to Venus just when
he has succeeded in negotiating the intricate spaces of Pandarus'
house and, by analogy, the elaborate plot which has brought him
to share a bed with Criseyde and experience a sense of personal
expansiveness. Again, in the *House of Fame*, Geffrey's sight of the
approaching eagle and the consequent sense of enveloping space
(492–508) is a response to prayer.

For Sargent, the hallmarks of meditative ideas minted in the
Franciscan tradition are imaginative participation in the key events
of Christ's passion; an emphasis on narrative sequence and dra-
matic incident; emotional empathy with the experiences of Christ
and Mary; and an intensification of interest in visual detail and of
the arrangement of people, objects and buildings. It is not difficult
to see why narratives inspired by Franciscan piety also had a
marked impact on pictorial composition. Transposed to another
representational mode, they demanded greater spatial realism and
a focus on significant narrative moments. David Wilkins links
Giotto's spatial realism specifically to the Franciscan religious
revolution of the thirteenth century. He maintains that St Francis's
attitude towards traditional religious stories was crucial because it
made a distinct effort to humanize otherwise remote and miracu-
lous happenings. The writings of the early Franciscans, such as
*Meditations on the Life of Christ*, include intimate details, a personal
style and evocative suggestions. Under Franciscan influence, the
period sees generally a growing interest in naturalism, of which
three-dimensional space is one aspect, and this is related to the
artists' concern with narrative. For the exploration of pictorial
space in paintings of the trecento is directly related to particular
narrative problems, to the demands of the plot and to its concern
with drama and emotion.[13]

Giotto's 'Marriage at Cana', at Padua, is for John White the
'starting point for all the later evolution of Giottesque perspec-
tive'.[14] It illustrates how the particular emphases of the narrative

---

13    Wilkins, 'Meaning of Space'. Cf. Hills, *Light of Early Italian Painting*, pp.
      12ff.; and Miles, *Image as Insight*, pp. 63–81.
14    White, *Birth and Rebirth*, p. 87.

are rendered in pictorial terms (Fig. 11.1). The patterned fretwork
of the canopy helps to set the recessional limits of the shallow
stage on which the action takes place but other details, such as the
averted and partially obscured figures and the large, foregrounded
wine-jars, are much stronger spatial cues. Eye contact among the
participants is also used to create a mesh of spatial relations. The
figures themselves are solid, sculptural, individualistic and, unlike
their early Gothic precursors, are depicted from a variety of angles.
They are placed in a dramatic situation and, as the participants in a
drama, seem to inhabit a space that is laden with emotion, tension
and atmosphere, thus validating human experience, however lowly.
It is the moment when a butler tests the truth of Christ's miracle.[15]

A picture such as this has many implications for an analysis of
Chaucer's spatial designs. It raises questions about the dependence
of coherent space upon realistic narrative; of the relations between
sight and space; of the suggestiveness of the human figure and
body language; of the importance of visual cues, including frames,
to signal depth; and of the synchronizing of three-dimensional
space with climactic dramatic episodes. As we have seen, Chaucer
was himself well versed in such techniques, which owe a good deal
to Boccaccio (himself an admirer of Giotto's work). Whether or
not Chaucer had direct access to trecento art, to the French
interpretations of it, or to its English variants,[16] he had a vivid
pictorial imagination, and one that could make deliberate and
strategic use of spatial effects. Already noted is the picture window
of the Knight's Tale, where a distant and vivid scene, one set to
change the direction of the narrative, is framed by the dark interior
of the prison at a moment of heightened drama. Within a few dec-
ades of Chaucer's death, Alberti made his famous formulation of a
painting as a window intersecting the rays of the visual pyramid

15    Ibid., pp. 65–6; and his *Art and Architecture*, p. 213. Cf. Edgerton, *Heritage of Giotto's Geometry*, ch. 2.
16    Binski and Park, 'Ducciesque Episode'; Hagiioannu, 'Giotto's Bardi Chapel Frescoes'; Kemp, *Science of Art*, pp. 9–12; Pächt, 'Giottesque Episode'; Pearsall, 'Visual World', pp. 310–13.

**Figure 11.1.** Giotto di Bondone, 'Marriage at Cana'
(1304–*c*.1312). Padua, Scrovegni Chapel.

(1435) and, a little later, Lorenzo Ghiberti used Alhacen's writings to formulate a theory of vanishing point perspective, or *perspectiva artificialis*.[17] Recent scholarship suggests that painters and architects made even earlier engagements with medieval optical theory.[18]

The links and analogies between Chaucer's spatial practices and those found in memorial practices, Franciscan writings or trecento art await further study. It is to be hoped that the present book has at least provided further justification – if any were needed – for examining the ways in which Chaucer deploys space in response to literary models and to writings with a more scientific bent. And just as Chaucer absorbed, reconstituted and revised spatial designs in Dante and Boccaccio, in part by incorporating new optical material, so fifteenth-century authors learnt from him some of the techniques and applications of narrative space. *The Kingis Quair*, written by King James I of Scotland between 1422 and 1437, adapts Palamon's view of Emelye from a prison window in order to articulate ideas of liberation and of connection to a network of social relations.[19] And Spearing observes that the most notable and distinctive descriptive skill of John Lydgate, a keen imitator of Chaucer, 'depends on the evocation of space, light, and color' to produce effects comparable to those found in late medieval manuscript illumination.[20] It is to be hoped that, as studies of the construction and use of space within medieval narrative become more frequent, the centrality of Chaucer as assimilator, innovator and model will become increasingly apparent.

---

17   Alberti, *De pictura*, I. 12, ed. Grayson, p. 48; Andrews, *Story and Space*, pp. 48–56; Edgerton, *Renaissance Rediscovery*, ch. 6; Romanyshyn, *Technology as Symptom and Dream*, pp. 35–57; White, *Birth and Rebirth*, p. 129.
18   Trachtenberg, *Dominion of the Eye*, pp. 232–4.
19   Boffey, 'Chaucerian Prisoners', pp. 90–9.
20   Spearing, 'Lydgate's Canterbury Tale', p. 36.

# Works Cited

## Primary Sources

Anon. *Liber exemplorum ad usum praedicantium*, ed. A. G. Little. British Society of Franciscan Studies, 1. Aberdeen: Aberdeen University Press, 1908.

―――― *Le Roman de Renart le contrefait*, ed. Gaston Raynaud and Henri Lemaitre. 2 vols. Paris: Champion, 1914.

―――― *Sidrak and Bokkus*, ed. T. L. Burton. 2 vols. EETS os 311 (1998) and 312 (1999).

Alan of Lille, *Anticlaudianus*, ed. R. Bossuat. Textes Philosophiques du Moyen Age, 1. Paris: Vrin, 1955.

―――― *Anticlaudianus, or The Good and Perfect Man*, trans. James J. Sheridan. Toronto: Pontifical Institute of Mediaeval Studies, 1973.

Alberti, Leon Battista. *De pictura. 'On Painting' and 'On Sculpture': The Latin Texts of 'De pictura' and 'De statua'*, ed. and trans. Cecil Grayson. London: Phaidon, 1972.

Albertus Magnus. *De anima*, ed. Clemens Stroick. In *Opera omnia*, vol. 1, pt 1. Weisbaden: Monasterii Westafalorum in aedibus Aschendorff, 1968.

Alhacen. *De aspectibus. As Alhacen's Theory of Visual Perception: A Critical Edition, with English Translation and Commentary, of the First Three Books of Alhacen's De aspectibus, the Medieval Latin Version of Ibn al-Haytham's Kitab al-Manazir*, ed. A. Mark Smith. 2 vols. Transactions of the American Philosophical Society, vol. 91, pts 4 and 5. Philadelphia: American Philosophical Society, 2001.

―――― *De aspectibus*. In *Opticae thesaurus: Alhazen arabis libri septem [...] Vitellonis Thuringpoloni libri X*, ed. F. Risner. Sources of Science, 94. Basel: 1572; repr. New York: Johnson, 1972.

―――― *The Optics of Ibn Al-Haytham, Books I–III On Direct Vision*, trans. A. I. Sabra. 2 vols. Studies of the Warburg Institute 40, i and ii. London: Warburg Institute, 1989.

Aristotle. *De anima. As Aristotle's De anima in the Version of William of Moerbeke and the Commentary of St Thomas Aquinas*, trans. Kenelm Foster and Silvester Humphries. London: Routledge, 1951.

Bacon, Roger. *De multiplicatione specierum. As Roger Bacon's Philosophy of Nature: A Critical Edition, with English Translation, Introduction, and Notes, of De multiplicatione specierum and De speculis comburentibus*, ed. and trans. David C. Lindberg. Oxford: Clarendon Press, 1983.

—— *Opus maius*, ed. John Henry Bridges. 3 vols. London: Williams and Norgate, 1897–1900.

—— *Perspectiva*. As *Roger Bacon and the Origins of* Perspectiva *in the Middle Ages: A Critical Edition and English Translation of Bacon's* Perspectiva, ed. and trans. David C. Lindberg. Oxford: Clarendon Press, 1996.

Bartholomaeus Anglicus. *On the Properties of Things: John Trevisa's Translation of* Bartholomaeus Anglicus De proprietatibus rerum, ed. M. C. Seymour et al. 3 vols. Oxford: Clarendon Press, 1975–88.

Bartholomew of Bononia. *Tractatus de luce*. Ed. Irenaeus Squadrani as '*Tractatus de luce* Fr. Bartholomaei de Bononia: inquisitiones et textus'. *Antonianum* 7 (1932), 201–38.

Berangar of Andorra. *Lumen animae*. As *Liber moralitatum elegantissimus magnarum rerum naturalium lumen anime dictus*, [ed. Mathias Farinator]. [Augsburg: ptd Günter Zainer], 1477.

Boccaccio, Giovanni. *Chaucer's Boccaccio: Sources of* Troilus *and the* Knight's *and* Franklin's *Tales*, ed. and trans. N. R. Havely. Chaucer Studies, 3. Cambridge: Brewer; Totowa, NJ: Rowman and Littlefield, 1980.

—— *Filostrato, Teseida, Chiose al Teseida*, ed. Mario Marti. In his *Opere minore*, vol. 4 (1970).

—— *Opere minore in volgare*, ed. Mario Marti. 4 vols. I Classici Rizzioli. Milan: Rizzoli, 1969–72.

—— *Teseida* [excerpts], trans. N. R. Havely. In his *Chaucer's Boccaccio* (1980), pp. 103–52.

Bozon, Nicole. *Les Contes moralisés de Nicole Bozon frère mineur*, ed. Lucy Toulmin Smith and Paul Meyer. SATF. Paris: 1889.

Bromyard, John. *Summa praedicantium omni eruditione refertissima, explicans praecipuos catholicae disciplinae sensus, et locos [...] nunc demum post alios aeditiones [...] recognita et [...] aucta, et illustrati* [by A. Ritius]. 2 pts. Venice: ptd Dominicus Nicolinus, 1586.

Charland, Th.–M. *Artes praedicandi: contribution à l'histoire de la rhétorique au moyen âge*. Publications de l'Institut d'Etudes Médiévales d'Ottawa, 7. Paris: Vrin; Ottawa: Institut d'Etudes Médiévales, 1936.

Chaucer, Geoffrey. *Astrolabe*. As *Chaucer and Messahalla on the Astrolabe*, ed. and trans. R. T. Gunther. Early Science in Oxford, 5. Oxford: ptd for subscribers at the University Press, 1929.

—— *Astrolabe. Chaucer's* Treatise on the Astrolabe: *MS. 4862–4869 of the Royal Library in Brussels* [Facsimile with intro. and notes by P. Pintelon]. Rijksuniversiteit te Gent Werken uitgegeven door de Faculteit van de Wijsbegeerte en Letteren, 89. Antwerp: de Sikkel, 1940.

—— *The Book of the Duchess*, ed. Helen Phillips, rev. edn. Durham and St Andrews Medieval Texts, 3. Durham and St Andrews: Durham and St Andrews Medieval Texts, 1984.

—— *Chaucer's Dream Poetry*, ed. Helen Phillips and Nick Havely. Longman Annotated Texts. London and New York: Longman, 1997.

—— *The House of Fame*, ed. Nicholas R. Havely. Durham Medieval Texts, 11. Durham: Durham Medieval Texts, 1994.

—— [*Works*.] *The Riverside Chaucer*, ed. Larry D. Benson et al. 3rd edn. Boston, Mass.: Houghton Mifflin, 1987.

—— *The Romaunt of the Rose and Le Roman de la Rose: A Parallel-Text Edition*, ed. Ronald Sutherland. Oxford: Blackwell, 1967.

—— *The Squire's Tale*, ed. Donald C. Baker. A Variorum Edition of the Works of Geoffrey Chaucer, vol. 2, pt 12. Norman, Okla., and London: University of Oklahome Press, 1990.

Clark, John Willis. *Fasciculus Ioanni Willis Clark dicatus*. Cambridge: Cambridge University Press, 1909.

Dante Alighieri. *The Divine Comedy*, ed. and trans. Charles S. Singleton. [Corrected text]. 6 vols. Bollingen series, 80. Princeton: Princeton University Press, 1977.

Denifle, Henricus and Chatelain, Aemilio. *Chartularium universitatis Parisiensis*. 4 vols. Paris: Delalain, 1889–97.

Duns Scotus. [*Commentary on the Sentences*.] As 'Medieval Light Theory and Optics and Duns Scotus' Treatment of Light in D.13 of Book II of his *Commentary on the Sentences*', ed. and trans. Edward Randal McCarthy. Diss. City University of New York, 1976.

Etienne de Besançon. *An Alphabet of Tales: An English 15th Century Translation of the* Alphabetum Narrationum *of Etienne de Besançon*, ed. Mary Macleod Banks. 2 vols. EETS os 126 (1904) and 127 (1905).

Euclid. *De visu*. As 'The Mediaeval Tradition of Euclid's *Optics*', ed. and trans. Wilfred R. Theisen. Diss. University of Wisconsin, 1972.

—— Ed. Wilfred Theisen as '*Liber de visu*: The Greco-Latin Translation of Euclid's Optics'. *Mediaeval Studies* 41 (1979), 44–105.

Faral, Edmond. *Les Arts poétiques du XIIè et du XIIIè siècle: recherches et documents sur la technique littéraire du moyen âge*. Bibliothèque de l'Ecole des Hautes Etudes, Section 4: Sciences Historiques et Philologiques, fasc. 238. Paris: Champion, 1924, repr. 1962.

Geoffrey of Vinsauf. *Poetria nova*, trans. Margaret F. Nims. Toronto: Pontifical Institute of Mediaeval Studies, 1967.

Gibson, Strickland (ed.) *Statuta antiqua universitatis Oxoniensis*. Oxford: Clarendon Press, 1931.

Gower, John. *Confessio Amantis*. In *English Works*, ed. Macaulay (1900–1).

—— *The Complete Works of John Gower*, ed. G. C. Macaulay. 4 vols. Oxford: Clarendon Press, 1899–1902.

—— *The English Works of John Gower*, ed. G. C. Macaulay. 2 vols. EETS es 81 (1900) and 82 (1901).

—— *Major Latin Works of John Gower: The Voice of One Crying and the Tripartite Chronicle*, trans. E. W. Stockton. Seattle: University of Washington Press, 1962.

—— *Vox Clamantis*. In *Complete Works*, ed. Macaulay, vol. 4 (1902).

Grant, Edward (ed.) *A Source Book in Medieval Science.* Source Books in the History of the Sciences. Cambridge, Mass.: Harvard University Press, 1974.

Grosseteste, Robert. *Commentary on the Posterior Analytics of Aristotle.* As *Divi Roberti Lincolniensis archiepiscopi Parisiensis ordinis praedicatorum in Aristotelis peripatheticorum principis posteriorum analeticorum librum* (Venice: 1521).

—— *Hexaëmeron,* ed. Richard C. Dales and Servus Gieben. Auctores Britannici Medii Aevi, 6. London: Oxford University Press for the British Academy, 1982.

—— *Hexameron,* ed. J. T. Muckle as 'The Hexameron of Robert Grosseteste: The First Twelve Chapters of Part Seven'. *Mediaeval Studies* 6 (1944), 151–74.

—— [*Letters.*] As *Roberti Grosseteste episcopi quondam Lincolniensis epistolae,* ed. Henry Richards Luard. Rolls ser., 25 (1861).

—— *On Light (De luce),* trans. C. Riedl. Milwaukee: Marquette University Press, 1942.

—— *On the Six Days of Creation: A Translation of the* Hexaëmeron, trans. C. F. J. Martin. Auctores Britannici Medii Aevi, 6 (2). Oxford: Oxford University Press for the British Academy, 1996.

—— [*Optical works.*] 'The Geometrical Optics of Robert Grosseteste', ed. Bruce S. Eastwood. Diss University of Wisconsin, 1964.

—— [*Optical works.*] *Die philosophischen Werke des Robert Grosseteste, Bishofs von Lincoln,* ed. Ludwig Baur. Beiträge zur Geschichte der Philosophie des Mittelalters, 9. Münster: 1912.

—— [*Sermons and Dicta.*] Ed. Edwin J. Westermann as 'A Comparison of Some of the Sermons and the *Dicta* of Robert Grosseteste'. *Mediaevalia et Humanistica* 3 (1945), 49–68.

—— [*Sermons and Dicta.*] As *Fasciculus rerum expetendarum et fugiendarum, prout ab O. G. editus est Coloniae. A.D. 1535,* ed. Edward Brown. 2 vols. London: Chiswell, 1690. Vol. 2, pp. 250-305.

Guillaume de Lorris and Jean de Meun. *The Romance of the Rose,* trans. Charles Dahlberg. Princeton: Princeton University Press, 1971.

—— *Le Roman de la Rose,* ed. Ernest Langlois. 5 vols. SATF (1914–24).

—— *The 'Romaunt of the Rose' and 'Le Roman de la Rose': A Parallel Text Edition,* ed. Ronald Sutherland. Oxford: Blackwell, 1967.

Holcot, Robert. *Super sapientiam Salomonis.* As *M. Roberti Holkoth […] in librum sapientiae regis Salomonis praelectiones CCXIII,* [ed. J. Ryterus] ([Basel]: 1586).

Love, Nicholas. *Nicholas Love's 'Mirror of the Blessed Life of Jesus Christ',* ed. Michael D. Sargent. Garland Reference Library of the Humanities, 1233; Garland Medieval Texts, 18. New York and London: Garland, 1992.

Neckham, Alexander. *'De naturis rerum libri duo' with the Poem of the Same Author: 'De laudibus divinae sapientiae',* ed. Thomas Wright. Rolls ser., (1863).

—— *De naturis rerum,* trans. [in part] David C. Lindberg and Greta J. Lindberg. In Grant (ed.), *Source Book,* pp. 380–3.

Oresme, Nicole. *Quaestiones super quatuor libros meteororum.* As 'Nicole Oresme on Light, Color and the Rainbow: An Edition and Translation, with Introduction and Critical Notes, of Part of Book 3 of his *Quaestiones super quatuor libros meteororum*', ed. Stephen Clement McCluskey, Jr. Diss. University of Wisconsin-Madison, 1974.

Ovid. *Metamorphoses*, ed. and trans. Frank Justus Miller. 2 vols. Loeb Classical Library. London: Heinemann; New York: Putnam's, 1916.

Pecham, John. *Perspectiva communis.* As *John Pecham and the Science of Optics: Perspectiva communis*, ed. and trans. David C. Lindberg. University of Wisconsin Publications in Medieval Science. Madison, Milwaukee and London: University of Wisconsin Press, 1970.

—— *Tractatus de perspectiva*, ed. David C. Lindberg. Franciscan Institute Publication, text ser. 16. St Bonaventure, NY: Franciscan Institute, 1972.

Peter of Limoges. *De oculo morali.* As *Johannis Pithsani archiepiscopi Canthuariensis [...] liber de oculo morali.* [Augsburg: ptd A. Sorg, 1475?].

Pseudo-Grosseteste. *Summa philosophiae.* As *A Study of the* Summa philosophiae *of the Pseudo-Grosseteste*, ed. Charles King McKeon. New York: Columbia University Press, 1948.

Rymer, T. and Sanderson, R. (eds). *Fœdera, conventions, litterae et cujuscunque generis acta publica inter reges Angliae, et alios*, ed. A. Clarke, F. Holbrooke, [and J. Caley]. 4 vols. in 6. London: [Record Commission], 1816–69.

Sandler, Lucy Freeman. *Omne bonum: A Fourteenth-Century Encyclopedia of Universal Knowledge, British Library MSS Royal E VI – 6 E VII.* 2 vols. London: Harvey Miller, 1996.

Seneca (Lucius Annaeus). *Ad Lucilium epistolae morales*, ed. and trans. Richard M. Gummere. 3 vols. Loeb Classical Library. London: Heinemann, 1917–25.

Shirley, Walter Waddington (ed.) *Royal and Other Historical Letters Illustrative of the Reign of Henry III.* 2 vols. Rolls series. London: Longmans, 1862–6.

Siegel, Rudolph E. *Galen on Sense Perception: His Doctrines, Observations and Experiments on Vision, Hearing, Smell, Taste, Touch and Pain and their Historical Sources.* Basel and New York: Karger, 1970.

Thomas of Eccleston, *De adventu fratrum minorum.* As *Fratris Thomae vulgo dicti de Eccleston tractatus de adventu fratrum minorum in Angliam*, ed. A. G. Little. Tout Memorial Publication Fund. Manchester: Manchester University Press, 1951.

Vincent of Beauvais. *Liber apologeticus.* As *Préface au* Speculum maius *de Vincent de Beauvais: réfraction et diffraction*, ed. Sergé Lusignan. Institut d'Etudes Médiévales de Montréal, Cahiers d'Etudes Médiévales, 5. Montréal: Bellarmin; Paris: Vrin, 1979.

—— *Speculum maius.* As *Bibliotheca mundi: Vincentii Bellovacensis speculum quadruplex; naturale, doctrinale, morale, historiale*, 4 vols. Douai: ptd B. Belleri, 1624.

Witelo. *Perspectiva.* In *Opticae thesaurus [...] item Vitellonis Thuringopoloni libri X*, ed. F. Risner [1572], intro. by David C. Lindberg. Sources of Science, 94. New York: Johnson, 1972.

—— *Witelonis perspectivae liber primus: Book I of Witelo's* Perspectiva, ed. and trans. Sabetai Unguru. Studia Copernica, 15. Wroclaw: Ossolineum/Polish Academy of Sciences Press, 1977.

—— *Witelonis perspectivae liber secundus et liber tertius: Books II and III of Witelo's* Perspectiva, ed. and trans. Sabetai Unguru. Studia Copernica, 28. Wroclaw: Ossolineum/Polish Academy of Sciences Press, 1991.

—— 'Witelonis Perspectivae Liber Quartus: Book IV of Witelo's *Perspectiva* – A Critical Edition and English Translation with Introduction, Notes and Commentary', ed. Carl J. Kelso, Jr. Diss. University of Missouri-Columbia, 2003.

—— *Witelonis perspectivae liber quintus: Book V of Witelo's* Perspectiva, ed. and trans. A. Mark Smith. Studia Copernica, 23. Wroclaw: Ossolineum/Polish Academy of Sciences Press, 1983.

Wyclif, John. *De actibus anime.* In *Johannis Wyclif miscellanea philosophica,* ed. Michael Henry Dziewicki. 2 vols. Wyclif's Latin Works, 19. London: Wyclif Society, 1902–5. Vol. 1 (1902 for 1901).

## Secondary Studies

Aerts, W. J.; Smits, E. R.; and Voorbij, J. B. (eds). *Vincent of Beauvais and Alexander the Great: Studies on the* Speculum maius *and its Translations into Medieval Vernaculars.* Mediaevalia Groningana, 7. Groningen: Forsten, 1986.

Aiken, Pauline. 'Arcite's Illness and Vincent of Beauvais'. *PMLA* 51 (1936), 361–9.

—— 'Chaucer's *Legend of Cleopatra* and the *Speculum Historiale*'. *Speculum* 13 (1938), 232–6.

—— 'The Summoner's Malady'. *Studies in Philology* 33 (1936), 40–4.

—— 'Vincent of Beauvais and Chaucer's Knowledge of Alchemy'. *Studies in Philology* 41 (1944), 371–89.

—— 'Vincent of Beauvais and Chaucer's Monk's Tale'. *Speculum* 17 (1942), 56–68.

—— 'Vincent of Beauvais and Dame Pertelote's Knowledge of Medicine'. *Speculum* 10 (1935), 281–7.

—— 'Vincent of Beauvais and the Green Yeoman's Lecture on Demonology'. *Studies in Philology* 35 (1938), 1–9.

—— 'Vincent of Beauvais and the "Houres" of Chaucer's Physician'. *Studies in Philology* 53 (1956), 22–4.

Akbari, Suzanne Conklin. 'Medieval Optics in Guillaume de Lorris' *Roman de la Rose*'. *Medievalia et Humanistica* ns 21 (1994) [*Convergences*, ed. Paul Maurice], 1–15.

—— *Seeing through the Veil: Optical Theory and Medieval Allegory*. Toronto, Buffalo and London: University of Toronto Press, 2004.

Alessio, Franco. 'Per uno studio sull'ottica del Trecento'. *Studi Medievali* ser. 3, 2 (1961), 444–504.

Alexander, J. J. G. and Gibson, M. T. (eds). *Medieval Learning and Literature: Essays Presented to Richard William Hunt*. Oxford: Clarendon Press, 1976.

Allen, Valerie. 'Portrait of a Lady: Blanche and the Descriptive Tradition'. *English Studies* 74 (1993), 324–42.

Andrew, Malcolm. 'Games'. In *Companion to Chaucer*, ed. Brown (2000), pp. 166–79.

Andrews, Lew. *Story and Space in Renaissance Art: The Rebirth of Continuous Narrative*. Cambridge: Cambridge University Press, 1995.

Bachelard, Gaston. *The Poetics of Space*, trans. Maria Jolas. New York: Orion Press, 1964. First published as *La Poétique de l'espace* (Paris: Presses Universitaires de France, 1958).

Baig, Bonnie Paulis. 'Vision and Visualization: Optics and Light Metaphysics in the Imagery and Poetic Form of Twelfth and Thirteenth Century Secular Allegory with Special Reference to the *Roman de la Rose*'. Diss. University of California, Berkeley, 1982.

Baldwin, Robert. '"Gates Pure and Shining and Serene": Mutual Gazing as an Amatory Motif in Western Literature and Art'. *Renaissance and Renascences* ns 10 (1986), 23–48.

Barney, Stephen A. *Allegories of History, Allegories of Love*. Hamden, Conn.: Archon Books, 1979.

—— 'Troilus Bound'. *Speculum* 47 (1972), 445–58.

—— (ed.) *Chaucer's 'Troilus': Essays in Criticism*. London: Scolar Press, 1980.

Barron, Caroline M. 'Centres of Conspicuous Consumption: The Aristocratic Town House in London 1200–1550'. *The London Journal* 20.1 (1995), 1–16.

Bauer, Hans. *Die Psychologie Alhazens auf Grund von Alhazens Optik*. Beiträge zur Geschichte der Philosophie des Mittelalters, 10, pt 5. Münster: 1911.

Baur, Ludwig. 'Das Licht in der Naturphilosophie des Robert Grosseteste'. In von Hertling, *Abhandlungen* (1913), pp. 41–55.

—— *Die Philosophie des Robert Grosseteste Bishofs von Lincoln*. Beiträge zur Geschichte der Philosophie des Mittelalters, 18, pts 4–6. Münster: 1917.

—— (ed.) *Die philosophischen Werke*. See Grosseteste, [*Optical works*].

Beckwith, Sarah. *Christ's Body: Identity, Culture and Society in Late Medieval Writings*. London and New York: Routledge, 1993.

Becq, Annie (ed.) *L'Encyclopédisme: actes du Colloque de Caen 12–16 janvier 1987*. Paris: Amateurs de Livres, 1991.

Beidler, Peter G. 'Chaucer's *Merchant's Tale* and the *Decameron*'. *Italica* 50 (1973), 266–84.

Benko, Georges and Strohmayer, Ulf (eds). *Space and Social Theory: Interpreting Modernity and Post-Modernity*. The Royal Geographical Society with the Institute of British Geographers Special Publications Series, 33. Oxford: Blackwell, 1997.

Bennett, J. A. W. *Chaucer at Oxford and at Cambridge* Oxford: Clarendon Press, 1974.
——— *Chaucer's 'Book of Fame': An Exposition of the* House of Fame. Oxford: Clarendon Press, 1968.
——— *The 'Parlement of Foules': An Interpretation.* Rev. edn. Oxford: Clarendon Press, 1965.
Benson, Larry D. (ed.) *The Learned and the Lewed: Studies in Chaucer and Medieval Literature.* Harvard English Studies, 5. Cambridge, Mass.: Harvard University Press, 1974.
Berger, Harry, Jr. 'The F-Fragment of the Canterbury Tales: Part I'. *Chaucer Review* 1 (1966–7), 88–102.
Berlioz, Jacques. 'Introduction à la recherche dans les *exempla* médiévaux'. In *Les Exempla médiévaux*, ed. Berlioz and Polo de Beaulieu (1992), pp. 15–73.
——— and Polo de Beaulieu, Marie Anne (eds). *Les Exempla médiévaux: introduction à la recherche suivie des tables critiques de Frederic C. Tubach.* Carcassonne: Garae/Hesiode, 1992.
Bethurum, Dorothy (ed.) *Critical Approaches to Medieval Literature: Selected Papers from the English Institute 1958–1959.* New York: Columbia University Press, 1960.
Bevan, Edwyn. *Symbolism and Belief.* Gifford Lectures. London: Allen and Unwin, 1938.
Biernoff, Suzannah. *Sight and Embodiment in the Middle Ages.* Houndmills: Palgrave Macmillan, 2002.
Binski, Paul and Park, David. 'A Ducciesque Episode at Ely: The Mural Decorations of Prior Crauden's Chapel'. In *England in the Fourteenth Century*, ed. Ormrod (1986), pp. 28–41.
Birkenmajer, Aleksander. *Etudes d'histoire des sciences en Pologne*, trans. Claire Brendel et al. Polska Akademia Nank. Zaklad Historii Nauki i Techniki. Studia Copernica, 4. Wroclaw: Zaklad Narodowy imienina Ossolínskich, 1972.
——— 'Etudes sur Witelo, 4è partie: Witelo et l'Université de Padoue' [1922]. In his *Etudes* (1972), pp. 361–407.
——— 'Pierre de Limoges commentateur de Richard de Fournival'. *Isis* 40 (1949), 18–31.
——— 'Robert Grosseteste and Richard Fournival'. *Medievalia et Humanistica* 5 (1948), 36–41.
——— 'Witelo, le plus ancien savant silesian' [1936]. In his *Etudes* (1972), pp. 413–34.
Blodgett, E. D. 'Chaucerian *Pryvetee* and the Opposition to Time'. *Speculum* 51 (1976), 477–93.
Boffey, Julia. 'Chaucerian Prisoners: The Context of *The Kingis Quair*'. In *Chaucer and Fifteenth-Century Poetry*, ed. Boffey and Cowen (1991), pp. 84–102.
——— and Cowen, Janet (eds). *Chaucer and Fifteenth-Century Poetry.* King's College London Medieval Studies, 5. London: King's College London Centre for Late Antique and Medieval Studies, 1991.

Boitani, Piero. *Chaucer and Boccaccio.* Medium Ævum Monographs, ns 8. Oxford: Society for the Study of Mediaeval Languages and Literature, 1977.

—— *Chaucer and the Imaginary World of Fame.* Chaucer Studies, 10. Cambridge: Brewer; Totowa, NJ: Barnes & Noble, 1984.

—— *English Medieval Narrative in the Thirteenth and Fourteenth Centuries,* trans. Joan Krakover Hall. Cambridge: Cambridge University Press, 1982.

—— 'What Dante Meant to Chaucer'. In *Chaucer and the Italian Trecento,* ed. Boitani (1983), pp. 115–39.

—— (ed.) *Chaucer and the Italian Trecento.* Cambridge: Cambridge University Press, 1983.

—— and Torti, Anna (eds). *Medieval and Pseudo-Medieval Literature: The J. A. W. Bennett Memorial Lectures, Perugia 1982–1983.* Tübingen: Narr; Cambridge: Brewer, 1984.

Bonnard, G. A. (ed.) *English Studies Today,* 2nd ser. Lectures and papers read at the fourth conference of the International Association of University Professors of English held at Lausanne and Berne, August 1959. Bern: Francke, 1961.

Borges, Jorge Luis. 'The Aleph'. In *The Aleph* (1971), pp. 15–30.

—— *The Aleph and Other Stories 1933–1969,* trans. Norman Thomas de Giovanni. London: Cape, 1971.

Boyde, Patrick. *Dante Philomythes and Philosopher: Man in the Cosmos.* Cambridge: Cambridge University Press, 1981.

—— *Perception and Passion in Dante's 'Comedy'.* Cambridge: Cambridge University Press, 1993.

Boyle, Leonard E. 'The Date of the *Summa praedicantium* of John Bromyard'. *Speculum* 48 (1973), 533–7. Repr. in his *Pastoral Care* (1981), item 10.

—— 'The *Oculus sacerdotis* and Some Other Works of William of Pagula (The Alexander Prize Essay)'. *Transactions of the Royal Historical Society* 5th ser., 5 (1955), 81–110.

—— *Pastoral Care, Clerical Education and Canon Law, 1200–1400.* London: Variorum, 1981.

Bradbury, S., and Turner, G. L'E (eds). *Historical Aspects of Microscopy: Papers Read at a One-Day Conference Held by The Royal Microscopical Society at Oxford, 18 March, 1966.* Cambridge: Heffer for the Royal Microscopical Society, 1967.

Bradley, Ritamary. 'Backgrounds of the Title *Speculum* in Mediaeval Literature'. *Speculum* 29 (1954), 100–15.

—— 'The Speculum Image in Medieval Mystical Writers'. In *Medieval Mystical Tradition,* ed. Glasscoe (1984), pp. 9–27.

Bremer, Dieter. 'Licht als universales Darstellungsmedium: Materialien und Bibliographie'. *Archiv für Begriffsgeschichte* 18, pt 2 (1974), 185–206.

Bremond, Claude; le Goff, Jacques; and Schmitt, Jean-Claude. *L'"Exemplum".* Typologie des Sources du Moyen Age Occidental, 40. Turnhout: Brepols, 1982.

Brewer, Derek (ed.) *Geoffrey Chaucer*. Writers and their Background. London: Bell, 1974.

Bridges, John Henry. *The Life and Work of Roger Bacon: An Introduction to the* Opus majus, ed. H. Gordon Jones. London: Williams and Norgate, 1914.

Brody, Saul N. 'Making a Play for Criseyde: The Staging of Pandarus's House in Chaucer's *Troilus and Criseyde*'. *Speculum* 73 (1998), 115–40.

Brown, Peter. *Chaucer at Work: The Making of the* Canterbury Tales. Harlow: Longman, 1994.

—— 'Chaucer's Visual World: A Study of His Poetry and the Medieval Optical Tradition'. 2 vols. Diss. University of York Centre for Medieval Studies, 1981.

—— 'The Containment of Symkyn: The Function of Space in the Reeve's Tale'. *Chaucer Review* 14 (1979–80), 225–36.

—— 'An Optical Theme in the Merchant's Tale'. *Studies in the Age of Chaucer: Proceedings*, 2 (1986), 231–43.

—— 'The Prison of Theseus'. *Chaucer Review*, 26 (1991–2), 147–52.

—— '"Shot Wyndowe" (Miller's Tale I. 3358 and 3695): An Open and Shut Case?' *Medium Ævum* 69 (2000), 96–103.

—— (ed.) *A Companion to Chaucer*. Oxford: Blackwell, 2000.

Brownlee, Kevin and Nichols, Stephen G. (eds). *Images of Power: Medieval History/Discourse/Literature*. Yale French Studies, 70. New Haven: Yale University Press, 1986.

Bruce, Vicki and Green, Patrick R. *Visual Perception: Physiology, Psychology and Ecology*. London and Hillsdale, NJ: Erlbaum, 1985.

Brusegan, Rosanna (ed.) *Un idea di città/L'Imaginaire de la ville médiévale*. Supplemento italo-francese di Nuovi Argomenti n. 43 dell'Istituto Italiano di Cultura di Parigi (Sep. 1992). Venice: Mondadori, 1992.

Buckmaster, Elizabeth. 'Meditation and Memory in Chaucer's *House of Fame*'. *Modern Language Studies* 16 (1986), 279–87.

Bundy, Murray Wright. *The Theory of Imagination in Classical and Mediaeval Thought*. University of Illinois Studies in Language and Literature, 12. Urbana, Ill.: University of Illinois Press, 1928. Repr. Norwood, 1978.

Burke, Peter (ed.). *New Perspectives on Historical Writing*. Cambridge: Polity Press, 1991.

Burlin, Robert B. *Chaucerian Fiction*. Princeton: Princeton University Press, 1977.

Burnley, J. D. 'Chaucer's *Termes*'. *Yearbook of English Studies* 7 (1977), 53–67.

——. 'Some Terminology of Perception in the *Book of the Duchess*'. *English Language Notes* 23 (1986), 15–22.

Burrow, J. A. *Gestures and Looks in Medieval Narrative*. Cambridge Studies in Medieval Literature. Cambridge: Cambridge University Press, 2002.

Butterfield, Ardis. 'Lyric and Elegy in the *Book of the Duchess*'. *Medium Ævum* 60 (1991), 33–60.

—— (ed.) *Chaucer and the City*. Chaucer Studies, 37. Cambridge: Brewer, 2006.

Callus, Daniel A. 'Introduction of Aristotelian Learning to Oxford'. *Proceedings of the British Academy* 29 (1943), 229–81.
—— 'The Oxford Career of Robert Grosseteste'. *Oxoniensia* 10 (1945), 42–72.
—— 'Robert Grosseteste as Scholar'. In *Grosseteste Scholar and Bishop*, ed. Callus (1955), pp. 1–69.
—— 'Robert Grosseteste's Place in the History of Philosophy'. In *Actes du XIème Congrès Internationale de Philosophie*, 12 (Brussels: 1953), pp. 161–5.
—— (ed.) *Robert Grosseteste Scholar and Bishop: Essays in Commemoration of the Seventh Centenary of His Death*. Oxford: Clarendon Press, 1955.
Cambier, Guy (ed.) *Hommages à André Boutemy*. Collection Latomus, 145. Brussels: Latomus, 1976.
Camille, Michael. 'Before the Gaze: The Internal Senses and Late Medieval Practices of Seeing'. In *Visuality*, ed. Nelson (2000), pp. 197–223.
—— *The Gothic Idol: Ideology and Image-Making in Medieval Art*. Cambridge New Art History and Criticism. Cambridge: Cambridge University Press, 1989.
—— 'Illustrations in Harley MS 3487 and the Perception of Aristotle's *Libri naturales* in Thirteenth-Century England'. In *England in the Thirteenth Century*, ed. Ormrod (1985), pp. 31–44.
—— 'Signs of the City: Place, Power, and Public Fantasy in Medieval Paris'. In *Medieval Practices of Space*, ed. Hanawalt and Kobialka (2000), pp. 1–36.
Campbell, Mary Baine. '"Nel mezzo del cammin di nostra vita": The Palpability of *Purgatorio*'. In *Text and Territory*, ed. Tomasch and Gilles (1998), pp. 15–28.
Carey, Hilary M. 'Devout Literate Laypeople and the Pursuit of the Mixed Life in Later Medieval England'. *Journal of Religious History* 14 (1987), 361–81.
Carruthers, Mary. *The Book of Memory: A Study of Memory in Medieval Culture*. Cambridge Studies in Medieval Literature. Cambridge: Cambridge University Press, 1990.
—— '"The Mystery of the Bed Chamber": Mnemotechnique and Vision in Chaucer's *The Book of the Duchess*'. In *Rhetorical Poetics*, ed. Hill and Sinnreich-Levi (2000), pp. 67–87.
—— 'Seeing Things: Locational Memory in Chaucer's Knight's Tale'. In *Art and Context*, ed. Edwards (1994), pp. 93–106.
Carter, Paul. *The Road to Botany Bay: An Essay in Spatial History*. London and Boston: Faber, 1987.
Casey, Edward S. *The Fate of Place: A Philosophical History*. Berkeley, Los Angeles and London: University of California Press, 1997.
Catto, J. I. (ed.) *The Early Oxford Schools*. History of the University of Oxford, vol. 1. Oxford: Clarendon Press, 1984.
Chapman, Coolidge Otis. 'Chaucer on Preachers and Preaching'. *PMLA* 44 (1929), 178–85.
Cipriani, Lisa. 'Studies in the Influence of the *Romance of the Rose* upon Chaucer'. *PMLA* 22 (1907), 552–95.

Clagett, Marshall. 'Some General Aspects of Physics in the Middle Ages'. *Isis* 39 (1948), 29–44.

Clanchy, M. T. *From Memory to Written Record: England 1066–1307*, 2nd edn. Oxford and Cambridge, Mass.: Blackwell, 1993.

Clark, David L. 'Optics for Preachers: The *De oculo morali* by Peter of Limoges'. *Michigan Academician* 9 (1977), 329–43.

Clark, S. L. and Wasserman, J. N. 'Jonah and the Whale: Narrative Perspective in *Patience*'. *Orbis Litterarum* 35 (1980), 1–19.

——— 'The Pearl Poet's City Imagery'. *Southern Quarterly* 16 (1978), 297–309.

Clemen, Wolfgang. *Chaucer's Early Poetry*, trans. C. A. M. Sym. London: Methuen, 1963. First published as *Der junge Chaucer*, Grundlagen und Entwicklung seiner Dichtung, Kölner anglistiche Arbeiten, 33 (Bochum: Poppinghaus, 1938).

Cline, Ruth H. 'Hearts and Eyes'. *Romance Philology* 25 (1971–2), 264–97.

Cobban, Alan B. *The Medieval English Universities: Oxford and Cambridge to c.1500*. Aldershot: Scolar Press, 1988.

——— *The Medieval Universities: Their Development and Organization*. London: Methuen, 1975.

Coleman, Janet. 'English Culture in the Fourteenth Century'. In *Chaucer and the Italian Trecento*, ed. Boitani (1983), pp. 33–63.

——— *Medieval Readers and Writers*. English Literature in History 1350–1400. London: Hutchinson, 1981.

Coleman, Joyce. *Public Reading and the Reading Public in Late Medieval England and France*. Cambridge Studies in Medieval Literature, 26. Cambridge: Cambridge University Press, 1996.

Coleman, William E. 'The Knight's Tale'. In *Sources and Analogues*, ed. Correale and Hamel, vol. 2 (2005), pp. 87–247.

Collette, Carolyn P. *Species, Phantasms and Images: Vision and Medieval Psychology in The Canterbury Tales*. Ann Arbor: University of Michigan Press, 2001.

Collison, Robert. *Encyclopedias: Their History throughout the Ages. A Bibliographical Guide with Extensive Historical Notes to the General Encyclopedias Issued throughout the World from 350 B.C. to the Present Day*, 2nd edn. New York and London: Hafner, 1966.

Coppleston, F. C. *A History of Medieval Philosophy*. London: Methuen, 1972.

Correale, Robert M. and Hamel, Mary (eds). *Sources and Analogues of the Canterbury Tales*, vol. 1. Chaucer Studies, 28. Cambridge: Brewer, 2002.

——— *Sources and Anaologues of the Canterbury Tales*, vol. 2. Chaucer Studies, 35. Cambridge: Brewer, 2005.

Courtenay, William J. *Schools and Scholars in Fourteenth-Century England*. Princeton, NJ: Princeton University Press, 1987.

Crane, Susan. 'Medieval Romance and Feminine Difference in the Knight's Tale'. *Studies in the Age of Chaucer* 12 (1990), 47–63.

——— *Gender and Romance in Chaucer's Canterbury Tales*. Princeton, NJ: Princeton University Press, 1994.

Crane, T. F. 'Mediaeval Sermon-Books and Stories'. *Proceedings of the American Philosophical Society* 21 (1883), 49–78.

Crombie, A. C. 'Expectation, Modelling and Assent in the History of Optics, Part I: Alhazen and the Medieval Tradition'. In his *Science, Art and Nature* (1996), pp. 301–28. Repr. from *Studies in History and Philosophy of Science* 21 (1990), 605–32.

—— 'Grosseteste's Position in the History of Science'. In *Grosseteste Scholar and Bishop*, ed. Callus (1955), pp. 98–120.

—— 'The Mechanistic Hypothesis and the Scientific Study of Vision: Some Optical Ideas as a Background to the Invention of the Microscope'. In *Historical Aspects of Microscopy*, ed. Bradbury and Turner (1967), pp. 3–112.

—— *Robert Grosseteste and the Origins of Experimental Science 1100–1700*. Oxford: Clarendon Press, 1953.

—— *Science, Art and Nature in Medieval and Modern Thought*. London and Rio Grande, Ohio: Hambledon Press, 1996.

—— *Science, Optics and Music in Medieval and Early Modern Thought*. London and Roncevale, WV: Hambledon Press, 1990.

Crow, Martin M. and Olson, Clair C. (eds). *Chaucer Life-Records*. Oxford: Clarendon Press, 1966.

Crowley, Theodore. *Roger Bacon: The Problem of the Soul in his Philosophical Discourses*. Louvain: Editions de l'Institut Supérieur de Philosophie; Dublin: Duffy, 1950.

Curry, Walter Clyde. *Chaucer and the Mediaeval Sciences*, 2nd edn. New York: Barnes and Noble, 1960.

Curtius, Ernst Robert. *European Literature and the Latin Middle Ages*, trans. Willard R. Trask. London: Routledge, 1953. First published as *Europäische Literatur und lateinisches Mittelalter* (Bern: Francke, 1948).

Dahlberg, Charles. 'Macrobius and the Unity of the *Roman de la Rose*'. *Studies in Philology* 58 (1961), 573–82.

Daiches, David and Thorlby, Anthony (eds). *The Mediaeval World*. Literature and Western Civilization. London: Aldus, 1973.

Dales, Richard C. 'Robert Grosseteste's Scientific Works'. *Isis* 52 (1961), 381–402.

Davenport, W. A. *Chaucer and his Contemporaries: Prologue and Tale in the* Canterbury Tales. Basingstoke: Macmillan, 1998.

d'Avray, D. L. *The Preaching of the Friars: Sermons Diffused from Paris before 1300*. Oxford: Clarendon Press, 1985.

Davy, M. M. *Les Sermons universitaires parisiens de 1230–1231: contribution à l'histoire de la prédication médiévale*. Etudes de Philosophie Médiévale, 15. Paris: Vrin, 1931.

Dear, Michael. 'Postmodern Bloodlines'. In *Space and Social Theory*, ed. Benko and Strohmayer (1997), pp. 49–71.

de Bruyne, Edgar. *Etudes d'esthétique médiévale*. 3 vols. Rijksuniverstat te Gent Werken uitgegeven door de Faculteit van de Wijsbegeerte en Letteren, 97–9. Bruges: de Tempel, 1946.

Debus, Allen G. (ed.) *Science, Medicine and Society in the Renaissance: Essays in Honor of Walter Pagel*. 2 vols. London: Heinemann, 1972.

de Certeau, Michel. *The Practice of Everyday Life*, trans. Steven Rendall. Berkeley, Los Angeles and London: University of California Press, 1984.

Dedeck–Héry, V. L. 'Le *Boèce* de Chaucer et les manuscrits français de la *Consolatio* de Jean de Meun'. *PMLA* 59 (1944), 18–25.

—— 'Jean de Meun et Chaucer, traducteurs de la *Consolation* de Boèce'. *PMLA* 52 (1937), 967–91.

Delcorno, Carlo. *L'Exemplum nella predicazione volgare di Giordano da Pisa*. Istituto Veneto, Memorie, Classe di Scienze Morali, Lettere ed Arti, 36, fasc. 1. Venice: 1972.

Delisle, Léopold. *Le Cabinet des manuscripts de la Bibliothèque Impériale [Nationale]: étude sur la formation de ce dépôt, comprenant les éléments d'une histoire de la calligraphie, de la miniature, de la reliure, et du commerce des livres à Paris avant l'invention de l'imprimerie*. 3 vols. Paris: Imprimerie Impériale, 1868–81.

Dempster, Germaine. 'On the Sources of the Deception Story in the Merchant's Tale'. *Modern Philology* 34 (1936–7), 133–54.

Denery, Dallas G., II. *Seeing and Being Seen in the Later Medieval World: Optics, Theology and Religious Life*. Cambridge Studies in Medieval Life and Thought, 4th ser., 63. Cambridge: Cambridge University Press, 2005.

de Ridder-Symoens (ed.) *A History of the University in Europe*, vol. 1: *Universities in the Middle Ages*. Cambridge: Cambridge University Press, 1992.

Despres, Denise. *Ghostly Sights: Visual Meditation in Late-Medieval Literature*. Norman, Oklahoma: Pilgrim Books, 1989.

Devons, Samuel. 'Optics through the Eyes of the Medieval Churchmen'. In *Science and Technology*, ed. Long (1985), pp. 205–24.

Dilts, Dorothy Arlene. 'Observations on Dante and the *Hous of Fame*'. *Modern Language Notes* 57 (1942), 26–8.

DiMarco, Vincent. 'The Dialogue of Science and Magic in Chaucer's Squire's Tale'. In *Dialogische Strukturen*, ed. Kühn and Schaefer (1996), pp. 50–68.

—— 'The Squire's Tale'. In *Sources and Analogues*, ed. Correale and Hamel, vol. 1 (2002), pp. 169–209.

Dobbs, Elizabeth A. 'Seeing through Windows in Chaucer's *Troilus*'. *Chaucer Review* 32 (1997–8), 400–22.

Donaldson-Evans, Lance K. 'Love's Fatal Glance: Eye Imagery and Maurice Scève's *Délie*'. *Neophilologus* 62 (1978), 202–11.

Doob, Penelope Reed. *The Idea of the Labyrinth from Classical Antiquity through the Middle Ages*. Ithaca and London: Cornell University Press, 1990.

Douie, Decima L. *Archbishop Pecham*. Oxford: Clarendon Press, 1952.

Dronke, Peter and Mann, Jill. 'Chaucer and the Medieval Latin Poets'. In *Geoffrey Chaucer*, ed. Brewer (1974), pp. 154–83.

Easton, Stewart C. *Roger Bacon and his Search for a Universal Science: A Reconsideration of the Life and Work of Roger Bacon in the Light of his Own Stated Purposes*. New York: Columbia University Press, 1952. Repr. New York: Russell and Russell, 1971.

Eastwood, Bruce S. 'Geometrical Optics of Grosseteste'. See Grosseteste, [*Optical works.*]

—— 'Mediaeval Empiricism: The Case of Grosseteste's Optics'. *Speculum* 43 (1968), 306–21.

Eberle, Patricia J. 'The Lovers' Glass: Nature's Discourse on Optics and the Optical Design of the *Romance of the Rose*'. *University of Toronto Quarterly* 46 (1976–7), 241–62.

Edgerton, Samuel Y., Jr. *The Heritage of Giotto's Geometry: Art and Science on the Eve of the Scientific Revolution*. Ithaca and London: Cornell University Press, 1991.

—— *The Renaissance Rediscovery of Linear Perspective*. Icon Editions. New York: Harper and Row, 1976.

Edwards, A. S. G. (ed.) *Middle English Prose: A Critical Guide to Major Authors and Genres*. New Brunswick, NJ: Rutgers University Press, 1984.

Edwards, Paul (ed.) *The Encyclopedia of Philosophy*. 8 vols. London and New York: Macmillan, 1967.

Edwards, Robert R. 'The Desolate Palace and the Solitary City: Chaucer, Boccaccio and Dante'. *Studies in Philology* 96 (1999), 394–416.

—— *The Dream of Chaucer: Representation and Reflection in the Early Narratives*. Durham, NC and London: Duke University Press, 1989.

—— 'The Franklin's Tale'. In *Sources and Analogues*, ed. Correale and Hamel, vol. 1 (2002), pp. 211–65.

—— *Ratio and Invention: A Study of Medieval Lyric and Narrative*. Nashville: Vanderbilt University Press, 1989.

—— (ed.) *Art and Context in Late Medieval English Narrative: Essays in Honor of Robert Worth Frank, Jr*. Cambridge: Brewer, 1994.

—— and Ziegler, Vickie (eds). *Matrons and Marginal Women in Medieval Society*. Woodbridge: Boydell and Brewer, 1995.

Eldredge, Laurence. 'Sheltering Space and Cosmic Space in the Middle English *Patience*'. *Annuale Mediaevale* 21 (1981), 121–33.

Elkins, James. *The Poetics of Perspective*. Ithaca and London: Cornell University Press, 1994.

Ellmann, Maud. 'Blanche'. In *Criticism and Critical Theory*, ed. Hawthorn (1984), pp. 99–110.

Erickson, Carolly. *The Medieval Vision: Essays in History and Perception*. New York: Oxford University Press, 1976.

Esch, Arno (ed.) *Chaucer und seine Zeit: Symposion für Walter F. Schirmer*. Buchreihe der Anglia Zeitschrift für Englische Philologie, 14. Tübingen: Niemeyer, 1968.

Evans, Ruth. 'The Production of Space in Chaucer's London'. In *Chaucer and the City*, ed. Butterfield (2006), pp. 41–56.

Fairclough, Graham. 'Meaningful Constructions: Spatial and Functional Analysis of Medieval Buildings'. *Antiquity* 66 (1992), 348–66.

Fansler, Dean Spruill. *Chaucer and 'Le Roman de la Rose'*. New York: Columbia University Press, 1914.

Faral, Edmond. '*Le Roman de la Rose* et la pensée française au XIIIè siècle'. *Revue des Deux Mondes*, 7è période, 35 (1926), 430–57.

Farrell, Thomas J. and Goodwin, Amy W. 'The Clerk's Tale'. In *Sources and Analogues*, ed. Correale and Hamel, vol. 1 (2002), pp. 101–67.

Federico, Sylvia. 'A Fourteenth-Century Erotics of Politics: London as a Feminine New Troy'. *Studies in the Age of Chaucer* 19 (1997), 121–55.

—— *New Troy: Fantasies of Empire in the Late Middle Ages*. Medieval Cultures, 36. Minneapolis and London: University of Minnesota Press, 2003.

Fein, Susanna Greer; Raybin, David; and Braeger, Peter C. (eds). *Rebels and Rivals: The Contestive Spirit in the* Canterbury Tales. Medieval Institute Publications, SMC 29. Kalamazoo, MI: Western Michigan University, 1991.

Fleming, John V. 'The Garden of the *Roman de la Rose*: Vision and Landscape or Landscape of Vision?' In *Medieval Gardens*, ed. MacDougall (1986), pp. 201–34.

—— *The 'Roman de la Rose': A Study in Allegory and Iconography*. Princeton: Princeton University Press, 1969.

Fletcher, Alan J. *Preaching, Politics and Poetry in Late-Medieval England*. Dublin: Four Courts Press, 1998.

Ford, Boris (ed.) *Medieval Literature: Chaucer and the Alliterative Tradition*. New Pelican Guide to English Literature, vol. 1, pt 1. Harmondsworth: Penguin, 1982.

Foucault, Michel. *Aesthetics, Method and Epistemology*, ed. James D. Faubion, trans. Robert Hurley et al. *Essential Works of Foucault 1954–1984*, vol. 2. London: Allen Lane, 1998. First published as *Dits et écrits 1954–1984* (Paris: Gallimard, 1994).

—— *Discipline and Punish: The Birth of the Prison*, trans. Alan Sheridan. London: Allen Lane, 1977. First published as *Surveiller et punir: naissance de la prison* (Paris: Gallimard, 1975).

—— 'The Eye of Power'. In his *Power/Knowledge*, ed. Gordon (1980), pp. 146–65. First published as 'L'Œil du pouvoir', preface to Jeremy Bentham, *Le Panoptique* (Paris: Belfond, 1977).

—— 'Of Other Spaces', trans Jay Miskowiec. *Diacritics* 16:1 (Spring 1986), 22–7. First published as 'Des autres espaces', *Architecture – Mouvement – Continuité*, 5 (October 1984), 46–9. Trans. Robert Hurley in Foucault, *Aesthetics* (1998), pp. 175–85.

—— *The Order of Things: An Archaeology of the Human Sciences.* London: Tavistock, 1970. First published as *Les Mots et les choses* (Paris: Gallimard, 1966).

—— *Power/Knowledge: Selected Interviews and Other Writings*, ed. Colin Gordon, trans. Colin Gordon, Leon Marshall, John Meopham and Kate Soper. Brighton: Harvester Press, 1980.

—— 'Questions on Geography'. In his *Power/Knowledge*, ed. Gordon (1980), pp. 63–77. First published as 'Questions à Michel Foucault sur la géographie', *Hérodote* 1 (1976).

—— 'Space, Knowledge and Power', trans Christian Hubert. In *Foucault Reader*, ed. Rabinow (1984), pp. 239–56. First published in *Skyline* (March 1982).

Frank, Robert Worth, Jr. 'The Reeve's Tale and the Comedy of Limitation'. In *Directions in Literary Criticism*, ed. Weintraub and Young (1973), pp. 53–69.

Frappier, Jean. 'Variations sur le thème du miroir de Bernard de Ventadour à Maurice Scève'. *Cahiers de l'Association Internationale des Etudes Françaises* 11 (1959), 134–58.

Freeman, Michelle A. 'Problems in Romance Composition: Ovid, Chrétien de Troyes and the *Romance of the Rose*'. *Romance Philology* 30 (1976), 159–68.

French, Roger and Cunningham, Andrew. *Before Science: The Invention of the Friars' Natural Philosophy.* Aldershot: Scolar Press, 1996.

Friedman, John Block. 'The Dreamer, the Whelp and Consolation in the *Book of the Duchess*'. *Chaucer Review* 3 (1968–9), 145–62.

Friend, Albert C. 'Chaucer's Version of the *Aeneid*'. *Speculum* 28 (1953), 317–23.

Fyler, John M. 'Domesticating the Exotic in the Squire's Tale'. *ELH* 55 (1988), 1–26. Repr. in *Chaucer's Cultural Geography*, ed. Lynch (2002), pp. 32–55.

Gallacher, Patrick J. 'Chaucer and the Rhetoric of the Body'. *Chaucer Review* 28 (1993–4), 216–36.

—— 'Perception and Reality in the Miller's Tale'. *Chaucer Review* 18 (1983–4), 38–48.

Gallick, Susan. 'A Look at Chaucer and his Preachers'. *Speculum* 50 (1975), 456–76.

Galloway, Andrew. 'Authority'. In *Companion to Chaucer*, ed. Brown (2000), pp. 23–39.

Ganim, John M. *Style and Consciousness in Middle English Narrative.* Princeton, NJ: Princeton University Press, 1983.

Gersh, Stephen. *From Iamblichus to Eriugena: An Investigation of the Prehistory and Evolution of the Pseudo-Dionysian Tradition.* Studien zur Problemgeschichte der antiken und mitteralterlichen Philosophie, 8. Leiden: Brill, 1978.

Gibson, J. J. *The Perception of the Visual World.* Boston: Houghton Mifflin, 1950; repr. Westport, Conn.: Greenwood Press, 1974.

Giddens, Anthony. 'Time, Space and Regionalisation'. In *Social Relations*, ed. Gregory and Urry (1985), pp. 265–95.

Gilchrist, Roberta. *Gender and Archaeology: Contesting the Past.* London and New York: Routledge, 1999.

—— *Gender and Material Culture: The Archaeology of Religious Women.* London and New York: Routledge, 1994.

—— 'Medieval Bodies in the Material World: Gender, Stigma and the Body'. In *Framing Medieval Bodies*, ed. Kay and Rubin (1994), pp. 43–61.

Gilson, Etienne. *Les Idées et les lettres.* Paris: Vrin, 1932.

—— 'Michel Menot et la technique du sermon médiéval'. In his *Idées et lettres* (1932), pp. 93–154. First published in *Revue d'Histoire Franciscaine* 2 (1925), 301–60.

—— *The Philosophy of St Bonaventure*, trans. Illtyd Trethowan and Frank J. Sheed. New York: Sheed and Ward, 1938; repr. Patterson, NY: St Anthony Guild Press, 1965. First published as *La Philosophie de saint Bonaventure*, Etudes de Philosophie Médiévale, 4 (Paris: Vrin, 1924).

Gilson, Stephen A. *Medieval Optics and Theories of Light in the Works of Dante.* Studies in Italian Literature, 8. Lewiston NY, Queenston Ont. and Lampeter: Edwin Mellen Press, 2000.

Ginsberg, Warren. 'Preaching and Avarice in the Pardoner's Tale'. *Mediaevalia* 2 (1976), 77–99.

Glasscoe, Marion (ed.) *The Medieval Mystical Tradition in England: Papers Read at Dartington Hall, July 1984.* Cambridge: Brewer, 1984.

Glorieux, P. *La Faculté des arts et ses maîtres au XIIIè siècle.* Etudes de Philosophie Médiévale, 59. Paris: Vrin, 1971.

—— *Répertoire des maîtres en théologie de Paris au XIIIè siècle.* 2 vols. Etudes de Philosophie Médiévale, 17–18. Paris: Vrin, 1933.

Goldberg, Benjamin. *The Mirror and Man.* Charlottesville: University Press of Virginia, 1985.

Goldin, Frederick. *The Mirror of Narcissus in the Courtly Love Lyric.* Ithaca, NY: Cornell University Press, 1967.

Gombrich, Ernst. *Art and Illusion: A Study in the Psychology of Pictorial Representation*, 4th edn. The A. W. Mellon Lectures in the Fine Arts, 1956. London: Phaidon, 1972.

Goodall, Peter. '"Allone, Withouten Any Compaignye": Privacy in the First Fragment of the *Canterbury Tales*'. *English Language Notes* 29 (1991), 5–15.

—— 'Being Alone in Chaucer'. *Chaucer Review* 27 (1992–3), 1–15.

Goodman, Jennifer R. 'Chaucer's Squire's Tale and the Rise of Chivalry'. *Studies in the Age of Chaucer* 5 (1983), 127–36.

Grabes, Herbert. *The Mutable Glass: Mirror-Imagery in Titles and Texts of the Middle Ages and Renaissance*, trans. Gordon Collier. Cambridge: Cambridge University Press, 1982. First published as *Speculum, Mirror und Looking-glass: Kontinuität und Originalität der Spiegelmatapher in der Buchtitlen des Mittelaters und der englischen Literatur des 13. bis 17. Jahrhunderts* (Tübingen: Niemeyer, 1973).

Grant, Edward. 'Place and Space in Medieval Physical Thought'. In *Motion and Time*, ed. Machamer and Turnbull (1976), pp. 137–67. Repr in Edward

Grant, *Studies in Medieval Science and Natural Philosophy* (London: Variorum Reprints, 1981).

—— and Murdoch, John E. (eds). *Mathematics and its Applications to Science and Natural Philosophy in the Middle Ages: Essays in Honor of Marshall Clagett.* Cambridge: Cambridge University Press, 1987.

Green, Victor G. *The Franciscans in Medieval English Life (1224–1348).* Paterson, NJ: St Anthony Guild Press, 1939.

Gregory, Derek. *Geographical Imaginations.* Oxford and Cambridge, Mass.: Blackwell, 1994.

—— and Urry, John (eds). *Social Relations and Spatial Structures.* Critical Human Geography. Basingstoke: Macmillan, 1985.

Grennen, Joseph E. 'The Calculating Reeve and his *Camera Obscura*'. *Journal of Medieval and Renaissance Studies* 14 (1984), 245–59.

—— 'Hert-Huntyng in the Book of the Duchess'. *Modern Language Quarterly* 25 (1964), 131–9.

Grenville, Jane. *Medieval Housing.* London and Washington: Leicester University Press, 1997.

Grosz, Elizabeth. 'Women, *Chora*, Dwelling'. In *Postmodern Cities*, ed. Watson and Gibson (1995), pp. 47–58.

Gunn, Alan M. F. *The Mirror of Love: A Reinterpretation of the* Romance of the Rose. Texas Technological College Research Publications in Literature (Lubbock, Texas: Texas Tech Press, 1951).

Gurevich, A. J. *Categories of Medieval Culture*, trans. G. L. Campbell. London: Routledge and Kegan Paul, 1985. First published as *Kategorii srednevekovoi kultury* (Moscow: Iskusstvo, 1972).

Hackett, Jeremiah. 'Epilogue: Roger Bacon's Moral Science'. In *Roger Bacon and the Sciences*, ed. Hackett (1997), pp. 405–9.

—— 'Roger Bacon: His Life, Career and Works'. In *Roger Bacon and the Sciences*, ed. Hackett (1997), pp. 9–23.

—— (ed.) *Roger Bacon and the Sciences: Commemorative Essays.* Studien und Texte zur Geistesgeschichte des Mittelalters, 57. Leiden: Brill, 1997.

Hagen, Susan K. *Allegorical Remembrance: A Study of* A Pilgrimage of the Life of Man *as a Medieval Treatise on Seeing and Remembering.* Athens, Ga. and London: University of Georgia Press, 1990.

Hagiioannu, Michael. 'Giotto's Bardi Chapel Frescoes and Chaucer's *House of Fame*: Influence, Evidence and Interpretations'. *Chaucer Review* 36 (2001–2), 28–47.

Haller, Robert S. 'Chaucer's Squire's Tale and the Uses of Rhetoric'. *Modern Philology* 62 (1965), 285–95.

Halverson, John. 'Aspects of Order in the Knight's Tale'. *Studies in Philology* 57 (1960), 606–21.

Hamel, Mary. 'The Pardoner's Prologue and Tale'. In *Sources and Analogues*, ed. Correale and Hamel, vol. 1 (2002), pp. 265–319.

Hanawalt, Barbara. 'At the Margin of Women's Space in Medieval Europe'. In *Matrons and Marginal Women*, ed. Edwards and Ziegler (1995), pp. 1–17. Repr. in her *'Of Good and Ill Repute'* (1998), pp. 70–87.

———— *'Of Good and Ill Repute': Gender and Social Control in Medieval England*. New York and Oxford: Oxford University Press, 1998.

———— and Kobialka, Michal (eds). *Medieval Practices of Space*. Medieval Cultures, 23. Minneapolis and London: University of Minnesota Press, 2000.

Hanna, Ralph and Lawler, Traugott. 'The Wife of Bath's Prologue'. In *Sources and Analogues*, ed. Correale and Hamel, vol. 2 (2005), pp. 351–403.

Harbert, Bruce. 'Chaucer and the Latin Classics'. In *Geoffrey Chaucer*, ed. Brewer (1974), pp. 137–53

Harrison, Dick. *Medieval Space: The Extent of Microspatial Knowledge in Western Europe during the Middle Ages*. Lund Studies in International History, 34. Lund: Lund University Press, 1996.

Harvey, David. *The Condition of Postmodernity: An Enquiry into the Origins of Cultural Change*. Oxford and Cambridge, Mass.: Blackwell, 1989.

Harvey, E. Ruth. *The Inward Wits: Psychological Theory in the Middle Ages and the Renaissance*. Warburg Institute Surveys, 6. London: Warburg Institute, 1975.

Haskins, Charles H. 'The University of Paris in the Sermons of the Thirteenth Century'. *American Historical Review* 10 (1904–5), 1–27.

Hatfield, Gary C. and Epstein, William. 'The Sensory Core and the Medieval Foundations of Early Modern Perceptual Theory'. *Isis* 70 (1979), 363–84.

Haug, Walter and Wachinger, Burghart (eds). *Exempel und Exempelsammlungen*. Furtuna Vitrea, 2. Tübingen: Niemeyer, 1991.

Hawthorn, Jeremy (ed.) *Criticism and Critical Theory*. Stratford-upon-Avon Studies, 2nd ser. London: Arnold, 1984.

Hazelton, Richard. 'Chaucer's Parson's Tale and the *Moralium dogma philosophorum*'. *Traditio* 16 (1960), 255–74.

Heffernan, Carol Falvo. *The Melancholy Muse: Chaucer, Shakespeare and Early Medicine*. Duquesne Studies: Language and Literature Series, 19. Pittsburgh: Duquesne University Press, 1995.

———— 'That Dog Again: *Melancholia Canina* and Chaucer's *Book of the Duchess*'. *Modern Philology* 84 (1986), 185–90.

Heffernan, Thomas J. 'Sermon Literature'. In *Middle English Prose*, ed. Edwards (1984), pp. 177–207.

Hertog, Erik. *Chaucer's Fabliaux as Analogues*. Mediaevalia Lovaniensia, series I, studia xix. Leuven: Leuven University Press, 1991.

Hessenauer, Matthias. 'The Impact of Grosseteste's Pastoral Care on Vernacular Religious Literature: *La Lumière as lais* by Pierre de Peckham'. In *Grosseteste: New Perspectives*, ed. McEvoy (1995), pp. 377–91.

Hill, John M. and Sinnreich-Levi, Deborah M. (eds.) *The Rhetorical Poetics of the Middle Ages: Reconstructive Polyphony: Essays in Honor of Robert O. Payne*. Madison: Fairleigh Dickinson University Press; London: Associated University Press, 2000.

Hillier, Bill and Hanson, Juliette. *The Social Logic of Space*. Cambridge: Cambridge University Press, 1984.

Hillman, Larry H. 'Another Look into the Mirror Perilous: The Role of the Crystals in the *Roman de la Rose*'. *Romania* 101 (1980), 225–38.

Hills, Paul. *The Light of Early Italian Painting*. New Haven and London: Yale University Press, 1987.

Hogg, James (ed.) *The Mystical Tradition and the Carthusians*, vol. 10. Analecta Carthusiana, 130. Salzburg: Institut für Anglistik und Amerikanistik Universität Salzburg, 1996.

Holley, Linda Tarte. *Chaucer's Measuring Eye*. Houston: Rice University Press, 1990.

—— 'Medieval Optics and the Framed Narrative in Chaucer's *Troilus and Criseyde*'. *Chaucer Review* 21 (1986–7), 26–44.

Howard, David R. *The Idea of the* Canterbury Tales. Berkeley, Los Angeles, and London: University of California Press, 1976.

Howie, Margaret D. *Studies in the Use of Exempla with Special Reference to Middle High German Literature*. London: University of London Press, 1923.

Hudson, Anne. 'Wycliffite Prose'. In *Middle English Prose*, ed. Edwards (1984), pp. 249–70.

—— and Wilks, Michael (eds). *From Ockham to Wyclif*. Studies in Church History, subsidia 5. Oxford: Blackwell for the Ecclesiastical History Society, 1987.

Hughes, Jonathan. *Pastors and Visionaries: Religion and Secular Life in Late Medieval Yorkshire*. Woodbridge: Boydell Press, 1988.

Hult, David F. 'The Allegorical Fountain: Narcissus in the *Roman de la Rose*'. *Romanic Review* 72 (1981), 125–48.

—— *Self-Fulfilling Prophecies: Readership and Authority in the First* Roman de la Rose. Cambridge: Cambridge University Press, 1986.

Humphreys, K. W. *The Book Provisions of the Mediaeval Friars 1215–1400*. Safaho Monographs, 2; Studies in the History of Libraries and Librarianship, 1. Amsterdam: Erasmus, 1964.

—— 'The Library of John Erghome and Personal Libraries of the Fourteenth Century in England'. *Proceedings of the Leeds Philosophical and Literary Society*, Literary and Historical Section, 18.2 (1982), 106–23.

—— (ed.) *The Friars' Libraries*. Corpus of British Medieval Library Catalogues. London: British Library in association with the British Academy, 1990.

Hunt, Richard William. 'The Library of Robert Grosseteste'. In *Grosseteste Scholar and Bishop*, ed. Callus (1955), pp. 121–45.

Ijsewijn, Jozef and Paquet, Jacques (eds). *The Universities in the Late Middle Ages*. Mediaevalia Lovaniensia, ser. 1, studia 6. Leuven: Leuven University Press and Institut d'Etudes Médiévales de l'Université Catholique de Leuven, 1978.

Jacquart, Danielle. 'Rapport de la Table ronde: les disciplines du quadrivium'. In *L'Enseignement des disciplines*, ed. Weijers and Holtz (1997), pp. 239–47.

James, M. R. (ed.) *The Catalogue of the Library of the Augustinian Friars at York*. Cambridge: Cambridge University Press, 1909.

Javelet, Robert. *Image et ressemblance au douzième siècle de saint Anselme à Alain de Lille*. 2 vols. Paris: Letouzey et Ané, 1967.

Jefferson, Bernard L. *Chaucer and the 'Consolation of Philosophy' of Boethius*. Princeton: Princeton University Press, 1917.

Jeffrey, David L. (ed.) *By Things Seen: Reference and Recognition in Medieval Thought*. Ottawa: University of Ottawa Press, 1979.

Jolivet, R. 'La Doctrine augustinienne de l'illumination'. *Revue de Philosophie* 1 (1930), 382–502.

Jonas, Hans. 'The Nobility of Sight: A Study in the Phenomenology of the Senses'. *Philosophy and Phenomenological Research* 14 (1954), 507–19.

Jordan, Robert M. *Chaucer and the Shape of Creation: The Aesthetic Possibilities of Inorganic Structure*. Cambridge, Mass.: Harvard University Press, 1967.

Joseph, Gerhard. 'Chaucerian "Game"-"Earnest" and the "Argument of Herbergage" in the *Canterbury Tales*.' *Chaucer Review* 5 (1970–1), 83–96.

Josipovici, Gabriel. *Touch*. New Haven and London: Yale University Press, 1996.

Kahrl, Stanley J. 'Chaucer's Squire's Tale and the Decline of Chivalry'. *Chaucer Review* 7 (1972–3), 194–209.

Kamerick, Kathleen. *Popular Piety and Art in the Late Middle Ages: Image Worship and Idolatry 1350–1500*. New York and Houndmills: Palgrave, 2002.

Kay, Sarah and Rubin, Miri (eds). *Framing Medieval Bodies*. Manchester and New York: Manchester University Press, 1994.

Keiser, George R. 'Middle English Passion Narratives and their Contemporaray Readers: The Vernacular Progeny of *Meditationes Vitae Christi*. In *The Mystical Tradition*, vol. 10, ed. Hogg (1996), pp. 85–99.

Kellogg, Alfred L. 'St Augustine and the Parson's Tale'. *Traditio* 8 (1952), 424–30.

Kemp, Martin. *The Science of Art: Optical Themes in Western Art from Brunelleschi to Seurat*. New Haven and London: Yale University Press, 1990.

Kenny, Anthony and Pinborg, Jan. 'Medieval Philosophical Literature'. In *Cambridge History of Later Medieval Philosophy*, ed. Kretzmann et al. (1982), pp. 11–42.

Ker, Neil. 'Oxford College Libraries before 1500'. In *Universities in the Late Middle Ages*, ed. Ijsewijn and Paquet (1978), pp. 293–311.

Kessler, Joan. 'La Quête amoureuse et poétique: la fontaine de Narcisse dans le *Roman de la Rose*'. *Romanic Review* 73 (1982), 133–46.

Kibre, Pearl and Siraisi, Nancy G. 'The Institutional Setting: The Universities'. In *Science in the Middle Ages*, ed. Lindberg (1978), pp. 120–44.

King, Pamela M. '"He pleyeth Herodes upon a scaffold hye"?' In *Porci ante Margaritam: Essays in Honour of Meg Twycross*, ed. Sarah Carpenter, Pamela M. King and Peter Meredith. *Leeds Studies in English* ns 32 (2001), 211–28.

Kittredge, George Lyman. *Chaucer and his Poetry*, 55th anniversary edn. Cambridge, Mass.: Harvard University Press, 1970. First published 1915.

Klassen, Norman. *Chaucer on Love, Knowledge and Sight*. Chaucer Studies, 21. Cambridge: Brewer, 1995.

––––– 'Optical Allusions and Chaucerian Realism: Aspects of Sight in Late Medieval Thought and *Troilus and Criseyde*'. *Stanford Humanities Review* 2 (1992), 129–46.

Knoespel, Kenneth J. *Narcissus and the Invention of Personal History*. Garland Publications in Comparative Literature. New York and London: Garland, 1985.

Köhler, Erich. 'Narcisse, la fontaine d'Amour et Guillaume de Lorris'. *Journal des Savants* (année 1963), 86–103

Kolve, V. A. *Chaucer and the Imagery of Narrative: The First Five Canterbury Tales*. London: Arnold, 1984.

––––– 'Chaucer and the Visual Arts'. In *Chaucer*, ed. Brewer (1974), pp. 290–320.

Koonce, *Chaucer and the Tradition of Fame: Symbolism in the* House of Fame. Princeton: Princeton University Press, 1966.

Kratzmann, Gregory and Simpson, James (eds). *Medieval English Religious and Ethical Literature: Essays in Honour of G. H. Russell*. Cambridge: Brewer, 1986.

Kretzmann, Norman; Kenny, Anthony; Pinborg, Jan; and Stump, Eleonore (eds). *The Cambridge History of Later Medieval Philosophy from the Rediscovery of Aristotle to the Disintegration of Scholasticism 1100–1600*. Cambridge: Cambridge University Press, 1982.

Kühn, Thomas and Schaefer, Ursula (eds). *Dialogische Strukturen/Dialogic Structures: Festschrift für Willi Erzgräber zum 70. Geburtstag*. Tübingen: Narr, 1996.

Lambert, Mark. '*Troilus*, Books I–III: A Criseydan Reading'. In *Essays on Troilus and Criseyde*, ed. Salu (1979), 105–25.

Langlois, Ernest. *Origines et sources du* Roman de la Rose. Paris: Thorin, 1891.

Latham, R. E. (comp.) *Revised Medieval Latin Word-List from British and Irish Sources*. London: Oxford University Press for the British Academy, 1965.

Lawrence, Denise L. and Low, Setha M. 'The Built Environment and Spatial Form'. *Annual Review of Anthropology* 19 (1990), 453–505.

Lawton, David. *Chaucer's Narrators*. Chaucer Studies, 13. Cambridge: Brewer, 1985.

Leader, Damian Riehl. *A History of the University of Cambridge*, vol. 1: *The University to 1546*. Cambridge: Cambridge University Press, 1988.

Lecoy de la Marche, A. *La Chaire française au moyen âge spécialement au XIIIe siècle d'après les manuscrits contemporains*, 2nd edn. Paris: Renouard, 1886.

Lefebvre, Henri. *The Production of Space*, trans. D. Nicolson–Smith. Oxford: Blackwell, 1991. First published as *La Production de l'espace* (Paris: Editions Anthropos, 1974).

Leff, Gordon. 'The *Trivium* and the Three Philosophies'. In *Universities in the Middle Ages*, ed. de Ridder-Symoens (1992), pp. 307–36.

le Goff, Jacques. *The Medieval Imagination*, trans. Arthur Goldhammer. Chicago and London: University of Chicago Press, 1988. First published as *L'Imaginaire médiévale* (Paris: Gallimard, 1985).

Lejeune, Albert. *Recherches sur la catoptrique grecque d'après les sources antiques et médiévales.* Académie Royale de Belgique, classe des letters, mémoires, 2è série, tome 52 (Brussels: 1956–7).

Lemoine, Michel. 'L'Oeuvre encyclopédique de Vincent de Beauvais'. *Journal of World History* 9 (1965–6), 571–79.

Lewis, C. S. *The Allegory of Love: A Study in Medieval Tradition.* London: Oxford University Press, 1936.

——— 'The Mirror of Love: A Reinterpretation of the *Romance of the Rose*' [Review of Gunn, *Mirror of Love*]. *Medium Ævum* 22 (1953), 27–31.

Lewis, N. B. 'The Anniversary Service for Blanche, Duchess of Lancaster, 12th September, 1374'. *Bulletin of the John Rylands Library* 21 (1937), 176–92.

Leyerle, John. 'The Rose-Wheel Design and Dante's *Paradiso*'. *University of Toronto Quarterly* 46 (1976–7), 280–308.

——— (ed.) 'The Language of Love and the Visual Imagination in the High Middle Ages'. *University of Toronto Quarterly* 46 (1976–7), 185–308.

Lindberg, David C. 'Alhazen's Theory of Vision and its Reception in the West'. *Isis* 58 (1967), 321–41. Repr. Lindberg, *Studies*, item 3.

——— 'Alkindi's Critique of Euclid's Theory of Vision'. *Isis* 62 (1971), 469–89. Repr. Lindberg, *Studies*, item 2.

——— *A Catalogue of Medieval and Renaissance Optical Manuscripts.* Pontifical Institute of Mediaeval Studies, subsidia mediaevalia, 4. Toronto: Pontifical Institute of Mediaeval Studies, 1975.

——— 'The Genesis of Kepler's Theory of Light: Light Metaphysics from Plotinus to Kepler'. *Osiris* 2nd ser., 2 (1986), 5–42.

——— 'Introduction' to Alhacen and Witelo, *Opticae thesaurus*, ed. Risner (repr. 1972), pp. v–xxxiv.

——— 'Introduction' to *Bacon and the Origins of* Perspectiva. See Bacon, *Perspectiva.*

——— 'Introduction' to *Bacon's Philosophy of Nature.* See Bacon, *De multiplicatione specierum.*

——— 'The Intromission-Extramission Controversy in Islamic Visual Theory: Alkindi versus Avicenna'. In *Studies in Perception*, ed. Machamer and Turnbull (1978), pp. 137–59. Repr. Lindberg, *Studies*, item 4.

——— 'Lines of Influence in Thirteenth-Century Optics: Bacon, Witelo and Pecham'. *Speculum* 46 (1971), 66–83. Repr. Lindberg, *Studies*, item 10.

——— 'The *Perspectiva communis* of John Pecham: Its Influence, Sources and Context'. *Archives Internationales d'Histoire des Sciences* 18 (1965), 37–53.

——— 'Roger Bacon and the Origins of *Perspectiva* in the West'. In *Mathematics and its Applications*, ed Grant and Murdoch (1987), pp. 249–68.

——— 'Roger Bacon on Light, Vision and the Universal Emanation of Force'. In *Roger Bacon*, ed. Hackett (1997), pp. 243–75.

—— 'The Science of Optics'. In *Science in the Middle Ages*, ed. Lindberg (1978), pp. 338–68. Repr. in Lindberg, *Studies*, item 1.

—— *Studies in the History of Medieval Optics*. London: Variorum, 1983.

—— *Theories of Vision from Al-Kindi to Kepler*. University of Chicago History of Science and Medicine. Chicago and London: University of Chicago Press, 1976.

—— (ed.) *Science in the Middle Ages*. Chicago History of Science and Medicine. Chicago: University of Chicago Press, 1978.

—— and Steneck, Nicholas M. 'The Sense of Vision and the Origins of Modern Science'. In *Science, Medicine and Society*, ed. Debus (1972), pp. 29–45. Repr. Lindberg, *Studies*, item 6.

Little, A. G. 'The Franciscan School at Oxford in the Thirteenth Century'. *Archivum Franciscum Historicum* 19 (1926), 803–74.

—— *The Grey Friars in Oxford, Part I: A History of the Convent; Part II: Biographical Notices of the Friars together with Appendices of Original Documents*. Oxford Historical Society, 20. Oxford: Clarendon Press, 1892.

—— (ed.) *Roger Bacon Essays Contributed by Various Writers on the Occasion of the Commemoration of the Seventh Centenary of his Birth*. Oxford: Clarendon Press, 1914.

Long, Pamela O. (ed.) *Science and Technology in Medieval Society*. Annals of the New York Academy of Sciences, 441. New York: New York Academy of Sciences, 1985.

Loomis, Dorothy Bethurum. 'Saturn in Chaucer's Knight's Tale'. In *Chaucer und seine Zeit*, ed. Esch (1968), pp. 149–61.

Looten, C. 'Chaucer et Dante'. *Revue de Littérature Comparée* 5 (1925), 545–71.

Luengo, A. 'Audience and Exempla in the Pardoner's Prologue and Tale'. *Chaucer Review* 11 (1976–7), 1–10.

Luscombe, David. 'Some Examples of the Use Made of the Works of the Pseudo-Dionysius by University Teachers in the Later Middle Ages'. In *Universities in the Late Middle Ages*, ed. Ijsewijn and Paquet (1978), pp. 228–41.

Lynch, Andrew. '"Taking Kep" of the *Book of the Duchess*', in *Medieval English Religious and Ethical Literature*, ed. Kratzmann and Simpson (1986), pp. 167–78.

Lynch, Kathryn L. 'East Meets West in Chaucer's Squire's and Franklin's Tales'. *Speculum* 70 (1995), 530–51. Repr. In *Chaucer's Cultural Geography*, ed. Lynch (2002), pp. 76–101.

—— 'Partitioned Fictions: The Meaning and Importance of Walls in Chaucer's Poetry'. In *Art and Context*, ed. Edwards (1994), pp. 107–25.

—— (ed.) *Chaucer's Cultural Geography*. Basic Readings in Chaucer and his Time. New York and London: Routledge, 2002.

Lynch, Lawrence E. 'The Doctrine of Divine Ideas and Illumination in Robert Grosseteste, Bishop of Lincoln'. *Mediaeval Studies* 3 (1941), 161–73.

McAlindon, T. 'Cosmology, Contrariety and the Knight's Tale'. *Medium Ævum* 55 (1986), 41–57.

McCall, John P. 'The Squire in Wonderland'. *Chaucer Review* 1 (1966–7), 103–9.

McCarthy 'Medieval Light Theory'. See Duns Scotus [*Commentary on the Sentences.*]

MacDougall, Elisabeth B. (ed.) *Medieval Gardens*. Dumbarton Oaks Colloquium on the History of Landscape Architecture, 9. Washington, DC: Dumbarton Oaks Research Library and Collection Trustees for Harvard University, 1986.

McEvoy, James. 'The Chronology of Robert Grosseteste's Writings on Nature and Natural Philosophy'. *Speculum* 58 (1983), 614–55. Repr. as McEvoy, *Grosseteste, Exegete and Philosopher* (1994), ch. 7.

—— 'The Metaphysics of Light in the Middle Ages'. *Philosophical Studies* [National University of Ireland] 26 (1979), 126–45.

—— 'Nature as Light in Eriugena and Grosseteste'. In *Man and Nature*, ed. Ridyard and Benson (1995), pp. 37–61.

—— 'Ein Paradigma der Lichtmetaphysik: Robert Grosseteste'. *Freiburger Zeitschrift für Philosophie und Theologie* 34 (1987), 91–110. Repr. in McEvoy, *Grosseteste, Exegete and Philosopher* (1994), item 8.

—— *The Philosophy of Robert Grosseteste*. Oxford: Clarendon Press, 1982.

—— *Robert Grosseteste, Exegete and Philosopher*. Variorum Collected Studies, CS 446. Aldershot: Variorum, 1994.

—— (ed.) *Robert Grosseteste: New Perspectives on his Thought and Scholarship*. Instrumenta Patristica, 27. Steenbrugge: Abbey of St Peter; Turnhout: Brepols, 1995.

McGerr, Rosemarie P. 'Medieval Concepts of Literary Closure: Theory and Practice'. *Exemplaria* 1 (1989), 149–79.

McKeon, *Study of the* Summa philosophiae. See pseudo-Grosseteste, *Summa philosophiae*.

Mabille, Madeleine. 'Pierre de Limoges et ses méthodes de travail'. In *Hommages à André Boutemy*, ed. Cambier (1976), pp. 244–51.

Machamer, Peter K. and Turnbull, Robert G. (eds). *Motion and Time, Space and Matter: Interrelations in the History of Philosophy and Science*. Columbus: Ohio State University Press, 1976.

—— (eds). *Studies in Perception: Interrelations in the History of Philosophy and Science*. Columbus: Ohio State University Press, 1978.

Mahler, Annemarie. 'Medieval Image Style and Saint Augustine's Theory of Threefold Vision'. *Mediaevalia* 4 (1978), 277–313.

Mahony, John and Keller, John Ester (eds). *Mediaeval Studies in Honor of Urban Tigner Holmes, Jr.* University of North Carolina Studies in the Romance Languages and Literatures, 56. Chapel Hill: University of North Carolina Press, 1965.

Manzalaoui, M. 'Chaucer and Science'. In *Geoffrey Chaucer*, ed. Brewer (1974), pp. 225–61.

Marshall, Peter. 'Nicole Oresme on the Nature, Reflection and Speed of Light'. *Isis* 72 (1981), 357–74.

—— 'Two Scholastic Discussions of the Perception of Depth by Shading'. *Journal of the Warburg and Courtauld Institutes* 44 (1981), 170–5.

Martin, Carol A. N. 'Mercurial Tradition in the *Book of the Duchess*'. *Chaucer Review* 28 (1993–4), 95–116.

Masi, Michael. 'Chaucer, Messahala and Bodleian Selden supra 78'. *Manuscripta* 19 (1975), 36–47.

Massey, Doreen. *Space, Place and Gender.* Cambridge: Polity Press, 1994.

Matthews, Gareth B. 'A Medieval Theory of Vision'. In *Studies in Perception*, ed. Machamer and Turnbull (1978), pp. 186–99.

Mazzeo, Joseph Anthony. *Medieval Cultural Tradition in Dante's* Comedy. Ithaca, NY: Cornell University Press, 1960. Repr. New York: Greenwood, 1968.

—— *Structure and Thought in the* Paradiso. Ithaca, NY: Cornell University Press, 1958. Repr. New York: Greenwood, 1968.

Metlitzki, Dorothee. *The Matter of Araby in Medieval England.* New Haven and London: Yale University Press, 1977.

Michaud-Quantin, Pierre. 'Les Champs semantiques de *species*: tradition latine et traductions du grec', in his *Etudes* (1970), pp. 113–62.

—— *Etudes sur le vocabulaire philosophique du moyen âge.* Lessico Intelletuale Europeo, 5. Rome: Edizioni dell'Ateneo, 1970.

—— 'Les petites Encyclopédies du XIIIè siècle'. *Journal of World History* 9 (1965–6), 580–95.

Miles, Margaret R. *Image as Insight: Visual Understanding in Western Christianity and Secular Culture.* Boston: Beacon Press, 1985.

Miller, James L. 'Three Mirrors of Dante's *Paradiso*'. *University of Toronto Quarterly* 46 (1976–7), 263–79.

Minnis, A. J. with Scattergood, V. J. and Smith, J. J. *The Shorter Poems.* Oxford Guides to Chaucer. Oxford: Clarendon Press, 1995.

Molland, A. G. 'The Geometrical Background to the "Merton School": An Exploration into the Application of Mathematics to Natural Philosophy in the Fourteenth Century'. *British Journal for the History of Science* 4 (1968), 108–25.

Montgomery, Robert L. *The Reader's Eye: Studies in Didactic Literary Theory from Dante to Tasso.* Berkeley, Los Angeles and London: University of California Press, 1979.

Moody, Ernest A. 'Ockham, Buridan and Nicholas of Autrecourt: The Parisian Statutes of 1339 and 1340'. *Franciscan Studies* 7 (1947), 113–46. Repr. in his *Studies in Medieval Philosophy* (1975), pp. 127–60.

—— *Studies in Medieval Philosophy, Science and Logic: Collected Papers 1933–1969.* Berkeley, Los Angeles and London: University of California Press, 1975.

—— 'William of Ockham'. In *Encyclopedia of Philosophy*, ed. Edwards, vol. 8 (1967), pp. 306–17.

Moore, Henrietta L. *Space, Text and Gender: An Anthropological Study of the Marakwet of Kenya.* Cambridge: Cambridge University Press, 1986.

Moore, Miriam. 'Troilus's Mirror: Vision and Desire in *Troilus and Criseyde*'. *Medieval Perspectives* 14 (1999), 152–65.

Moran, Joann H. *Education and Learning in the City of York 1300–1560.* Borthwick Papers, 55. York: University of York Borthwick Institute for Historical Research, 1979.

Mosher, Joseph Albert. *The Exemplum in the Early Religious and Didactic Literature of England.* New York: Columbia University Press, 1911.

Mroczkowsi, Przemyslaw. 'The Friar's Tale and its Pulpit Background'. In *English Studies Today*, ed. Bonnard (1961), pp. 107–20.

Muscatine, Charles. 'Locus of Action in Medieval Narrative'. *Romance Philology* 17 (1963–4), 115–22.

——— *Medieval Literature, Style and Culture: Essays.* Columbia, SC: University of South Carolina Press, 1999.

——— *Poetry and Crisis in the Age of Chaucer.* University of Notre-Dame Ward-Phillips Lectures in English Language and Literature, 4. Notre Dame, IN and London: University of Notre Dame Press, 1972.

Nash, Ronald H. *The Light of the Mind: St Augustine's Theory of Knowledge.* Lexington: University Press of Kentucky, 1969.

Natter, Wolfgang and Jones, John Paul III. 'Identity, Space and Other Uncertainties'. In *Space and Social Theory*, ed. Benko and Strohmayer (1997), pp. 141–61.

Neaman, Judith S. 'Sight and Insight: Vision and the Mystics'. *Fourteenth Century English Mystical Newsletter* [now *Mystics Quarterly*] 5, pt 3 (1979), 27–43.

Nelson, Robert S. (ed.) *Visuality before and beyond the Renaissance: Seeing as Others Saw.* Cambridge Studies in New Art History and Criticism. Cambridge: Cambridge University Press, 2000.

Newhauser, Richard. 'Nature's Moral Eye: Peter of Limoges' *Tractatus moralis de oculo*'. In *Man and Nature*, ed. Ridyard and Benson (1995), pp 125–36. Revised and translated version of his 'Der *Tractatus moralis de oculo*', in *Exempel und Exempelsammlunger*, ed. Haug and Wachinger (1991), pp. 95–136.

——— 'The Parson's Tale'. In *Sources and Analogues*, ed. Correale and Hamer, vol. 1 (2002), pp. 529–611.

Nicholson, Peter. 'The Friar's Tale'. In *Sources and Analogues*, ed. Correale and Hamel, vol. 1 (2002), pp. 87–99.

Nolan, Barbara. 'Chaucer's Poetics of Dwelling in *Troilus and Criseyde*'. In *Chaucer and the City*, ed. Butterfield (2006), pp. 57–75.

North, John. 'The Quadrivium'. In *Universities in the Middle Ages*, ed. de Ridder-Symoens (1992), pp. 337–59.

Orme, Nicholas. 'Chaucer and Education'. *Chaucer Review* 16 (1981–2), 38–59. Repr. in his *Education and Society* (1989), pp. 221–42.

——— *English Schools in the Middle Ages.* London: Methuen, 1973.

—— *Education and Society in Medieval and Renaissance England.* London and Ronceverte: Hambledon Press, 1989.

Ormrod, W. M. (ed.) *England in the Fourteenth Century: Proceedings of the 1985 Harlaxton Symposium.* Woodbridge: Boydell Press, 1986.

—— *England in the Thirteenth Century: Proceedings of the 1984 Harlaxton Symposium.* Woodbridge: Boydell Press, 1985.

Owen, Nancy H. 'The Pardoner's Introduction, Prologue, and Tale: Sermon and Fabliau'. *Journal of English and Germanic Philology* 66 (1967), 541–49.

Owst, G. R. *Literature and Pulpit in Medieval England: A Neglected Chapter in the History of English Letters and of the English People,* 2nd edn. Oxford: Blackwell, 1961.

—— *Preaching in Medieval England: An Introduction to Sermon Manuscripts of the Period* c.*1350–1450.* Cambridge: Cambridge University Press, 1926. Repr. New York: Russell and Russell, 1965.

Pächt, Otto. 'A Giottesque Episode in English Medieval Art'. *Journal of the Warburg and Courtauld Institutes* 6 (1943), 51–70. Repr. In *England and the Mediterranean Tradition,* ed. Warburg and Courtauld Institutes (1945), pp. 40–59; and *British Art and the Mediterranean,* ed. Saxl and Wittkower (1969), ch. 33.

Padolsky, Enoch P. 'Steering the Reader's Heart in *Patience*'. *Revue de l'Université d'Ottawa* 53 (1983), 169–80.

Panofsky, Erwin. *Early Netherlandish Painting: Its Origins and Character.* The Charles Eliot Norton Lectures, 1947–8. 2 vols. Cambridge, Mass.: Harvard University Press, 1966.

Pantin, W. A. *The English Church in the Fourteenth Century.* Cambridge: Cambridge University Press, 1954.

Paré, Gérard. *Les Idées et les lettres au XIIIè siècle: Le Roman de la Rose.* Université de Montréal Bibliothèque de Philosophie, 1; Publications de l'Instituit d'Etudes Médiévales Albert-le-Grand. Montréal: Centre de Psychologie et de Pédagogie, 1947.

—— *Le 'Roman de la Rose' et la scolastique courtoise.* Publications de l'Institut d'Etudes Médiévales d'Ottawa, 10. Paris: Vrin; Ottawa: Institut d'Etudes Médiévales, 1941.

Parkes, Malcolm Beckwith. *English Cursive Book Hands,* rev. edn. London: Scolar Press, 1979.

—— 'The Influence of the Concepts of *Ordinatio* and *Compilatio* on the Development of the Book'. In *Medieval Learning and Literature,* ed. Alexander and Gibson (1976), pp. 115–41.

—— 'The Literacy of the Laity'. In *Mediaeval World,* ed. Daiches and Thorlby (1973), pp. 555–77.

Parronchi, Alessandro. 'La perspettiva dantesca'. *Studi Danteschi* 36 (1959), 5–103. Repr. in his *Studi su la 'dolce' prospettiva* (1964), pp. 3–90.

—— *Studi su la 'dolce' prospettiva.* Milan: Martello, 1964.

Pasnau, Robert. *Theories of Cognition in the Later Middle Ages*. Cambridge: Cambridge University Press, 1997.

Patterson, Lee. *Chaucer and the Subject of History*. London: Routledge, 1991.

—— '"Rapt with Pleasaunce": Vision and Narration in the Epic'. *ELH* 48 (1981), 455–75.

Paulmier-Foucart, Monique. 'Ordre encyclopédique et organisation de la matière dans le *Speculum maius* de Vincent de Beauvais'. In *L'Encyclopédisme*, ed. Becq (1991), pp. 201–26.

—— with Duchenne, Marie-Christine. *Vincent de Beauvais at le 'Grand miroir du monde'*. Turnhout: Brepols, 2004.

Pearsall, Derek. *The Canterbury Tales*. London: Allen and Unwin, 1985.

—— *The Life of Geoffrey Chaucer*. Blackwell Critical Biographies. Oxford: Blackwell, 1992.

—— 'The Squire as Story-Teller'. *University of Toronto Quarterly* 34 (1964), 82–92.

——. 'The Visual World of the Middle Ages'. In *Medieval Literature*, ed. Ford (1982), pp. 290–317.

Pearson, Mike Parker and Richards, Colin. 'Ordering the World: Perceptions of Architecture, Space and Time'. In *Architecture and Order*, ed. Pearson and Richards (1994), pp. 1–37.

—— (eds). *Architecture and Order: Approaches to Social Space*. Material Cultures. London and New York: Routledge, 1994.

Pelster, Fr. 'An Oxford Collection of Sermons of the End of the Thirteenth Century (MS. Laud Misc. 511, SC. 969)'. *Bodleian Library Record* 6 (1930), 168–72.

—— [and Little, A. G.]. 'Sermons and Preachers at the University of Oxford in the Years 1290–3'. *Oxford Historical Society Publications* 96 (1934), 149–215.

Penhallurick, Robert (ed.) *Debating Dialect: Essays on the Philosophy of Dialect Study*. Cardiff: University of Wales Press, 2000.

Petersen, Kate Oelzner. *On the Sources of the Nonne Prestes Tale*. Radcliffe College Monographs, 10. Boston: Ginn, 1898.

—— *The Sources of the Parson's Tale*. Radcliffe College Monographs, 12. Boston: Ginn, 1901.

Peterson, Joyce E. 'The Finished Fragment: A Reassessment of the Squire's Tale'. *Chaucer Review* 5 (1970–1), 62–74.

Pfander, H. G. 'The Mediaeval Friars and Some Alphabetical Reference-Books for Sermons'. *Medium Ævum* 3 (1934), 19–29.

—— 'Some Medieval Manuals of Religious Instruction in England and Observations on Chaucer's Parson's Tale'. *Journal of English and Germanic Philology* 35 (1936), 243–58.

Phillips, Heather. 'John Wyclif and the Optics of the Eucharist'. In *Ockham to Wyclif*, ed. Hudson and Wilks (1987), pp. 245–58.

Pintelon, 'Introduction' to *Chaucer's Treatise on the Astrolabe*. See Chaucer, *Astrolabe*.

Plassmann, P. Thomas. 'Bartholomaeus Anglicus'. *Archivum Franciscanum Historicum* 12 (1919), 68–109.

Polyak, S. L. *The Retina: The Anatomy and the Histology of the Retina in Man, Ape and Monkey, including the Consideration of Visual Functions, the History of Physiological Optics and the Histological Laboratory Technique*. Fiftieth Anniversary Publication of the University of Chicago Press. Chicago: University of Chicago Press, 1941.

Porter, Roy. 'History of the Body'. In *New Perspectives*, ed. Burke (1991), pp. 206–32.

Pouchelle, Marie-Christine. *The Body and Surgery in the Middle Ages*, trans. Rosemary Morris. Cambridge: Polity Press, 1990. First published as *Corps et chirurgie à l'apogée du moyen-âge* (Paris: Flammarion, 1983).

Powicke, F. M. *The Medieval Books of Merton College*. Oxford: Clarendon Press, 1931.

Pratt, Robert A. 'Chaucer and the Hand that Fed him'. *Speculum* 41 (1966), 619–42.

—— 'Karl Young's Work on the Learning of Chaucer'. In Young, *Memorial* (1946), pp. 45–55.

—— 'Some Latin Sources of the Nonnes Preest on Dreams'. *Speculum* 52 (1977), 538–70.

Praz, Mario. 'Chaucer and the Great Italian Writers of the Trecento' (1927), rev. and repr. in his *Flaming Heart* (1958), pp. 29-89.

—— *The Flaming Heart: Essays on Crashaw, Machiavelli and Other Studies in the Relations between Italian and English Literature from Chaucer to T. S. Eliot*. Garden City, NY: Doubleday Anchor, 1958.

Prior, Sandra Pierson. 'Routhe and Hert-Huntyng in the Book of the Duchess'. *Journal of English and Germanic Philology* 85 (1986), 1–19.

Pugh, Ralph B. *Imprisonment in Medieval England*. Cambridge: Cambridge University Press, 1968.

Rabinow, Paul (ed.). *The Foucault Reader*. Harmondsworth: Penguin, 1984.

Raguin, Virginia Chieffo and Stanbury, Sarah (eds). *Women's Space: Patronage, Place and Gender in the Medieval Church*. Albany: State University of New York Press, 2005.

Rashed, Roshdi. 'Optique géométrique et doctrine optique chez Ibn Al Haytham'. *Archive for History of Exact Sciences* 6 (1970), 271–98.

Reed, Edward S. *James J. Gibson and the Psychology of Perception*. New Haven and London: Yale University Press, 1988.

Reidy, John. 'The Education of Chaucer's Duke Theseus', in *Epic in Medieval Society*, ed. Scholler (1977), pp. 391–408.

Renoir, Alain. 'Descriptive Technique in *Sir Gawain and the Green Knight*'. *Orbis Litterarum* 13 (1958), 126–32.

—— 'The Progressive Magnification: An Instance of Psychological Description in *Sir Gawain and the Green Knight*'. *Moderna Språk* 54 (1960), 245–53.

Rickert, Edith (comp.) *Chaucer's World*, ed. Clair C. Olson and Martin Crow. New York and London: Columbia University Press, 1948.

Ridyard, Susan J. and Benson, Robert G. (eds). *Man and Nature in the Middle Ages*. Sewanee Mediaeval Studies, 6. Sewanee, TN: University of the South, 1995.

Robertson, D. W., Jr. 'The Historical Setting of Chaucer's *Book of the Duchess*', in *Mediaeval Studies*, ed. Mahoney and Keller (1965), pp. 169–95.

—— *A Preface to Chaucer: Studies in Medieval Perspectives*. Princeton, NJ: Princeton University Press, 1962.

Robertson, Stuart. 'Elements of Realism in the Knight's Tale'. *Journal of English and Germanic Philology* 14 (1915), 226–55.

Robinson, F. N. 'Chaucer and Dante'. [Review of C. Chiarini, *Di una imitazione inglese della* Divina commedia, La Casa della Fama *di G. Chaucer* (Bari: Laterza, 1902)]. *Journal of Comparative Literature* 1 (1903), 292–7.

Romanyshyn, Robert D. *Technology as Symptom and Dream*. London and New York: Routledge, 1989.

Ronchi, Vasco. *The Nature of Light: An Historical Survey*, trans. V. Barocas. London: Heinemann, 1970. First published as *Storia della luce* (1939); English version includes new material by the author.

—— *Optics: The Science of Vision*, trans. Edward Rosen. New York: New York University Press, 1957. Originally published as *L'Ottica scienza della visione* (Bologna: Zanichelli, 1955).

Rooney, Anne. *Hunting in Middle English Literature*. Cambridge: Brewer, 1993.

Root, Robert Kilburn. 'Chaucer's Dares'. *Modern Philology* 15 (1917–18), 1–22.

Rouse, Mary A. and Rouse, Richard H. 'The Texts Called *Lumen anime*'. *Archivum Fratrum Praedicantium* 41 (1971), 1–113.

Rowland, Beryl. 'The Whelp in Chaucer's *Book of the Duchess*'. *Neuphilologische Mitteilungen* 66 (1965), 148–60.

Russell, Josiah C. 'Phases of Grosseteste's Intellectual Life'. *Harvard Theological Review* 43 (1950), 93–116.

Sabra, A. I. 'Ibn Al-Haytham's Criticisms of Ptolemy's *Optics*'. *Journal of the History of Philosophy* 4 (1966), 145–9.

—— 'Sensation and Inference in Alhazen's Theory of Visual Perception'. In *Studies in Perception*, ed. Machamer and Turnbull (1978), pp. 160–85.

Salda, Michael Norman. 'Pages from History: The Medieval Palace of Westminster as a Source for the Dreamer's Chamber in the *Book of the Duchess*'. *Chaucer Review* 27 (1992–3), 109–25.

Salter, Elizabeth. *Nicholas Love's 'Myrrour of the Blessed Lyf of Jesu Christ'*. Analecta Cartusiana, 10. Salzburg: Institut für Englische Sprache und Literatur, 1974.

Salu, Mary (ed.) *Essays on* Troilus and Criseyde. Chaucer Studies, 3. Cambridge: Brewer, 1979.

Sargent, Michael G. 'Bonaventura English: A Survey of the Middle English Prose Translations of Early Franciscan Literature'. *Analecta Cartusiana* 106 (1984), 145–76.

Savage, Ernest A. *Old English Libraries: The Making, Collection and Use of Books during the Middle Ages.* The Antiquary's Books. London: Methuen, 1911.

Saxl, F. and Wittkower, R. *British Art and the Mediterranean.* 2nd edn. London: Oxford University Press, 1969. First published 1948.

Scattergood, V. J. 'Literary Culture at the Court of Richard II'. In *English Court Culture,* ed. Scattergood and Sherborne (1983), pp. 29–43.

—— 'Two Medieval Book Lists'. *The Library* 5th ser., 23 (1968), 236–9.

—— and Sherborne, J. W. (eds). *English Court Culture in the Later Middle Ages.* London: Duckworth, 1983.

Scheps, Walter. 'Chaucer's Theseus and the Knight's Tale'. *Leeds Studies in English* ns 9 (1977), 19–34.

Schibanoff, Susan. 'Prudence and Artificial Memory in Chaucer's *Troilus*'. *English Literary History* 42 (1975), 507–17.

Schless, Howard H. *Chaucer and Dante: A Revaluation.* Norman, Okla.: Pilgrim Books, 1984.

Schleusener-Eichholz, Gudrun. 'Naturwissenschaft und Allegorese: der *Tractatus de oculo morali* des Petrus von Limoges'. *Frühmittelalterliche Studien* 12 (1978), 258–309.

Schmitt, Jean-Claude (ed.) *Prêcher d'exemples: récits de prédicateurs du moyen âge.* Paris: Stock, 1985.

Schneyer, Johannes Baptiste. *Repertorium der lateinischen Sermones des Mittelalters für die Zeit von 1150–1350.* 7 vols. Beiträge zur Geschichte der Philosophie des Mittelalters, 43. Münster, 1969–74.

Schoeck, Richard and Taylor, Jerome (eds). *Chaucer Criticism,* 2 vols. Notre Dame, Ind. and London: University of Notre Dame Press, 1960–1.

Scholler, Harald (ed.) *The Epic in Medieval Society: Aesthetic and Moral Values.* Tübingen: Niemeyer, 1977.

Se Boyar, Gerald E. 'Bartholomaeus Anglicus and his Encyclopaedia'. *Journal of English and Germanic Philology* 19 (1920), 168–89.

Sedgewick, G. G. 'The Progress of Chaucer's Pardoner, 1880–1940'. *Modern Language Quarterly* 1 (1940), 431–58. Repr. In *Chaucer Criticism,* ed. Schoeck and Taylor, vol. 1 (1960), pp. 190–220.

Severs, J. Burke. *The Literary Relationships of Chaucer's Clerk's Tale.* Yale Studies in English, 96. New Haven: Yale University Press, 1942.

Seymour, M. C. 'Some Medieval English Owners of *De proprietatibus rerum*'. *Bodleian Library Record* 9 (1973–7), 156–65.

—— et al. *Bartholomaeus Anglicus and his Encyclopedia.* Aldershot: Variorum, 1992.

Shain, Charles E. 'Pulpit Rhetoric in Three Canterbury Tales'. *Modern Language Notes* 70 (1955), 235–45.

Sharon-Zisser, Shirley. 'The Squire's Tale and the Limits of Non-Mimetic Fiction'. *Chaucer Review* 26 (1991–2), 377–94.

Shoaf, R. A. with Cox, Catherine S. (eds). *Chaucer's* Troilus and Criseyde *'subgit to alle poesye': Essays in Criticism*. Medieval and Renaissance Texts and Studies, 104. Binghampton, NY: Medieval and Renaissance Texts and Studies, 1992.

Singer, Charles (ed.) *Studies in the History and Method of Science*. 2 vols. Oxford: Clarendon Press, 1917–21.

Singleton, Charles S. *Journey to Beatrice*. Dante Studies, 2. Cambridge, Mass.: Harvard University Press, 1958.

Smalley, Beryl. *English Friars and Antiquity in the Early Fourteenth Century*. Oxford: Blackwell, 1960.

—— 'Oxford University Sermons 1290–1293'. In *Learning and Literature*, ed. Alexander and Gibson (1976), pp. 307–27.

—— 'Robert Bacon and the Early Dominican School at Oxford'. *Transactions of the Royal Historical Society*, 4th ser. 30 (1948), 1–19.

—— 'Robert Holcot O.P.' *Archivum Fratrum Praedicatorum* 26 (1956), 5–97.

Smith, A. Mark. 'Getting the Big Picture in Perspectivist Optics'. *Isis* 72 (1981), 568–89.

—— (ed.) *Alhacen's Theory of Visual Perception*. See Alhacen, *De aspectibus*.

Smith, D. Vance. 'Plague, Panic Space and the Tragic Medieval Household'. *Southern Atlantic Quarterly* 98 (1999), 367–414.

Smits, E. R. 'Vincent of Beauvais: A Note on the Background of the Speculum'. In *Vincent of Beauvais*, ed. Aerts, Smits and Voorbij (1986), pp. 1–9.

Smyser, H. M. 'The Domestic Background of *Troilus and Criseyde*'. *Speculum* 31 (1956), 297–315.

Soja, Edward W. *Postmodern Geographies: The Reassertion of Space in Critical Social Theory*. London: Verso, 1989.

—— 'The Spatiality of Social Life: Towards a Transformative Rhetorisation'. In *Social Relations*, ed. Gregory and Urry (1985), pp. 90–127.

—— *Thirdspace: Journeys to Los Angeles and Other Real and Imagined Places*. Oxford and Malden, Mass.: Blackwell, 1996.

Southern, R. W. *Robert Grosseteste: The Growth of an English Mind in Medieval Europe*, 2nd edn. Oxford: Clarendon Press, 1992.

Spade, Paul Vincent (ed.) *The Cambridge Companion to Ockham*. Cambridge Companions to Philosophy. Cambridge: Cambridge University Press, 1999.

Spargo, John Webster. *Virgil the Necromancer: Studies in Virgilian Legends*. Harvard Studies in Comparative Literature, 10. Cambridge, Mass.: Harvard University Press; London: Oxford University Press, 1934.

Spearing, A. C. *The Gawain-Poet: A Critical Study*. Cambridge: Cambridge University Press, 1970.

—— 'Lydgate's Canterbury Tale: *The Siege of Thebes* and Fifteenth-Century Chaucerianism'. In *Fifteenth-Century Studies*, ed. Yeager (1984), pp. 335–64.

—— *The Medieval Poet as Voyeur: Looking and Listening in Medieval Love-Narratives.* Cambridge: Cambridge University Press, 1993.

Spencer, H. Leith. *English Preaching in the Late Middle Ages.* Oxford: Clarendon Press, 1993.

Spettman, Hieronymus. 'Das Schriftchen *De oculo morali* und sein Verfasser'. *Archivum Franciscanum Historicum* 16 (1923), 309–22.

Sprung, Andrew. 'The *Townes Wak* A Frame for *Fre Chois* in Chaucer's *Troilus and Criseyde*'. *Mediaevalia* 14 (1988), 127–42.

Stakel, Susan. *False Roses: Structures of Duality and Deceit in Jean de Meun's Roman de la Rose.* Stanford French and Italian Studies, 69. Saratoga, Ca.: ANMA Libri, 1991.

Stanbury, Sarah. 'The Lover's Gaze in *Troilus and Criseyde*'. In *Chaucer's* Troilus, ed. Shoaf (1992), pp. 224–38.

—— *Seeing the Gawain-Poet: Description and the Act of Perception.* Middle Ages series. Philadelphia: University of Pennsylvania Press, 1991.

—— 'Space and Visual Hermeneutics in the *Gawain*-Poet'. *Chaucer Review* 21 (1986–7), 476–89.

—— 'Visualizing'. In *Companion to Chaucer*, ed. Brown (2000), 459–79.

—— 'The Voyeur and the Private Life in *Troilus and Criseyde*'. *Studies in the Age of Chaucer* 13 (1991), 141–58.

Steele, Robert. 'Roger Bacon and the State of Science in the Thirteenth Century'. In *Studies*, ed. Singer, vol. 2 (1921), pp. 121–50.

Steinberg, Diane Vanner. '"We Do Usen Here No Wommen for to Selle": Embodiment of Social Practices in *Troilus and Criseyde*'. *Chaucer Review* 29 (1994–5), 259–73.

Steneck, Nicholas H. 'Albert on the Psychology of Sense Perception'. In *Albertus Magnus*, ed. Weisheipl (1980), pp. 265–90.

Stillwell, Gardiner. 'Chaucer in Tartary'. *Review of English Studies* 24 (1948), 177–88.

Strohm, Paul. 'Chaucer's Audience(s): Fictional, Implied, Intended, Actual'. *Chaucer Review* 18 (1983–4), 137–45.

—— *Social Chaucer.* Cambridge, Mass.: Harvard University Press, 1989.

—— *Theory and the Premodern Text.* Medieval Cultures, 26. Minneapolis and London: University of Minnesota Press, 2000.

—— 'Three London Itineraries: Aesthetic Purity and the Composing Process'. In his *Theory and the Premodern Text* (2000), pp. 3–19.

Stump, Eleonore. 'The Mechanisms of Cognition: Ockham on Mediating Species', in *Cambridge Companion to Ockham*, ed. Spade (1999), pp. 168–203.

Summers, David. *The Judgment of Sense: Renaissance Naturalism and the Rise of Aesthetics.* Ideas in Context. Cambridge: Cambridge University Press, 1987.

Sutherland, Ronald. 'The *Romaunt of the Rose* and Source Manuscripts'. *PMLA* 74 (1959), 178–83.

Sylla, Edith D. 'Mathematical Physics and Imagination in the Work of the Oxford Calculators: Roger Swineshead's *On Natural Motions*'. In *Mathematics and its Applications*, ed. Grant and Murdoch (1987), pp. 69–101.

Tachau, Katherine H. 'The Problem of the *Species in Medio* at Oxford in the Generation after Ockham'. *Mediaeval Studies* 44 (1982), 394–443.

—— *Vision and Certitude in the Age of Ockham: Optics, Epistemology and the Foundations of Semantics 1250–1345*. Studien und Texte zur Geistegeschichte des Mittelalters, 22. Leiden: Brill, 1988.

Tea, Eva. 'Witelo prospettico del secolo XIII'. *L'Arte* 30 (1927), 3–30.

ten Doesschate, Gezenius. 'Oxford and the Revival of Optics in the Thirteenth Century'. *Vision Research* 1 (1962), 313–42.

Theisen, Wilfred. 'Euclid's Optics in the Medieval Curriculum'. *Archives Internationales d'Histoire des Sciences* 32 (1982), 159–76.

—— 'Witelo's Recension of Euclid's *De visu*'. *Traditio* 33 (1977), 394–402.

Thomas, Julian. *Time, Culture and Identity: An Interpretive Archaeology*. Material Cultures. London and New York: Routledge, 1996.

Thompson, N. S. 'The Merchant's Tale'. In *Sources and Analogues*, ed. Correale and Hamel, vol. 2 (2005), pp. 479–534.

Thomson, S. Harrison. *The Writings of Robert Grosseteste Bishop of Lincoln 1235–1253*. Cambridge: Cambridge University Press, 1940.

Thorndike, Lynn. *A History of Magic and Experimental Science*. 8 vols. New York: Columbia University Press, 1923–58.

—— 'Peter of Limoges on the Comet of 1299'. *Isis* 36 (1945–6), 3–6.

—— *Science and Thought in the Fifteenth Century: Studies in the History of Medicine and Surgery, Natural and Methematical Science, Philosophy and Politics*. New York: Columbia University Press, 1929.

Thrupp, Sylvia L. *The Merchant Class of Medieval London [1300–1500]*. Chicago: University of Chicago Press, 1948.

Tomasch, Sylvia, and Gilles, Sealy (eds). *Text and Territory: Geographical Imagination in the European Middle Ages*. The Middle Ages series. Philadelphia: University of Pennyslvania Press, 1998.

Torti, Anna. *The Glass of Form: Mirroring Structures from Chaucer to Skelton*. Cambridge: Brewer, 1991.

Trachtenberg, Marvin. *Dominion of the Eye: Urbanism, Art and Power in Early Modern Florence*. Cambridge: Cambridge University Press, 1997.

Tuan, Yi-Fi. *Space and Place: The Perspective of Experience*. London: Arnold, 1977.

Turner, Marion. 'Greater London'. In *Chaucer and the City*, ed. Butterfield (2006), pp. 25–40.

—— '*Troilus and Criseyde* and the "Treasonous Aldermen" of 1382: Tales of the City in Late Fourteenth-Century London'. *Studies in the Age of Chaucer* 25 (2003), 225–57.

Ullman, B. L. 'A Project for a New Edition of Vincent of Beauvais'. *Speculum* 8 (1933), 312–26.

Van, Thomas A. 'Imprisoning and Ensnarement in *Troilus* and the Knight's Tale'. *Papers in Language and Literature* 7 (1971), 3–12.

Vaughan, M. F. 'Chaucer's Imaginative One-Day Flood'. *Philological Quarterly* 60 (1981), 117–23.

Vescovini, Graziella Federici. 'Contributo per la storia della fortuna de Alhazen in Italia: il volgarizzamento del MS. Vat. 4595 e il *Commentario terzo* del Ghiberti'. *Rinascimento* ser. 2, 5 (1965), 17–49.

—— 'La Fortune de l'optique d'Ibn al-Haitham: le livre *De aspectibus* (*Kitab al-Manazir*) dans le moyen-âge latin'. *Archives Internationales d'Histoire des Sciences* 40 (1990), 220–38.

—— 'La *perspectiva* nell'enciclopedia del sapere medievale'. *Vivarium* 6 (1968), 35–45.

—— 'Le questioni di *Perspectiva* di Biagio Pelacani da Parma'. *Rinascimento* ser. 2, 1 (1961), 163–243.

—— 'Les Questions de *perspective* de Dominus de Clivaxo'. *Centaurus* 10 (1964), 232–46.

—— *Studi sulla prospettiva medievale*. Università di Torino, Pubblicazioni della Facoltà di Lettere e Filosofia, 16, fasc. 1. Turin: Giappichelli, 1965.

Vogl, Sebastian. 'Roger Bacons Lehre von der sinnlichen Spezies und vom Schvorgange'. In *Roger Bacon Essays*, ed. Little (1914), pp. 205–27.

von Hertling, Georg Freiherrn. *Abhandlungen aus dem Gebiete der Philosophie und ihrer Geschichte: eine Festgabe zum 70. Geburtstag Georg Freiherrn von Hertling*. Freiburg: Herdersche, 1913.

Warburg and Courtauld Institutes (eds). *England and the Mediterranean Tradition: Studies in Art, History and Literature*. London: Oxford University Press, 1945.

Watkins, Charles A. 'Modern Irish Variants of the Enchanted Pear Tree'. *Southern Folklore Quarterly* 30 (1966), 202–13.

Watson, Nicholas. 'Christian Ideologies'. In *Companion to Chaucer*, ed. Brown (2000), pp. 75–89.

Watson, Sophie and Gibson, Katherine. *Postmodern Cities and Spaces*. Oxford and Cambridge, Mass.: Blackwell, 1995.

Weijers, Olga and Holtz, Louis (eds). *L'Enseignement des disciplines à la Faculté des arts (Paris et Oxford, XIIIè–XVè siècles): actes du colloque international*. Studia Artistarum, 4. Turnhout: Brepols, 1997.

Weintraub, Stanley and Young, Philip (eds). *Directions in Literary Criticism: Contemporary Approaches to Literature*. University Park, Pa., and London: Pennyslvania State University Press, 1973.

Weisheipl, James A. 'Classification of the Sciences in Medieval Thought'. *Mediaeval Studies* 27 (1965), 54–90.

—— 'Curriculum of the Faculty of Arts at Oxford in the Early Fourteenth Century'. *Mediaeval Studies* 26 (1964), 143–85.

—— 'The Interpretation of Aristotle's Physics and the Science of Motion'. In *Cambridge History of Later Medieval Philosophy*, ed. Kretzmann et al. (1982), pp. 521–36.

—— 'The Nature, Scope and Classification of the Sciences'. In *Science in the Middle Ages*, ed. Lindberg (1978), pp. 461–82.

—— 'The Place of John Dumbleton in the Merton School'. *Isis* 1 (1959), 439–54.

—— 'Science in the Thirteenth Century'. In *Early Oxford Schools*, ed. Catto (1984), pp. 435–69.

—— (ed.) *Albertus Magnus and the Sciences: Commemorative Essays 1980*. Studies and Texts, 49. Toronto: Pontifical Institute of Mediaeval Studies, 1980.

Welter, J.-Th. *L'Exemplum dans la littérature religieuse et didactique du moyen âge*. Paris and Toulouse: Guitard, 1927. Repr. Geneva: Slatkine, 1973.

Wentersdorf, Karl P. 'Chaucer's Merchant's Tale and its Irish Analogues'. *Studies in Philology* 63 (1966), 604–29.

——. 'A Spanish Analogue of the Pear-Tree Episode in the Merchant's Tale'. *Modern Philology* 64 (1967), 320–1.

Wenzel, Siegfried. 'Chaucer and the Language of Contemporary Preaching'. *Studies in Philology* 73 (1976), 138–61.

—— 'Medieval Sermons and the Study of Literature'. In *Medieval and Pseudo-Medieval Literature*, ed. Boitani and Torti (1984), pp. 19–32.

Westermann, 'Comparison'. See Grosseteste, *Sermons and dicta*.

Wheatley, Edward. 'The Nun's Priest's Tale'. In *Sources and Analogues*, ed. Correale and Hamel, vol. 1 (2002), pp. 449–89.

Wheatley, Paul. *The Pivot of the Four Quarters: A Preliminary Enquiry into the Origins and Character of the Ancient Chinese City*. Edinburgh: Edinburgh University Press, 1971.

White, John. *Art and Architecture in Italy 1250 to 1400*. Pelican History of Art. Harmondsworth: Penguin, 1966.

—— *The Birth and Rebirth of Pictorial Space*, 2nd edn. London: Faber, 1967.

Whitehead, Christiania. *Castles of the Mind: A Study of Medieval Architectural Allegory*. Religion and Culture in the Middle Ages. Cardiff: University of Wales Press, 2003.

Wiedemann, Eilhard. 'Roger Bacon und seine Verdienste um die Optik'. In *Roger Bacon Essays*, ed. Little (1914), pp. 185–203.

Wilkins, 'The Meaning of Space in Fourteenth-Century Tuscan Painting'. In *By Things Seen*, ed. Jeffrey (1979), pp. 109–21.

Williams, Jeni. 'Competing Spaces: Dialectology and the Place of Dialect in Chaucer's Reeve's Tale'. In *Debating Dialect*, ed. Penhallurick (2000), pp. 46–65.

Wilson, Elizabeth. 'The Invisible *Flâneur*'. In *Postmodern Cities*, ed. Watson and Gibson (1995), pp. 59–79.

Wilson, R. M. 'The Contents of the Mediaeval Library'. In *English Library*, ed. Wormald and Wright (1958), pp. 85–111.

Wimsatt, James I. *Allegory and Mirror: Tradition and Structure in Middle English Literature*. New York: Pegasus, 1970.

—— *Chaucer and the French Love Poets: The Literary Background of the Book of the Duchess*. University of North Carolina Studies in Comparative Literature, 43. Chapel Hill: University of North Carolina Press, 1968.

Wimsatt, W. K., Jr. 'Vincent of Beauvais and Chaucer's Cleopatra and Crœsus'. *Speculum* 12 (1937), 375–81.

Windeatt, Barry. 'Chaucer and the *Filostrato*'. In *Chaucer and the Italian Trecento*, ed. Boitani (1983), pp. 163–83.

—— 'Gesture in Chaucer'. *Medievalia et Humanistica* ns 9 (1979), 143–61.

Winter, H. J. J. 'The Optical Researches of Ibn al-Haitham'. *Centaurus* 3 (1954), 190–210.

Wittreich, Joseph Anthony (ed.) *Milton and the Line of Vision*. Madison: University of Wisconsin Press, 1975.

Woods, William F. 'Private and Public Space in the Miller's Tale'. *Chaucer Review* 29 (1994–5), 166–78.

—— 'Symkyn's Place in the Reeve's Tale'. *Chaucer Review* 39 (2004–5), 17–40.

—— 'Up and Down, To and Fro: Spatial Relationships in the Knight's Tale'. In *Rebels and Rivals*, ed. Fein, Raybin and Braeger (1991), pp. 37–57.

Workman, Graham. 'The Science of Light and Reflection in the *Paradiso*'. Diss. University of York Centre for Medieval Studies, 1975.

Wormald, Francis and Wright, C. E. (eds). *The English Library before 1700: Studies in its History*. London: Athlone Press, 1958.

Yager, Susan. 'Visual Perception in Chaucer'. Diss. University of Pennsylvania, 1991.

—— '"A Whit Thyng in Hir Ye": Perception and Error in the Reeve's Tale'. *Chaucer Review* 28 (1993–4), 393–404.

Yates, Frances A. *The Art of Memory*. Harmondsworth: Penguin, 1969.

Yeager, Robert F. (ed.) *Fifteenth-Century Studies: Recent Essays*. Hamden, Conn.: Archon Books, 1984.

Young, Carl. 'The *Speculum majus* of Vincent of Beauvais'. *Yale University Library Gazette* 5 (1930), 1–13.

Young, Karl. *A Memorial of Karl Young*. New Haven: privately printed, 1946.

Zink, Michel. 'The Allegorical Poem as Interior Memoir', in *Images of Power*, ed. Brownlee and Nichols (1986), pp. 100–26.

Zinn, Grover A., Jr. 'Personification Allegory and Visions of Light in Richard of St Victor's Teaching on Contemplation'. *University of Toronto Quarterly* 46 (1976–7), 190–214.

Zumthor, Paul. 'L'Espace de la cité dans l'imaginaire médiéval'. In *Idea di città*, ed. Brusegan (1992), pp. 17–26.

—— *La Mesure du monde: représentation de l'espace au moyen âge*. Collection poétique. Paris: Editions du Seuil, 1993.

# Index

368

*Index*